ALLIED TANKS OF WORLD WAR II

1939–1945

THE WORLD'S GREAT WEAPONS

ALLIED TANKS OF WORLD WAR II
1939–1945
THE WORLD'S GREAT WEAPONS

David Porter

amber
BOOKS

The material in this volume has previously appeared in:
The Essential Vehicle Identification Guide: Western Allied Tanks 1939–45 and *The Essential Vehicle Identification Guide: Soviet Tank Units 1939–45*.

Published by
Amber Books Ltd
74–77 White Lion Street
London
N1 9PF
United Kingdom
www.amberbooks.co.uk
Appstore: itunes.com/apps/amberbooksltd
Facebook: www.facebook.com/amberbooks
Twitter: @amberbooks

ISBN: 978-1-78274-208-1

Project Editor: Michael Spilling
Design: Colin Hawes and Andrew Easton
Picture Research: Terry Forshaw

Printed in China

Picture Credits
Art-Tech: 22, 27, 71 top, 77, 89, 91, 94, 97, 104, 107, 108, 110, 115, 116 (bottom), 118, 122, 126, 143, 154, 161, 163, 168, 177, 197
Courtesy of the Central Museum of the Armed Forces Moscow: 190, 332
Cody Images: 8, 10, 11, 12, 17, 18 (both), 24, 30, 37, 46, 52, 54, 59, 66, 67, 71 (bottom), 74, 78, 82, 101, 103, 116 (top), 124, 130, 131, 135, 151, 152, 165, 227, 243, 273 (top), 313
Corbis: 199
Nik Cornish @ STAVKA: 264, 277, 294
Public Domain: 14, 308
From the Fonds of the RGAKFD at Krasnogorsk: 194, 288
TopFoto: 214, 310
Ukrainian State Archive: 188/189, 192, 193, 206, 216, 234, 236, 240, 248, 258–263 (all), 266, 271, 273 (bottom), 282, 285, 292, 298, 300, 302, 315, 317, 320, 322, 324, 329, 331, 347–368 (both)
U.S. National Archives: 6/7, 138, 148

All artworks are courtesy of Oliver Missing, Alcaniz Fresno's S.A. and Art-Tech/Aerospace

Contents

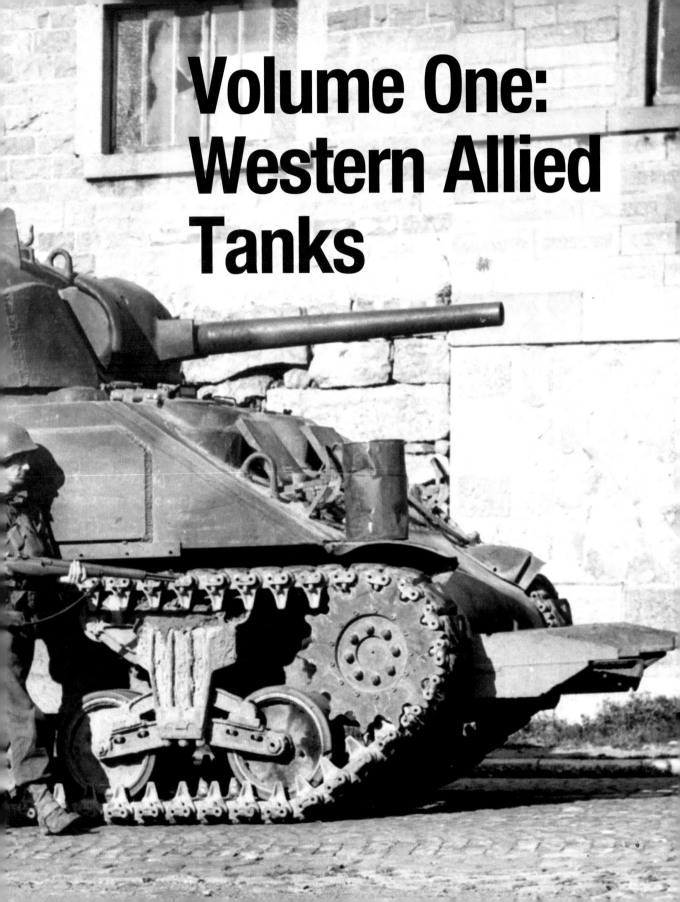

Volume One: Western Allied Tanks

Introduction

On 8 August 1918, a British force of 414
combat tanks and 120 supply tanks, supported by
800 aircraft, played a key role in the decisive Allied victory
at Amiens. The impression was given that a true revolution
in military technology had occurred that would change the
face of warfare forever. The events of the next few months
would show that Amiens had been a false dawn and that
it would be another 20 years before technology caught up
with the theories of visionaries such as J.F.C. Fuller, who
devised the futuristic Plan 1919. The process of creating the
tanks and other essential equipment that would transform
the theory and practice of armoured warfare between
1939 and 1945 was to be long and hard.

◀ Pre-war trials
During the inter-war period, much research was carried out using the large stock of French
Renault FT-17s. This vehicle is one of a number fitted with new tracks and suspension and
designated the FT Kegresse-Hinstin M26/27.

▲ **Elite French armour**

A column of H-35 light tanks of the 18e Dragons, part of the elite 1re DLM.

IN 1918, IT SEEMED that a revolution in land warfare was imminent – British and French practical experience of armoured warfare was on the point of being linked to the industrial strength of the United States to produce a huge Allied mechanized force. However, this proved to be a false dawn – the unexpectedly swift collapse of the Central Powers drastically changed military priorities as the United States withdrew into isolationism, whilst the British and French armies largely reverted to their old 'colonial policing' roles.

Although US and French armoured forces soon came under infantry control, in Britain the Tank Corps just retained its independence. Most importantly, in 1923 it also managed to acquire a modern tank, the Vickers Medium. Whilst the design had many faults, it was able to serve as a test-bed for establishing which of the many theories of armoured warfare were truly practical. The most important trials were the exercises carried out in 1927–31 by the Experimental Mechanized Force, which pioneered the techniques of tanks, artillery, infantry and engineers all operating together under radio control.

Radio technology

The development of reliable radio was arguably one of the most significant technological advances affecting armoured warfare in the inter-war years, but improved weapons, engines, tracks and suspension systems were also vital in allowing theories to be transformed into reality. Possibly the greatest innovator of the period was an eccentric American inventor, J. Walter Christie, who devised a variety of amphibious and airmobile tanks.

Whilst these projects were asking too much of the technology of the time, his 'big wheel' suspension system, soon to be known as the Christie suspension, offered an immense improvement in cross-country performance and was adopted for a host of British and Soviet tank designs, including the Crusader, Cromwell and T-34.

French designers pioneered the use of very large castings for gun mantlets, turrets and eventually entire tank hulls, a technique also taken up by the US and USSR and, to a lesser extent, the UK. Most early tanks had used riveted or bolted armour, which was inherently dangerous as hostile fire could shear off the rivets and bolts, which became lethal projectiles flying around inside the vehicle. Welding overcame this vulnerability, although the welds had to be subjected to stringent quality control to ensure they could withstand hits from high-velocity weapons.

New weapons technology

The inter-war years were also marked by significant improvements in weapons technology as the machine guns and low-velocity guns of World War I gradually gave way to high-velocity weapons capable of destroying tanks at ranges out to 1000m (1095 yards) or more. Even so, the chances of acquiring and hitting a target at that sort of range remained minimal until well into the war.

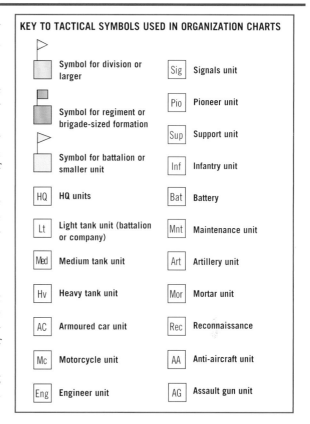

KEY TO TACTICAL SYMBOLS USED IN ORGANIZATION CHARTS

	Symbol for division or larger	Sig	Signals unit
	Symbol for regiment or brigade-sized formation	Pio	Pioneer unit
	Symbol for battalion or smaller unit	Sup	Support unit
HQ	HQ units	Inf	Infantry unit
Lt	Light tank unit (battalion or company)	Bat	Battery
Med	Medium tank unit	Mnt	Maintenance unit
Hv	Heavy tank unit	Art	Artillery unit
AC	Armoured car unit	Mor	Mortar unit
Mc	Motorcycle unit	Rec	Reconnaissance
Eng	Engineer unit	AA	Anti-aircraft unit
		AG	Assault gun unit

▲ **Autotransport**
In 1931, a small number of tankette transporters, dubbed 'autotransports', were produced on modified Ursus truck chassis. The tankette was driven onto the autotransport, its tracks were removed and a chain drive was taken from the drive sprocket to the rear axle of the transporter. The tankette's driver was then able to control the combination from his usual position inside the tankette.

Chapter 1

Defence of Poland

The first Polish-crewed tanks were 150 Renault
FT-17s that were delivered in 1919–20. In 1929, modified
versions of Vickers-Carden-Loyd tankettes (TK and TKS) and
Vickers 6-ton tanks (generally known as the Vickers E) were
adopted after extensive trials. These formed the mainstay
of the *Bron Pancerna*, or Armoured Forces, an organization
set up in 1930 to administer all tanks, armoured cars
and armoured trains. By 1935, a total of nine armoured
battalions had formed, although these were actually
deployed in company units (usually of 13 vehicles each)
supporting infantry divisions and cavalry brigades.

◀ Training
A column of Polish 7TPs, based on the Vickers 6-Ton tank, on pre-war manoeuvres.

On the road to war

The increasing threat from German and Soviet forces led to Poland's adoption of an ambitious six-year plan in 1936 under which a total of 479 20mm (0.79in) gun armed 4TP light tanks were to be built for infantry and cavalry support.

EIGHT BATTALIONS OF 7TPs (the latest version of the 6-Tonner) were to be allotted to army group commanders. The most radical feature of the plan was the formation of four Mechanized Brigades (OMs), each of which was to include two tank battalions: one of 7TPs and the other a mixed unit of 4TPs and new 10TP fast medium tanks, the latter model to have Christie suspension, 20mm (0.79in) armour and 37mm (1.5in) main armament. Each OM would also have two battalions of motorized infantry, and a battalion each of artillery, anti-tank guns and engineers.

Imported tanks

Poland could not pay for such an ambitious modernization programme and in 1936 France agreed to supply tanks and to make a loan to cover their cost. Even this did not solve the problem as French defence industries were working flat out to supply their own forces and little could be spared for export. An order for Somua S-35s had to be turned down, and although it was agreed to supply 100

Armoured Fighting Vehicles (AFVs), September 1939	Strength
TK and TKS Tankettes	440
7TPs	130
Vickers E	30
R-35s	49
Renault FT-17s	55
wz.29 and wz.34 Armoured Cars	95

R-35s instead, only 53 had been delivered before the German invasion. Besides these tanks and tankettes, almost 100 armoured cars were in service with the reconnaissance squadrons of the 11 cavalry brigades, generally deployed in troops of eight cars each. The approximate totals of operational Polish AFVs as at 1 September 1939 are set out in the table above.

The German *Panzerwaffe*

The evolution of major German armoured units began in 1934 with the formation of the first operational Panzer I battalion. The pace of events quickened throughout the 1930s as German confidence grew, especially after Hitler formally announced his intention to ignore military restrictions imposed on Germany by the 1919 Treaty of Versailles. By 1938, when Heinz Guderian, General Oswald Lutz's former chief of staff, was appointed *General der Panzertruppen*, the first four Panzer divisions had been formed.

All this effort could not alter the fact that Germany's resources were limited and that tank production had to compete with the needs of the growing *Luftwaffe* and *Kriegsmarine*. As a result, although the official strength of a Panzer division at the beginning of the war totalled 562 tanks, the reality was very different, with the strongest formations only fielding 328 tanks each.

Of these, the vast majority were Panzer Is and IIs, which even by 1939 standards were only really fit for training and reconnaissance. The Panzer IIIs and IVs – intended to be the main combat tanks

▲ **Polish Vickers Mark E light tank**

An example of the Polish twin-turreted Vickers E in its initial configuration – a total of 38 were delivered. The tank is armed with two 7.92mm (0.31in) wz.25 Hotchkiss machine guns, which were later replaced with water-cooled wz.30 weapons in 16 vehicles. (Most of the remainder received a wz.30 in the left-hand turret and a 13.2mm (0.52in) Hotchkiss heavy machine gun in the right.)

– were in short supply and formed only a small proportion of the total armoured strength. It was only the reinforcement of the *Panzerwaffe* with the excellent Czech Panzer 35(t)s and 38(t)s which made it a truly battleworthy force. Most of these were distributed among the five Panzer divisions and four light divisions, which were assigned to the Polish operation.

Tank Formations, 1939	Sub-Unit	TK	TKS	7TP	R–35	Vickers	FT–17	wz.29	wz.34
Mazowska BK	11 dp	–	13	–	–	–	–	8	–
Wolynska BK	21 dp	–	13	–	–	–	–	–	8
Suwalska BK	31 dp	–	13	–	–	–	–	–	8
Podlaska BK	32 dp	–	13	–	–	–	–	–	8
Wilenska BK	33 dp	–	13	–	–	–	–	–	8
Krakowska BK	51 dp	13	–	–	–	–	–	–	8
Kresowa BK	61 dp	–	13	–	–	–	–	–	8
Podolska BK	62 dp	–	13	–	–	–	–	–	8
Wielkopolska BK	71 dp	–	13	–	–	–	–	–	8
Pomorska BK	81 dp	13	–	–	–	–	–	–	8
Nowogrodzka BK	91 dp	13	–	–	–	–	–	–	8
WBP–M	11 sk	–	13	–	–	–	–	–	–
WBP–M	12 sk	–	13	–	–	–	–	–	–
25 DP	31 sk	–	13	–	–	–	–	–	–
10 DP	32 sk	–	13	–	–	–	–	–	–
30 DP	41 sk	13	–	–	–	–	–	–	–
Kresowa BK	42 sk	13	–	–	–	–	–	–	–
GO Bielsko	51 sk	13	–	–	–	–	–	–	–
GO Slask	52 sk	13	–	–	–	–	–	–	–
GO Slask	61 sk	–	13	–	–	–	–	–	–
20 DP	62 sk	–	13	–	–	–	–	–	–
8 DP	63 sk	–	13	–	–	–	–	–	–
26 DP	71 sk	–	13	–	–	–	–	–	–
14 DP	72 sk	–	13	–	–	–	–	–	–
4 DP	81 sk	13	–	–	–	–	–	–	–
26 DP	82 sk	13	–	–	–	–	–	–	–
10 DP	91 sk	13	–	–	–	–	–	–	–
10 DP	92 sk	13	–	–	–	–	–	–	–
10 BKM	101 sk	13	–	–	–	–	–	–	–
10 BKM	121 sk	–	13	–	–	–	–	–	–
	1 bcl	–	–	49	–	–	–	–	–
	2 bcl	–	–	49	–	–	–	–	–
	21 bcl	–	–	–	45	–	–	–	–
	111, 112, 113 kcl	–	–	–	–	–	45	–	–
WBP–M	12 kcl	–	–	–	–	17	–	–	–
10 BKM	121 kcl	–	–	–	–	17	–	–	–

KEY

BK	*Brygada kawalerii*	Cavalry brigade
BKM	*Brygada kawalerii mechanizowanej*	Mechanized cavalry brigade
DP	*Dywizja piechoty*	Infantry division
dp	*Dywizjon pancerny*	Armoured troop
GO	*Grupa operacjna*	Operational group
kcl	*Kompanja czogow lekkich*	Light tank company
sk	*Samodziena kompanja*	Scout tank company
WBP-M	*Warszawska Brygada Pancerno-Motorowa*	Warsaw Mechanized Brigade

First clash of armour
1 SEPTEMBER 1939

Although relations with Germany had been strained for months, the invasion caught the Poles in the throes of mobilization, which had only been ordered on 30 August when signs of the coming attack were unmistakable.

THE GERMAN TAKEOVER of the Sudetenland in October 1938 followed by what was left of Czechoslovakia in March 1939, allowed offensives to be launched from an arc of territory stretching for over 1000km (625 miles) along Poland's northern, western and southern frontiers from East Prussia, through Pomerania and Silesia to Slovakia. The overall objective was to encircle the Polish armies in a great pincer movement, with the jaws of the pincer closing east of Warsaw, before destroying the trapped units in a classic *Kesselschlacht*, or cauldron battle.

Plan Z
In contrast, the Polish 'Plan Z', adopted in March 1939, intended to concentrate forces against each main German attack to slow its progress before gradually falling back on Warsaw, taking up successive delaying positions along the rivers of central Poland. It was estimated that this strategy could hold the Germans for up to six months, giving time for the French to launch their promised offensives against the weakly garrisoned Rhineland and Ruhr in the West.

A number of factors combined to wreck this plan, including German air superiority and the concentrated armoured punch provided by the six Panzer and four light divisions. Only one of the four planned OMs was ready for action and this, the 10th Mechanized Brigade, was well under strength. Although heavily outnumbered, this formation mauled 2nd Panzer and 4th Light Divisions as they advanced on Cracow, but it could not hope to win a decisive victory.

Polish armoured attack
Apart from the action near Cracow, the only major clash of armoured units came when the incomplete Warsaw Mechanized Brigade played a key role in defeating 4th Panzer Division's attempt to take the city on 9 September.

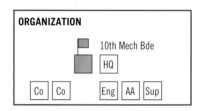

ORGANIZATION

10th Mech Bde

HQ

Co | Co | Eng | AA | Sup

This attack was launched before the tired German infantry divisions (which remained mainly dependent on horse-drawn transportation throughout the war) could catch up with the Panzers. As a result, the only infantry available were 4th Panzer's own two battalions, which were easily held by the city's garrison whilst the Warsaw Mechanized Brigade and anti-tank guns dealt with the German AFVs.

By the end of the day's fighting, 57 German tanks had been destroyed, 40 of them by a single platoon of 7TPs and a company of nine Bofors 37mm (1.5in) anti-tank guns. After this, attacks on the capital were left to infantry units with heavy air and artillery support until the garrison surrendered on 27 September.

Small-scale actions
A few small-scale armoured actions were fought after 4th Panzer's abortive attack on Warsaw. Pre-war plans had called for a high proportion of the TK and TKS tankettes to be rearmed with 20mm (0.79in) cannon, but only 20–25 TKSs had been converted by the time of the invasion in September 1939. A few cannon-armed tankettes saw action with the first platoon of the 71st Armoured Battalion of the *Wielkopolska* Cavalry Brigade.

On 14 September, its tankettes supported an attack by the brigade's 7th Mounted Rifles Regiment at Brochów (on the River Bzura, east of Warsaw). During the skirmish, a cannon-armed TKS fired across the river, knocking out two or three tanks of 4th Panzer Division. In a further action on 18 September near Pociecha in Puszcza Kampinoska forest east of Warsaw, three tankettes sprang an ambush at a forest crossroads.

▲ Awaiting the scrap heap

Burnt-out Renault FT-17s are examined by German troops following the invasion of Poland, September 1939.

▶ wz.34 Armoured Car

11th Experimental Armoured Battalion, Modlin

As a result of mechanical problems, it was decided to rebuild the 90 wz.28 armoured halftracks in Polish service as wz.34 armoured cars. The leisurely conversion programme ran from 1934 to 1938. Roughly 60 vehicles were completed as shown, armed with a single Hotchkiss wz.25 machine gun.

 Most Polish vehicles were camouflaged in a three-colour scheme of light sand, olive green and a very dark chestnut brown. These colours were spray-painted in irregular horizontal patterns, with feathered edges. The main exception to this was the R-35 battalion, whose tanks were left in their original olive green. No Polish nationality markings were used and the few authorized peacetime unit insignia were removed on mobilization.

Specifications

Crew: 2	Engine: 17.88kW (24hp) FIAT-108-III
Weight: 2.2 tonnes (2.16 tons)	(PZInż.117) petrol
Length: 3.62m (11ft 11in)	Speed: 50km/h (31mph)
Width: 1.91m (6ft 3in)	Range: 250km (155 miles)
Height: 2.22m (7ft 3in)	Armament: 1 x 7.92mm (0.31in)
	Hotchkiss wz.25 MG

One of these was a cannon-armed vehicle, commanded by Cadet Roman Orlik, who destroyed a patrol of three Panzer 35(t)s of 11th Panzer Regiment, 1st Light Division, with hits on their side armour. On the following day, the tankette platoon supported the defenders of Sieraków village in Puszcza Kampinoska against an attack by 11th Panzer Regiment. Orlik's TKS carried out short forays from tank scrapes on the left flank of the German advance and claimed the destruction of seven tanks. (Unconfirmed Polish reports claimed that the Germans lost a total of 20 tanks in the action, mostly due to anti-tank and field artillery.) A single surviving cannon-armed tankette of the 71st Armoured Battalion got through to Warsaw and took part in its defence, but no further details have emerged.

By this time, the Poles' last chance of holding out had been wrecked by the Soviet invasion of their country, which began on 17 September. Stalin quickly achieved his objective of securing eastern Poland, as had been agreed by the Russo-German Non-Aggression Pact signed in August 1939. Caught between the attacks from east and west, by the beginning of October the remnants of *Bron Pancerna* had been destroyed or had escaped across the frontier to internment in neutral Rumania.

▲ **Booty**
A captured TKS tankette. A number were taken into German service as the TKS(p).

▼ **Winter manoeuvres**
A TKS tankette tows a detachment of ski troops on pre-war winter manoeuvres.

▶ wz.34 Armoured Car

Lodz Army / Wolynska Cavalry Brigade / 21st Armoured Battalion / Armoured Car Squadron

About 30 vehicles were fitted with an L/21 37mm (1.5in) SA-18 Puteaux gun instead of the Hotchkiss machine gun. These gun-armed cars were generally used by squadron and troop commanders.

Specifications

Crew: 2	Engine: 17.88kW (24hp) FIAT-108-III
Weight: 2.2 tonnes (2.16 tons)	(PZIn˝.117) petrol
Length: 3.62m (11ft 11in)	Speed: 50km/h (31mph)
Width: 1.91m (6ft 3in)	Range: 250km (155 miles)
Height: 2.22m (7ft 3in)	Armament: 1 x 37mm (1.5in) wz.18
	(SA-18) Puteaux gun

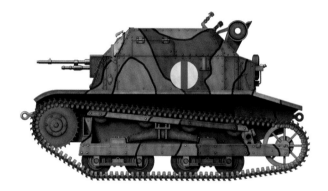

Specifications

Crew: 2	Engine: 29.8kW (40hp) Ford A 4-cylinder petrol
Weight: 2.43 tonnes (2.39 tons)	Speed: 46km/h (28.58mph)
Length: 2.58m (8ft 5in)	Range: 200km (124 miles)
Width: 1.78m (5ft 10in)	Armament: 1 x 7.92mm (0.31in) Hotchkiss
Height: 1.32m (4ft 4in)	wz.25 MG

▲ TK Tankette

Cracow Army / Operational Group Bielsko / 51st Independent Reconnaissance Tank Company

The TK tankette was developed from the Carden-Loyd carrier series. A total of possibly 300 TK tankettes were built between 1931 and 1933.

▶ TKS Tankette

Poznan Army / Podolska Cavalry Brigade / 62nd Armoured Battalion / Reconnaissance Tank Squadron

The TKS closely resembled the TK tankette but incorporated a number of improvements, including thicker armour, a more powerful engine and wider tracks.

Specifications

Crew: 2	Engine: 34.27kW (46hp) Polski FIAT 122BC
Weight: 2.65 tonnes (2.60 tons)	6-cylinder petrol
Length: 2.58m (8ft 5in)	Speed: 40km/h (25mph)
Width: 1.78m (5ft 10in)	Range: 180km (112 miles)
Height: 1.32m (4ft 4in)	Armament: 1 x 7.92mm (0.31in) Hotchkiss
	wz.25 MG

▶ 7TP Light Tank

Warsaw Defence HQ / Light Tank Company

A total of 24 twin-turreted 7TP light tanks were produced between 1935 and 1936. These vehicles were developed from the Vickers E, but were fitted with the new licence-built Saurer diesel engines and slightly thicker armour. These were always regarded as an interim type and were scheduled to be rebuilt as single-turreted vehicles, although not all had been converted by September 1939.

Specifications

Crew: 3	Engine: 80kW (110hp) Saurer VBLDd
Weight: 9.4 tonnes (9.25 tons)	diesel
Length: 4.56m (14ft 11in)	Speed: 37km/h (23mph)
Width: 2.43m (7ft 11in)	Range: 160km (99.42 miles)
Height: 2.19m (7ft 2in)	Armament: 2 x 7.92mm (0.31in) Ckm
	wz.30 MGs (1 in each turret)

◀ 7TP Light Tank

Reserve Army 'Prussia' / 2nd Light Tank Battalion

At the time of the German invasion, the bulk of the operational 7TPs (98 vehicles) were serving with the 1st and 2nd Light Tank Battalions, both of which were assigned to Reserve Army 'Prussia'. The tank's L/45 37mm (1.5in) wz.37 gun (a licence-built copy of a Bofors design) proved highly effective against all German AFVs encountered during the campaign.

Specifications

Crew: 3	Engine: 80kW (110hp) Saurer VBLDd diesel
Weight: 9.9 tonnes (9.74 tons)	Speed: 37km/h (23mph)
Length: 4.56m (14ft 11in)	Range: 160km (99 miles)
Width: 2.43m (7ft 11in)	Armament: 1 x 37mm (1.45in) Bofors
Height: 2.3m (7ft 6in)	wz.37 gun, plus 1 coaxial Ckm wz.30 MG

Specifications

Crew: 1	Height: 2.11m (6ft 11in)
Weight: 1.85 tonnes (1.82 tons)	Engine: 38.75kW (52hp) petrol
Length: 4.72m (15ft 6in)	Speed: 60km/h (37mph)
Width: 2m (6ft 7in)	Range: 400km (248 miles)

▲ Polski Fiat PF-618 Light Truck

Poznan Army / 26th Infantry Division / 82nd Independent Reconnaissance Tank Company / Maintenance Platoon

The PF-618 was a relatively modern light truck, which equipped the support units of many armoured formations.

▼ Warsaw Mechanized Brigade

A second OM, the Warsaw Mechanized Brigade, was forming at the time of the German invasion. It had one 7TP company (16 vehicles – one command tank plus three platoons each of five tanks) and two TKS companies (13 vehicles each – one command tankette plus a supply platoon of two vehicles and two platoons with five tankettes each). Most of the remaining Polish tank units fought as battalions – the 1st and 2nd Light Tank Battalions each had 49 7TPs, whilst the 21st was equipped with 45 R-35s.

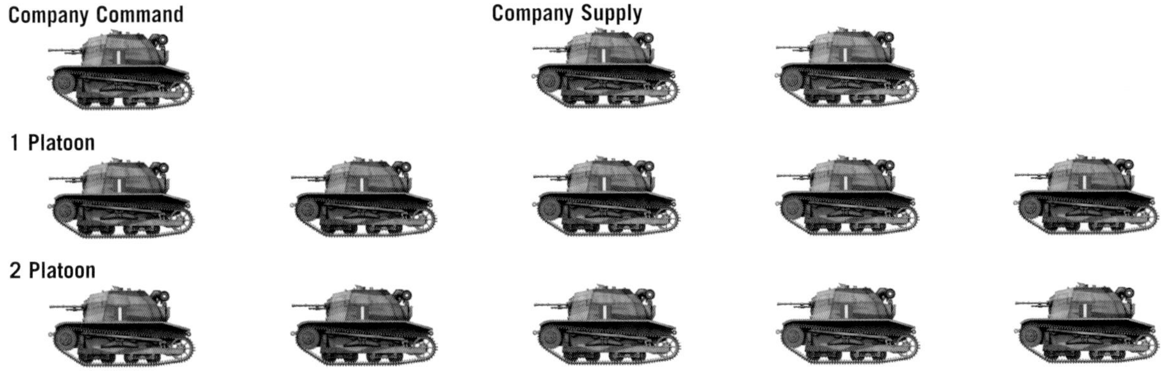

Company Command

1 Platoon

2 Platoon

3 Platoon

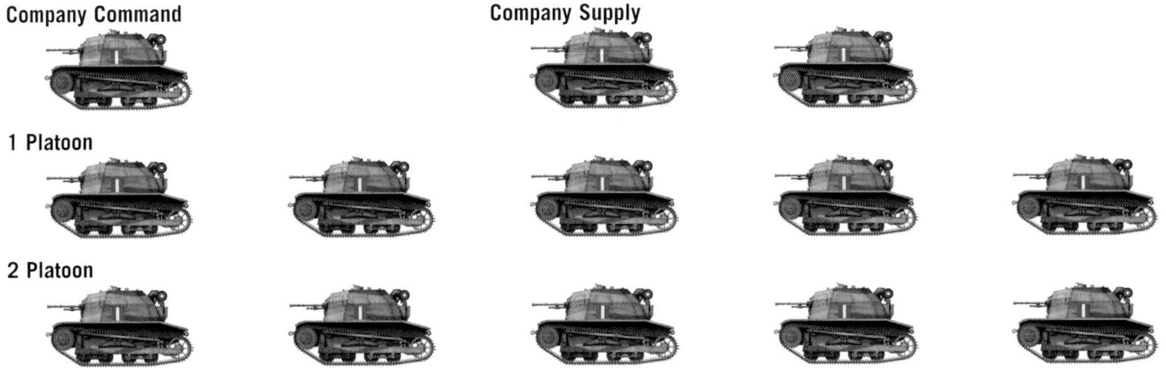

Company Command

Company Supply

1 Platoon

2 Platoon

Company Command

Company Supply

1 Platoon

2 Platoon

Chapter 2

France and the Low Countries

In 1939, the prestige of the French Army
was immense. Its performance on the battlefields of World
War I had won the respect of allies and enemies alike.
During the inter-war years it had constructed the impressive
fortifications of the Maginot Line and developed some of
the most formidable tanks in the world. Despite this show of
power, it was crippled by weaknesses, especially
in its command structure, that were only apparent to a small
minority of observers. As the Germans prepared to launch
Fall Gelb (Case Yellow), the great offensive in
Western Europe, everything depended on how far they
could exploit those failings in their opponents.

◀ **Alpine manoeuvres**
Char Léger R-35 tanks move through an Alpine pass on training manoeuvres, August 1938.

Netherlands and Belgium

As World War II began, the Netherlands had not fought a war since the Belgian Revolution of 1830. The country had a very small military industrial base and its army was in a sorry state after the economic crises of the inter-war years.

THE BELGIAN ARMY had used armoured cars as early as 1914, but the economic crises of the 1920s and 1930s, coupled with a foreign policy of strict neutrality, had prevented the development of any significant armoured forces. Whilst almost 300 AFVs were in service at the time of the German invasion in May 1940, they were parcelled out in 'penny packets' to various infantry and cavalry divisions for use as support weapons.

Poor relation

The Dutch Army was in an even worse position than its Belgian counterpart – it had been subjected to massive budget cuts before World War II, and at the time of the German invasion of the Netherlands its only AFVs were 41 armoured cars and five Carden-Loyd machine-gun carriers.

The Great Depression had hit the Dutch Army especially hard – conscripts' terms of service were progressively cut from two years to six months, barely sufficient for basic training. As early as 1925, a report indicated that the army required 350 million guilders for modernization, but all that happened was a further cut of 100 million guilders. A Dutch parliamentary committee set up to investigate the possibility of further cuts in the military budget reported that the army was in such a poor state that any more cutbacks would seriously endanger its sustainability. The committee was dissolved and

Belgian Armoured Distribution, May 1940	T.13	T.15	ACG-1
1re Division d'Infanterie	12	–	–
2e Division d'Infanterie	12	–	–
3e Division d'Infanterie	12	–	–
4e Division d'Infanterie	12	–	–
7e Division d'Infanterie (R)	12	–	–
8e Division d'Infanterie (R)	12	–	–
9e Division d'Infanterie (R)	12	–	–
10e Division d'Infanterie (R)	12	–	–
11e Division d'Infanterie (R)	12	–	–
1re Division des Chasseurs Ardennais	48	3	–
2e Division des Chasseurs Ardennais	–	3	–
Compagnie Ind. de l'Unité Cyclistes Frontière	12	–	–
8e Companie de l'Unité Cyclistes Frontière	12	–	–
Compagnie PFL de l'Unité de Forteresse	12	–	–
1re Division de Cavalerie			
1er Régiment de Guides	6	6	–
2e Régiment de Lanciers	6	6	–
3e Régiment de Lanciers	6	6	–
2e Division de Cavalerie			
1er Régiment de Lanciers	6	6	–
1er Régiment de Chasseurs	6	6	–
2e Régiment de Chasseurs	6	6	–
Escadron d'Autoblindées	–	–	8

▲ **Phoney War**

A Belgian T.15 light tank and motorcycle despatch rider wait by the roadside during the Phoney War period.

replaced by a new body that was far more ruthless and managed to make cuts totalling an additional 160 million guilders.

Although funding was reluctantly made available for some modernization in the late 1930s, its effects were limited. A total of 400 modern Bohler 47mm (1.9in) anti-tank guns were bought, but much of the army's light artillery was archaic – over 100 of its field guns dated back to 1878 and a further 200 were of 1894 vintage. As late as February 1940, the defence

minister refused to release funding to modernize all the Dutch defence lines, provoking the resignation of the commander-in-chief.

In the circumstances, it is hardly surprising that Dutch armoured forces were minimal. Nonetheless, the traditional Dutch expertise in the use of water obstacles was still highly effective, and the handful of armoured cars that did manage to get into action against German paratroops indicated the value of even light armour against airborne forces.

▶ **M39 Pantserwagen**

3e Eskadron Pantserwagens

The M39 was a DAF-designed armoured car that was just entering Dutch service at the time of the German invasion.

Specifications

Crew: 6	Speed: 60km/h (37mph)
Weight: 6.9 tonnes (6.79 tons)	Range: 300km (180 miles)
Length: 4.63m (15ft 2in)	Armament: 1 x 37mm (1.5in) Bofors
Width: 2m (6ft 7in)	gun, plus 3 x 7.92mm (0.31in) MGs (1
Height: 2m (6ft 7in)	coaxial, 1 ball-mounted in hull front and
Engine: 70.77kW (95hp) Ford 8-cylinder	1 ball-mounted in hull rear)
petrol	

◀ **M39 Pantserwagen**

3e Eskadron Pantserwagens

It seems likely that no more than a dozen or so M39s were completed, of which one or two may have seen action alongside the earlier M36 and M38 armoured cars in 1940.

Specifications

Crew: 6	Speed: 60km/h (37mph)
Weight: 6.9 tonnes (6.79 tons)	Range: 300km (180 miles)
Length: 4.63m (15ft 2in)	Armament: 1 x 37mm (1.5in) Bofors
Width: 2m (6ft 7in)	gun, plus 3 x 7.92mm (0.31in) MGs (1
Height: 2m (6ft 7in)	coaxial, 1 ball-mounted in hull front
Engine: 70.77kW (95hp) Ford 8-cylinder	and 1 ball-mounted in hull rear)
petrol	

▶ **Vickers Utility Tractor**

1re Division d'Infanterie

This armoured version of the Vickers one-man utility tractor was widely used by the Belgian Army for towing anti-tank guns and for front-line supply duties.

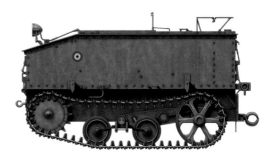

Specifications

Crew: 1	Height: 1.52m (5ft) (estimated)
Weight: not known (n/k)	Engine: 38.74kW (52hp) Ford 4-cylinder petrol
Length: 2.13m (7ft)	Speed: 16km/h (10 mph) (estimated)
Width: 1.22m (4ft)	Range: n/k

Belgium, meanwhile, had adopted, in 1936, a policy of 'armed independence', rather than a stance of strict neutrality, entailing an increase in defence expenditure to almost 25 per cent of the national budget. Belgian attitudes towards both Britain and France were ambivalent – both countries had been allies during World War I, but post-war disagreements had soured relations. This was especially true in the case of France – there was a popular perception in Belgium that French generals and politicians saw Belgium not as an independent state but as an ideal battlefield for any future war with Germany. This perception was strengthened by the failure to extend the Maginot Line to the Channel coast – to Belgian public opinion, this was tantamount to a French invitation to the Germans to attack France through Belgium. The French government turned down several requests to extend the fortifications, which increased Belgian suspicions of French intentions.

Belgian armour

By 1940, the Belgian Army totalled 650,000 men in 22 divisions. It lacked modern AA guns, but some of its equipment was good, such as the 750-plus 47mm (1.9in) FRC Model 1931 anti-tank guns, which were issued on a scale of 32 per division. Each division also had a company of 12 T.13 tank destroyers, light AFVs mounting the same 47mm (1.9in) gun.

In all, the Belgian Army fielded almost 300 AFVs at the time of the German invasion, but their effectiveness was greatly reduced by being spread thinly among infantry and cavalry divisions as mentioned above. The only exception to this type of deployment was the *1re Division des Chasseurs Ardennais*, which had 48 T.13s.

◀ **Renault ACG-1 Light Tank**

Escadron d'Autoblindées

The ACG-1 was the most potent AFV in the Belgian inventory in 1940, but only eight vehicles were operational at the time of the German invasion.

Specifications

Crew: 3	Engine: 134.1kW (180hp) Renault water-cooled
Weight: 14.5 tonnes (14.27 tons)	4-cylinder petrol
Length: 4.57m (15ft)	Speed: 40km/h (24.85mph)
Width: 2.23m (7ft 3in)	Range: 161km (100 miles)
Height: 2.33m (7ft 8in)	Armament: 1 x 47mm (1.85in) SA35 L/32 gun,
	plus 1 x coaxial 13.2mm (0.52in) HMG

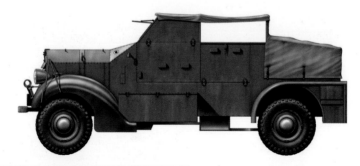

Specifications

Crew: 2	Engine: Ford V8 cylinder 63.38kW (85hp) petrol
Weight: 3.49 tons (7710lbs)	Speed: n/k
Length: 4.82m (15ft 9in)	Range: n/k
Width: 1.9m (6ft 3in)	Radio: none
Height: 1.77m (5ft 9in)	

▲ **Ford/Marmon-Herrington Armoured Car**

2e Division de Cavalerie / 1er Régiment de Chasseurs

A total of 90 of these vehicles were produced. The chassis were built by Ford at Antwerp and the armoured bodies by Rageno at Malines. They were issued to cavalry regiments as prime movers for the 47mm (1.9in) anti-tank gun.

▶ **T.15 Light Tank**

1re Division de Cavalerie / 3e Régiment de Lanciers

The T.15 was another Vickers design developed specifically to meet Belgian requirements, with a tall conical turret mounting a Hotchkiss 13.2mm (0.52in) heavy machine gun.

Specifications

Crew: 2	Engine: 67kW (90hp) Meadows petrol
Weight: 6 tonnes (5.9 tons)	Speed: 62km/h (38.5mph)
Length: 3.4m (11ft 2in)	Range: n/k
Width: n/k	Armament: 1 x 13.2mm (0.52in) Hotchkiss HMG
Height: n/k	

The evolution of French armour
1918–40

By 1918, French tank design and production had reached an advanced stage under the energetic guidance of General Jean-Baptiste Estienne, the commander of all armoured units, which were termed *Artillerie d'Assaut*.

THEIR MOST IMPORTANT equipment was the Renault FT, the first turreted tank of modern layout to be produced in quantity, with a total of over 3000 delivered by November 1918. On occasions these had been used en masse to considerable effect, most notably near Soissons on 18 July 1918, where 225 FTs played the key role in the success of a major French counterattack that captured 10,000 prisoners and 200 guns in a single day.

After the end of World War I, General Estienne remained in charge of the technical development of French AFVs and his influence led to an army directive of July 1920 calling for a full range of vehicles to include:

- Light tanks
- Howitzer-armed support tanks
- *Chars de Rupture* – heavy breakthrough tanks. (Prototypes of these had been tested by 1918 and the definitive 69-tonne/68-ton Char 2C was ready for production. An order for 300 vehicles was placed in February 1918, but this was cut back to 10, all of which were delivered by 1922)
- Armoured supply and command vehicles.

All this was far too radical for the French military establishment, and the headquarters of the *Artillerie d'Assaut* was disbanded in 1920, whilst in 1921 a special commission ordered that the earlier directive should be cancelled. In future, tanks were to be committed to infantry support and were to come under infantry control.

Stalled development

This move stifled any major development of French armour during the 1920s and early 1930s when

▲ **On parade**

H-35 light tanks on parade during the Phoney War period, late 1939.

ORGANIZATION

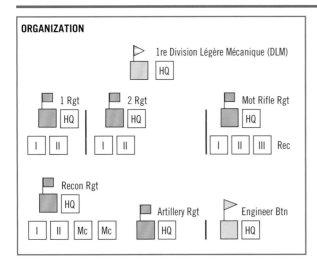

1re Division Légère Mécanique (DLM)

HQ

1 Rgt
HQ
I | II

2 Rgt
HQ
I | II

Mot Rifle Rgt
HQ
I | II | III | Rec

Recon Rgt
HQ
I | II | Mc | Mc

Artillery Rgt
HQ

Engineer Btn
HQ

1RE DIVISION LEGERE MECANIQUE (1935)	Strength
Regiments x 2	
H-35s (per rgt)	40
S-35s (per rgt)	40
Recon Rgt with P-178s	40
Motorcycle Squadrons x 2	
Motorized Rifle Regiment (3 battalions)	
AMR-33/AMR-35s	60
Artillery Regiment	
75mm (2.9in) Field Guns	24
105mm (4.1in) Howitzers	12
Engineer Battalion x 1	

the planning and construction of the Maginot Line claimed the lion's share of the limited defence budget.

Largely as a result, any real progress had to wait until 1934 with the formation of the *1re Division Légère Mécanique* (DLM). This was a mechanized cavalry division trained to operate in the classic cavalry roles of screening, strategic reconnaissance and pursuit. At first, there was very little modern equipment but gradually a range of new AFVs came into service, including the Somua S-35, the Renault R-35 and the Hotchkiss H-35.

Independent tank battalions

The impressive Char B, constructed by several producers, including Renault, entered service in 1935–36 with independent tank battalions and these were (in theory) combined with units of older

medium tanks such as the Char D. All such tanks were officially described as *Chars de manoeuvre d'ensemble* ('operating together') and were tasked with the breakthrough role, but it was not until September 1939 that they were brought together in a larger permanent formation. This was the *1re Division Cuirassée de Réserve* (DCR).

The French tank industry could not produce enough Char B vehicles to equip further divisions on this scale and, to allow the 2e DCR to form by January 1940, it was decided to standardize the tank strengths of all DCRs as two battalions of Char Bs and two battalions of H-39s, each with 45 tanks. The other elements of the division remained unchanged.

The 3e DCR assembled in March 1940 and the 4e DCR, commanded by General Charles de

▶ **Renault Chenillette UE, experimental armed prototype**

In November 1931, the Section Technique de la Cavalerie asked Renault to rebuild one of its six chenillette prototypes as an armed tankette. Accordingly, Prototype No. 77982 was converted to an Automitrailleuse légère de contact tout terrain. A ball-mounted machine gun was installed in the front plate of a small rectangular superstructure fitted over the commander's position, but the type was rejected for service due to its low speed.

Specifications

Crew: 2

Weight: 2.64 tonnes (2.6 tons)

Length: 2.8m (9ft 2in)

Width: 1.74m (5ft 8in)

Height: 1.25m (4ft 1in)

Engine: 28.31kW (38hp) Renault 85 4-cylinder petrol

Speed: 30km/h (19mph)

Range: 100 km (62 miles)

Armament: 1 x 7.5mm (0.295in) MG in hull front (prototype only)

Specifications

Crew: 2

Weight: 12.1 tonnes (11.9 tons)

Length: 4.23m (13ft 10in)

Width: 1.96m (6ft 5in)

Height: 2.16m (7ft 1in)

Engine: 90W (120hp) Hotchkiss 1938

  6-cylinder petrol

Speed: 36.5km/h (22.7mph)

Range: 150km (93 miles)

Armament: 1 x 37mm (1.5in) SA-38 gun, plus

  1 x coaxial 7.5mm (0.295in) MG

▲ Char de Cavalerie 38H (H-39)

3e DLM / 1e Cuirassiers

The H-39 was a modernized H-35, fitted with a more powerful (90kW/120hp) engine, together with improved suspension and tracks. From April 1940, the L/35 37mm (1.5in) SA-38 gun was fitted to all new vehicles, with older H-39s being refitted with the weapon as supplies became available.

◀ Char de Cavalerie 35H (H-35)

13e Bataillon de Chars de Combat (BCC)

Roughly 400 H-35s were in service in September 1939. It was intended to update them with improved vision devices and the L/35 37mm (1.5in) SA-38 gun with a much improved anti-tank capacity. The programme was never completed and many tanks went into action in their original configuration.

Specifications

Crew: 2

Weight: 10.6 tonnes (10.43 tons)

Length: 4.22m (13ft 10in)

Width: 1.96m (6ft 5in)

Height: 2.62m (8ft 7in)

Engine: 55.91kW (75hp) Hotchkiss 1935,

  6-cylinder petrol

Speed: 27.4km/h (17mph)

Range: 150km (93 miles)

Armament: 1 x 37mm (1.5in) SA-18 gun, plus

  1 x coaxial 7.5mm (0.295in) MG

▶ Char Léger 35R (R-35)

4e DCR / 24e Bataillon de Chars de Combat

The R-35 was a 1934 design intended to replace the venerable Renault FT-17 as the French Army's standard infantry support tank. Production began in 1936, but technical difficulties with the turrets delayed deliveries and the FT-17 had to remain in service for far longer than expected. Roughly 900 R-35s equipped front-line units by May 1940.

Specifications

Crew: 2

Weight: 14.5 tonnes (14.3 tons)

Length: 4.55m (14ft 11in)

Width: 2.2m (7ft 2.5in)

Height: 2.3m (7ft 6.5in)

Engine: 134.2kW (180hp) Renault 4-cylinder

Speed: 42km/h (26mph)

Range: 160km (99 miles)

Armament: 1 x 37mm (1.5in) SA-18 gun, plus

  1 x coaxial 7.5mm (0.295in) MG

▲ **AMR-33**

AMR-33 light tanks taking part in a pre-war Bastille Day parade.

Gaulle, was still incomplete when it was rushed into action following the German invasion in May 1940. In addition to these divisions, a total of five partially mechanized *Divisions Légères de Cavalerie* (DLCs) had formed during the winter and spring of

1939/40. These were little more than smaller and weaker versions of the DLMs. A total of over 3400 French tanks were available to oppose the German offensive that began in May 1940 – almost 2900 of these were modern types, with the balance being made up with old FTs and a few Char 2Cs. Their battlefield effectiveness was severely hampered by technical problems (especially short range, a lack

▶ **Char Léger 35R (R-35)**

4e DCR, 24e Bataillon de Chars de Combat

By the standards of 1940, the R-35 was an exceptionally well protected light tank, with much of the vehicle covered with 40mm (1.57in) of armour, giving a high degree of immunity to contemporary German tank and anti-tank guns.

Specifications

Crew: 2	Engine: 134.2kW (180hp) Renault 4-cylinder
Weight: 14.5 tonnes (14.3 tons)	petrol
Length: 4.55m (14ft 11in)	Speed: 42 km/h (26.1mph)
Width: 2.2m (7ft 2.5in)	Range: 160km (99.4 miles)
Height: 2.3m (7ft 6.5in)	Armament: 1 x 37mm (1.5in) SA-18 gun, plus
	1 x coaxial 7.5mm (0.295in) MG

of radios and, in most cases, one-man turrets). The deployment of nearly half the total strength in small units each of less than 50 vehicles scattered across the front under infantry command created added difficulties, making it impossible for the French to exploit their numerical superiority.

German AFV developments

Analysis of the victory in Poland had shown that the *Panzerwaffe* was working along the right lines, but that improvements were needed. The Panzer I was clearly in need of replacement, whilst the Panzer II was also obsolescent. As a result, every effort was made to re-equip units running these tanks with Panzer IIIs or Panzer 35(t)s and 38(t)s which had demonstrated their superiority over both these earlier types in the Polish campaign.

Work to meet the requirement for more specialized AFVs to support the main Panzer striking force was beginning to show results, with the first halftrack Armoured Personnel Carriers (APCs) coming into service along with small numbers of Stug III assault guns. A few heavier self-propelled (SP) guns and *Panzerjägers* ('Panzer hunters'), both types initially using obsolete Panzer I hulls, were also issued during the winter of 1939/40.

The *Wehrmacht*'s total first line tank strength for the campaign against France stood at 640 Panzer

Specifications

Crew: 2	Engine: 134.2kW (180hp) Renault 4-cylinder
Weight: 14.5 tonnes (14.3 tons)	petrol
Length: 4.55m (14ft 11in)	Speed: 42km/h (26mph)
Width: 2.2m (7ft 2.5in)	Range: 160km (99 miles)
Height: 2.3m (7ft 6.5in)	Armament: 1 x 37mm (1.5in) SA-18 gun, plus
	1 x coaxial 7.5mm (0.295in) MG

Specifications

Crew: 3	Engine: 141.7kW (190hp) V8 petrol
Weight: 19.5 tonnes (19.2 tons)	Speed: 41km/h (25mph)
Length: 5.38m (17ft 7.8in)	Range: 257km (160 miles)
Width: 2.12m (6ft 11.5in)	Armament: 1 x 47mm (1.9in) SA-35 gun, plus
Height: 2.62m (8ft 7in)	1 x coaxial 7.5mm (0.295in) MG

▲ **Char de Cavalerie 35S (Somua)**

3e DLM / 2e Cuirassiers

The Somua was one of the best tanks of its time – with up to 47mm (1.9in) of armour and the potent L/32 47mm (1.9in) SA-35 gun, it was a formidable opponent for any German AFV.

ORGANIZATION

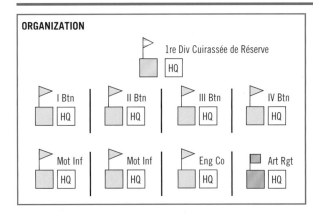

1re Div Cuirassée de Réserve
HQ

I Btn HQ | II Btn HQ | III Btn HQ | IV Btn HQ

Mot Inf HQ | Mot Inf HQ | Eng Co HQ | Art Rgt HQ

Is, 825 Panzer IIs, 456 Panzer IIIs, 366 Panzer IVs, 151 Panzer 35(t)s and 264 Panzer 38(t)s.

In addition, there were nine batteries of six 150mm (5.9in) SP infantry guns as well as four independent Stug III batteries, with six assault guns in each. The infantry divisions also had the support of five *Panzerjäger* companies (two with 18 vehicles each, the remainder each having 27 vehicles).

Finally, there was a single heavy anti-tank company of 10 self-propelled 88mm (3.5in) Flak 18s mounted on armoured Sd Kfz 8 halftracks.

Specifications

Crew: 4

Weight: 32.5 tonnes (32 tons)

Length: 6.52m (21ft 5in)

Width: 2.5m (8ft 2in)

Height: 2.79m (9ft 2in)

Engine: 223.7kW (300hp) Renault 6-cylinder
petrol

Speed: 28km/h (17mph)

Range: 180km (112 miles)

Armament: 1 x 75mm (2.9in) ABS SA-35
howitzer in the hull, 1 x 47mm (1.9in) SA-35
gun in turret, plus 2 x 7.5mm (0.295in) MGs
(1 coaxial, 1 fixed forward-firing in hull)

Radio: ER51 or ER53

▲ **Char B1 bis**

1re DCR / 37e Bataillon de Chars de Combat

The Char B1 bis was a much-improved development of the earlier Char B. Orders were placed in 1937 for a total of 1144 vehicles, but only 369 examples of the B1 bis had been delivered by June 1940.

▶ **Panhard 178 Armoured Car**

6e Groupe de Reconnaissance de Division d'Infanterie (GRDI)

The Panhard 178 entered service in 1937, and 218 vehicles had been completed by September 1939. The three DLMs each had 40 vehicles, whilst each of the seven GRDIs fielded 12.

Specifications

Crew: 3

Weight: 8.63 tones (8.5 tons)

Length: 4.79m (15ft 8in)

Width: 2.01m (6ft 7in)

Height: 2.31m (7ft 7in)

Engine: 78KW (105hp) Panhard SK 4-cylinder petrol

Speed: 72 km/h (45mph)

Range: 300km (186 miles)

Armament: 1 x 25mm (0.98in) gun,
plus 1 x coaxial 7.5mm (0.295in) MG

Radio: ER 26 or ER29

▼ 1re Division Cuirassée de Réserve

The 33-strong Char B battalions of the DCRs were formidable assault forces, but required careful tactical handling due to the tanks' low speed. They were particularly vulnerable during the frequent refuelling halts imposed by their short range – 1re DCR was badly mauled by 7th Panzer Division whilst refuelling near Flavion on 15 May 1940.

Battalion

The battle for France

MAY–JUNE 1940

'La France a perdu une bataille, mais la France n'a pas perdu la guerre.' ('France has lost a battle, but France has not lost the war.') – General de Gaulle, BBC broadcast, 18 June 1940

THE MAGINOT LINE had an enormous impact on military planning in Europe throughout the 1930s. The popular press ran colourful articles often giving greatly exaggerated accounts of the strength of these fortifications, which covered the key areas of the French frontiers with Germany and Italy. To a large extent, the French fell victim to their own propaganda and came to rely too heavily on such fixed defences, whilst German planners naturally sought ways to avoid them. Until the beginning of 1940, the Germans were convinced that the only realistic option for a major attack on France was an offensive sweeping through Holland and Belgium to outflank the Maginot Line.

Standby

Most Allied experts agreed with this evaluation and from the beginning of the conflict, the British Expeditionary Force (BEF) and the strongest French field armies were on standby to move into Belgium and Holland as soon as the Germans attacked. The scene was set for stalemate, with both sides' most powerful forces meeting head-on in long, indecisive battles until an accident began a series of events leading to a stunning German victory.

On 10 January 1940, top secret documents outlining the plans for the German offensive were retrieved from a *Luftwaffe* communications aircraft that force-landed in Belgium after the pilot lost his way in bad weather. These papers were passed to French military intelligence and were welcomed as confirmation of their assessment of the situation. As a result, this compromised plan was replaced by General Erich von Manstein's radical proposal for a feint attack along the lines of the original plan by Army Group B (including three Panzer divisions) to draw Allied armour into Belgium.

Panzer thrust

The main offensive by Army Group A, spearheaded by seven Panzer divisions, would then strike through the weakly held wooded hills of the Ardennes and drive for the Channel coast. The Allied armies which had been drawn into Belgium would then be cut off and destroyed, virtually guaranteeing the final defeat of their remaining forces.

The German operation, designated *Fall Gelb* ('Case Yellow'), began on 10 May 1940 as airborne units landed at key points in Holland and Belgium whilst Army Group B advanced to link up with them. (The airborne landings in Holland suffered particularly heavy casualties, in part from the intervention of a handful of Dutch armoured cars.) The Allies reacted as planned, advancing to take up positions along the line of the River Dyle to meet the anticipated attack. As they moved up, the main German striking force was slowly pushing through the Ardennes, brushing aside light Belgian and French screening forces.

First encounter

The first major armoured action of the campaign took place in Belgium near the Gembloux Gap between the Rivers Meuse and Dyle, where the 2e and 3e DLMs clashed with the 3rd and 4th Panzer Divisions, which were significantly weaker than those deployed further south. Each of these Panzer divisions fielded 140 Panzer Is, 110 Panzer IIs, 150 Panzer IIIs and 40 Panzer IVs.

These were markedly inferior to the DLMs, each of which had 80 Somua S-35s plus 80 Hotchkiss H-35s or H-39s. The S-35s were particularly formidable as their 47mm (1.9in) guns could penetrate all the Panzers at normal battle ranges whilst they were immune to the German 37mm (1.5in) and short-barrelled 75mm (2.9in) guns except at point-blank range. It was only poor French battlefield tactics plus the slow, inaccurate fire of their one-man turrets that allowed the Panzers to manoeuvre and close the range to pick out their opponents' weak spots.

At the end of the action, each side had lost about 100 AFVs, but the DLMs withdrew to the main French positions, abandoning many damaged but repairable tanks. In contrast, the Panzer divisions were able to salvage most of their losses to help maintain their combat strengths.

As this two-day action ended on 13 May, the main German offensive developed along the Meuse. Six hours of intense *Luftwaffe* attacks cracked open the defences that were largely held by low-grade French reserve infantry divisions, allowing bridgeheads to be established at Dinant, Montherme and Sedan. After the failure of the first counterattacks launched against these bridgeheads with local reserves, a larger-scale operation using all three DCRs was planned for 14 May. The lack of a unified command structure ruled out a prompt, properly coordinated attack, allowing each DCR to be defeated in detail.

1re DCR was destroyed as an effective fighting force after being caught refuelling by the 5th and 7th Panzer Divisions as they broke out from the Dinant

AFV Units, 10 May 1940	R-35	H-39	D2	B1	FT-17
1re Division Cuirassée					
25e BCC	–	45	–	–	–
26e BCC	–	45	–	–	–
28e BCC	–	–	–	35	–
37e BCC	–	–	–	33	–
2e Division Cuirassée					
8e BCC	–	–	–	35	–
14e BCC	–	45	–	–	–
15e BCC	–	–	–	35	–
27e BCC	–	45	–	–	–
3e Division Cuirassée					
41e BCC	–	–	–	35	–
42e BCC	–	45	–	–	–
45e BCC	–	45	–	–	–
49e BCC	–	–	–	35	–
4e Division Cuirassée					
2e BCC	45	–	–	–	–
19e BCC	–	–	45	–	–
24e BCC	45	–	–	–	–
44e BCC	45	–	–	–	–
46e BCC	–	–	–	25	–
47e BCC	–	–	–	25	–
Compagnies Autonomes de Chars					
342e Cie A	–	15	–	–	–
343e Cie A	–	–	–	–	10
344e Cie A	–	–	–	–	10
345e Cie A	–	–	15	–	–
346e Cie A	–	–	15	–	–
347e Cie A	–	–	–	11	–
348e Cie A	–	–	–	11	–
349e Cie A	–	–	–	11	–
350e Cie A	–	–	–	–	10
351e Cie A	–	15	–	–	–
352e Cie A	–	–	–	11	–
353e Cie A	–	–	–	11	–

AFV Units, 10 May 1940	R-35	H-35	FCM-36	2C	FT-17
Bataillons Organiques					
1er BCC	45	–	–	–	–
3e BCC	45	–	–	–	–
4e BCC	–	–	45	–	–
5e BCC	45	–	–	–	–
6e BCC	45	–	–	–	–
7e BCC	–	–	45	–	–
9e BCC	45	–	–	–	–
10e BCC	45	–	–	–	–
11e BCC	–	–	–	–	63
12e BCC	45	–	–	–	–
13e BCC	–	45	–	–	–
16e BCC	45	–	–	–	–
17e BCC	45	–	–	–	–
18e BCC	–	–	–	–	63
20e BCC	45	–	–	–	–
21e BCC	45	–	–	–	–
22e BCC	45	–	–	–	–
23e BCC	45	–	–	–	–
29e BCC	–	–	–	–	63
30e BCC	–	–	–	–	63
31e BCC	–	–	–	–	63
32e BCC	45	–	–	–	–
33e BCC	–	–	–	–	63
34e BCC	45	–	–	–	–
35e BCC	45	–	–	–	–
36e BCC	–	–	–	–	63
38e BCC	–	45	–	–	–
39e BCC	45	–	–	–	–
40e BCC	45	–	–	–	–
43e BCC	45	–	–	–	–
48e BCC	45	–	–	–	–
51e BCC	–	–	–	6	–
Bataillon Colonial	–	–	–	–	63

bridgehead. XLI Panzer Corps (6th and 8th Panzer Divisions) struck 2e DCR as it attempted to deploy against the Montherme bridgehead, overrunning

part of its artillery and scattering its transport. The DCR's armour fought on in battalions and smaller groups under local control, but it had lost the ability to inflict decisive damage on the Panzers.

Formidable opponent

Misguided orders rather than enemy action caused the destruction of 3e DCR, which was ready to attack the Sedan bridgehead when its tanks were ordered to be dispersed to form a 12.8km (8-mile) chain of mobile pillboxes along the front-line. This thin screen was easily broken when Guderian's XIX Panzer Corps (consisting of 1st, 2nd and 10th Panzer Divisions) advanced from Sedan. In these actions against the French DCRs, the Germans found that the Char B was an even more formidable

Cavalry units, 10 May 1940	H-35	H-39	S-35	P178	AMR
1re Div Légère Mécanique					
4e Cuirassiers	40	–	40	–	–
18e Dragons	40	–	40	–	–
6e Cuirassiers	–	–	–	40	–
4e Dragons	–	–	–	–	60
2e Div Légère Mécanique					
13e Dragons	40	–	40	–	–
29e Dragons	40	–	40	–	–
8e Cuirassiers	–	–	–	40	–
1er Dragons	–	–	–	–	60
3e Div Légère Mécanique					
1er Cuirassiers	–	40	40	–	–
2e Cuirassiers	–	40	40	–	–
12e Cuirassiers	–	–	–	40	–
11e Dragons	60	–	–	–	–
1re Div Légère de Cavalerie					
1er RAM	12	–	–	12	–
5e Dragons	–	–	–	–	20
2e Div Légère de Cavalerie					
2e RAM	12	–	–	12	–
3e Dragons	–	–	–	–	20
3e Div Légère de Cavalerie					
3e RAM	12	–	3	12	–
2e Dragons	–	–	–	–	–
4e Div Légère de Cavalerie					
4e RAM	12	–	–	12	–
14e Dragons	–	–	–	–	20
5e Div Légère de Cavalerie					
5e RAM	–	12	–	12	–
15e Dragons	–	–	–	–	20
1er GRDI (1DIM)	–	–	–	12	20
2e GRDI (2 DIM)	20	–	–	12	–
3e GRDI (3 DIM)	–	–	–	12	20
4e GRDI (9 DIM)	–	–	–	12	20
5e GRDI (12 DIM)	20	–	–	12	–
6e GRDI (15 DIM)	–	–	–	12	20
7e GRDI (25 DIM)	–	–	–	12	20

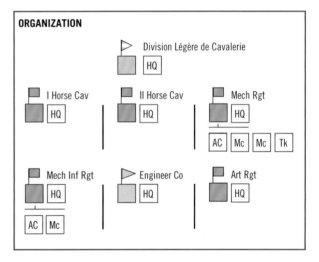

ORGANIZATION

Division Légère de Cavalerie — HQ

I Horse Cav — HQ
II Horse Cav — HQ
Mech Rgt — HQ — AC | Mc | Mc | Tk

Mech Inf Rgt — HQ — AC | Mc
Engineer Co — HQ
Art Rgt — HQ

Division Légère de Cavalerie	Strength
Regiments of Horsed Cavalry x 2	
Mechanized Regiment	
Motorcycle Squadrons x 2	
P-178s	12
H-35/H-39s	12
Mechanized Infantry Regiment	
AMR-33/AMR-35s	12
Motorcycle Squadron x 1	
Artillery Regiment	
75mm (2.9in) Field Guns	12
105mm (4.1in) Howitzers	12
Engineer Company x 1	

opponent than the Somua, due to its thicker armour and heavier armament. It was only the usual combination of failings in the Char B-equipped units (poor tactics, lack of radios and the one-man turrets) that allowed the Panzers to win through.

Most of the major French armoured formations were now effectively crippled and the German commanders (especially Guderian) exploited the freedom of movement that this provided by driving hard for the Channel coast, covering up to 90km (56 miles) per day until they reached the sea near Abbeville on 20 May. The first phase of the German plan had been completed and it seemed that the Allied units trapped in Belgium were finished (Holland had surrendered on 15 May).

Taking stock

The Panzers had won a spectacular victory, but the practical difficulties of dealing with the heavily armoured French tanks had come as a shock. The German 37mm (1.5in) tank and anti-tank guns had proved to be almost useless against not only the massive Char B but also the Somua and they were only marginally effective against the R-35/H-35 light tanks. In contrast, the 47mm (1.9in) guns of the Char B and Somua were easily capable of penetrating contemporary Panzers, none of which had armour more than 30mm (1.18in) thick. (The first production models of the Stug III assault gun with 50mm/2in frontal armour were just entering service, but only four batteries fielding a total of 24 vehicles took part in the French campaign.) These experiences accelerated existing plans to up-armour serving and future Panzers and to replace the 37mm (1.5in) tank and anti-tank guns with 50mm (2in) weapons.

The French were equally shocked at the speed of the German advance and had the appallingly difficult task of restructuring their forces in the midst of a fiercely fought campaign. The best-

▲ **Char D2**
The Char D2 was intended as the main battle tank for the DCRs, but only 100 were produced before it was replaced by the more heavily armed and better-armoured Char B.

◀ Char de Cavalerie 38H (H-39)

3e DLM / 1er Cuirassiers

H-39 units were given priority in the up-gunning programme in 1939–40 and a high proportion of their vehicles had been refitted with the L/35 37mm (1.5in) SA-38 gun by the time of the German invasion.

Specifications

Crew: 2	Engine: 89.5kW (120hp) Hotchkiss 1938
Weight: 12.1 tonnes (11.9 tons)	6-cylinder petrol
Length: 4.23m (13ft 10in)	Speed: 36.5km/h (22.7mph)
Width: 1.96m (6ft 5in)	Range: 150km (93 miles)
Height: 2.16m (7ft 1in)	Armament: 1 x 37mm (1.5in) SA-38 gun, plus
	1 x coaxial 7.5mm (0.295in) MG

Specifications

Crew: 4	Speed: 28km/h (17mph)
Weight: 32.5 tonnes (32 tons)	Range: 180km (112 miles)
Length: 6.52m (21ft 5in)	Armament: 1 x 75mm (2.9in) ABS SA-35 howitzer
Width: 2.5m (8ft 2in)	in the hull, 1 x 47mm (1.9in) SA-35 gun
Height: 2.79m (9ft 2in)	in turret, plus 2 x 7.5mm (0.295in) MGs (1
Engine: 223.7kW (300hp) Renault 6-cylinder petrol	coaxial, 1 fixed forward firing in hull)
	Radio: ER51 or ER53

▲ Char B1 bis

2e DCR / 8e Bataillon de Chars de Combat

Although the B1 bis was handicapped by its one-man turret, the combination of the turreted 47mm (1.9in) gun and hull-mounted 75mm (2.9in) howitzer was formidable by the standards of 1940.

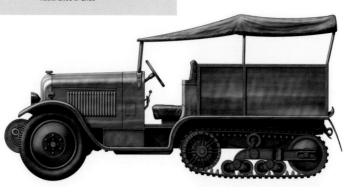

▲ Unic P107 Halftrack

1re DLM / 74e Regiment d'Artillerie

This vehicle was designed by Citroen in the early 1930s as an artillery tractor, but most production was undertaken by Unic. Over 2000 of these vehicles were in service in 1940.

Specifications

Crew: 1 plus up to 6 passengers	Height: 1.95m (6ft 4in)
Weight: 2.35 tonnes (2.31 tons)	Engine: 41kW (55hp) 4-cylinder petrol
Length: 4.85m (15ft 11in)	Speed: 45km/h (28mph)
Width: 1.8m (5ft 11in)	Range: 400km (248.5 miles)

equipped French armies, including the most effective armoured formations, had been sent north and were lost in the resulting encirclement.

A front from Sedan to the Channel now had to be defended with greatly reduced forces – 64 French divisions were available, together with a single British division, the 51st Highland Division. They had to cover a front of 600km (375 miles), which theoretically required 60 divisions, leaving a totally inadequate reserve. If the Germans broke through at any point along this line, it would be almost impossible to stop them.

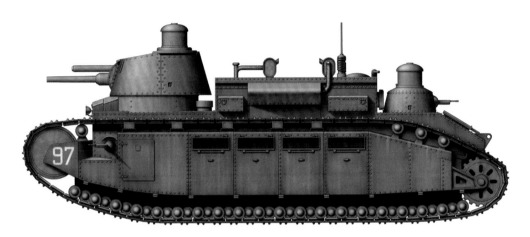

Specifications

Crew: 12	Speed: 12km/h (7.5mph)
Weight: 69 tonnes (67.9 tons)	Range: 100km (62 miles)
Length: 10.26m (33ft 8in)	Armament: 1 x 75mm (2.9in) gun, plus 4 x
Width: 2.95m (9ft 8in)	8mm (0.315in) Hotchkiss MGs (1 in rear
Height: 4m (13ft 1in)	sub-turret, 1 ball-mounted in hull front, 1
Engine: 2 x 186.25kW (250hp) Daimler or	ball-mounted each side of hull)
Maybach 6-cylinder petrol	Radio: ER53

▲ Char 2C (FCM-2C)
51e Bataillon de Chars de Combat

The Char 2C was designed in 1917–18 as a 'breakthrough tank'. An order for 300 vehicles was placed in February 1918, but only 10 were finally completed between 1919 and 1921. It seems probable that by 1940 only eight tanks were still operational and all but one of these were destroyed by their crews on their rail transport wagons to avoid capture.

▶ Char Léger FCM-36
7e Bataillon de Chars de Combat

The FCM-36 was designed by the Société des Forges et Chantiers de la Mediterranée for the infantry support role. The 100 vehicles produced were only issued to the 4e and 7e BCC. The design incorporated sloped armour and an octagonal FCM turret but was poorly armed with an L/21 37mm (1.5in) SA-18 gun and a coaxial machine gun. (A very small number may have been rearmed with the L/33 37mm/1.5in SA-38 gun.)

Specifications

Crew: 2	Engine: 67.9kW (91hp) Berliet 4-cylinder diesel
Weight: 12.35 tonnes (12.15 tons)	Speed: 24km/h (15mph)
Length: 4.22m (13ft 10in)	Range: 225km (140 miles)
Width: 1.95m (6ft 4.75in)	Armament: 1 x 37mm (1.5in) SA-18 gun, plus
Height: 2.15m (7ft 0.61in)	1 x 7.5mm (0.295in) coaxial MG

The battalion insignia of *7e Bataillion de Chars de Combat* shows a stylized depiction of a tank gunner. The red spade on the rear turret indicates that this tank is from the 1st section.

Counterattacks

MAY 1940

The German forces that had reached the Channel coast on 20 May sought to establish bridgeheads across the River Somme and to tighten the ring around the Allied armies trapped against the Channel.

HOWEVER, THEY WERE themselves dependent on a long, narrow corridor stretching back to the River Meuse. Until the infantry with their horse-drawn artillery and supply columns could catch up with the Panzers, there was still a chance for the Allies to turn

the tables. Forces holding the line of the Somme tried to eliminate the German bridgeheads on the south bank. These forces included the newly arrived but under-strength British 1st Armoured Division. Its initial operations west of Amiens on the 24th were

▲ Char B1 bis

3e DCR / 41e Bataillon de Chars de Combat

When boldly handled, the B1 bis was truly formidable. On 16 May 1940, at Stonne, a single vehicle ('Eure' commanded by Lieutenant Bilotte) attacked a column of tanks of 8th Panzer Regiment, destroying two Panzer IVs, 11 Panzer IIIs and two 37mm (1.5in) anti-tank guns. The B1 bis took an estimated 140 hits from return fire, none of which penetrated the armour.

 Some French tank battalions and regiments used colourful symbols – *4e Régiment de Cuirassiers*, for example, adopted a red and white Joan of Arc badge.

Specifications

Crew: 4

Weight: 32.5 tonnes (32 tons)

Length: 6.52m (21ft 5in)

Width: 2.5m (8ft 2in)

Height: 2.79m (9ft 2in)

Engine: 223.7kW (300hp) Renault 6-cylinder petrol

Speed: 28km/h (17mph)

Range: 180km (112 miles)

Armament: 1 x 75mm (2.9in) ABS SA-35 howitzer
in the hull, 1 x 47mm (1.9in) SA-35 gun in
turret, plus 2 x 7.5mm (0.295in) MGs (1 coaxial,
1 fixed forward-firing in hull)

Radio: ER51 or ER53

▶ Char de Cavalerie 35H (H-35)

1re DLM / 4e Cuirassiers

This H-35 was one of the relatively small number of radio-equipped French tanks in 1940. Widespread reliance on verbal briefings and flag signals played an important part in slowing the tempo of French armoured operations.

Specifications

Crew: 2

Weight: 10.6 tonnes (10.43 tons)

Length: 4.22m (13ft 10in)

Width: 1.96m (6ft 5in)

Height: 2.62m (8ft 7in)

Engine: 55.91kW (75hp) Hotchkiss 1935,
6-cylinder petrol

Speed: 27km/h (17mph)

Range: 150km (93 miles)

Armament: 1 x 37mm (1.5in) SA-18 gun,
plus 1 x coaxial 7.5mm (0.295in) MG

Radio: ER51

partially successful, but the ground gained could not be held against increasing German resistance. Further attacks, supported by the re-formed 2e and 5e DLCs, were mounted on 27 May in which 1st Armoured Division lost 110 of its 257 tanks. French armoured units, including the rebuilt 2e DCR, continued the attacks until 4 June, by which time they had suffered such heavy losses that they were no longer effective

fighting units. These losses sealed the fate of the Weygand Line, the defences along the Rivers Somme and Aisne that were intended to buy time to rebuild the battered French forces. In themselves, these defences were highly effective, comprising deep belts of fortified villages and other mutually supporting strongpoints. Their crucial weakness lay in the lack of adequate mobile forces to seal off any penetration of

Specifications

Crew: 3	Engine: 141.7kw (190hp) V8 petrol
Weight: 19.5 tonnes (19.2 tons)	Speed: 41km/h (25mph)
Length: 5.38m (17ft 7.8in)	Range: 257km (160 miles)
Width: 2.12m (6ft 11.5in)	Armament: 1 x 47mm (1.9in) SA-35 gun, plus
Height: 2.62m (8ft 7in)	1 x coaxial 7.5mm (0.295in) MG

▲ Char de Cavalerie 35S (Somua)
1re DLM / 18e Dragons

The use of national roundels on French tanks became widespread at the time of the German invasion after several 'friendly fire' incidents, such as that on 19 May 1940, when Char Bs of the newly formed 4e DCR took several casualties from the fire of Somuas of 3e Cuirassiers.

▲ Char B1 bis
4e DCR / 47e Bataillon de Chars de Combat

The B1 bis rapidly acquired a fearsome reputation amongst German troops from its ability to shrug off repeated hits from 37mm (1.5in) tank and anti-tank guns. The tanks were often referred to as: Stahlkolosse ('iron colossus'), Stahlriesen ('iron giants'), Stahlfestungen ('iron fortresses'), stählerne Kasten ('iron boxes'), Riesentiere ('giant beasts'), Ungeheuer, Ungetüme or Untiere ('monsters').

Specifications

Crew: 4	Speed: 28km/h (17mph)
Weight: 32.5 tonnes (32 tons)	Range: 180km (112 miles)
Length: 6.52m (21ft 5in)	Armament: 1 x 75mm (2.9in) ABS SA-35
Width: 2.5m (8ft 2in)	howitzer in the hull, 1 x 47mm (1.9in) SA-35
Height: 2.79m (9ft 2in)	gun in turret, plus 2 x 7.5mm (0.295in) MGs
Engine: 223.7kW (300hp) Renault	(1 coaxial, 1 fixed forward-firing in hull)
6-cylinder petrol	Radio: ER51 or ER53

the line. General Maxime Weygand concentrated his best remaining units in the coastal sector, where he expected the Germans to strike for the ports to cut off reinforcements and supplies from Britain, and on the plain of Champagne east of Reims, which was ideal terrain for armoured operations. He had correctly assessed German intentions, but the entire Somme portion of the new line was weak from the outset because of German bridgeheads established during their advance to the Channel.

On 5 June, Army Group B launched what was considered a secondary effort north-west of Paris. Although French resistance was fierce, German reinforcements were instrumental in achieving a decisive breakthrough on the 8th. Success was largely due to the lack of fully combat-worthy major French

▲ Char B1 bis

4e DCR / 46e Bataillon de Chars de Combat

Primarily designed as a close support weapon for firing high explosive (HE) against anti-tank guns and field fortifications, the B1 bis' L/17.1 75mm (2.9in) SA-35 howitzer also had a useful armour-piercing high explosive (APHE) shell that could penetrate 40mm (1.57in) of armour at 400m (438 yards).

Specifications

Crew: 4	Speed: 28km/h (17mph)
Weight: 32.5 tonnes (32 tons)	Range: 180km (112 miles)
Length: 6.52m (21ft 5in)	Armament: 1 x 75mm (2.9in) ABS SA-35
Width: 2.5m (8ft 2in)	howitzer in the hull, 1 x 47mm (1.85in) SA-35
Height: 2.79m (9ft 2in)	gun in turret, plus 2 x 7.5mm (0.295in) MGs
Engine: 223.7kW (300hp) Renault	(1 coaxial, 1 fixed forward-firing in hull)
6-cylinder petrol	Radio: ER51 or ER53

▲ Char Léger 17R (Renault FT-17)

Armée des Alpes / Bataillon Colonial

Over 3700 FT-17s were built in French factories between 1917 and 1921, almost 1300 of which were still in service in 1940. Eight tank battalions each fielded 63 FT-17s and the type also equipped some independent tank companies.

Specifications

Crew: 2	Engine: 26.1kw (35hp) Renault
Weight: 6.6 tonnes (6.5 tons)	4-cylinder petrol
Length: 4.09m (13ft 5in)	Speed: 7.7km/h (4.8mph)
Width: 1.7m (5ft 7in)	Range: 35km (21.7 miles)
Height: 2.13m (7ft)	Armament: 1 x 37mm (1.5in) SA-18 gun or 1 x
	7.5mm (0.295in) MG

armoured formations. The 2e, 3e and 4e DCRs could field only 150 tanks between them, whilst the newly raised 7e DLM had a further 174 AFVs.

As the French forces north-west of Paris retreated, they exposed the left flank of the armies defending the line of the Aisne. It was in this sector that General Gerd von Rundstedt's Army Group A launched the German main effort on 9 June. It managed only limited advances during the first three days in the face of repeated French counterattacks, but the constant German pressure and an increasingly exposed left flank forced the defenders to pull back to the Marne on the 11th. The next day Guderian's four Panzer divisions penetrated this flimsy line and rapidly exploited the breakthrough. Although the remnants of the French armoured formations fought a series of fierce small-scale actions until 16 June, they could do no more than delay the German advance, which only ended with the French surrender on the 22nd.

Specifications

Crew: 3	Engine: 44.7kW (60hp) Panhard 17 petrol
Weight: 6.91 tonnes (6.8 tons)	Speed: 50km/h (31mph)
Length: 4.83m (16ft 1in)	Range: 251km (156 miles)
Width: 1.73m (5ft 9.5in)	Armament: 1 x 37mm (1.5in) SA-18 gun, plus
Height: 2.6m (8ft 8in)	1 x coaxial 7.5mm (0.295in) MG

▲ **AMC Schneider P16**

1er Groupe de Reconnaissance de Division d'Infanterie

Roughly 100 P16s were produced from 1928 to 1930. They originally served with cavalry divisions in Escadrons d'Automitrailleuses de Combat (EAMCs), but were subsequently transferred to five of the GRDIs, each of which had 12 vehicles. The remaining serviceable P16s were sent to North Africa to operate in support of the Chasseurs d'Afrique.

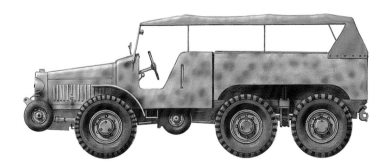

Specifications

Crew: 1	Height: 2.15m (7ft 1in)
Weight: 2.85 tonnes (2.8 tons)	Engine: 40.98kW (55hp) 4-cylinder petrol
Length: 4.64m (15ft 2.7in)	Speed: 51km/h (32mph)
Width: 1.85m (6ft 1in)	Range: n/k

▲ **Laffly S15T**

German occupation forces, France 1943

The Laffly S15T was a French artillery tractor designed to tow light weapons such as the 75mm (2.9in) field gun and the 105mm (4.1in) howitzer. Captured examples were widely used by German occupation forces.

▲ Lorraine 38L (VBCP)

1re DCR / Bataillon de Chasseurs Portés

The Lorraine 38L – also known as a VBCP (Voiture Blindée de Chasseurs Portés, or 'Armoured Mounted Infantry Vehicle') – was the world's first fully tracked armoured personnel carrier to go into action. Orders were placed for 440 vehicles, but only 150 were delivered by May 1940 and most of these were issued to the DCRs' mechanized chasseur (infantry) battalions on a scale of 40 per battalion. The Lorraine 38L could carry six men in the tractor, with a further six in the armoured trailer and most vehicles were fitted with one or two AA mountings.

Specifications	
Crew: 2 plus 8 passengers	Engine: 52.15kW (70hp) Delahaye Type 135
Weight: 6.2 tonnes (6.1 tons)	6-cylinder petrol
Length: 4.22m (13ft 10in)	Speed: 35km/h (22mph)
Width: 1.57m (5ft 3in)	Range: 137km (85 miles)
Height: 2.13m (7ft) (estimated)	

▲ Citroen-Kegresse P19 (CK P19)

1re DLC / 5e Dragons

The P19 entered production in 1932 and a total of 547 remained in service in 1940. Most vehicles were used as personnel carriers in French cavalry formations.

Specifications	
Crew: 5–7	Height: 1.95m (6ft 5in)
Weight: 4.05 tonnes (3.9 tons)	Engine: 41kW (55hp) 4-cylinder petrol
Length: 4.85m (15ft 11in)	Speed: 45km/h (28mph)
Width: 1.8m (5ft 11in)	Range: 400km (248.5miles)

▶ Panhard 178 Armoured Car

German occupation forces, France 1942

In June 1941, a total of 190 Panhards were issued to German units. Forty-three were fitted with flanged steel wheels for use on railways. In 1943, some were fitted with a new open-topped turret mounting a 50mm (2in) L/42 or L/60.

Specifications	
Crew: 3	Speed: 72km/h (45mph)
Weight: 8.63 tones (8.5 tons)	Range: 300km (186 miles)
Length: 4.79m (15ft 8in)	Armament: 1 x 25mm (1in) gun, plus 1 x coaxial
Width: 2.01m (6ft 7in)	7.5mm (0.295in) MG
Height: 2.31m (7ft 7in)	Radio: ER 26 or ER29
Engine: 78kW (105hp) Panhard SK 4-cylinder petrol	

BEF in France
MAY 1940

In 1918 the British Army had built up great expertise in the battlefield handling of AFVs and was now rapidly developing a wide range of special-purpose vehicles.

SUPPLY TANKS AND GUN carriers that could transport medium artillery had been in service as early as 1917 whilst prototypes of APCs and engineer tanks were being trialled. At Amiens in August 1918, a total of almost 450 British AFVs inflicted 26,000 casualties on the Germans and captured 400 guns, scoring an even greater success than that achieved by the French at Soissons the previous month. In recognition of the value of AFVs, the Tank Corps had grown to a total of strength of 25 battalions by the Armistice of November 1918.

Post-war austerity

In the first years of peace a rapid run-down in tank numbers meant that by 1921 only five battalions and 12 armoured car companies remained. Although there was often great pressure to bring AFVs under infantry control, the Royal Tank Corps survived and during the early 1920s received its first major new tank type, the Vickers Medium.

Although it was very thinly armoured, by the standards of the time the Vickers Medium was a fast and reliable tank that played a vital role in testing the theories of armoured warfare during the 1920s and 1930s. The most important of these tests came with the formation of the Experimental Mechanised Force in 1927.

This was the ancestor of all armoured divisions and in a series of exercises it showed the potential battle-winning capabilities of such formations. Foreign military observers were deeply impressed and their

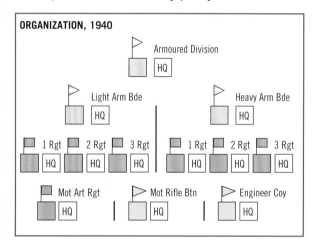

BEF Armoured Units, 10 May 1940	Mark VI	Matilda I	Matilda II	Cruiser Tank	Carrier	Daimler	Morris	Guy
4th/7th Dragoon Guards	28	–	–	–	44	–	–	–
5th Dragoon Guards	28	–	–	–	44	–	–	–
13th/18th Hussars	28	–	–	–	44	–	–	–
15th/19th Hussars	28	–	–	–	44	–	–	–
1st Lothians	28	–	–	–	44	–	–	–
1st Fife and Forfar	28	–	–	–	44	–	–	–
East Riding Yeomanry	28	–	–	–	44	–	–	–
12th Lancers	–	–	–	–	–	–	38	–
4th Northumberland Fusiliers (infantry)	–	–	–	–	–	12	–	–
1st Army Tank Bde 4 RTR (Royal Tank Regiment) 7 RTR	5 7	50 27	– 23	– –	8 8	– –	– –	– –
No. 3 Air Mission Phantom	–	–	–	–	–	–	–	6

 Training

Mark VIB light tanks and Scout carriers of the BEF participate in manoeuvres during the winter of 1939/40.

reports influenced the development of German, Soviet and United States armoured units.

By the late 1930s rearmament programmes were slowly beginning to produce desperately needed new tanks and enough were available for the first two Mobile Divisions to form in 1938. In 1940 these formations were retitled, becoming 1st and 7th Armoured Divisions.

Separate role

The armoured divisions (one based in the United Kingdom and the other, the 7th, later the 'Desert Rats', in Egypt) were not designed for the infantry support role, which was assigned to specialist army tank brigades, each of which was supposed to have three regiments equipped with heavily armoured infantry tanks. Infantry divisions had some light AFVs of their own in the form of Bren, Scout and (later) Universal Carriers (a total of 96 per division). A mechanized cavalry regiment with 28 light tanks

and 44 carriers was also attached to each infantry division to provide close reconnaissance.

When the German offensive opened on 10 May 1940, the BEF's principal armoured units were the 1st Army Tank Brigade (77 Matilda Is, 23 Matilda IIs and 12 Mark VI light tanks, plus 16 carriers) and eight mechanized cavalry regiments, seven with the mix of light tanks and carriers given above and an eighth with 38 Morris CS9/LAC armoured cars.

INSIGNIA

The most conspicuous tactical markings were a solid white recognition square (see top left) about 30cm x 30cm (12in x 12in) carried on the hull front, rear and sides, and company/squadron outlined symbols, which were applied to each side of the turret (or hull side for non-turreted vehicles).

These latter symbols were:

Diamond	HQ
Triangle	A Company or Squadron (see above)
Square	B Company or Squadron
Circle	C Company or Squadron

Although these symbols were supposed to be colour-coded, in practice a wide variety of colours were used, including red, white, yellow, blue and purple.

INSIGNIA

British vehicles were khaki green, over-painted with an irregular disruptive pattern of dark green.

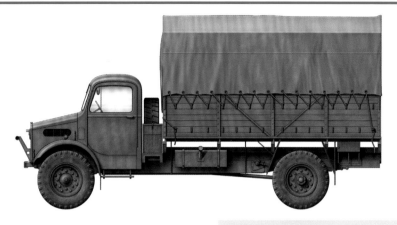

▲ Bedford OYD GS 3-Ton Truck

1st Armoured Division / 2nd Armoured Brigade / 10th Royal Hussars / HQ
Squadron / F Echelon

Over 72,000 OY series '3-Tonners' were produced between 1939 and 1945.
Officially, each armoured regiment fielded 22 such vehicles.

Specifications

Crew: 1	Engine: 53.64kW (72hp) Bedford WD
Weight: 6.57 tonnes (6.46 tons)	6-cylinder petrol
Length: 6.22m (20ft 4.9in)	Speed: 72.5km/h (45mph) (estimated)
Width: 2.18m (7ft 2in)	Range: 450km (280 miles)
Height: 3.09m (10ft 1.6in)	

▶ Light Tank Mark VIC

1st Armoured Division / 2nd Armoured Brigade / 10th Royal Hussars

The Mark VIC was fitted with a new turret, mounting a 15mm (0.59in) Besa heavy
machine gun and a coaxial 7.92mm (0.31in) Besa machine gun.

Specifications

Crew: 3	Speed: 56km/h (35mph)
Weight: 5.08 tonnes (5 ton)	Range: 200km (124 miles)
Length: 4.01m (13ft 2in)	Armament: 1 x 15mm (0.59in) Besa HMG,
Width: 2.08m (6ft 10in)	plus 1 x coaxial 7.92mm (0.31in) Besa MG
Height: 2.13m (6ft 11in)	Radio: Wireless Set No. 9
Engine: 65.6kW (88hp) Meadows 6-cylinder petrol	

▶ Light Tank Mark VIB

2nd Infantry Division / 4th/7th Royal Dragoon Guards

Over 200 of these tanks were in service with the BEF in May 1940. Whilst they
were effective as reconnaissance vehicles, their thin armour and feeble armament
caused heavy losses when they were forced to act in the role of 'substitute cruiser
or infantry tank'.

Specifications

Crew: 3	Speed: 56km/h (34.78mph)
Weight: 5.08 tonnes (5 ton)	Range: 200km (124.2 miles)
Length: 4.01m (13ft 2in)	Armament: 1 x 12.7mm (0.5in) Vickers HMG, plus
Width: 2.08m (6ft 10in)	1 x coaxial 7.62mm (0.3in) Vickers MG
Height: 2.26m (7ft 5in)	Radio: Wireless Set No. 9
Engine: 65.6kW (88hp) Meadows 6-cylinder petrol	

Specifications

Crew: 4

Weight: 15.04 tonnes (14.8 tons)

Length: 6.02m (19ft 9in)

Width: 2.59m (8ft 6in)

Height: 2.59 (8ft 6in)

Engine: 253.64kW (340hp) Nuffield Liberty V12 petrol

Speed: 48km/h (30mph)

Range: 145km (90 miles)

Armament: 1 x 40mm (1.57in) 2pdr Ordnance Quick Firing (OQF)

   gun, plus 1 x coaxial 7.92mm (0.31in) Besa MG

Radio: Wireless Set No. 9

▲ **Cruiser Tank Mark IV, A13 Mark II**

1st Armoured Division / 2nd Armoured Brigade / 2nd Dragoon Guards (Queen's Bays)

Despite being used for tasks better suited to heavily armoured infantry tanks, the cruiser tanks of 1st Armoured Division scored some notable tactical successes before being overwhelmed by superior German weaponry and tactics.

◀ **Morris CS9 Armoured Car**

GHQ BEF / 12th Royal Lancers

The Morris CS9 armoured car was based on the chassis of the Morris 4x2 15cwt truck. A total of 99 were built in 1938, of which 38 equipped the 12th Royal Lancers, the only armoured car unit in the BEF.

Specifications

Crew: 4	Speed: 72km/h (45mph)
Weight: 4.26 tonnes (4.2 tons)	Range: 386km (240 miles)
Length: 4.78m (15ft 8in)	Armament: 1 x 14mm (0.55in) Boys
Width: 2.06m (6ft 9in)	anti-tank rifle, plus 1 x 7.7mm (0.303in)
Height: 2.21m (7ft 3in)	Bren MG
Engine: 52kW (70hp) Morris Commercial	Radio: Wireless Set No. 9
4-cylinder petrol	

▲ **Morris CS8 GS 15cwt Truck**

1st Armoured Division / 2nd Armoured Brigade / 2nd Dragoon Guards (Queen's Bays) / HQ Squadron / F Echelon

The CS8 entered service in 1934 and over 21,000 vehicles were built before production ceased in 1941. A total of 12 GS 15cwt trucks were held by each armoured regiment. Many were captured in May/June 1940 and were taken into service with the Wehrmacht.

Specifications

Crew: 1	Engine: 3.5 litre (213ci) 4-cylinder petrol
Weight: 0.99 tonnes (0.9 tons)	Speed: 75km/h (47mph)
Length: 4.80m (15ft 9in)	Range: 225km (136 miles)
Width: 1.80m (5ft 11in)	Radio: None
Height: 1.85m (6ft 1in)	

▶ **Light Tank Mark VIB**

1st Armoured Reconnaissance Brigade / East Riding Yeomanry

Only a handful of the 300-plus British light tanks deployed to France were successfully evacuated, contributing to Britain's desperate shortage of AFVs in the summer of 1940.

Specifications

Crew: 3	petrol
Weight: 5.08 tonnes (5 tons)	Speed: 56km/h (34.78mph)
Length: 4.01m (13ft 2in)	Range: 200km (124 miles)
Width: 2.08m (6ft 10in)	Armament: 1 x 12.7mm (0.5in) Vickers HMG,
Height: 2.26m (7ft 5in)	plus 1 x coaxial 7.62mm (0.303in) Vickers MG
Engine: 65.6kW (88hp) Meadows6-cylinder	Radio: Wireless Set No. 9

▶ **Bren Gun Carrier**

2nd Infantry Division / 4th Brigade / 1st Battalion The Royal Scots

Each of the BEF's infantry divisions had a total of 96 Bren and Scout Carriers. These were scheduled to be replaced by the more versatile Universal Carrier, but few, if any, of these new vehicles reached the BEF before the Dunkirk evacuation.

Specifications

Crew: 3	Speed: 48km/h (30mph)
Weight: 3.81 tonnes (3.75 tons)	Range: 210km (130 miles)
Length: 3.65m (11ft 11in)	Armament: 1 x 14mm (0.55in) Boys anti-tank
Width: 2.05m (6ft 9in)	rifle, plus 1 x 7.7mm (0.303in) Bren MG or 2 x
Height: 1.45m (4ft 9in)	7.7mm (0.303in) Bren MGs
Engine: 52.2kW (70hp) Ford 8-cylinder petrol	

Counterattack at Arras
21 MAY 1940

Both sides of the 'Panzer corridor' from the Meuse to the Channel were potentially vulnerable to counterattacks. Repeated attempts were made by the Allies to break through from the south, but it was the Arras counterattack launched by the forces trapped against the Channel coast that was to have the greatest impact on the outcome of the campaign.

IN MANY RESPECTS, the Arras counterattack was improvised rather than planned. It was launched on 21 May by 58 Matilda Is and 16 Matilda IIs of the BEF's 1st Army Tank Brigade, supported by the remaining 60 Somuas of 3e DLM. Their advance hit the SS Motorized Infantry Regiment *Totenkopf* and 7th Panzer Division's rifle battalions, who found to their horror that the Matildas were immune to the fire of their 37mm (1.5in) anti-tank guns. As the tanks pushed on into the German rear, General Erwin

Rommel frantically formed a defence line using 7th Panzer Division's 88mm (3.5in) Flak guns and its medium artillery. These weapons were decisive as the British armour had outrun its supporting infantry and artillery. Eight Matildas were knocked out and the rest were forced to withdraw, but when the Panzer 38(t)s of 25th Panzer Regiment attempted to cut off the retreat, they ran into a screen of 2pdr anti-tank guns backed up by Somuas and were beaten off. A total of about 40 Matildas were lost in exchange for six Panzer 38(t)s, three Panzer IVs and many lighter AFVs and anti-tank guns.

The importance of this action went far beyond the losses on either side – Rommel was convinced that further attacks were imminent and halted his advance for 24 hours, giving the British time to reinforce the vital Channel coast, especially the ports of Boulogne and Calais, which held out against XIX Panzer Corps until 25 and 27 May respectively. Coupled with reports of continuing small-scale French counter-attacks, the Arras fighting raised fears amongst many of the more senior German generals that the Panzer divisions might be cut off from the infantry

divisions who were making epic forced marches to catch up with them. Understandably, most were relieved when, on 24 May, Hitler ordered the Panzer divisions out of the line to allow time for them to refit before the next stage of the campaign. Although Guderian protested strongly against this ruling, it was not rescinded until two days later, by which point the Dunkirk evacuation (Operation *Dynamo*) was about to begin. The Allied defences were able to hold the renewed German attacks until 4 June, by which time over 330,000 troops (one third of them French) had been rescued, although virtually all their AFVs, artillery and heavy equipment had to be abandoned.

Specifications

Crew: 2	Speed: 13km/h (8mph)
Weight: 11.16 tonnes (11 tons)	Range: 129km (80 miles)
Length: 4.85m (15ft 11in)	Armament: 1 x 12.7mm (0.5in) Vickers HMG or
Width: 2.29m (7ft 6in)	1 x 7.7mm (0.303in) Vickers MG
Height: 1.85m (6ft 1in)	Radio: Wireless Set No. 9
Engine: 52.2kW (70hp) Ford V8 petrol	

▲ Matilda I Infantry Tank

1st Army Tank Brigade / 4 RTR

A total of 77 Matilda Is were issued to the 1st Army Tank Brigade by May 1940. The armour of the 58 vehicles that took part in the Arras counterattack proved to be virtually immune to the German 37mm (1.5in) anti-tank gun, although the vehicles' exposed tracks were vulnerable.

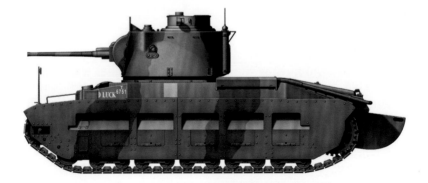

▲ Matilda II Infantry Tank

1st Army Tank Brigade / 7 RTR

Only 16 of 7 RTR's 23 Matilda IIs were available for the Arras counterattack, but their apparent invulnerability and aggressive handling had an immense psychological impact on the German chain of command.

Specifications

Crew: 4	Speed: 13km/h (8mph)
Weight: 26.92 tonnes (26.5 tons)	Range: 258km (160 miles)
Length: 5.61m (18ft 5in)	Armament: 1 x 40mm (1.57in) 2pdr Ordnance
Width: 2.59m (8ft 6in)	Quick-Firing (OQF) gun, plus 1 x coaxial
Height: 2.52m (8ft 3in)	7.92mm (0.31in) Besa MG
Engine: 2 x 64.8kW (87hp) AEC 6-cylinder diesel	Radio: Wireless Set No. 11

▼ Counterattack force at Arras

The Allied tank forces that formed the main striking force of the Arras counterattack were an ad hoc collection of units, with no experience of working together. Battlefield procedures were improvised and unreliable communications hampered the co-ordination of the disparate elements of the force. In the circumstances, their achievements were truly remarkable.

4 RTR at Arras (7 x Matilda II, 29 Matilda I)

7 RTR at Arras (9 x Matilda II, 27 Matilda I)

3e DLM (60 Somuas)

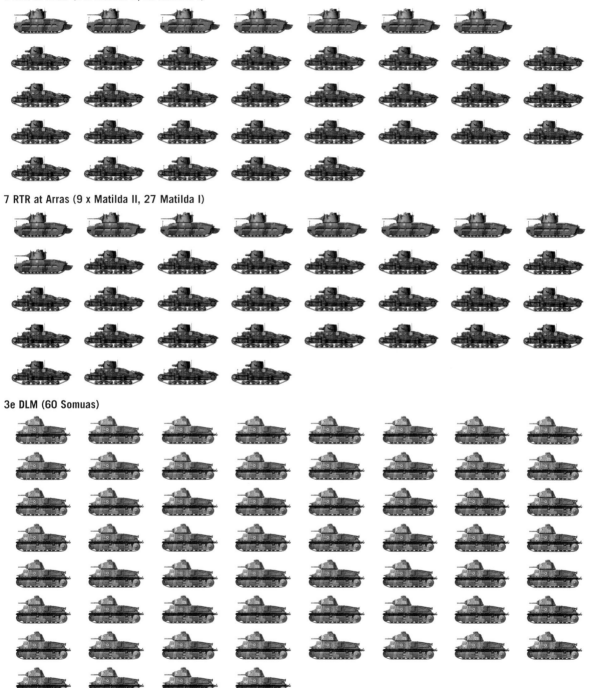

Chapter 3

North Africa: 1940–43

For almost three years, the deserts of North Africa
were the setting for some of the most dramatic battles in the
history of armoured warfare. They ruined the reputations of a
string of British generals, but created two legends. Rommel
gained fame as the 'Desert Fox' and acquired the grudging
admiration of his opponents, who came to refer to any
successful job as 'a Rommel'. Montgomery's victory at
the Second Battle of El Alamein made his name as a
great commander and set him on the road that would
lead to the command of Twenty-first Army Group and
a field-marshal's baton.

◀ **Moving up**
A newly delivered Grant en route to the front-line. This vehicle is from an early production batch with the
short (L/31) M2 75mm (2.9in) gun. Later Grants and Lees had the longer (L/40) M3 75mm (2.9in) gun.

Early operations

Italy's conquest of Ethiopia in the mid-1930s raised British fears that Mussolini's ambitions included the seizure of Egypt and the Suez Canal.

A SCRATCH FORCE OF AFVs was assembled at Mersa Matruh during 1936 to act as a deterrent to any hostile move by the large Italian garrison of Cyrenaica, less than 160km (100 miles) away to the west. This British force was slowly strengthened as tensions mounted in Europe during the 1930s until it became the Mobile Division Egypt following the 1938 Munich crisis. The division's first commander was General Percy Hobart, one of the pioneers of armoured warfare, whose fierce training made it the most formidable unit in North Africa. He made high-ranking enemies at HQ in Cairo with his prickly nature, coupled with his insistence that AFVs were the only real battle winners, and he was sacked in September 1939. For all Hobart's faults, the first desert victory was largely due to his old division,

which General Richard O'Connor described as 'the best trained division I have ever seen'. Indeed, the division's training was soon to be tested in action, for the French surrender on 22 June 1940 released all 250,000 Italian troops in North Africa for operations against Egypt. They were opposed by the 10,000 British troops of the Western Desert Force – truly daunting odds by any standards.

▶ **Hot pursuit**
Mark VI light tanks follow up the retreating Italian forces, December 1940.

A classic victory – the desert war
JUNE 1940–FEBRUARY 1941

Immediately after Mussolini's declaration of war on 10 June 1940, Morris and Rolls Royce armoured cars of the 11th Hussars began a series of raids into Libya.

THEIR AMBUSHES DISRUPTED convoys and began hitting Italian morale, which took another blow on 28 June when the able and popular Italian commander-in-chief, Air Marshal Italo Balbo, was killed when his aircraft was shot down. He had been demanding vast quantities of equipment before launching the offensive that Mussolini demanded – 100 water tankers, 1000 lorries and more medium tanks and anti-tank guns, all of which were essential.

His replacement, Marshal Rodolfo Graziani, repeated these demands but, despite airy promises, only a fraction of the required equipment was delivered after long delays. Under intense pressure from Mussolini, the much-postponed Italian

British Tank Units, June 1940	Vehicles
2 RTR	A9, A10, A13 cruisers
7 RTR	Matilda II infantry tanks
3rd Hussars	Mark VI light tanks

offensive was finally launched by five divisions on 13 September. The heavily outnumbered British screening forces covering the border fell back, fighting a series of delaying actions, until the Italians halted around Sidi Barrani, about 96km (60 miles) inside Egypt. This halt surprised the British, but Graziani had little choice as his tanks and motor transport were suffering frequent breakdowns whilst the infantry, which made up most of his force, were exhausted after three days of marching in the searing heat.

The small-scale armoured actions since the opening of the desert war had shown just how inferior Italian AFVs were to their British counterparts. This was most obvious as far as armament was concerned, for the L3s had no anti-armour weapons, but could be knocked out by the heavy machine guns and anti-tank rifles of the opposing light tanks, carriers and armoured cars. The M11/39 was little better off as its hull-mounted 37mm (1.5in) gun proved to be ineffective against A10 and A13 tanks except at point-blank range.

In contrast, the 2pdr guns of the British cruiser tanks could easily penetrate the M11/39's frontal armour at normal battlefield ranges. Equally important was the scale of issue of radios – almost all British AFVs had them, but very few Italian tanks were so equipped. This meant that Italian armoured operations were slowed by the need to halt for new orders as the tactical situation changed – the only alternative was for junior officers to issue 'follow me' orders – a practice that could cause disaster if they became casualties.

Given these factors, plus the continuing shortages of fuel and artillery ammunition, Graziani's decision to secure his new positions with a line of fortified

▶ **Light Tank Mark VIB**

Western Desert Force / 7th Armoured Division / 7th Armoured Brigade / 1 RTR

In the first months of the desert war, the Mark VI light tanks were found to be markedly superior to their Italian counterparts.

Specifications

Crew: 3	Speed: 56km/h (35mph)
Weight: 5.08 tonnes (5 tons)	Range: 200km (124 miles)
Length: 4.01m (13ft 2in)	Armament: 1 x 12.7mm (0.5in) Vickers HMG,
Width: 2.08m (6ft 10in)	plus 1 x coaxial 7.62mm (0.3in) Vickers MG
Height: 2.26m (7ft 5in)	Radio: Wireless Set No. 9
Engine: 65.6kW (88hp) Meadows 6-cylinder petrol	

▲ **Cruiser Tank Mark II, A10 Mark IA**

Western Desert Force / 7th Armoured Division / 4th Armoured Brigade / 7th Hussars

The A10's 2pdr gun was capable of destroying any Italian tank at normal battlefield ranges.

Specifications

Crew: 5	Speed: 26km/h (16mph)
Weight: 13.97 tonnes (13.75 tons)	Range: 161km (100 miles)
Length: 5.51m (18ft 1in)	Armament: 1 x 40mm (1.57in) 2pdr OQF gun,
Width: 2.54m (8ft 4in)	plus 2 x 7.92mm (0.31in) Besa MGs (1 coaxial
Height: 2.59m (8ft 6in)	and 1 ball-mounted in hull front)
Engine: 111.9kW (150hp) AEC Type 179 6-cylinder petrol	Radio: Wireless Set No. 9

camps is understandable. Greatly exaggerated reports of British reinforcements also played a part in this decision and strengthened his reluctance to attempt any further advance until more of the long-awaited equipment arrived.

Italian caution prompted both General O'Connor, commanding the Western Desert Force at Mersa Matruh, and General Archibald Wavell, commander-in-chief in Cairo, to plan counter-offensives. Since

June, their commands had received reinforcements that had greatly increased their fighting power.

Operation *Compass*

Although Graziani still had a vast front-line numerical superiority (80,000 to 30,000 troops), the position was reversed as far as the vital AFVs were concerned, with 275 British tanks opposing 120 greatly inferior Italian vehicles. Preparations for the counter-offensive

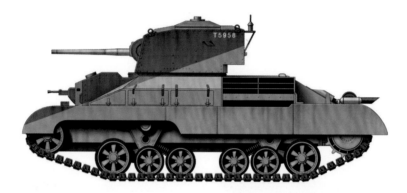

▲ **Cruiser Tank Mark II, A10 Mark IA**

Western Desert Force / 7th Armoured Division / 4th Armoured Brigade / 2 RTR

The A10's 30mm (1.18in) frontal armour was proof against most Italian tank guns except at very close range.

Specifications

Crew: 5	Speed: 26km/h (16mph)
Weight: 13.97 tonnes (13.75 tons)	Range: 161km (100 miles)
Length: 5.51m (18ft 1in)	Armament: 1 x 40mm (1.57in) 2pdr OQF
Width: 2.54m (8ft 4in)	gun, plus 2 x 7.92mm (0.31in) Besa MGs (1
Height: 2.59m (8ft 6in)	coaxial and 1 ball-mounted in hull front)
Engine: 111.9kW (150hp) AEC Type 179	Radio: Wireless Set No. 9
6-cylinder petrol	

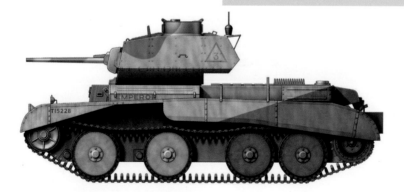

Specifications

Crew: 4	Speed: 48km/h (30mph)
Weight: 15.04 tonnes (14.8 tons)	Range: 145km (90 miles)
Length: 6.02m (19ft 9in)	Armament: 1 x 40mm (1.57in) 2pdr OQF gun,
Width: 2.59m (8ft 6in)	plus 1 x coaxial 7.92mm (0.31in) Besa MG
Height: 2.59 (8ft 6in)	Radio: Wireless Set No. 9
Engine: 253.64kW (340hp) Nuffield Liberty V12 petrol	

▲ **Cruiser Tank Mark IV, A13 Mark II**

Western Desert Force / 7th Armoured Division / 4th Armoured Brigade / 2 RTR

The A13's high speed proved invaluable during Operation Compass.

went on in great secrecy throughout the next few months and were completed by early December.

The detailed plans only covered the initial five-day Operation *Compass* in which 4th Indian and 7th Armoured Divisions were to attack each of the widely separated Italian camps in turn. After the first five days, 4th Indian Division was scheduled to be redeployed to protect the Sudan from Italian forces in Ethiopia and Eritrea, which meant that exploitation

of any success would have to be left to 7th Armoured Division and 16th Infantry Brigade.

The first attack by 7 RTR and elements of 4th Indian Division went in against Nibeiwa Camp at dawn on 9 December under cover of a 200-gun barrage. The motorized *Gruppo* Maletti, which formed the camp's garrison, included 23 M11/39s, which were the only Italian medium tanks in the front-line. These were surprised and scarcely had

Specifications

Crew: 4	Speed: 48km/h (30mph)
Weight: 15.04 tonnes (14.8 tons)	Range: 145km (90 miles)
Length: 6.02m (19ft 9in)	Armament: 1 x 40mm (1.57in) 2pdr OQF gun,
Width: 2.59m (8ft 6in)	plus 1 x coaxial 7.92mm (0.31in) Besa MG
Height: 2.59 (8ft 6in)	Radio: Wireless Set No. 9
Engine: 253.64kW (340hp) Nuffield Liberty V12 petrol	

▲ **Cruiser Tank Mark IV, A13 Mark II**

Western Desert Force / 7th Armoured Division / 4th Armoured Brigade / 7th Hussars

In common with most other British cruiser and infantry tanks of the period, most A13s were armed with the 2pdr, although a small percentage were fitted with a 76mm (3in) howitzer for the close support role.

▲ **Matilda II Infantry Tank**

Western Desert Force / 4th Indian Infantry Division / 7 RTR

In their first major actions, Matildas were found to be virtually immune to all Italian weapons, except for heavy artillery. Even direct hits by the 13.6kg (30lb) high explosive shells of 100mm (3.9in) howitzers rarely inflicted serious damage.

Specifications

Crew: 4	Speed: 13km/h (8mph)
Weight: 26.92 tonnes (26.5 tons)	Range: 258km (160 miles)
Length: 5.61m (18ft 5in)	Armament: 1 x 40mm (1.57in) 2pdr OQF gun,
Width: 2.59m (8ft 6in)	plus 1 x coaxial 7.92mm (0.31in) Besa MG
Height: 2.52m (8ft 3in)	Radio: Wireless Set No. 11
Engine: 2 x 64.8kW (87hp) AEC 6-cylinder diesel	

Specifications

Crew: 4

Weight: 26.92 tonnes (26.5 tons)

Length: 5.61m (18ft 5in)

Width: 2.59m (8ft 6in)

Height: 2.52m (8ft 3in)

Engine: 2 x 64.8kW (87hp) AEC 6-cylinder diesel

Speed: 13km/h (8mph)

Range: 258km (160 miles)

Armament: 1 x 40mm (1.57in) 2pdr OQF gun, plus

   1 x coaxial 7.92mm (0.31in) Besa MG

Radio: Wireless Set No. 11

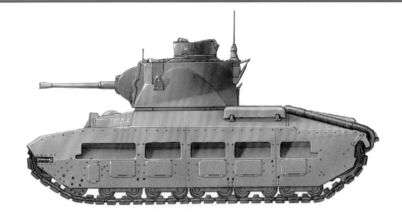

▼ Matilda II Infantry Tank

Western Desert Force / 7th Armoured Division / 7th Armoured Brigade / 4 RTR

This Matilda carries the prominent white-red-white recognition stripes applied to many British AFVs in North Africa.

▲ Matilda II Infantry Tank

Western Desert Force / 7th Armoured Division / 4th Armoured Brigade / 2 RTR

A wide variety of desert camouflage schemes were tried at different times – including desert pink. Prolonged exposure to the sun and sandstorms frequently faded camouflage paints, producing strange colours.

Specifications

Crew: 4

Weight: 26.92 tonnes (26.5 tons)

Length: 5.61m (18ft 5in)

Width: 2.59m (8ft 6in)

Height: 2.52m (8ft 3in)

Engine: 2 x 64.8kW (87hp) AEC 6-cylinder diesel

Speed: 13km/h (8mph)

Range: 258km (160 miles)

Armament: 1 x 40mm (1.57in) 2pdr OQF gun, plus

   1 x coaxial 7.92mm (0.31in) Besa MG

Radio: Wireless Set No. 11

Specifications

Crew: 4	Speed: 13km/h (8mph)
Weight: 26.92 tonnes (26.5 tons)	Range: 258km (160 miles)
Length: 5.61m (18ft 5in)	Armament: 1 x 40mm (1.57in) 2pdr OQF gun,
Width: 2.59m (8ft 6in)	plus 1 x coaxial 7.92mm (0.31in) Besa MG
Height: 2.52m (8ft 3in)	Radio: Wireless Set No. 11
Engine: 2 x 64.8kW (87hp) AEC 6-cylinder diesel	

▲ Matilda II Infantry Tank

Western Desert Force / 7th Armoured Division / 1st Army Tank Brigade / 7 RTR

This Matilda has a version of the 'radiating lines' camouflage pattern widely used in 1940–41. The lightest colour was primarily applied at the bottom, to lighten shadows around the suspension, with the darkest on top, to lessen the contrast of reflected light.

▲ **Hunting for the enemy**

A Matilda advances through a minor sandstorm. Poor visibility caused by dust, heat haze and mirages often made accurate gunnery all but impossible.

Italians' morale began to crack, and the death of General Pietro Maletti hastened the final surrender of the 4000 surviving members of the garrison. Attacks on the other camps followed much the same pattern as at Nibeiwa and (after only 48 hours and at the cost of 600 British casualties) their garrisons were destroyed with total losses of 20,000 prisoners, 180 guns and 60 tanks.

This defeat thoroughly demoralized Graziani, who believed that there was no chance of holding the key ports of Bardia and Tobruk against a further British offensive. In his despair he even voiced doubts about the chances of holding the rest of Libya, which undermined his credibility with Mussolini and the *Comando Supremo* in Rome.

Bardia and Tobruk

Even as the Western Desert Force drove the Italians back across the Egyptian frontier, O'Connor and Wavell began working on plans for the next stage of the campaign, with the capture of Bardia and Tobruk as the first priority. Given the urgency of the situation, 6th Australian Division began immediate intensive training for the assault on Bardia as soon as it arrived to replace 4th Indian Division. (In a further reorganization, the Western

time to fire a shot before they were destroyed by the Matildas, which were in any case invulnerable to their feeble 37mm (1.5in) guns.

After dealing with the M11/39s, 7 RTR, with close infantry support, concentrated on overrunning the dug-in Italian artillery. Most gun crews fought to the death, although even hits from the 13.6kg (30lb) shells of the Italians' 100mm (3.9in) howitzers did little more than jam the turrets of one or two Matildas. With the destruction of their guns, the

▲ **Fiat-Ansaldo M11/39**

XIII Corps / 6th Australian Division Cavalry Regiment

The M11/39 was a poorly designed vehicle developed in the late 1930s as a 'breakthrough tank' for the Italian Army. By the time it went into action in 1940, it was already obsolescent and took heavy losses from British 2pdr tank and anti-tank guns. A small number of M11/39s and the later M13/40s were captured in running order and issued to 6th Australian Division Cavalry Regiment to support their Universal Carriers in the assault on Tobruk in January 1941. The large white kangaroo recognition markings were applied to the front, sides and rear of all captured AFVs used by the regiment to minimise the risk of 'friendly fire'.

Specifications

Crew: 3	Speed: 32.2km/h (20mph)
Weight: 11.175 tonnes (11 tons)	Range: 200km (125 miles)
Length: 4.7m (15ft 5in)	Armament: 1 x 37mm (1.45in) Vickers-Terni
Width: 2.2m (7ft 2.5in)	L/40 in limited traverse mount in hull front,
Height: 2.3m (7ft 6.5in)	plus 2 x 8mm (0.31in) MGs in turret
Engine: 78.225kW (105hp) Fiat SPA 8T V-8	Radio: None fitted
diesel	

Desert Force was retitled XIII Corps at about this time.)

The port's garrison included the battered 62nd, 63rd and 64th Divisions, plus the untried 1st and 2nd Blackshirt Divisions. In addition, there were over 100 tanks (mainly L3s, with a handful of M11/39s and the first few M13/40s), plus over 400 guns of all types. These forces held a fortified perimeter complete with anti-tank ditches, wire entanglements and concrete strongpoints stretching for 29km (18 miles) around the harbour.

In theory, the 40,000-strong garrison should easily have been able to hold out for the duration of their one month's water supply, but demoralization had already spread after earlier defeats. The defenders were further shaken by raids of up to 100 RAF bombers during the first nights of 1941. On top of all this, a final blow to Italian morale came in the early hours of 3 January as the battleships *Barham*, *Valiant* and *Warspite* gave impressive naval gunfire support to thicken up the fire of the corps' 160 guns.

The initial barrage concentrated on the area of the defences held by the 1st Blackshirt Division, which was subsequently in no state to put up much resistance to the following Australian assault. Sections of the anti-tank ditch were quickly levelled to allow 7 RTR (which was now down to 23 serviceable Matildas) to support the next phase of the attack. Most Italian positions were only too ready to surrender, but a single counterattack by six M11/39s and M13/40s made some progress before it was broken up by accurate fire from three portee 2pdrs. After this, the attackers were able to work steadily through the defences until the last positions surrendered on 5 January. The majority of the garrison were captured, together with almost all their tanks and guns.

The advance to Bardia had strained O'Connor's supply columns to the limit and made the capture of Tobruk's harbour facilities vital for the next phase of the offensive. The anti-tank ditches, wire and emplacements of the port's perimeter defences, which stretched for almost 48km (30 miles), were held by a total garrison of 25,000 with 200 guns and 87 tanks (including 25 mediums). The old armoured cruiser *San Giorgio* had been damaged in earlier attacks, but was beached in the harbour so that its guns could be used in the defence of the port area.

Tobruk taken

The 7th Armoured Division reached Tobruk on the evening of 6 January, whilst the Australians and 7 RTR followed to complete the process of sealing off the perimeter. Preparations for the attack included the now usual air raids and naval bombardments before the assault went in on the 21st. This used similar tactics to those employed at Bardia, but took into account the lessons learnt in the earlier operation and was influenced by the need to minimize the risks to the invaluable Matildas, only 16 of which could be brought forward in time.

Within an hour of moving off, the Australians had broken through the defences and were widening the breach in the Italian line. Two hours later the attackers were approaching the central strongpoints of Fort Pilastrino and Fort Solaro when they came under fire from a line of 22 dug-in tanks, one of which was destroyed and the rest captured by a daring infantry assault. Counterattacks by other armoured formations were quickly defeated by small groups of Matildas and infantry with

▶ **Universal Carrier**

Western Desert Force / 6th Australian Division / 16th Australian Infantry Brigade

Almost invariably referred to as the 'Bren Carrier', the Universal Carrier was as indispensable in North Africa as elsewhere for resupply, casualty evacuation and a thousand and one other tasks.

Specifications

Crew: 3	Engine: 63.4kW (85hp) Ford V8 8-cylinder petrol
Weight: 4.06 tonnes (4 tons)	Speed: 52km/h (32mph)
Length: 3.76m (12ft 4in)	Range: 258km (160 miles)
Width: 2.11m (6ft 11in)	Armament: 1 x 14mm (0.55in) Boys anti-tank
Height: 1.63m (5ft 4in)	rifle, plus 1 or 2 x 7.7mm (0.303in) Bren MGs

artillery support. The failure of these counterattacks triggered the collapse of the garrison's morale and most units had surrendered by the evening of the 21st, although those holding the port area did not give in until the next morning. The real importance of the capture of Tobruk lay in its resources, including fuel depots, harbour installations and a water distillation plant that O'Connor desperately needed to supply his planned advance to Benghazi

and beyond. The next move was directed against the key crossroads at Mechili, which was held by the *Bambini* Armoured Brigade with a total of 120 M13/40s. Most of these had only just arrived from Benghazi and were scarcely ready for action when the brigade was ordered to attack the leading elements of 7th Armoured Division, which were threatening the desert flank of the main Italian defences covering the coast road at Derna. In

Specifications

Crew: 4	4-cylinder petrol
Weight: 4.26 tonnes (4.2 tons)	Speed: 72km/h (45mph)
Length: 4.78m (15ft 8in)	Range: 386km (240 miles)
Width: 2.06m (6ft 9in)	Armament: 1 x 14mm (0.55in) Boys anti-tank
Height: 2.21m (7ft 3in)	rifle, plus 1 x 7.7mm (0.303in) Bren MG
Engine: 52kW (70hp) Morris Commercial	Radio: Wireless Set No. 9

▲ Morris CS9 Armoured Car

Western Desert Force / 7th Armoured Division / 7th Armoured Brigade / 11th Hussars

The 11th Hussars were equipped with 30 of these armoured cars in the early months of the desert war. Although their armament of a Boys anti-tank rifle and Bren gun was feeble, they were popular for their ability to cross soft sand.

▲ Marmon-Herrington Armoured Car Mark II

Eighth Army / 2nd Armoured Division / 3rd Armoured Brigade / King's Dragoon Guards

Marmon-Herrington armoured cars were built in South Africa using a variety of imported components. Almost 900 Mark IIs were produced, the majority of which were sent to North Africa.

Specifications

Crew: 4	Speed: 80km/h (50mph)
Weight: 6.096 tonnes (6 tons)	Range: 322km (200 miles)
Length: 5.18m (17ft)	Armament: 1 x 14mm (0.55in) Boys anti-tank
Width: 2m (6ft 6in)	rifle, plus 2 x 7.7mm (0.303in) Bren MGs (1
Height: 2.67m (8ft 9in)	in the turret and 1 AA)
Engine: 63kW (85hp) Ford V8 petrol	Radio: Wireless Set No. 9

their first action on 24 January, a detachment of the brigade's M13/40s forced the 7th Hussars' light tanks to withdraw after knocking out two of their three cruisers. The pursuing Italian armour was ambushed by a squadron of 2 RTR's cruisers which, firing from hull-down positions, destroyed seven M13/40s in as many minutes. This action, combined with the usual greatly exaggerated reports of British strength, prompted the withdrawal of the

Bambini Armoured Brigade before 7th Armoured Division could completely surround their positions. The way was now clear for probing attacks against the desert flank of the Derna position, which was evacuated during the night of 28/29 January.

As the Italians withdrew westwards along the coast road, O'Connor planned a 240km (150-mile) advance across the desert by 7th Armoured Division to cut off their retreat near Beda Fomm. Whilst

▲ Marmon-Herrington Armoured Car Mark II

Eighth Army / 7th Armoured Division / 4th South African Armoured Car Regiment

The Marmon-Herrington's small turret with a standard armament of a Boys anti-tank rifle and a Bren, plus one or two AA machine guns, was frequently up-gunned with heavier weapons such as captured 20mm (0.79in) AA guns.

Specifications

Crew: 4	Speed: 80km/h (50mph)
Weight: 6.096 tonnes (6 tons)	Range: 322km (200 miles)
Length: 5.18m (17ft)	Armament: 1 x 14mm (0.55in) Boys anti-tank
Width: 2m (6ft 6in)	rifle, plus 2 x 7.7mm (0.303in) Bren MGs (1
Height: 2.67m (8ft 9in)	in the turret and 1 AA)
Engine: 63kW (85hp) Ford V8 petrol	Radio: Wireless Set No. 9

Specifications

Crew: 1	Height: 3m (9ft 9in)
Weight: 3.05 tonnes (3 tons)	Engine: 71kW (95hp) Ford V8 petrol
Length: 6.58m (21ft 7in)	Speed: 80km/h (50mph)
Width: 2.49m (8ft 2in)	Range: 274km (170 miles)

▲ Chevrolet WA

Eighth Army / Long Range Desert Group

This Chevrolet is typical of the wide range of 'soft-skinned' vehicles used by the Long Range Desert Group for raiding and reconnaissance missions far behind enemy lines. A vast assortment of weaponry was carried, ranging from machine guns to anti-tank and light AA guns.

▼ B Squadron, 2nd Royal Tank Regiment, 1940

During the first months of the desert war, 2 RTR operated a mixed bag of A9, A10 and A13 cruiser tanks. All three types had differing levels of mobility and armour protection, but were nonetheless used very effectively against far larger Italian forces.

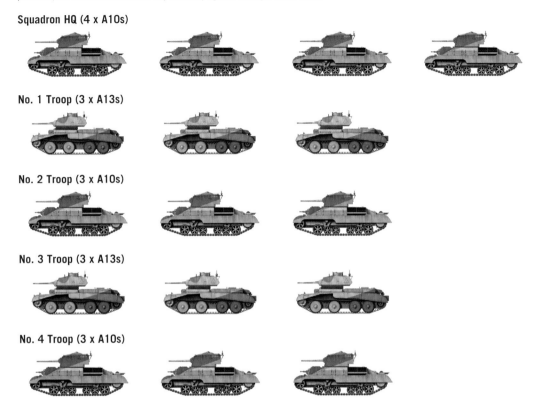

Squadron HQ (4 x A10s)

No. 1 Troop (3 x A13s)

No. 2 Troop (3 x A10s)

No. 3 Troop (3 x A13s)

No. 4 Troop (3 x A10s)

this was going on, the Australians were to keep up the pressure of the pursuit along the coast road to convince Graziani that this was still the main threat. The spearhead of the dash for Beda Fomm was a small group equipped with wheeled vehicles and designated 'Combeforce' after its commander, Lieutenant-Colonel John Combe. It had a total strength of only 2000 men and comprised: 11th Hussars with Rolls Royce and Morris armoured cars; 2nd Battalion, The Rifle Brigade; C Battery, 4th Royal Horse Artillery, with six 25pdr guns; and 106th Battery, Royal Artillery, with nine 37mm (1.5in) Bofors portee anti-tank guns.

Combeforce in position

By midday on 5 February, Combeforce had set up an ambush on the coast road at Sidi Saleh, a few kilometres south-west of Beda Fomm. They were just a couple of hours ahead of the retreating

Italians, who made a series of increasingly desperate but uncoordinated attacks in their attempts to break through. Initially these attacks were small-scale affairs as of all the varied units heading the retreat only the 10th *Bersaglieri* were first-line combat troops and they were without any armoured support. Inevitably, the pressure against Combeforce began to mount as more Italian units arrived, and the situation was becoming serious when the leading elements of 4th Armoured Brigade arrived late that afternoon. These were directed against the flanks of the steadily lengthening enemy column, shooting up seemingly endless lines of halted soft-skinned vehicles and taking 800 prisoners. The most valuable prizes were petrol tankers, which were immediately used to refuel the brigade's tanks, several of which had run dry on the battlefield itself.

That night, both sides gathered their tank strengths for the coming battle. The *Bambini* Armoured

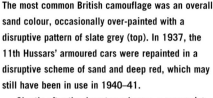

of C Squadron were able to join the battle, but their combined efforts accounted for an estimated total of 79 M13/40s.

By the end of the day's fighting, the Italians were down to barely 30 serviceable tanks, all of which were committed to a final desperate attack at first light on 7 February. This was launched with the support of all the remaining artillery and came close to breaking through Combeforce's positions before being destroyed by accurate fire from 106th Battery's guns. Italian morale collapsed with this defeat and the mass surrenders began, the final total for this action reaching 25,000 prisoners, plus over 100 tanks, 216 guns and 1500 other vehicles.

No further advance

O'Connor pressed for the exploitation of the victory, proposing a further advance to occupy the whole of Libya, which would have been a massive blow to Mussolini's prestige and might well have forced Italy out of the war. He was overruled by political pressures to divert forces to support Greece in its counter-offensive against the Italian forces that had invaded from Albania. Despite this, the campaign had ended in a stunning British success, amply illustrated by a comparison of the losses on each side:

• British: 500 dead, 55 missing and 1373 wounded.
• Italian: 10 divisions destroyed (130,000 prisoners); 180 medium tanks and over 200 light tanks captured; 845 guns captured.

Brigade was ordered to detach 60 of its M13/40s from the rearguard to help batter a way through with support from all the available artillery. The British also frantically worked to raise the number of AFVs fit for action, which eventually totalled 32 cruisers and 53 light tanks plus some armoured cars.

Throughout the next day, a succession of Italian attacks were beaten off, notably at the small hill known as the Pimple, where accurate fire from nine hull-down A13s of A Squadron, 2 RTR, broke up two assaults, each led by at least 20 M13/40s. The A13s were running critically short of 2pdr ammunition by the time the slower A9s and A10s

El Agheila to El Alamein
1941–42

The string of victories that culminated at Beda Fomm had made British commanders dangerously overconfident. Matters were made worse by the transfer of battle-hardened formations to Greece and their replacement by inexperienced units that would inevitably take time to adjust to the demands of desert warfare.

THE EASY VICTORIES of the opening months of the desert war had left the impression that mobility and surprise were guarantees of success, and conventional formations tended to be broken up to form large numbers of small raiding units, each with their own detachments of armour, artillery and infantry. Although some of these small units were very effective, they became used to fighting their own 'private wars' and lost the knack of efficient cooperation with other formations in larger actions. The breaking-up of the sophisticated artillery command structure was perhaps the worst single effect of this process. As a result, intense, concentrated bombardments could rarely be laid when they were really needed, most notably to counter Rommel's expertly sited anti-tank batteries, which inflicted such heavy losses on British armour. Dug-in 88s (3.5in weapons) and 50mm (2in) Pak

38s gave bloody reminders of lessons that should have been learnt after Arras. In the early stages of Operation *Battleaxe*, the towed artillery assigned to support 4 RTR's Matildas bogged down in soft sand, leaving the tanks to be picked off by 88mm (3.5in) weapons dug-in on Halfaya Ridge.

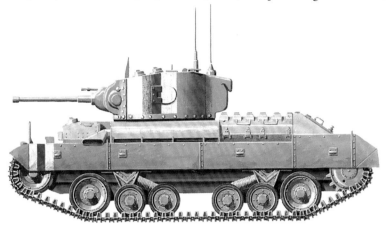

▲ Infantry Tank Mark III, Valentine Mark II

Eighth Army / XIII Corps / 1st Army Tank Brigade

Valentines were introduced to supplement the Matildas in 1941 and first went into action with 8 RTR during Operation Crusader in November of that year. During 1942 they steadily replaced Matildas in the infantry tank regiments.

Specifications

Crew: 3	Speed: 24km/h (14.9mph)
Weight: 17.27 tonnes (17 tons)	Range: 145km (90 miles)
Length: 5.89m (19ft 4in)	Armament: 1 x 40mm (1.57in) 2pdr OQF gun,
Width: 2.64m (8ft 8in)	plus 1 x coaxial 7.92mm (0.31in) Besa MG
Height: 2.29m (7ft 6in)	Radio: Wireless Set No. 11
Engine: 97.73kW (131hp) AEC 6-cylinder diesel	

Specifications

Crew: 3	Speed: 24km/h (15mph)
Weight: 17.27 tonnes (17 tons)	Range: 145km (90 miles)
Length: 5.89m (19ft 4in)	Armament: 1 x 40mm (1.57in) 2pdr OQF gun,
Width: 2.64m (8ft 8in)	plus 1 x coaxial 7.92mm (0.31in) Besa MG
Height: 2.29m (7ft 6in)	Radio: Wireless Set No. 11
Engine: 97.73kW (131hp) AEC 6-cylinder diesel	

▲ Infantry Tank Mark III, Valentine Mark II

Eighth Army / XIII Corps / 1st Army Tank Brigade

The Valentine was greatly appreciated for its mechanical reliability, which was far higher than that of most contemporary British tanks.

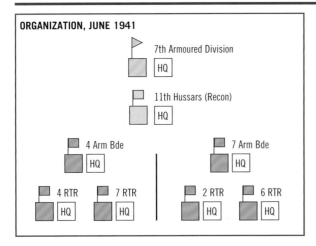

ORGANIZATION, JUNE 1941

7th Armoured Division
HQ

11th Hussars (Recon)
HQ

4 Arm Bde
HQ

7 Arm Bde
HQ

4 RTR
HQ

7 RTR
HQ

2 RTR
HQ

6 RTR
HQ

These problems were worsened by the totally inadequate provision for HE-firing weapons in British tank designs; it was confined to the small number of close support (CS) versions of each type, which were armed with the 76mm (3in) CS howitzer. (In 1941 only six of the 52 cruiser tanks in each armoured regiment were CS variants.) Not only were the numbers of CS tanks too low, but the weapon itself was unimpressive, with a badly designed HE round of poor lethality that had a maximum range of no more than 2200m (2407 yards). (Contrary to popular belief, there was a 2pdr HE shell, but very little has come to light on this ammunition, which seems only to have been issued to AFVs in the Far East from 1943 onwards.)

All too often these factors resulted in British tanks being committed to costly frontal charges in desperate attempts to get within machine-gun range of the enemy anti-tank guns.

No real solution was found until the US-supplied Grants and Lees began to enter service in May 1942, armed with 75mm (2.9in) M2 and M3 guns firing a good HE shell (much more effective than that of the 76mm/3in CS howitzer) out to 12,000m (13,130 yards). The M2 and M3 also had a respectable anti-tank performance for the time, although the limited traverse sponson mounting made it impossible to fire from hull-down positions.

The same 75mm (2.9in) M3 weapon, but now in a conventional turret, was the main armament of the Shermans which began to be issued a few months later. This layout solved most of the tactical problems posed by the earlier sponson mountings, and long-range indirect HE fire was made more effective by the fitting of the Azimuth Indicator M19.

Enter the Desert Fox

Rommel arrived in North Africa on 12 February 1941 and quickly appreciated the urgency of boosting the Italians' morale, which had been badly shaken by their defeat at Beda Fomm. The first probing attacks were launched as early as 24 February and were followed up by a full-blown offensive on 24 March when the German 5th Light Division had completed its concentration.

▲ **Heat and dust**
A column of Crusaders kicks up dust. Vehicles could rarely move in the desert without creating large clouds of dust that could be seen for kilometres.

This timing totally surprised Rommel's opponents, who had assumed that no major operations would be launched until the Germans had taken a month or so to acclimatize and settle in. Aided by the inexperience of so many Allied front-line units, this surprise attack achieved a striking success, including the capture of General O'Connor, who had masterminded the victorious Beda Fomm campaign. After little more than a month, Axis forces had recaptured almost all the territory lost during the previous winter and were again on the Egyptian frontier. Only the fortified port of Tobruk, which Rommel desperately needed to ease his acute supply problems, stubbornly held out against all attacks.

Stung by the dramatic Axis advance, General Wavell in Cairo planned a counterattack, codenamed Operation *Brevity*, which opened on 15 May. The objective was the recapture of the vital Halfaya Pass together with Sollum and Fort Capuzzo as a preliminary to raising the siege of Tobruk. The pass and Fort Capuzzo were seized, but Rommel reacted quickly and retook both by 27 May.

By 15 June, Wavell had been reinforced and launched Operation *Battleaxe* with a total of almost 400 tanks, again aimed at breaking through to Tobruk before driving westwards to secure a line from Derna to Mechili. Although British reading of the German 'Enigma' codes provided useful information, Rommel's own expert signals intelligence staff were

▲ **Get a move on!**

Crews race to their Stuart Is, autumn 1941. They all wear early pattern US tankers' helmets, which were supplied with Lend-Lease AFVs in 1941–42.

able to counter this through their intercepts of many of Wavell's orders. With neither side having a clear advantage in the 'intelligence war', superior German tactical ability proved to be the decisive factor – especially their expertise in deploying anti-tank batteries, which had a distinct edge over AFVs provided that the gun crews had time to measure ranges and set up range markers. (This was largely due to the special conditions of desert warfare in which mirages, heat shimmer and dust clouds made it very difficult to identify targets and even harder to accurately judge ranges.)

Specifications

Crew: 5	Speed: 44km/h (27mph)
Weight: 19.26 tonnes (18.95 tons)	Range: 161km (100 miles)
Length: 5.99m (19ft 8in)	Armament: 1 x 40mm (1.57in) 2pdr OQF gun,
Width: 2.64m (8ft 8in)	plus 2 x 7.92mm (0.31in) Besa MGs
Height: 2.24m (7ft 4in)	(1 coaxial and 1 in sub-turret)
Engine: 253.64kW (340hp) Nuffield Liberty	Radio: Wireless Set No. 11
Mark III V12 petrol	

▲ **Cruiser Tank Mark VI, Crusader Mark I**

Eighth Army / 7th Armoured Division / HQ / 22nd Armoured Brigade

Crusaders began to replace the earlier cruiser tanks in North Africa from mid-1941. A9s were phased out of service at about this time, but A10s and A13s soldiered on until the end of the year.

In tank-versus-tank actions, the British and Germans were quite evenly matched, although 2pdr shot tended to shatter against the Panzers' face-hardened armour at close range, a fault which was not cured until capped shot (APCBC, or armour-piercing cap ballistic cap) was issued in May 1942. After making some initial gains, the British offensive was fought to a standstill within a couple of days and their outmanoeuvred armour only just escaped being surrounded. The respective losses (220 British tanks lost, of which 87 were complete write-offs, against 25 Panzers destroyed) clearly showed how well Rommel had done with his outnumbered forces and marked the beginning of his reputation as the 'Desert Fox'.

Tobruk campaign

In the aftermath of the failure of Brevity and Battleaxe, Wavell was posted to India and replaced by General Claude Auchinleck as commander-in-chief in Cairo, whilst General Alan Cunningham took over command of the forces in the desert, which were now reorganized as the Eighth Army. Rommel's victories were recognized by his promotion to *General der Panzertruppe* (lieutenant-general) on 1 July and his command was redesignated *Panzergruppe Afrika* on 15 August. The first operation of the *Panzergruppe* (in September 1941) was a raid on what was believed to be a major British supply dump to build up stocks of fuel before renewing the assault on Tobruk, which was planned for 23 November. This raid was a failure with the loss of 30 AFVs and the delay allowed Auchinleck to launch his own offensive (Operation *Crusader*) on 18 November with over 750 tanks,

including 280 of the newly supplied M3 Stuarts, supported by 600 guns.

Once again, the objective was to raise the siege of Tobruk and the opening moves went well – the major airfield at Sidi Rezegh was captured and 19 Axis aircraft were destroyed on the ground. The inevitable German counterattacks began the next day, with each of the two Panzer divisions massing all available resources to strike concentrated blows at the scattered British brigades. In four days of fighting two of these brigades lost some 300 tanks between them. As Rommel was later to remark to a captured British officer: 'What does it matter if you have two tanks to my one, when you spread them out and let me smash them in detail?'

New broom

General Cunningham wanted to withdraw, but was replaced by General Neil Ritchie, who was under strict orders to continue with the offensive. Rommel was convinced that the Eighth Army would indeed be forced to fall back and he led the bulk of his forces in a dash for the Egyptian frontier to cut off its line of retreat. This spectacular advance caused a temporary panic in Egypt, but by abandoning the battlefield around Sidi Rezegh, Rommel took the pressure off the battered British armoured units, which were allowed time to recover and repair many of their damaged tanks whilst New Zealand forces broke through to the Tobruk garrison.

By the time that the *Deutsches Afrikakorps* (DAK) was able to regroup, it was down to 40 battleworthy tanks whilst the Italians were even worse off with

▶ **M3 Stuart I Light Tank**

Eighth Army / XXX Corps / 7th Armoured Division / 4th Armoured Brigade / 8th Hussars

Eighty-four Stuarts arrived in North Africa in July 1941 and by November the total had risen to 280, which equipped all three battalions of 4th Armoured Brigade.

Specifications

Crew: 4	Speed: 58km/h (36mph)
Weight: 12.7 tonnes (12.5 tons)	Range: 110km (70 miles)
Length: 4.53m (14ft 10in)	Armament: 1 x 37mm (1.5in) M5 gun,
Width: 2.24m (7ft 4in)	plus 3 x 7.62mm (0.3in) MGs (1 AA, 1 coaxial
Height: 2.64m (8ft 8in)	and 1 ball-mounted in hull front)
Engine: 186.25kW (250hp) Continental	Radio: SCR210
W-670-9A 7-cylinder petrol	

only 30 serviceable tanks. However, it was the chronic supply problems that posed the greatest threat to the Axis cause in the theatre as virtually two-thirds of the 122,000 tonnes (120,000 tons) of stores sent to North Africa in recent weeks had been sunk en route. In early December a determined British attack convinced Rommel that he had to retreat, and by Christmas he was back where he had started 10 months earlier.

The next round in the desert war opened at the beginning of 1942 with the long-awaited arrival of reinforcements for the DAK, including 74 AFVs, which allowed Rommel to launch his next offensive on 21 January. Within a couple of weeks this pushed the front-line almost 400km (250 miles) eastwards to the fortified Gazala Line covering Tobruk, where it

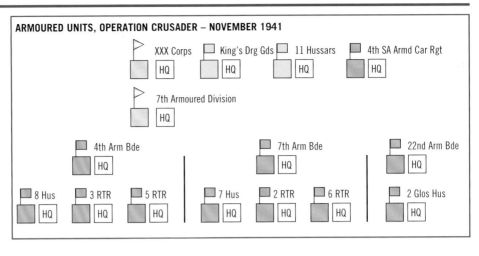

ARMOURED UNITS, OPERATION CRUSADER – NOVEMBER 1941

▼ C Squadron, 8th Hussars

The Stuart was highly popular with its crews for its reliability and speed. It was widely referred to as the 'Honey', supposedly after a driver remarked 'She's a honey!' on returning from his first test drive.

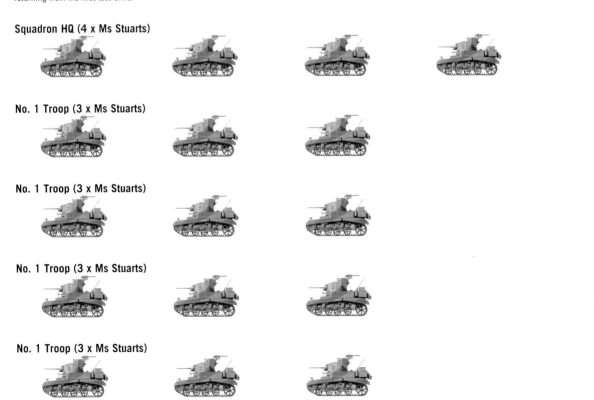

Squadron HQ (4 x Ms Stuarts)

No. 1 Troop (3 x Ms Stuarts)

No. 1 Troop (3 x Ms Stuarts)

No. 1 Troop (3 x Ms Stuarts)

No. 1 Troop (3 x Ms Stuarts)

remained for the next four months as both sides built up their strength for the next move.

By the end of May, the Axis forces were heavily outnumbered in terms of tanks, although they had a distinct edge in numbers of aircraft. Despite the obvious difficulties posed by Allied tank strengths, which for the first time included the Grant, Rommel considered that his forces still had sufficient tactical superiority to ensure victory and attacked again on 26 May, only just before Ritchie was ready to launch his own offensive. Whilst Italian infantry divisions attacked the coastal end of the Gazala Line, the DAK plus the *Ariete* Armoured Division moved to outflank the southern end of the Allied line, held by the Free French at Bir Hacheim. Although the Bir Hacheim garrison beat off all assaults, the main Axis armoured thrust was able to push into the Eighth Army's rear areas before any major counterattacks developed. These were determined efforts which, for a few critical days, trapped Rommel against the Allied minefields in an area which became known as the Cauldron. Eventually the pressure was eased by the defeat of a major Allied assault followed by the evacuation of Bir Hacheim on 10/11 June.

Barely 24 hours later, the DAK broke out of the Cauldron and raced for the Tobruk perimeter, reimposing the siege on 18 June. This time, however,

the port's garrison was in no condition to hold out for more than a few days and, on 21 June, it surrendered to a jubilant Rommel, who was promoted to field-marshal in recognition of his victory, having been in the rank of full general for less than six months.

In the aftermath of defeat, command of the Eighth Army changed again as Auchinleck dismissed Ritchie and took over in person. Allied forces fell back on Mersa Matruh before continuing their retreat to El Alamein, the final defensible line covering the Nile Delta. The DAK was in hot pursuit and had closed up to the El Alamein positions by 1 July, but failed to break through in a series of attacks launched over the next few days.

CAMOUFLAGE & MARKINGS, 1942

In general, there were only minor changes to camouflage and markings from those described in the preceding section. Most British AFVs were simply painted in overall sand yellow or sand brown (top), but no matter what the nationality, the actual colours could vary greatly after prolonged exposure to the fierce sun and an occasional sandstorm. A few units used more elaborate camouflage schemes, adding disruptive patterns of darker brown, green, grey or black to the original sand finish (bottom).

▲ **M3 Lee Medium Tank**

Eighth Army / 1st Armoured Brigade / 1 RTR

The Grants-M3s modified to meet British specifications by the adoption of a new low turret without a cupola were first used in action at Gazala in May 1942 when a total of 167 equipped three armoured brigades. Standard M3s, designated Lees in British service, were also sent to North Africa to replace combat losses and a total of 210 Grants/Lees were in service by October 1942.

Specifications

Crew: 7

Weight: 27.22 tonnes (26.7 tons)

Length: 5.64m (18ft 6in)

Width: 2.72m (8ft 11in)

Height: 3.12m (10ft 3in)

Engine: 253.5kW (340hp) Continental

R-975-EC2 radial petrol

Speed: 42km/h (26mph)

Range: 193km (120 miles)

Armament: 1 x 75mm (2.9in) M2 or M3 gun,

1 x 37mm (1.5in) M4 or M5 gun, plus

4 x 7.62mm (0.3in) MGs (1 in commander's

cupola, 1 coaxial and 2 fixed forward-firing)

Radio: SCR508

▲ Covering fire

A Daimler Mk I armoured car provides fire support for a British infantry attack, October 1942.

▼ 'Bombing-up'

A Sherman's crew stow ammunition for the tank's 75mm (2.9in) main armament. Early Shermans carried 90 rounds of 75mm (2.9in) ammunition; later models stowed 97 rounds.

Allied counterattacks later in July had only limited success, and stalemate set in with neither side able to achieve a decisive result. This led to yet another change in command of the Allied forces, with Auchinleck replaced by General Harold Alexander whilst General Bernard Montgomery took over the Eighth Army. His efforts to rebuild its self-confidence were greatly helped by the stream of new AFVs arriving to re-equip its armoured formations. Rommel realized that he could not hope to match the scale of the Allied build-up and decided to attack on 30 August before the odds became too great.

Failed attack

The plan was similar to that used at Gazala, with holding attacks launched near the coast, whilst the main effort was aimed at outflanking the southern end of the Allied line. Once this was achieved, the attack would swing north-eastwards to take the Alam el Halfa ridge, cutting the Allied supply lines and unhinging the entire El Alamein position. Even before the offensive began, there were disturbing signs of increased Allied strength – Axis armour was heavily bombed as it began to concentrate in the days leading up to the attack.

The early stages of the advance were slowed by the extensive minefields and once through these, the DAK found that Alam el Halfa was held in strength

by two armoured brigades backed up by ample artillery and air support. After two days of fruitless attacks, Rommel admitted that a breakthrough was impossible and pulled back to his start line, with the loss of more than 50 tanks. British losses totalled almost 70 tanks, but, unlike Rommel's, these could easily be replaced and the balance of forces had now swung decisively in the Allies' favour.

El Alamein to Tunis
1942–43

The defensive victories at the First Battle of El Alamein and Alam el Halfa had boosted confidence throughout the Eighth Army and had created an atmosphere in which Montgomery's reorganization and retraining were readily accepted.

THE FORMATION ONCE again became a key battlefield player, curbing the tendency to deploy armour in small units each of which could be defeated in succession by properly concentrated Panzer divisions. Most importantly, Montgomery emphasized training in all-arms cooperation, in which armour, infantry and artillery worked together as battlefield teams. A steadily increasing flow of new AFVs, notably Shermans and Priests plus the first Matilda Scorpion flail tanks, provided the essential equipment for these teams to operate effectively and gave them a decisive advantage over their opponents.

Axis armour 1942–43

This period saw the introduction of a new generation of German AFVs, including up-gunned Stugs, Panzer IVs and the first Tiger Is. A generous allocation of these AFVs to the DAK might have

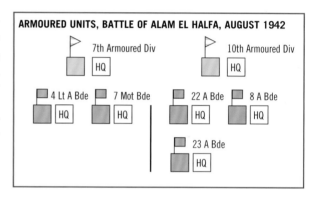

ARMOURED UNITS, BATTLE OF ALAM EL HALFA, AUGUST 1942

7th Armoured Div — HQ

10th Armoured Div — HQ

4 Lt A Bde — HQ   7 Mot Bde — HQ

22 A Bde — HQ   8 A Bde — HQ

23 A Bde — HQ

partially offset Allied numerical superiority, but even Rommel could not compete with the overriding needs of the Eastern Front until the prospect of the complete loss of North Africa prompted panic measures in a futile attempt to stave off defeat. If German problems were bad, they were trivial

Specifications

Crew: 3	Speed: 44km/h (27mph)
Weight: 20.07 tonnes (19.75 tons)	Range: 161km (100 miles)
Length: 6.3m (20ft 8in)	Armament: 1 x 57mm (2.24in) 6pdr OQF gun,
Width: 2.64m (8ft 8in)	plus 1 coaxial 7.92mm (0.31in) Besa MG
Height: 2.2m (7ft 4in)	Radio: Wireless Set No. 11
Engine: 253.64kW (340hp) Nuffield Liberty	
Mark IV V12 petrol	

▲ **Cruiser Tank Mark VI, Crusader Mark III**

Eighth Army / XXX Corps / HQ 23rd Armoured Brigade

The first towed 6pdr anti-tank guns were issued to front-line units in May 1942, but the Crusader III, which carried the 6pdr, was not ready until August of that year. Despite the 6pdr's anti-tank performance being better than that of the US 75mm (2.9in) in the Lee/Grant and Sherman, it was not as popular, because the American gun's superior HE shell was far more useful in dealing with the enemy anti-tank batteries, which posed the greatest threat at that time. Moreover, 6pdr HE was rarely issued and its very existence was often forgotten.

compared with those confronting Italian armoured units, whose equipment was increasingly outclassed by Allied AFVs. The various types of Semovente self-propelled guns were useful assault weapons, but the majority mounted short 75mm (2.9in) L/18 guns that had a poor anti-tank performance. Deliveries of more powerfully armed AFVs were slow – barely 30 of the potent Semovente 90/53 were available by late 1942 and several promising types had only just entered production by the time that Italy surrendered in September 1943.

El Alamein

The failure of his offensives at the First Battle of El Alamein and at Alam el Halfa in July/August 1942 left Rommel with seriously weakened armoured forces. His losses, totalling more than 50 tanks, were especially grave given the slow trickle of replacements along a lengthy and dangerously exposed supply line that was being subjected to increasingly heavy air attacks. One of the most damaging effects of these interdiction operations was to cause a chronic fuel shortage throughout the Axis forces, which severely limited their freedom of manoeuvre.

Rommel's priority was now to establish strong defence lines in readiness for the offensive that Montgomery was certain to launch once his build-up was complete. Wherever possible, Allied minefields in captured sectors were used to form part of the Axis defences. These were thickened and extended until the 65km (41-mile) front from the Mediterranean to the virtually impassable terrain of the Qattara Depression was clogged with 500,000 mines. Behind the minefields lay defence lines up to 3km (1.9 miles) deep, held by infantry and artillery (and with the Italian formations bolstered by flanking German units). Axis armour waited in reserve, ready to counterattack as soon as the Allied offensive was blunted by the minefields and fortified positions.

By late October 1942, Montgomery's preparations were complete and he launched the Second Battle of El Alamein on the 23rd. His offensive began at 21:40 with a 30-minute bombardment by 1000 guns and a series of air attacks before the assaults went in, directed against the northern and southern ends of the Axis line.

Eighth Army AFV Units, Oct 1942	Constituent Units	Commanding Officer	Vehicles	Strength
British 7th Armoured Div	1st Household Cav Rgt 11th Hussars	Maj-Gen John Harding		
– 4th Light Armoured Bde	Royal Scots Greys 4th/8th Hussars	Brig Marcus G. Roddick	Stuart Grant	57 14
– 22nd Armoured Bde	1st Royal Tank Regiment 5th Royal Tank Regiment	Brig George 'Pip' Roberts	Grant Crusader Stuart	57 46 19
British 1st Armoured Div	12th Royal Lancers 4th/6th South African Armd Car Rgt	Maj-Gen Raymond Briggs		
– 2nd Armoured Bde	2nd Dragoon Guards (Queen's Bays) 9th Queen's Royal Lancers 10th Royal Hussars Yorkshire Dragoons	Brig Arthur Fisher	Sherman Crusader	92 68
– 7th Motor Bde	2nd Btn King's Royal Rifle Corps 2nd Btn Rifle Brigade 7th Btn Rifle Brigade	Brig Thomas J. Bosville		
British 10th Armoured Div	Royal Dragoons	Maj-Gen Alexander Gatehouse		
– 8th Armoured Bde	3rd Royal Tank Regiment The Nottinghamshire Yeomanry Staffordshire Yeomanry	Brig Edward C.N. Custance	Crusader Grant Sherman	45 57 31
– 24th Armoured Bde	41st Royal Tank Regiment 45th Royal Tank Regiment 47th Royal Tank Regiment	Brig Arthur G. Kenchington	Sherman Crusader	93 45

Rommel was on sick leave in Germany when the battle began, thoroughly exhausted by 18 months of intensive operations in gruelling desert conditions. He had handed over to General Georg Stumme, who suffered a fatal heart attack just as the battle began, but despite this, the DAK put up a fierce fight over 11 days, inflicting losses of up to 90 per cent on some Allied armoured units.

Rommel's return to the front to resume command on 25 October boosted morale, but could do nothing to alter the two-to-one Allied superiority in AFVs. Over 1000 Allied tanks, including 250 Shermans, faced barely 500 Axis tanks, of which more than half were obsolescent Italian vehicles. This numerical superiority meant that the Allies could accept heavy losses in exchange for the destruction of the DAK's armour – on 24/25 October 15th Panzer Division's counterattack was halted with the loss of all but 31 of its 119 tanks.

Torch landings

Sheer weight of enemy numbers coupled with ever worsening fuel shortages eventually forced Rommel to acknowledge that, despite 'stand fast' orders from Hitler and Mussolini, a retreat was unavoidable if he was going to save any of his units. The withdrawal

CAMOUFLAGE & MARKINGS

There was very little change to camouflage schemes until the fighting spread to Tunisia, where there was more vegetation, especially during the wetter winter months. Both sides began to make more use of camouflage schemes, which included at least some greenish paint – a few of the Tiger Is encountered may well have been painted in overall olive green as were some British and most US AFVs during the final stages of the North Africa campaign.

began on 4 November, and four days later the Allies began Operation *Torch* – major landings in Morocco and Algeria (then French North Africa) aimed at Rommel's base areas, particularly the key ports of Tunis and Bizerta.

No one was certain how the Vichy French garrisons would react to this invasion, and American forces led the first wave in the hope of avoiding open fighting. There was some resistance to the first landings, but within 48 hours a ceasefire had been negotiated and the route to Tunis seemed to be open. The deadly threat posed by Operation Torch was immediately apparent to the Germans, who reacted swiftly, flying in reinforcements to protect their Tunisian bases and establishing a 15,000-strong garrison (with 130

▲ **Dominating the desert**

The Sherman represented a major advance in American AFV design, as it was the first US tank with a turret-mounted 75mm (2.9in) gun. Deliveries to North Africa began in August 1942 and a total of 270 had arrived by October of that year.

AFVs) by the end of November. This proved to be sufficient to halt the First Army's advance from French North Africa, which had made alarming progress – on 27 November Stuarts of the US 1st Tank Battalion and the Derbyshire Yeomanry's Daimler armoured cars raided Djedeida airfield, less than 15km (9 miles) from Tunis.

German counterattack

By early December, General Hans-Jürgen von Arnim, commanding the German forces in Tunisia, was ready to launch his own offensive against the opposing Allied units, which were by now seriously overstretched. Heavy winter rains slowed operations, but affected the inexperienced American forces far more than their veteran German opponents, most notably on 10 December when Combat Command B (CCB), 1st US Armored Division, panicked during a night withdrawal and drove off wildly, eventually abandoning a total of 18 tanks, 41 guns and 130 other vehicles, all bogged down in thick mud. Further German spoiling attacks in January 1943 imposed more delays on the Allied build-up in Tunisia and confirmed the dangerous amateurishness of the American command and control structure.

Whilst these events were unfolding, Rommel, away to the east, was conducting an expertly handled withdrawal westwards towards Tunisia, imposing temporary halts on the Eighth Army's pursuit at El Agheila (23 November–13 December) and at Buerat (26 December–15 January). The Buerat Line was significantly weakened by the transfer of

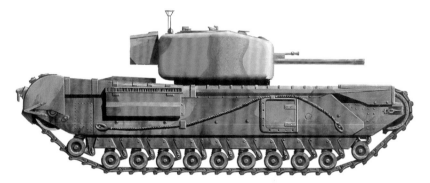

▲ Infantry Tank Mark IV, Churchill Mark IV

First Army / 4th Infantry Division / 21st Tank Brigade

A trials unit fielded six Churchill IIIs in the Second Battle of El Alamein, but it was not until the Tunisian campaign that the Mark IV was first used in any numbers, sometimes serving alongside Churchill Is in the same units.

Specifications

Weight: 39.62 tonnes (39 tons)	Speed: 25km/h (15.5mph)
Length: 7.44m (24ft 5in)	Range: 193km (120 miles)
Width: 2.74m (9ft)	Armament: 1 x 57mm (2.24in) 6pdr OQF
Height: 3.25m (10ft 8in)	gun, plus 2 x 7.92mm (0.31in) Besa MGs (1
Engine: 261.1kW (350hp) Bedford	coaxial and 1 ball-mounted in hull front)
12-cylinder petrol	Radio: Wireless Set No. 19

▶ Humber Armoured Car Mark II

Eighth Army / 7th Armoured Division / 11th Hussars

The Humber Mark II was a 4 x 4 vehicle armed with a 15mm (0.59in) Besa heavy machine gun and a coaxial 7.92mm (0.31in) Besa machine gun. A total of 440 vehicles were produced, many of which saw service in North Africa.

Specifications

Crew: 3	Speed: 72km/h (45mph)
Weight: 7.213 tonnes (7.1 tons)	Range: 402km (250 miles)
Length: 4.57m (15ft)	Armament: 1 x 15mm (0.59in) Besa HMG,
Width: 2.18m (7ft 2in)	plus 1 x coaxial 7.92mm (0.31in) Besa MG
Height: 2.34m (7ft 10in)	Radio: Wireless Set No. 19
Engine: 67kW (95hp) Rootes 6-cylinder petrol	

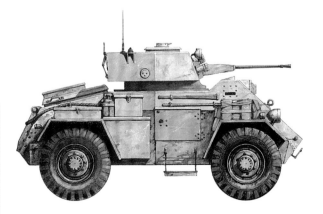

21st Panzer Division to reinforce von Arnim, and when the position was outflanked by Montgomery's next attack, the DAK was pulled back to eastern Tunisia. Its new positions were based on the old French fortifications of the Mareth Line, which were strengthened by German and Italian engineers so that the bulk of Rommel's forces could be freed for operations against the First Army's front.

Kasserine Pass

In the meantime, it was von Arnim who began the offensive on 14 February with a drive by 10th and 21st Panzer Divisions against the Faid Pass. This broke through the front-line held by American infantry, swiftly deploying to hull-down fire positions against a clumsy counterattack by 1st Armored's CCA, which was beaten off with the loss of 55 US AFVs. On the following day, a further ill-directed effort, this time by CCB, was defeated, during which 46 American tanks were captured or destroyed.

As von Arnim's spearheads moved westwards, Rommel struck north to link up with his attack at the Kasserine Pass, hoping to be able to exploit the breakthrough with a drive against the Allied rear and their key Algerian supply centres at Bone and Constantine. After punching through the Kasserine Pass on 18 February, Axis armour swept on to Thala and Sbiba where it was beaten off by defences with massive artillery support, backed up by the British 6th Armoured Division.

Despite having inflicted 10,000 casualties for the loss of only 2000, Rommel realized that it was time to break off the attack and by the end of the month, the Axis forces were back on their old front-lines.

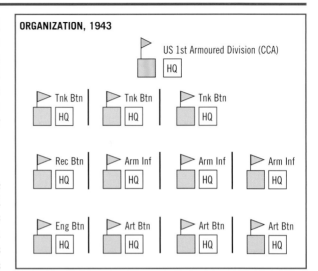

ORGANIZATION, 1943

US 1st Armoured Division (CCA)
HQ

Tnk Btn — HQ | Tnk Btn — HQ | Tnk Btn — HQ

Rec Btn — HQ | Arm Inf — HQ | Arm Inf — HQ | Arm Inf — HQ

Eng Btn — HQ | Art Btn — HQ | Art Btn — HQ | Art Btn — HQ

The DAK's final offensive was launched by three Panzer divisions with a total of 142 tanks and 200 guns against the Eighth Army's positions at Medinine. Good intelligence and reconnaissance ensured that Montgomery was well aware of what was coming and over 450 anti-tank guns (including the new 17pdrs) supported by 350 pieces of field and medium artillery broke up the attack, knocking out 50 of the Panzers.

Rommel was now desperately concerned by the overwhelming odds his men were facing and he handed over to von Arnim before returning to Germany to try to convince Hitler of just how critical the situation had become. Hitler refused to accept Rommel's bleak assessment of the chances of holding Tunisia and ordered him to take further sick leave.

▶ **M3A1 Light Tank**

First Army / 1st Armored Division / 12th Armored Regiment / 1st Battalion

In common with the Eighth Army, US forces in North Africa quickly appreciated the M3's qualities as a reconnaissance vehicle.

Specifications

Crew: 4	Speed: 58km/h (36mph)
Weight: 12.9 tonnes (12.69 tons)	Range: 110km (70 miles)
Length: 4.53m (14ft 10in)	Armament: 1 x 37mm (1.5in) M6 gun, plus
Width: 2.24m (7ft 4in)	3 x 7.62mm (0.3in) MGs (1 AA, 1 coaxial and
Height: 2.64m (8ft 8in)	1 ball-mounted in hull front)
Engine: 186.25kW (250hp) Continental	Radio: SCR508
W-670-9A 7-cylinder petrol	

▶ **Link-up**

M3 light tanks of US II Corps meet leading elements of the Eighth Army in Tunisia, April 1943. Axis forces in North Africa were now trapped in a shrinking pocket around Tunis, finally surrendering in mid-May.

Any chances that Rommel might be able to return to Africa were soon overtaken by the final Allied offensives, which squeezed the Axis forces into a shrinking perimeter around Tunis and Bizerta by mid-April. It was clearly only a matter of time before the enormous Allied superiority (1200 AFVs and 1500 guns to 130 tanks and 500 guns) would prove decisive. Despite some effective rearguard actions, notably by the handful of available Tigers, all Axis forces in North Africa surrendered on 12 May, ending almost three years of desert warfare.

Specifications

Crew: 7	Speed: 42km/h (26mph)
Weight: 27.22 tonnes (26.7 tons)	Range: 193km (120 miles)
Length: 5.64m (18ft 6in)	Armament: 1 x 75mm (2.9in) M2 or M3 gun,
Width: 2.72m (8ft 11in)	1 x 37mm (1.5in) M4 or M5 gun, plus
Height: 3.12m (10ft 3in)	4 x 7.62mm (0.3in) MGs (1 in commander's
Engine: 253.5kW (340hp) Continental	cupola, 1 coaxial and 2 fixed forward-firing)
R-975-EC2 radial petrol	Radio: SCR508

▲ **M3 Medium Tank**

First Army / 1st Armored Division / 12th Armored Regiment / 2nd Battalion

If handled carefully, the M3 was still an effective medium tank in 1942–43, but US armoured units in North Africa initially lacked the necessary tactical expertise to overcome its design limitations.

Chapter 4

Sicily and Italy: 1943–45

Winston Churchill was a keen proponent
of the 'Mediterranean strategy' – exploiting the
Axis collapse in North Africa by invading Italy,
which he memorably (and inaccurately) termed
'the soft underbelly of Europe'.
Allied hesitancy and German doggedness
were to ensure that it was anything but soft.
Indeed, to those who fought from Sicily to Turin
it became 'the tough old gut'.

◀ **Desolation**
A Canadian Sherman stops in the ruins of Ortona, Italy, December 1943.

Invasion of Sicily
10 JULY–17 AUGUST 1943

In early 1943, the Allies finally agreed that an invasion of France was not feasible that year and to adopt elements of Churchill's Mediterranean strategy, beginning with the invasion of Sicily.

THE ISLAND WAS DEFENDED by General Alfredo Guzzoni's Italian Sixth Army, with over 240,000 men, and the roughly 40,000 German troops of XIV Panzer Corps, comprising the *Hermann Göring* Panzer Division and 15th *Panzergrenadier* Division. The force had at least 270 AFVs and about 220 guns.

The invasion force, meanwhile, was built around General George Patton's US Seventh Army and Montgomery's Eighth Army, a total of 160,000 men, 600 tanks and 1800 guns carried by a fleet of 2500 vessels. Crucially, the fleet included battleships and cruisers, whose long-range gunfire support would do much to ensure the success of the landings on 10 July.

Airborne assault

Although the Allied airborne assault that was intended to block the routes to the beachheads was badly scattered, it did confuse the defenders, slowing their reaction to the landings. Patton's Seventh Army, including 2nd Armored Division, landed in the Gulf of Gela, in south-central Sicily, on a frontage of over 50km (31 miles). Montgomery's forces landed in south-eastern Sicily, also on a 50km (31-mile) front, with a 40km (25-mile) gap between the two armies. The plan called for the armies to link up and secure a large beachhead area before Eighth Army drove north to Messina, whilst Seventh Army covered its left flank and cleared the rest of the island.

Inevitably, there were setbacks and delays – whilst many Italian units were only too happy to surrender, others fought with surprising ferocity. As ever, German forces were able opponents, skilfully exploiting the terrain to delay the Allied advance and launching sharp counterattacks.

On 10 July, US forces around Gela fought off an Italian counterattack by the *Livorno* Division supported by tanks of the *Niscemi* Armoured Combat Group. Two days later the *Livorno* Division tried again in conjunction with the *Hermann Göring* Panzer Division, but this attack was also beaten off with the help of accurate naval gunfire support.

British advance

In contrast, British forces had only met light opposition in their capture of Syracuse, but on 13 July, they had to fight off counterattacks by infantry and ex-French R-35 tanks of General Giulio Porcinari's *Napoli* Infantry Division. (Elements of 4th Armoured Brigade captured Porcinari and his staff in this action.)

As the Allied advances continued, there was little tank-versus-tank action, but scores of small engagements such as those recorded in the report for 22 July of the US 2nd Armored Division (nicknamed 'Hell on Wheels'). 'Each defile was strongly defended by A-T weapons and machine-guns cleverly emplaced and protected by infantry. Each of these elements had to be reduced one by one. Not until surrounded by infantry and shelled by artillery and/or tanks was there

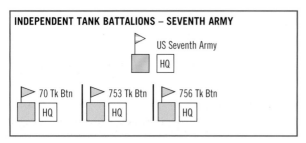

INDEPENDENT TANK BATTALIONS – SEVENTH ARMY

US Seventh Army — HQ

70 Tk Btn — HQ | 753 Tk Btn — HQ | 756 Tk Btn — HQ

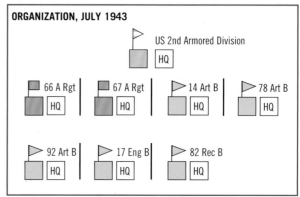

ORGANIZATION, JULY 1943

US 2nd Armored Division — HQ

66 A Rgt — HQ | 67 A Rgt — HQ | 14 Art B — HQ | 78 Art B — HQ

92 Art B — HQ | 17 Eng B — HQ | 82 Rec B — HQ

any sign of surrender. For the most part, the antitank guns were manned by Germans and the infantry furnished by the Italians.… Leading elements of the division on arrival at the pass 4 miles [6.5km] NE of San Guisseppe were held up by a determined defense in depth by A-T guns including German 88mm's [3.5in]. These guns were well emplaced in the sides of the canyons, cleverly concealed and in an extremely strong natural position. This resistance was overcome by flanking action of dismounted patrols, covered by

▲ M4 Dozer

US Seventh Army / 2nd Armored Division / 17th Armored Engineer Battalion

The Sherman's great virtue was its adaptability, an early modification being the installation of a dozer blade. The resulting vehicle proved invaluable for a host of tasks, from clearing rubble-strewn roads to acting as a recovery vehicle.

Specifications*

Crew: 5

Weight: 30.3 tonnes (29.82 tons)

Length: 5.89m (19ft 4in)

Width: 2.62m (8ft 7in)

Height: 2.74m (8ft 11in)

Engine: 298kW (400hp) Continental R975
  C1 radial petrol

Speed: 34km/h (21mph)

Range: 193km (120 miles)

Armament: 1 x 75mm (2.9in) M3 gun,
  plus 2 x 7.62mm (0.3in) MGs (1 coaxial,
  1 ball-mounted in hull front)

Radio: SCR 508

*Data is for standard M4 - the dozer attachment increased weight, length and width, but no figures are available

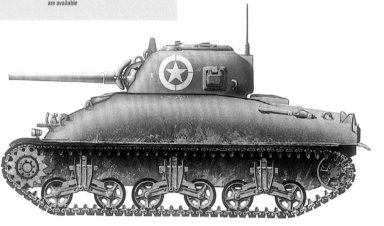

▲ M4A1 Sherman Medium Tank

US Seventh Army / 2nd Armored Division / 66th Armored Regiment

Successful operations in Sicily demonstrated the vast improvement in US armoured formations since the debacle at Kasserine Pass in North Africa only a few months earlier.

Specifications

Crew: 5

Weight: 30.3 tonnes (29.82 tons)

Length: 5.84m (19ft 2in)

Width: 2.62m (8ft 7in)

Height: 2.74m (8ft 11in)

Engine: 298kW (400hp) Continental R975
  C1 radial petrol

Speed: 34km/h (21mph)

Range: 193km (120 miles)

Armament: 1 x 75mm (2.9in) M3 gun,
  plus 2 x 7.62mm (0.3in) MGs (1 coaxial,
  1 ball-mounted in hull front)

Radio: SCR 508

▲ Safely ashore
An M4A1 Sherman of 2nd Armored Division departs from Red Beach 2, Sicily.

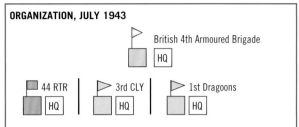

ORGANIZATION, JULY 1943

British 4th Armoured Brigade
HQ

44 RTR — 3rd CLY — 1st Dragoons
HQ   HQ   HQ

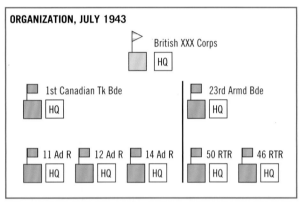

ORGANIZATION, JULY 1943

British XXX Corps
HQ

1st Canadian Tk Bde   23rd Armd Bde
HQ   HQ

11 Ad R   12 Ad R   14 Ad R   50 RTR   46 RTR
HQ   HQ   HQ   HQ   HQ

artillery, tank and supporting cannon gun fire. In the meantime, reconnaissance was being pushed around the flanks to determine routes to by-pass this defile.'

After much bitter fighting, Sicily was finally cleared of Axis forces on 17 August 1943. In a brilliantly executed operation, the Germans evacuated 40,000 men, hundreds of vehicles, including 44 tanks, together with thousands of tonnes of ammunition and supplies under constant air attack. The Sicilian campaign had been a sharp reminder of the importance of good logistical support in successful armoured actions. The US 2nd Armored Division's report ruefully concluded: 'The operation against PALERMO served to emphasize the tremendous supply problem involved in sustaining an armored division on the move and in action. It is estimated

Specifications

Crew: 7	Speed: 41.8km/h (26mph)
Weight: 26.01 tonnes (25.6 tons)	Range: 201km (125 miles)
Length: 6.02m (19ft 9in)	Armament: 1 x 105mm (4.1in) M1A2 howitzer,
Width: 2.88m (9ft 5in)	plus 1 x 12.7mm (0.5in) HMG on 'pulpit'
Height: 2.54m (8ft 4in)	AA mount.
Engine: 298kW (400hp) Continental R975	Radio: SCR 608
C1 radial petrol	

▲ 105mm Howitzer Motor Carriage (HMC) M7 (Priest)
US Seventh Army / 2nd Armored Division / 14th Armored Field Artillery Battalion

This was a heavily modified M3 medium tank hull, fitted with the standard US 105mm (4.1in) howitzer in a thinly armoured, open-topped fighting compartment. In British service, it was referred to as the Priest due to the pulpit-like machine-gun position.

that the organic vehicles within an armored division can keep the division supplied as long as the Army rail or truck head is within 30 miles [48km] of the combat elements and a reasonable road net exists.

In 1942, red-and-white recognition stripes were applied to British AFVs. These were retained until at least mid-1944, when they were largely superseded by the Allied white star.

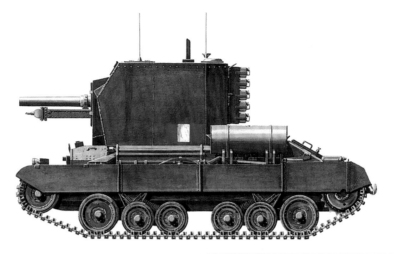

▲ Bishop SP 25pdr

Eighth Army / XIII Corps / 24th Armoured Field Regiment RA

This was an early attempt to provide a fully tracked SP version of the 25pdr gun/howitzer, based on the Valentine's hull. It is possible that the original intention was to use the vehicle as a stop-gap tank destroyer until the 6pdr-armed Crusaders and Valentines were ready. This would account for the awkward gun mounting in a fixed, fully enclosed armoured fighting compartment with limited traverse. More importantly, the mounting severely restricted elevation, which almost halved the gun's maximum range – 5850m (6400 yards), compared with the towed gun's 10,900m (11,925 yards). The 100 or so Bishops produced entered service in the first half of 1942 and were used throughout the remainder of the desert war and in Sicily, before being replaced by US-supplied Priest SP 105mm (4.1in) howitzers during the early stages of the Italian campaign.

Specifications

Crew: 4	Speed: 24km/h (15mph)
Weight: 20.32 tonnes (20 tons)	Range: 177km (110 miles)
Length: 5.62m (18ft 6in)	Armament: 1 x 87.6mm (3.45in) 25pdr gun/
Width: 2.77m (9ft 1in)	howitzer
Height: 3.05m (10ft)	Radio: Wireless Set No. 19
Engine: 98kW (131hp) AEC 6-cylinder diesel	

Specifications

Crew: 6	Engine: 109.5kW (147hp) White 160AX
Weight: 9.1 tonnes (8.95 tons)	6-cylinder petrol
Length: 6.16 m (20ft 2.5in)	Speed: 72km/h (45mph)
Width: 1.96m (6ft 5in)	Range: 320km (200 miles)
Height: 2.3m (7ft 6.5in)	Armament: 1 x 105mm (4.1in) M1A2 howitzer
	Radio: SCR 608

▲ T19 105mm Howitzer Motor Carriage (HMC)

US Seventh Army / 2nd Armored Division / 92nd Armored Field Artillery Battalion

The T19 HMC was an M3 halftrack mounting the M2A1 105mm (4.1in) howitzer. The M3 could only stow eight rounds of 105mm (4.1in) ammunition, whilst the chassis was only just able to withstand the howitzer's weight and recoil. The type was phased out as more Priests became available.

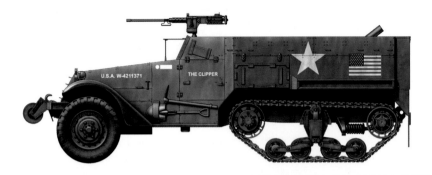

▲ **M4 81mm Motor Mortar Carriage (MMC)**

US Seventh Army / 2nd Armored Division / 41st Armored Infantry Regiment

The M4 was a version of the M2 halftrack fitted with the M1 81mm (3.19in) mortar, which was intended to be fired dismounted but could also be fired to the rear from a mounting inside the vehicle.

Specifications

Crew: 6

Weight: 7.97 tonnes (7.84 tons)

Length: 6.01m (19ft 8.6in)

Width: 1.96m (6ft 5in)

Height: 2.27m (7ft 5in)

Engine: 109.5kW (147hp) White 160AX

6-cylinder petrol

Speed: 72km/h (45mph)

Range: 320km (200 miles)

Armament: 1 x 81mm (3.19in) M1 mortar,
plus 1 x 12.7mm (0.5in) HMG

Radio: n/k

▲ **Car, Heavy Utility, 4x2, Ford C11 ADF**

Eighth Army / HQ XXX Corps

The C11 was a slightly modified version of the civilian Ford Fordor station wagon and was widely used as a staff car. This example flies a lieutenant-general's pennant, indicating its use by the corps commander, Sir Oliver Leese.

Specifications

Crew: 1

Weight: 1.8 tonnes (1.78 tons)

Length: 4.83m (16ft 2in)

Width: 2.01m (6ft 7in)

Height: 1.83m (6ft)

Engine: 70.8kW (95hp) Ford Mercury V8 petrol

Speed: 89km/h (55mph) (estimated)

Range: 370km (230 miles) (estimated)

▶ **Car, Heavy Utility, 4x4 (FWD) Humber**

HQ Eighth Army

Generally referred to as the 'Humber Box', this was the only British-built 4x4 vehicle of its type to enter British Army service during the war years, seeing extensive service as a staff car.

Specifications

Crew: 1

Weight: 2.41 tonnes (2.37 tons)

Length: 4.29m (14ft 1in)

Width: 1.88m (6ft 2in)

Height: 1.96m (6ft 5in)

Engine: 63.4kW (85hp) Humber 6-cylinder petrol

Speed: 80km/h (50mph) (estimated)

Range: 300km (186 miles) (estimated)

As this division landed with a very limited number of trucks due to shortage of shipping, it was able to maintain itself only by a close margin. All trucks hauled 24 hours a day, being forced to draw from beach dumps. Due to the rapid movement of the division, the distance from these dumps increased until it reached 140 miles [224km].

Fortunately, ammunition requirements for the operation were not heavy. Had the action been sustained and the demand for ammunition tonnage been heavy, it would have been impossible to have supplied the division with both gasoline and ammunition with the trucks available. The entire operation would have been seriously impeded and might have been entirely jeopardized.'

Mountain warning

The Sicilian campaign also gave a taste of some of the conditions that were to become all too familiar in Italy itself. The Axis defences in the mountainous north-east of the island (the Etna Line) had largely relegated Allied armour to acting in the infantry support role or as improvised artillery. It was the shape of things to come.

Specifications

Crew: 1	Height: 1.96m (6ft 5in)
Weight: n/k	Engine: 21.97kW (29.5hp) Austin 4-cylinder petrol
Length: 3.98m (13ft 1in)	Speed: 80km/h (50mph) (estimated)
Width: 1.6m (5ft 3in)	Range: 300km (186 miles) (estimated)

▲ **Austin 10 Light Utility Truck**

Eighth Army / XIII Corps / HQ 50th (Northumbrian) Division

The Austin 10 utility truck (better known as the Austin Tilly) was the military version of the Austin 10 saloon and was widely used for a host of light transport duties. About 30,000 vehicles were built.

Specifications

Crew: 4 or 5	Height: 1.89m (6ft 2.4in)
Weight: 2.17 tonnes (2.14 tons)	Engine: 64kW (86hp) Humber 6-cylinder petrol
Length: 4.29m (14ft 1in)	Speed: 75km/h (46mph)
Width: 1.88m (6ft 2in)	Range: 500km (310 miles)

▲ **Humber Snipe Light Utility Truck**

Eighth Army / XXX Corps / HQ 51st (Highland) Division

Humber built large numbers of light utility trucks based on the civilian Snipe. This is the FFW (Fitted For Wireless) version, with a detachable body for use as a ground wireless station.

▼ US 2nd Armored Division, Combat Command A – Sicily, July 1943

The US armoured divisions were especially flexible formations. The abolition of their armoured brigades in March 1942 and their replacement by the combat command structure allowed units to be switched between combat commands to meet the changing needs of each particular mission.

Combat Command HQ (10 x M3 half-tracks, 3 x M3A1 Stuarts)

66th Armored Rgt (detachment)

Battalion HQ (2 x M3 half-tracks, 2 x M4 Shermans)

Tank Company x 3

Company HQ (2 x M4 Shermans, 1 x M3 half-track, 1 x recovery vehicle)

1 Tank Platoon (5 x M4 Shermans)

2 Tank Platoon (5 x M4 Shermans)

3 Tank Platoon (5 x M4 Shermans)

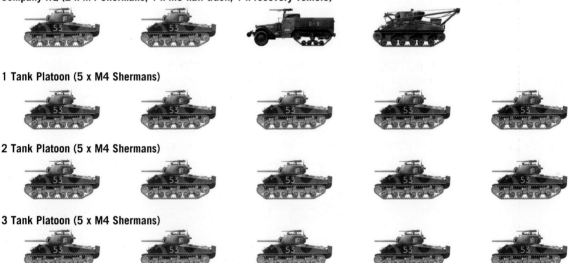

Field Artillery Battery, from 78th Armored Field Artillery Battalion (3 x M3 half-tracks, 6 x HMC M7s)

Battalion HQ   **Fire Control Section**

▲ **DUKW**

US Seventh Army / 2nd Armored Division / Quartermaster Corps (QMC)
Battalion

The DUKW was an amphibious version of the General Motors 2½-ton cargo truck, which entered service in 1942. It proved to be a highly successful means of delivering supplies directly to shore from ships at sea.

Specifications

Crew: 1	Height: 2.69m (8ft 10in)
Weight: 6.75 tonnes (6.64 tons)	Engine: 68.2kW (91.5hp) GMC Model 270 petrol
Length: 9.75m (32ft)	Speed: 80km/h (50mph)
Width: 2.51m (8ft 2.9in)	Range: n/k

Into Italy: Salerno landings

SEPTEMBER–DECEMBER 1943

The realization that there was no prospect of defeating the Allied forces in Sicily was the final blow to Mussolini's already shaky regime. He was deposed and arrested on 25 July whilst Marshal Pietro Badoglio's new Italian government began negotiations with the Allies with a view to changing sides.

UNFORTUNATELY, DIPLOMATIC leaks alerted the Germans, who massively reinforced their units in Italy and disarmed most Italian forces as soon as the Badoglio government signed an armistice on 3 September. Soon after the armistice, Mussolini was rescued from his imprisonment in the Campo Imperatore Hotel at Gran Sasso by German Special Forces and installed as head of state of the puppet Italian Social Republic in northern Italy.

Landings

On the same day that the armistice was signed in Cassibile, Sicily, Montgomery's forces made unopposed landings at Reggio di Calabria, whilst General Mark Clark's US Fifth Army (including British units) landed at Salerno, south of Naples, on 9 September. The plan was daring but flawed – Fifth Army's landings were made on a very broad 56km (35-mile) front, using only three assault divisions, and the army's two corps were widely separated.

This was potentially a recipe for disaster, especially as 16th Panzer Division was deployed within easy reach of the beachheads and Clark had specifically ruled out any preliminary naval bombardment.

By 12 September, the Germans were able to launch a concentrated assault by two *Panzergrenadier* and four Panzer divisions which destroyed a US infantry battalion and came close to overrunning the entire beachhead before it was halted by massed artillery and air attacks, backed up by naval gunfire support from the battleships *Warspite* and *Valiant*. As soon as it became clear that there was no realistic chance of driving the Allies back into the sea, the Germans skilfully disengaged and withdrew to the north.

With the Salerno beachhead secure, Fifth Army began its attack towards Naples on 19 September. The Eighth Army's 7th Armoured Division was ordered to take Naples, which fell to A Squadron, King's Dragoon Guards, on 1 October after the occupying German forces withdrew following a popular uprising in the city. By 6 October, Fifth Army had closed up to the line of the River Volturno, the first of many German defence lines that were to slow the Allied advance up the Italian peninsula to a long, bloody crawl. Narrow Italian roads and bridges were obvious targets for demolitions and it was said with feeling that the best Allied weapon of the campaign was the bulldozer rather than the tank.

On 6 November, Hitler appointed the *Luftwaffe*'s Field-Marshal Albert Kesselring as commander-in-chief in Italy, approving his plans for a 'forward defence' of the country. The Volturno Line was defended just long enough to give time for the completion of the Winter Line, the main fortified zone south of Rome.

It was not until mid-January 1944 that the Allies managed to fight their way through to the key element of the Winter Line defences, the Gustav Line. This made use of some of the most difficult terrain in Europe, strengthened by an array of gun pits, concrete bunkers, machine-gun turrets, barbed wire and minefields. It was ably defended by 15 German divisions until late May 1944 and was the setting for the four battles of Monte Cassino.

▲ Ford GPA Seagoing Jeep (Seep)
US Seventh Army / 540th Engineer Shore Regiment
The GPA was intended to be a fully amphibious version of the jeep, but its greater weight and poor waterborne performance led to its withdrawal from front-line US service shortly after the campaign in Sicily.

Specifications

Crew: 1	Height: 1.75m (5ft 9in)
Weight: 1.63 tonnes (1.6 tons)	Engine: 44.7kW (60hp) Ford 4-cylinder petrol
Length: 4.62m (15ft 2in)	Speed: 105km/h (65mph)
Width: 1.63m (5ft 4in)	Range: n/k

▲ M2A1 Halftrack
US Fifth Army / VI Corps / 1st Armored Division / 11th Armored Infantry Battalion
The M2A1 was fitted with the armoured M49 machine-gun ring mount over the right-hand front seat. Two or three fixed pintle mounts for 7.62mm (0.3in) machine guns were often fitted at the unit level in the field.

Specifications

Crew: 2 plus 8 passengers	6-cylinder petrol
Weight: 8.89 tonnes (8.75 tons)	Speed: 72km/h (45mph)
Length: 6.14m (20ft 1in)	Range: 320km (200 miles)
Width: 2.22m (7ft 3in)	Armament: 1 x 12.7mm (0.5in) HMG,
Height: 2.69m (8ft 10in)	plus 2 x 7.62mm (0.3in) MGs
Engine: 109.5kW (147hp) White 160AX	

▲ **Amphibious landings**

American Sherman tanks splash through the surf at Salerno. Although the Sherman was inferior to German tanks in terms of firepower and armour, it was mechanically reliable and produced in large numbers.

▲ **M8 Armoured Car**

US Fifth Army / IV Corps / 1st Armored Division / Cavalry Reconnaissance Squadron

Many users felt that the M8's armour was inadequate and that the vehicle was especially vulnerable to mines. Crews often lined the floor of the fighting compartment with sandbags to give a measure of protection against mines.

Specifications

Crew: 4

Weight: 8.12 tonnes (8 tons)

Length: 5m (16ft 5in)

Width: 2.54m (8ft 4in)

Height: 2.25m (7ft 5in)

Engine: 82kW (110hp) Hercules JXD
6-cylinder petrol

Speed: 89km/h (55mph)

Range: 563km (350 miles)

Armament: 1 x 37mm (1.5in) M6 gun,
plus 1 x 12.7mm (0.5in) AA HMG and
1 x coaxial 7.62mm (0.3in) MG

Radio: SCR508

▶ **Willys MB Jeep**

US Seventh Army / 45th Infantry Division / 45th Reconnaissance Troop

The versatile jeep appeared in many guises during (and long after) the war. This reconnaissance vehicle is armed with a pintle-mounted 12.7mm (0.5in) heavy machine gun.

Specifications

Crew: 1 plus 2/3 passengers

Weight: 1.04 tonnes (1.02 tons)

Length: 3.33m (10ft 11in)

Width: 1.57m (5ft 2in)

Height: 1.83m (6ft)

Engine: 40.23kW (54hp) L head 134 I4
4-cylinder petrol

Speed: 105km/h (65mph)

Range: 482.8km (300 miles)

Armament: 1 x 12.7mm (0.5in) HMG or
1 x 7.62mm (0.3in) MG

Anzio

JANUARY–MAY 1944

As Allied forces struggled to punch through the Winter Line, a further effort was made to break the stalemate, by means of an amphibious assault at Anzio, south of Rome.

A SHORTAGE OF TANK LANDING SHIPS, which were urgently required for the preparations for the Normandy landings, limited the scale of the initial assault to little more than two divisions. This force, comprising the British 1st Infantry Division and the US 3rd Infantry Division, landed practically unopposed on 22 January 1944 but passively awaited reinforcements instead of advancing inland. As usual, Kesselring reacted swiftly and within three days the beachheads were sealed off by 40,000 German troops, and the chance of a quick breakthrough had been lost. Yet the terrain was once again a limiting

▲ M4A3 Sherman Medium Tank

US Fifth Army / VI Corps / 1st Armored Division

As the Italian campaign dragged on, increasingly frequent encounters with Panthers, Tigers and powerful tank destroyers convinced many Sherman crews that their vehicles were becoming obsolete. US and British officials were reluctant to accept this and much time was lost before work got under way on a successor.

▶ Staghound Mark I Armoured Car

Eighth Army / 2nd New Zealand Division / Divisional Cavalry Regiment

'Staghound' was the British designation for the Ford T17E1 armoured car. The vehicle was not adopted by the US Army and only saw service with British and Commonwealth forces.

Specifications

Crew: 5	Speed: 42km/h (26mph)
Weight: 30.3 tonnes (29.82 tons)	Range: 210km (130 miles)
Length: 5.9m (19ft 4in)	Armament: 1 x 75mm (2.9in) M3 gun,
Width: 2.62m (8ft 7in)	plus 1 x 12.7mm (0.5in) AA HMG and
Height: 2.74m (8ft 11in)	2 x 7.62mm (0.3in) MGs (1 coaxial,
Engine: 372.5kW (500hp) Ford GAA	1 ball-mounted in hull front)
8-cylinder petrol	Radio: SCR 508

Specifications

Crew: 5	Speed: 89km/h (55mph)
Weight: 14.12 tonnes (13.9 tons)	Range: 724km (450 miles)
Length: 5.49m (18ft)	Armament: 1 x 37mm (1.5in) M6 gun plus
Width: 2.69m (8ft 10in)	3 x 7.62mm (0.3in) MGs (1 AA, 1 coaxial
Height: 2.36m (7ft 9in)	and 1 ball-mounted in hull front)
Engine: 2 x 72kW (97hp) GMC 270 CID	Radio: Wireless Set No. 19
6-cylinder in-line petrol	

factor – in the initial stages of the landings a single Sherman of the Scots Greys commanded by Sergeant McMeeking was the only tank able to get through the marshy ground at the beach exits. He arrived at the forward infantry positions just in time to break up a German counterattack by single-handedly destroying four Panzer IVs in quick succession.

Stalemate

Both sides reinforced the area, and a series of attacks and counterattacks in February ended in another bloody stalemate that lasted until late May when the Allies finally broke through the Gustav Line in the Fourth Battle of Monte Cassino. At this point, on 23 May, the US VI Corps, comprising three US and two British divisions, broke out of the Anzio beachhead. The opposing German Fourteenth Army had been weakened by the need to reinforce the Gustav Line but still managed to inflict heavy losses – on the first day of the offensive 1st Armored Division lost 100 tanks whilst 3rd Infantry Division suffered 955 casualties, the highest losses sustained in a single day by any US division in World War II.

By 25 May, the seven divisions of the German Tenth Army were in full retreat from the Gustav Line and VI Corps was poised to cut off their retreat towards Rome along Route 6. At this point, Clark

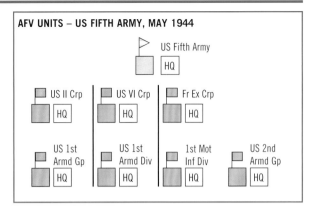

AFV UNITS – US FIFTH ARMY, MAY 1944

▶ **Mud and guts**
Shermans and British infantry move up through the mud to the front-line, 1944.

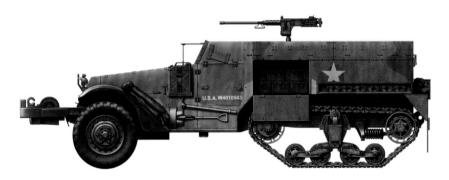

Specifications

Crew: 2 plus 8 passengers	Engine: 109.5kW (147hp) White 160AX
Weight: 8.7 tonnes (8.56 tons)	6-cylinder petrol
Length: 5.96m (19ft 6in)	Speed: 72km/h (45mph)
Width: 1.96m (6ft 5in)	Range: 320km (200 miles)
Height: 2.3m (7ft 6in)	Armament: 1 x 12.7mm (0.5in) HMG

▲ **M2 Halftrack**

US Fifth Army / VI Corps / 1st Armored Division

This M2 shows some of the stowage arrangements – a side compartment, in this case packed with ammunition boxes, and an external rack for anti-tank mines.

ordered General Lucian Truscott, commanding VI Corps, to abandon the advance on Route 6 and move directly on Rome. It seems likely that this was simply down to Clark's personal ambition to go down in history as the liberator of the Eternal City. Whatever the motivation, it is certain that a great opportunity was missed, and General Heinrich von Vietinghoff's Tenth Army was able to retreat to the next line of defence, the Trasimene Line, where it linked up with Fourteenth Army, under General Joachim Lemelsen, before making a fighting withdrawal to the Gothic Line north of Florence.

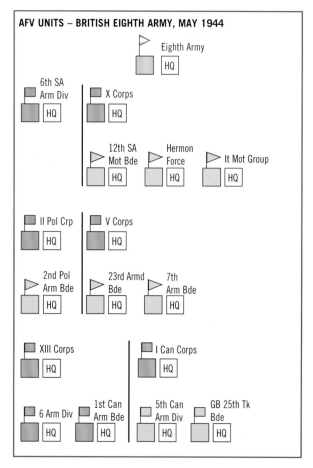

AFV UNITS – BRITISH EIGHTH ARMY, MAY 1944

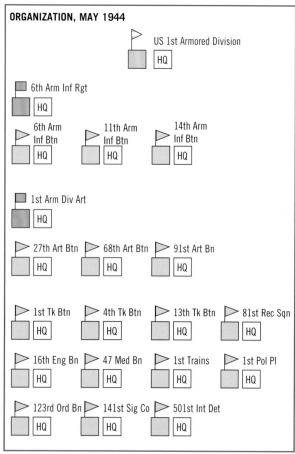

ORGANIZATION, MAY 1944

▶ **Staghound AA Armoured Car**

Eighth Army / 2nd New Zealand Division / Divisional Cavalry Regiment

This was the Staghound Mark I fitted with an open-topped Frazer-Nash turret mounting two 12.7mm (0.5in) M2 Browning heavy machine guns with 1305 rounds per gun. Allied air superiority meant that the type was most commonly used in the fire support role. (The high elevation of the guns often proved useful in the mountainous terrain encountered in much of Italy.)

Specifications

Crew: 5

Weight: 12.05 tonnes (11.86 tons)

Length: 5.43m (17ft 10in)

Width: 2.69m (8ft 10in)

Height: 2.42m (7ft 11in)

Engine: 2 x 72kW (97hp) GMC 270 CID 6-cylinder in-line petrol

Speed: 89km/h (55mph)

Range: 320km (200 miles)

Armament: 2 x 12.7mm (0.5in) HMGs

Radio: Wireless Set No. 19

Gothic Line

SEPTEMBER 1944

Rome fell to units of Clark's US Fifth Army on 4 June, only two days before the Italian campaign was overshadowed by the Normandy landings.

THE GOTHIC LINE was a belt of fortifications 16km (10 miles) deep, running from south of La Spezia on the Mediterranean coast to the Adriatic near Ravenna. It passed through the superb defensive terrain of the Apennine mountains, which ran unbroken nearly from coast to coast, 80km (50 miles) deep, with peaks rising to 2100m (6890ft).

The line's defences included numerous concrete-reinforced gun pits and trenches, 2376 machine-gun nests with interlocking fields of fire, 479 anti-tank gun, mortar and assault-gun positions, 120km (75 miles) of barbed wire and anti-tank ditches.

Some positions included the imposing *Pantherturm* – a Panther tank turret, complete with 75mm (2.9in) gun, built on to a concrete or armoured emplacement to create a deadly anti-tank position.

Attacks on the outposts of the Gothic Line began on 25 August, but it was not until 12 September that Allied forces were able to close up on the line itself. The experience of Allied armour in Italy was typified by the ordeal of 21st Tank Brigade, which was heavily involved in innumerable infantry support actions throughout September. These imposed immense stress on men and tanks alike: a tank driver spoke of

▶ **Daimler Scout Car Mark IA (Dingo)**

US Fifth Army / XIII Corps / 6th Armoured Division / 1st Derbyshire Yeomanry

The Daimler Scout Car, almost invariably known as the Dingo, was one of the most successful light AFVs of the war. It was an ideal reconnaissance vehicle with a quiet engine, high speed in forward and reverse gears and a low silhouette.

Specifications

Crew: 2	Engine: 41kW (55hp) Daimler 6-cylinder petrol
Weight: 3.22 tonnes (3.2 tons)	Speed: 89km/h (55mph)
Length: 3.23m (10ft 5in)	Range: 322km (200 miles)
Width: 1.72m (5ft 8in)	Armament: 1 x 7.7mm (0.303in) Bren MG
Height: 1,5m (4ft 11in)	Radio: Wireless Set No. 19

▶ **Daimler Armoured Car**

US Fifth Army / XIII Corps / 6th Armoured Division / 1st Derbyshire Yeomanry

The Daimler Armoured Car was essentially an enlarged development of the Daimler Scout Car, fitted with the two-man turret of the Tetrarch light tank. Almost 2700 vehicles were produced and many remained in service well after the end of the war.

Specifications

Crew: 3	Speed: 80km/h (50mph)
Weight: 7.62 tonnes (7.5 tons)	Range: 330km (205 miles)
Length: 3.96m (13ft)	Armament: 1 x 40mm (1.57in) 2pdr OQF gun,
Width: 2.44m (8ft)	plus 1 x coaxial 7.92mm (0.31in) Besa MG
Height: 2.24m (7ft 4in)	Radio: Wireless Set No. 19
Engine: 71kW (95hp) Daimler 6-cylinder petrol	

▲ **Look out for Panzerfausts!**
A Sherman of the Canadian Three Rivers Regiment advances through the ruins of Ortona.

'Hideous nights pressed on days of horror – we lost men, we lost tanks, we almost lost hope of survival.'

The brigade, part of I Canadian Corps within the Eighth Army, lost 52 Churchills, 29 Shermans and four Stuarts from the reconnaissance squadron. During the month it fired off 2828 armour-piercing rounds, 9632 HE shells and just under one million rounds of machine-gun ammunition.

Weather and terrain

Weather conditions and the terrain posed as many problems as the enemy – cloud cover often ruled out close air support, whilst the steep mountain slopes confined Allied armour to the muddy valley roads. These were heavily mined and booby-trapped besides being covered by German artillery and anti-tank guns. Even Allied artillery was not much use, the poor roads, washed-out bridges and mud limited

the numbers of shells that could be brought forward, and most German bunkers were proof against all but a direct hit. Allied forces had to resort to infantry attacks under cover of artillery bombardments to take the German positions one at a time with grenades and small-arms fire, a very slow way indeed to advance. A locally produced German forces' news-sheet described these attacks:

'The Americans use quasi-Indian tactics. They search for the boundary between battalions or regiments, they look for gaps between our strongest points, they look for the steepest mountain passages (guided by treacherous civilians). They infiltrate through these passages with a patrol, a platoon at first, mostly at dusk. At night they reinforce the infiltrated units, and in the morning they are often in the rear of a German unit, which is simultaneously being attacked from the flanks …'

▼ Armoured Car Squadron, 1st Derbyshire Yeomanry, 1944

The armoured car squadron was a highly mobile reconnaissance force. Whilst always attempting to carry out its missions by stealth, it had sufficient strength to fight its way through when necessary.

Squadron HQ (4 x Daimler AC, 1 x Daimler scout car)

1 Troop (2 x Daimler AC, 2 x Daimler scout car)

2 Troop (2 x Daimler AC, 2 x Daimler scout car)

3 Troop (2 x Daimler AC, 2 x Daimler scout car)

4 Troop (2 x Daimler AC, 2 x Daimler scout car)

5 Troop (2 x Daimler AC, 2 x Daimler scout car)

Heavy Troop (1 x Daimler scout car, 2 x AEC AC)

Support Troop (1 x Daimler scout car, 3 x M2/M3 half-tracks)

AA Troop (5 x Staghound AC)

Battering down the door

It took a further week's hard fighting to break through the main defences, only for the advance to bog down. Torrential rain caused mudslides that frequently blocked roads and tracks, creating a logistical nightmare. Although the Allies were through the mountains, the Lombardy plains were waterlogged and Eighth Army found itself confronted, as in the previous autumn, by a succession of swollen rivers running across its line of advance. Once again, conditions (and losses totalling 480 AFVs) prevented Eighth Army's armour from exploiting the breakthrough. Both sides settled into their positions for what was to be the war's final winter.

▲ M5 High-Speed Tractor

US Fifth Army / II Corps / 88th Infantry Division / 337th Field Artillery Battalion

The M5 entered service with the US Army in 1942 and was extensively used by field artillery battalions.

Specifications	
Crew: 1	Engine: 154kW (207hp) Continental R6572
Weight: 13.8 tonnes (13.58 tons)	6-cylinder petrol
Length: 5.03m (16ft 6in)	Speed: 48km/h (30 mph)
Width: 2.54m (8ft 4in)	Range: 290km (180 miles)
Height: 2.69m (8ft 10in)	

▲ WC54 Dodge 4x4 Ambulance

US Fifth Army / IV Corps / 1st Armored Division / Armored Medical Battalion

A total of 26,000 of these ambulances were produced between 1942 and 1944. Each could carry four stretchers or seven seated casualties.

Specifications	
Crew: 2	Engine: 68.6kW (92hp) Dodge T2155
Weight: 2.04 tonnes (2.01 tons)	6-cylinder petrol
Length: 4.67m (15ft 4in)	Speed: 89km/h (55mph) (estimated)
Width: 1.93m (6ft 4in)	Range: 402km (250 miles) (estimated)
Height: 2.13m (7ft 10in)	

▲ **Shelling the enemy**

An M36 tank destroyer shells German positions on the plains of Lombardy, autumn 1944.

▲ **3in Gun Motor Carriage (GMC) M10**

US Fifth Army / VI Corps / 3rd Infantry Division / 601st Tank Destroyer Battalion

The M10 was the first US fully tracked tank destroyer design to enter service, utilizing the chassis of the Sherman with a new, thinly armoured superstructure and an open-topped turret mounting a 76mm (3in) M7 high-velocity gun.

Specifications

Crew: 5	Speed: 48km/h (30mph)
Weight: 29.05 tonnes (28.6 tons)	Range: 320km (200 miles)
Length: 5.82m (19ft 1in)	Armament: 1 x 76mm (3in) M7 gun,
Width: 3.05m (10ft)	plus 1 x 12.7mm (0.5in) HMG on AA mount
Height: 2.49m (8ft 2in)	Radio: SCR610
Engine: 305.45kW (410hp) General Motors	
6046 12-cylinder twin in-line diesel	

▶ Universal Carrier

US Fifth Army / 6th Armoured Division / 61st Infantry Brigade / 2nd Battalion Rifle Brigade

The Universal Carrier was found to be as useful in Italy as in every other theatre of war. The 13-vehicle Carrier Platoons in each infantry battalion were always in demand for a bewildering variety of tasks.

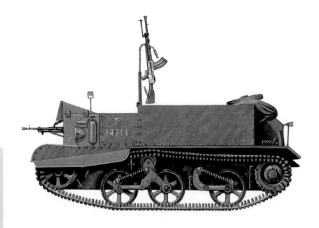

Specifications

Crew: 3	Engine: 63.4kW (85hp) Ford V8
Weight: 4.06 tonnes (4 tons)	8-cylinder petrol
Length: 3.76m (12ft 4in)	Speed: 52km/h (32mph)
Width: 2.11m (6ft 11in)	Range: 258km (160 miles)
Height: 1.63m (5ft 4in)	Armament: 2 x 7.7mm (0.303in) Bren MGs

▶ Dodge WC58 Command Reconnaissance Radio Car

US Fifth Army / IV Corps / 1st Armored Division

This dedicated radio vehicle was a relative rarity – just over 2300 were built between 1942 and 1945.

Specifications

Crew: 3	Engine: 68.54kW (92hp) Dodge T214
Weight: 2.42 tonnes (2.38 tons)	6-cylinder petrol
Length: 4.46m (14ft 7in)	Speed: 89km/h (55mph)
Width: 2m (6ft 7in)	Range: 384km (240 miles)
Height: 2.07m (6ft 9in)	Radio: SCR506-AFII

Specifications

Crew: 1	Engine: 68.54kW (92hp) Dodge T214
Weight: 3.3 tonnes (3.24 tons)	6-cylinder petrol
Length: 4.47m (14ft 8in)	Speed: 89km/h (55mph)
Width: 2.1m (6ft 10in)	Range: 384km (240 miles)
Height: 2.15m (7ft)	

▲ Dodge WC51 Weapons Carrier

US Fifth Army / IV Corps / 1st Armored Division

Although officially designated as weapons carriers, the 98,000 or so WC51s produced during the war were mainly used for general transport duties.

▲ **Sherman Firefly**

Eighth Army / Polish II Corps / 2nd Armoured Brigade / 1st Krechowiecki
Lancers / 2nd Squadron

Roughly 100 Fireflies were sent to Italy, where they were issued to the 2nd,
4th and 7th New Zealand and 5th Canadian armoured brigades, as well as the
Polish 2nd Armoured Brigade.

Specifications

Crew: 4	Speed: 40km/h (25mph)
Weight: 32.7 tonnes (32.18 tons)	Range: 161km (100 miles)
Length: 7.85m (25ft 9in)	Armament: 1 x 76mm (3in) 17pdr OQF,
Width: 2.67m (8ft 9in)	plus 1 coaxial 7.62mm (0.3in) MG
Height: 2.74m (8ft 11in)	Radio: Wireless Set No. 19
Engine: 316.6kW (425hp) Chrysler Multibank	
A57 petrol	

The last battles
MARCH–MAY 1945

**By late March 1945, Allied strength amounted to 17 divisions plus eight independent brigades –
equivalent overall to almost 20 divisions. These forces included four groups of volunteers from
the former Italian Army, equipped and trained by the British.**

THEY FACED 21 MUCH WEAKER German divisions
and four Italian Fascist divisions. Three of the
Italian divisions formed part of the Ligurian Army
under Marshal Graziani, covering La Spezia and
Genoa, whilst the fourth came under command
of Fourteenth Army and was deployed in a sector
thought less likely to be attacked.

Final offensive
The Allied offensive began on 9 April 1945, preceded
by carpet-bombing (using 175,000 fragmentation
bombs) and heavy artillery bombardment. Wasps –
flamethrower-armed Universal Carriers – and Buffalo

amphibians helped the assaults across the various
water obstacles and by 20 April Allied armies were
racing across the Po Valley. Kesselring had always
counted on the River Po as another defensive line,
but Allied aircraft had destroyed all the bridges and
now the river became a death trap, although some
German troops managed to escape after abandoning
their heavy equipment. Allied forces quickly followed
up, crossing the Po and advancing towards the Alps.

Surrender
By 28 April, the Axis position was clearly hopeless
and, on the 29th, von Vietinghoff, who had replaced

AFV Units, Italy, December 1944	Commander
US FIFTH ARMY	Lt-Gen M.L.K. Truscott
US IV Corps	Maj-Gen W.D. Crittenberger
US 1st Armoured Div	Maj-Gen V.E. Prichard
6th S African Armoured Div	Maj-Gen W. Poole
BRITISH 8TH ARMY	Lt-Gen Sir R. McCreery
British V Corps	Lt-Gen C. Keightley
British 1st Armoured Div	Maj-Gen R. Hull
British XIII Corps	Lt-Gen S. Kirkman
British 6th Armoured Div	Maj-Gen H. Murray
Canadian I Corps	Lt-Gen C. Foulkes
Canadian 5th Armoured Div	Maj-Gen B. Hoffmeister
Polish II Corps	Lt-Gen W. Anders
Polish 2nd Armoured Bde	Brig-Gen B. Rakowski

Kesselring, signed the surrender of all German forces in Italy, which came into effect on 2 May.

Postscript

Whilst war is a grim business, it does have its lighter moments. In April 1945, Shermans of the 10th Hussars were supporting 167th Brigade's attack on Bastia, in Umbria, central Italy. One of the objectives was a thoroughly bombed treacle factory. Its damaged storage tanks had leaked thousands of litres of treacle across the surrounding area.

Fortunately, there was no opposition, as the attack quite literally bogged down in the sticky mess and the crew of one Sherman had to be rescued after their tank fell into a treacle-filled bomb crater!

▶ Wasp Mark IIC Flamethrower

Eighth Army / I Canadian Corps / 5th Canadian Armoured Division

The Wasp Mark IIC was a highly effective weapon that was widely used from August 1944 until the end of the war in Europe. On occasions Wasps were used in considerable numbers, notably in the Senio River offensive in northern Italy in April 1945, in which 127 took part.

Specifications

Crew: 3	Engine: 63.4kW (85hp) Ford V8
Weight: 4.06 tonnes (4 tons)	8-cylinder petrol
Length: 3.76m (12ft 4in)	Speed: 52km/h (32mph)
Width: 2.11m (6ft 11in)	Range: 258km (160 miles)
Height: 1.63m (5ft 4in)	Armament: 1 x flame gun

▲ Landing Vehicle Tracked (LVT-4) Buffalo IV

Eighth Army / 27th Lancers

The LVT-4 was a highly capable amphibious assault vehicle, capable of carrying troops, supplies or artillery as large as a 105mm (4.1in) howitzer. The type was extensively used in river crossings in the final stages of the Italian campaign.

Specifications

Crew: 2 plus up 35 infantry	Engine: 186kW (250hp) Continental W670-9A
Weight: 12.42 tonnes (12.2 tons)	7-cylinder diesel
Length: 7.95m (26ft 1in)	Speed: 32km/h (20mph)
Width: 3.25m (10ft 8in)	Range: 240km (150 miles)
Height: 2.46m (8ft 1in)	Armament: 1 x 12.7mm (0.5in) HMG,
	plus 2 x 7.62mm (0.3in) MGs

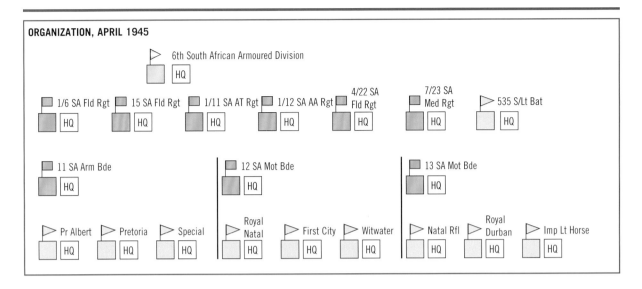

ORGANIZATION, APRIL 1945

6th South African Armoured Division
HQ

1/6 SA Fld Rgt
HQ

15 SA Fld Rgt
HQ

1/11 SA AT Rgt
HQ

1/12 SA AA Rgt
HQ

4/22 SA Fld Rgt
HQ

7/23 SA Med Rgt
HQ

535 S/Lt Bat
HQ

11 SA Arm Bde
HQ

12 SA Mot Bde
HQ

13 SA Mot Bde
HQ

Pr Albert
HQ

Pretoria
HQ

Special
HQ

Royal Natal
HQ

First City
HQ

Witwater
HQ

Natal Rfl
HQ

Royal Durban
HQ

Imp Lt Horse
HQ

▲ **Taking a break**

A unit of Achilles tank destroyers and infantry in northern Italy, 1945. The powerful 17 pounder British gun was used to equip the US-supplied M10 Wolverine to produce the Achilles.

Specifications

Crew: 4	Speed: 60km/h (37mph)
Weight: 14.93 tonnes (14.7 tons)	Range: 161km (100 miles)
Length: 4.34m (14ft 3in)	Armament: 1 x 37mm (1.5in) M6 gun,
Width: 2.26m (7ft 5in)	plus 3 x 7.62mm (0.3in) MGs (1 AA, 1 coaxial,
Height: 2.31m (7ft 7in)	1 ball-mounted in hull front)
Engine: 2 x 82kW (110hp) Cadillac Series 42	Radio: SCR 508
V8 8-cylinder petrol	

▲ M5A1 Light Tank

US Fifth Army / IV Corps / 1st Armored Division / 13th Tank Battalion

The M5A1 was the final development of the basic 'M3 design'. Although it was fast and mechanically reliable, by the end of the war it was highly vulnerable to all Axis anti-tank weapons.

▲ M24 Chaffee Light Tank

US Fifth Army / IV Corps / 1st Armored Division / 1st Tank Battalion

The Chaffee was the most advanced light tank of the late-war period, with firepower equivalent to many of the earlier Sherman medium tanks that were still in service.

Specifications

Crew: 5	Speed: 55km/h (34mph)
Weight: 18.28 tonnes (18 tons)	Range: 282km (175 miles)
Length: 5.49m (18ft)	Armament: 1 x 75mm (2.9in) M6 gun, plus
Width: 2.95m (9ft 8in)	1 x 12.7mm (0.5in) HMG on AA mount and
Height: 2.46m (8ft 1in)	2 x 7.62mm (0.3in) MGs (1 x coaxial,
Engine: 2 x 82kW (110hp) Cadillac 44T24	1 ball-mounted in hull front)
V8 8-cylinder petrol	Radio: SCR 508

▲ M24 Chaffee Light Tank

US Fifth Army / IV Corps / 1st Armored Division / 4th Tank Battalion

The M24's torsion bar suspension allowed it to maintain high cross-country speeds and its reliability equalled that of the M3/M5 series.

Specifications

Crew: 5	Speed: 55km/h (34mph)
Weight: 18.28 tonnes (18 tons)	Range: 282km (175 miles)
Length: 5.49m (18ft)	Armament: 1 x 75mm (2.9in) M6 gun, plus
Width: 2.95m (9ft 8in)	1 x 12.7mm (0.5in) HMG on AA mount and
Height: 2.46m (8ft 1in)	2 x 7.62mm (0.3in) MGs (1 x coaxial,
Engine: 2 x 82kW (110hp) Cadillac 44T24	1 ball-mounted in hull front)
V8 8-cylinder petrol	Radio: SCR 508

▲ Up hill and down dale

Churchills and Universal Carriers in the hills of Italy, 1945. The Churchill's superb hill-climbing ability proved to be invaluable in this sort of terrain.

Chapter 5

D-Day to Arnhem: 1944

The Allied planners responsible for the Normandy
landings faced a daunting task – the disastrous Dieppe
Raid had been a dire warning of what might happen if
things went wrong. The sheer scale of the amphibious and
airborne operations, subject to the vagaries of tide and
weather conditions, posed enormous challenges. Even
if these could be overcome, there remained the threat
of Rommel's ingenious Atlantic Wall defences and his
potentially devastating Panzer counterattacks. The 'funnies'
of 79th Armoured Division provided a partial solution to the
problems, but, in the final analysis, it was Allied numerical
superiority and air power that proved to be
the decisive factors.

◀ AVRE
An AVRE (Armoured Vehicle, Royal Engineers) moves up to the front-line, its turret festooned with kit.

79th Armoured Division

Despite their bizarre appearance, the 'funnies' of 79th Armoured Division proved to be invaluable during the long advance from Normandy to the Baltic, whether in cracking open the grandiose fortifications of the Atlantic Wall or in breaching improvised roadblocks.

IN MANY RESPECTS the Dieppe Raid of August 1942 proved to be a bloody fiasco, not least for the tanks that were landed – most of the 29 Churchills involved were unable to cross the sea wall and were knocked out on the beach. This experience convinced the British of the need for specialized AFVs, and an intensive development programme was launched that produced a vast range of such vehicles – the 'funnies' of 79th Armoured Division.

The first major step was taken in April 1943, with the appointment of Major-General Percy Hobart to command the 79th Armoured Division. His remit was to convert the division into a formation to develop and administer all specialized AFVs. Hobart was reputedly suspicious at first and would not accept

command until formally assured that it would be an operational formation with a proper combat role. Under his leadership, the division rapidly developed units of extensively modified vehicles that were to become known as 'Hobart's Funnies'.

Specialist troops

From the outset, it was recognized that the division would never go into action as a single formation – its

INSIGNIA

The badge of 79th Armoured Division was derived from the black bull of the family crest of Major-General Percy Hobart, the divisional commander.

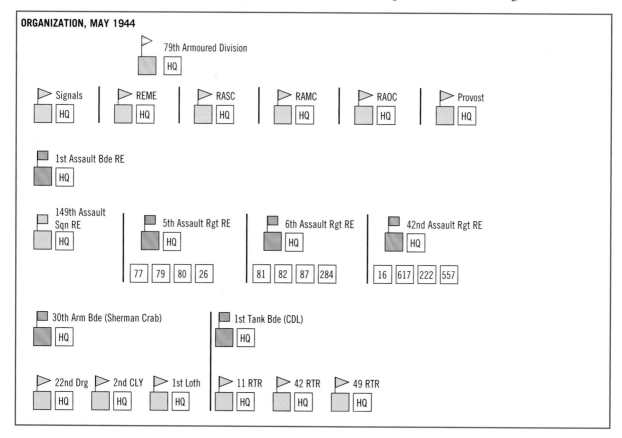

ORGANIZATION, MAY 1944

79th Armoured Division HQ

Signals HQ | REME HQ | RASC HQ | RAMC HQ | RAOC HQ | Provost HQ

1st Assault Bde RE HQ

149th Assault Sqn RE HQ | 5th Assault Rgt RE HQ — 77 | 79 | 80 | 26 | 6th Assault Rgt RE HQ — 81 | 82 | 87 | 284 | 42nd Assault Rgt RE HQ — 16 | 617 | 222 | 557

30th Arm Bde (Sherman Crab) HQ | 1st Tank Bde (CDL) HQ

22nd Drg HQ | 2nd CLY HQ | 1st Loth HQ | 11 RTR HQ | 42 RTR HQ | 49 RTR HQ

◀ On target!

A Churchill Crocodile and its blazing target, Holland, 1944.

function was to organize detachments to carry out whatever special tasks were required. Training went ahead at a furious rate, with the first major exercise at Linney Head followed by extensive 'breaching trials' against replica Atlantic Wall fortifications built at Orford training area in Suffolk. Despite spectacular demonstrations laid on for General Eisenhower and other senior American officers, US forces were

▲ Churchill Crocodile Flamethrower

79th Armoured Division / 31st Armoured Brigade / 1st Fife and Forfar Yeomanry

The Crocodile proved to be highly effective against all types of bunkers and pillboxes. The tank's psychological effect was such that many fortifications surrendered after the first ranging shots from a Crocodile's flame gun.

Specifications

Crew: 5

Weight: 46.5 tonnes (45.7 tons)

Length: 12.3m (40ft 6.5in)

Width: 3.2m (10ft 8in)

Height: 2.4m (8ft 2in)

Engine: 261.1kW (350hp) Bedford 12-cylinder petrol

Speed: 21km/h (13.5mph)

Range: 144km (90 miles)

Armament: 1 x 75mm (2.9in) OQF gun plus 1 x coaxial 7.92mm (0.31in) Besa MG and 1 x flame gun

Radio: Wireless Sets Nos. 19 and 38

Specifications

Crew: 5

Weight: 46.5 tonnes (45.7 tons)

Length: 12.3m (40ft 6.5in)

Width: 3.2m (10ft 8in)

Height: 2.4m (8ft 2in)

Engine: 261.1kW (350hp) Bedford 12-cylinder petrol

Speed: 21km/h (13.5mph)

Range: 144km (90 miles)

Armament: 1 x 75mm (2.9in) OQF gun, plus 1 x coaxial 7.92mm (0.31in) Besa MG and 1 x flame gun

Radio: Wireless Sets Nos. 19 and 38

▲ Churchill Crocodile Flamethrower

79th Armoured Division / 31st Armoured Brigade / 7 RTR

The Crocodile's armoured trailer carried a total of 1820 litres (400 gallons) of flame fuel, sufficient for up to 80 one-second shots out to a maximum range of roughly 91m (100 yards).

▲ Take cover!

A Sherman Crab, a mine-clearing variant equipped with a flail, comes under fire as the Allies push through Normandy, July 1944.

Specifications

Crew: 5	Speed: 46km/h (29mph)
Weight: 31.8 tonnes (31.3 tonnes)	Range: 100km (62 miles)
Length: 8.23m (27ft)	Armament: 1 x 75mm (2.9in) M3 gun,
Width: 3.5m (11ft 6in)	plus 1 x 12.7mm (0.5in) AA HMG and
Height: 2.7m (9ft)	1 x 7.62mm (0.3in) MG
Engine: 373kW (500hp) Ford GAA V8 petrol	Radio: Wireless Set No. 19

▲ Sherman Crab Flail Tank

79th Armoured Division / 30th Armoured Brigade / 22nd Dragoons

This Crab, with guns and mantlet covered for transit, is unusual in retaining the 12.7mm (0.5in) Browning heavy machine gun on the turret roof. The odd-looking 'stalks' on the hull and turret held station-keeping lights for use when several Crabs were flailing together, throwing up clouds of dust and debris. In such poor visibility careful control was essential to ensure that the tanks didn't drift apart, leaving an uncleared strip of ground between them.

sceptical of the ability of the strange-looking 'funnies' to operate effectively on the battlefield and refused to adopt any of them except for the amphibious Sherman DD.

Battlefield experience was to show that this was a dire mistake and after the Normandy landings detachments of 'funnies' were in great demand to support US assaults on heavily fortified positions such as the Channel ports. By the end of the war the division had 21,430 men and 1566 AFVs – a conventional armoured division's strength was 14,400 men and 350 AFVs.

The vast majority of the division's AFVs were modified versions of the Churchill or the Sherman,

Specifications

Crew: 5	Speed: 46km/h (29mph)
Weight: 31.8 tonnes (31.3 tonnes)	Range: 100km (62 miles)
Length: 8.23m (27ft)	Armament: 1 x 75mm (2.9in) M3 gun,
Width: 3.5m (11ft 6in)	plus 1 x 7.62mm (0.3in) MG
Height: 2.7m (9ft)	Radio: n/k
Engine: 373kW (500hp) Ford GAA V8 petrol	

▲ **Sherman Crab Flail Tank**

79th Armoured Division / 30th Armoured Brigade / 2nd County of London Yeomanry (Westminster Dragoons)

The serrated edges of the flail drum acted as wire cutters, preventing the flail chains becoming entangled in barbed-wire obstacles.

▲ **Sherman Crab Flail Tank**

79th Armoured Division / 30th Armoured Brigade / 1st Lothian and Border Horse Yeomanry

A variety of special equipment was added to Crabs as a result of operational experience, including side-mounted angled boxes containing powdered chalk that trickled out to mark the swept lane.

Specifications

Crew: 5	Speed: 46km/h (29mph)
Weight: 31.8 tonnes (31.3 tonnes)	Range: 100km (62 miles)
Length: 8.23m (27ft)	Armament: 1 x 75mm (2.9in) M3 gun,
Width: 3.5m (11ft 6in)	plus 1 x 7.62mm (0.3in) MG
Height: 2.7m (9ft)	Radio: n/k
Engine: 373kW (500hp) Ford GAA V8 petrol	

both of which were readily available in large numbers. Although relatively slow, the Churchill had a roomy interior, thick armour and a good cross-country performance. Whilst the Sherman was less well armoured, its greater speed and exceptional mechanical reliability made it particularly suitable for other roles undertaken by the formation.

Types of 'funnies'

Churchill and Sherman tanks were adapted to perform a multitude of battlefield tasks beyond the capabilities of conventional AFVs. Among the many 'funnies' developed by Hobart's division were:

• **Churchill Crocodile** – The first Crocodiles were converted from Churchill IVs, but production models were all based on the more heavily armoured Churchill VII. This conversion involved fitting the flame gun of the Wasp Mark II Flamethrower in the Churchill's hull machine-gun mount and installing piping for the flame fuel which was run back to the 'Link', a three-way coupling on the hull rear plate. This was the connection to the armoured trailer that contained 1820 litres (400 gallons) of

▲ **Up and over!**
An AVRE practicing obstacle-crossing using fascines.

▲ **Churchill AVRE**

79th Armoured Division / 1st Assault Brigade RE / 6th Assault Regiment RE

AVREs landed in the first assault waves were carefully waterproofed and fitted with deep-wading equipment, including trunking over the air intakes and extended exhausts. This example mounts a 'Bobbin Carpet' – a reinforced mat that was laid over soft sand to provide a temporary trackway for following vehicles.

Specifications (without attachments)

Crew: 6	Speed: 25km/h (15.5mph)
Weight: 38.6 tonnes (38 tons)	Range: 193km (120 miles)
Length: 7.67m (25ft 2in)	Armament: 1 x 290mm (11.4in) Petard
Width: 3.25m (10ft 8in)	demolition mortar, plus 2 x 7.92mm (0.31in)
Height: 2.79m (9ft 2in)	Besa MGs (1 coaxial and 1 ball-mounted in
Engine: 261.1kW (350hp) Bedford	hull front)
12-cylinder petrol	Radio: Wireless Set No. 19

▾ 79th Armoured Division – Assault Detachment

The 'funnies' were constantly on the move, forming and re-forming detachments tailored to meet the varying needs of specific operations. This force is representative of a typical grouping for an assault on a fortified sector of the German front-line.

Troop 1 (3 x Sherman Crabs)   **Troop 2 (3 x Sherman Crabs)**

Troop 1 (3 x Churchill Crocodiles)

Troop 2 (3 x Churchill Crocodiles)

Troop 3 (3 x Churchill Crocodiles)

Troop 1 (3 x AVRE)   **Troop 2 (3 x AVRE)**

Troop 3 (3 x AVRE)

Troop (3 x ARK)

Troop (12 x Ram Kangaroos)

flame fuel, sufficient for 80 one-second bursts. The trailer, which proved unexpectedly resistant to battle damage, also carried five nitrogen cylinders that pressurized the fuel. A total of 800 Crocodiles were eventually produced.

• **Churchill Armoured Vehicle, Royal Engineers (AVRE)** – Several hundred Churchill IIIs and IVs were converted to AVREs by having their turret armament replaced with the Petard, a 290mm (11.4in) spigot mortar. This had a practical range of 73m (80 yards) with its standard ammunition, a fin- stabilized 18kg (40lb) hollow-charge bomb that proved highly effective against a wide range of obstacles and fortifications. (An attempt to improve

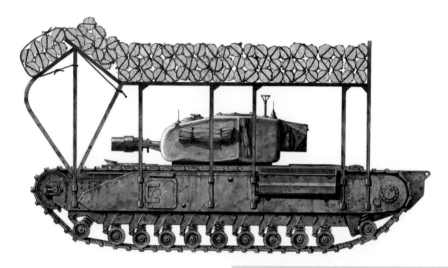

▲ **Churchill AVRE**

79th Armoured Division / 1st Assault Brigade RE / 5th Assault Regiment RE

This AVRE carries a 'Log Carpet', a more durable version of the 'Bobbin Carpet'.

Specifications (without attachments)

Crew: 6	Speed: 25km/h (15.5mph)
Weight: 38.6 tonnes (38 tons)	Range: 193km (120 miles)
Length: 7.67m (25ft 2in)	Armament: 1 x 290mm (11.4in) Petard
Width: 3.25m (10ft 8in)	demolition mortar, plus 2 x 7.92mm (0.31in)
Height: 2.79m (9ft 2in)	Besa MGs (1 coaxial and 1 ball-mounted in
Engine: 261.1kW (350hp) Bedford	hull front)
12-cylinder petrol	Radio: Wireless Set No. 19

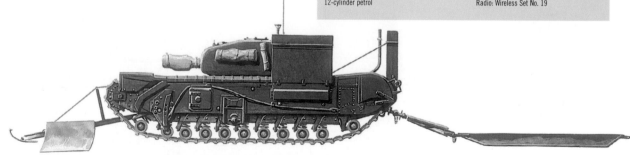

Specifications (without attachments)

Crew: 6	Speed: 25km/h (15.5mph)
Weight: 38.6 tonnes (38 tons)	Range: 193km (120 miles)
Length: 7.67m (25ft 2in)	Armament: 1 x 290mm (11.4in) Petard
Width: 3.25m (10ft 8in)	demolition mortar, plus 2 x 7.92mm (0.31in)
Height: 2.79m (9ft 2in)	Besa MGs (1 coaxial and 1 ball-mounted in
Engine: 261.1kW (350hp) Bedford	hull front)
12-cylinder petrol	Radio: Wireless Set No. 19

▲ **Churchill AVRE**

79th Armoured Division / 1st Assault Brigade RE / 42nd Assault Regiment RE

Another AVRE in full deep-wading kit, fitted with a Bullshorn mine plough and towing a Porpoise skid trailer. These skid trailers were designed to carry a wide variety of supplies.

on the Petard resulted in the conversion of a single AVRE to mount 'Ardeer Aggie', a large-calibre recoilless demolition gun. This weapon operated on the principle of the World War I Davis Gun, which was developed for use on aircraft and in which recoil was eliminated by firing a counterweight to the rear. Ardeer Aggie used sand as a counterweight, but trials showed that the idea was impractical – the risk of sand-blasting the AVRE's engine decks or nearby infantry with every shot was just too great.

On a more practical level, AVREs were adapted to carry and operate a wide range of special equipment such as:

The Bobbin: A reel of 3m (10ft) wide canvas cloth reinforced with steel poles carried above the tank and unrolled onto patches of soft ground to form a 'carpet' to prevent vehicles bogging down.

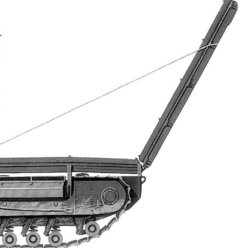

▲ Churchill ARK Mark I

79th Armoured Division / 1st Assault Brigade RE / 5th Assault Regiment RE

ARKs were highly effective – in one case, two were used, one on top of the other, to bridge a deep ravine in Italy.

Specifications

Crew: 2/3	Engine: 261.1kW (350hp) Bedford 12-cylinder
Weight: 35 tonnes (34.44 tons) (estimated)	petrol
Length: 7.67m (25ft 2in)	Speed: 25km/h (15.5mph)
Width: 3.25m (10ft 8in)	Range: 193km (120 miles)
Height: 1.83m (6ft) (estimated)	Armament: 1 or 2 x 7.7mm (0.303in) Bren MGs
	Radio: Wireless Set No. 19

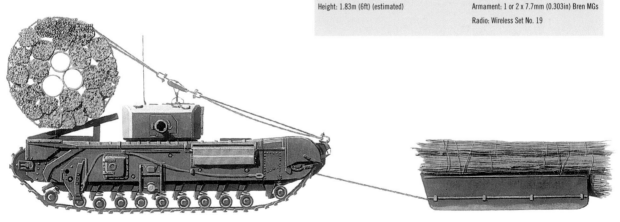

▲ Churchill AVRE

79th Armoured Division / 1st Assault Brigade RE / 6th Assault Regiment RE

This AVRE carries one fascine and tows another on an AVRE skid trailer. Fascines were simple and highly effective obstacle-crossing devices, but badly obscured the driver's vision. In most cases another crew member had to perch on top of the fascine to guide the driver.

Specifications (without attachments)

Crew: 6	Speed: 25km/h (15.5mph)
Weight: 38.6 tonnes (38 tons)	Range: 193km (120 miles)
Length: 7.67m (25ft 2in)	Armament: 1 x 290mm (11.4in) Petard
Width: 3.25m (10ft 8in)	demolition mortar, plus 2 x 7.92mm (0.31in)
Height: 2.79m (9ft 2in)	Besa MGs (1 coaxial and 1 ball-mounted in
Engine: 261.1kW (350hp) Bedford	hull front)
12-cylinder petrol	Radio: Wireless Set No. 19

Fascines: Bundles of wooden poles or brushwood lashed together with wire. These were carried on the front of the tank and could be released to fill a ditch or form a step. Metal pipes in the centre of the fascine allowed water to flow through.

Small Box Girder (SBG) Assault Bridge: A bridge carried on the front of the tank, which could be dropped to span a 9.1m (30ft) gap in 30 seconds.

– Bullshorn Plough: This mine plough proved to be effective on soft ground, lifting and turning aside mines for subsequent defusing.

Specifications

Crew: 5	Speed (water): 7.4km/h (4 knots)
Weight: 32.3 tonnes (31.8 tons)	Range: 240km (149 miles)
Length: 6.35m (20ft 10in)	Armament: 1 x 75mm (2.9in) M3 gun,
Width: 2.81m (9ft 3in)	1 x coaxial 7.62mm (0.3in) MG
Height: 3.96m (13ft)	Radio: Wireless Set No. 19
Engine: 373kW (500hp) Ford GAA V8 petrol	

▲ **Sherman DD**

3rd Infantry Division / 27th Armoured Brigade / 4th/7th Royal Dragoon Guards

Although the waterproofed canvas flotation screen of the Sherman DD looked fragile, operational experience showed that it could withstand surprisingly rough sea conditions.

Specifications

Crew: 5	Speed (water): 7.4km/h (4 knots)
Weight: 32.3 tonnes (31.8 tons)	Range: 240km (149 miles)
Length: 6.35m (20ft 10in)	Armament: 1 x 75mm (2.9in) M3 gun,
Width: 2.81m (9ft 3in)	1 x coaxial 7.62mm (0.3in) MG
Height: 3.96m (13ft)	Radio: Wireless Set No. 19
Engine: 373kW (500hp) Ford GAA V8 petrol	

▲ **Sherman DD**

3rd Infantry Division / 27th Armoured Brigade / 13th/18th Royal Hussars

Although best known for their role in the Normandy landings, Sherman DD tanks were also used in the assault crossings of the Rhine and Elbe.

ORGANIZATION, JUNE 1944

27th Armoured Brigade
HQ

148 Rgt RAC
HQ

4/7 R Dr Gds
HQ

13/18 R Hus
HQ

1 E Riding
HQ

Staffs Yeo
HQ

1 Q Vic Rfls
HQ

7 King's Rfls
HQ

▲ DD column

Sherman DD tanks move along a road in Normandy shortly after the Allied invasion, June 1944. The DD tanks would again prove their usefulness in the Rhine and Elbe crossings of 1945.

Double Onion: Two large demolition charges on a metal frame that could be placed against a concrete wall and then detonated from a safe distance. It was the successor to the single-charge devices Carrot and Light Carrot, which were trialled but never used in combat.

• **Churchill Armoured Ramp Carrier (ARK)** – A number of Churchills were converted to ARKs by the removal of their turrets and the fitting of moveable ramps at each end. When the tank was driven up to a sea wall (or into a crater or gulley), the ramps were deployed, allowing other vehicles to drive up the first ramp, over the ARK, then along the second ramp, enabling the obstacle to be scaled.

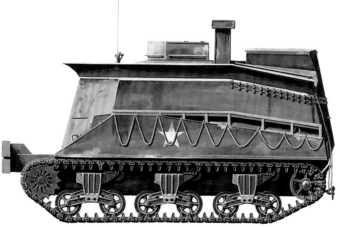

Specifications

Crew: 4	Engine: 305.45kw (410hp) General Motors
Weight: 28.45 tonnes (28 tons)	6046 12-cylinder twin in-line diesel
Length: 5.63m (18ft 5in)	Speed: 48km/h (30mph)
Width: 2.58m (8ft 6in)	Range: 240km (150 miles)
Height: 2.83m (9ft 2in)	Radio: Wireless Set No. 19

▲ Sherman BARV

79th Armoured Division / REME

Roughly 60 Sherman BARVs were used on the invasion beaches of Normandy. Unusually for a tank, the crew included a diver, whose job was to attach towing gear to 'drowned' vehicles.

- **Sherman Crab** – A modified Sherman tank which was equipped with a mine-clearing flail: a rotating drum fitted with weighted chains that beat the ground to detonate mines in the path of the tank.
- **Sherman DD** – From 'Duplex Drive', this was an amphibious Sherman able to swim ashore after launching from a landing craft well offshore to give support to the first waves of infantry immediately on landing. (Similarly adapted Valentines were used only for trials and training.)
- **Sherman Beach Armoured Recovery Vehicle (BARV)** – These were M4A2 Shermans that were waterproofed and had their turrets replaced with tall armoured superstructures. These tanks were capable of operating in up to 2.7m (9ft) of water to remove broken-down or swamped vehicles that were blocking access to the beaches. BARVs were also used to refloat small landing craft that had become stuck on the beach.
- **Buffalo** – The British version of the American LVT-4 amphibious landing vehicle, the Buffalo was frequently fitted with appliqué armour and up-gunned, with some examples carrying a forward-

▶ **'Hobo'**
Major-General Percy Hobart, commander of the 79th Armoured Division and the driving force behind the creation of the 'funnies'.

▲ **Tank recovery**
A Cromwell ARV (Armoured Recovery Vehicle) tows a captured Panzer Mk IV. The Cromwell ARV was a turretless conversion of a Cromwell tank.

firing Browning machine gun in a ball mount operated by the co-driver, a 20mm (0.79in) Polsten cannon on the cab roof and a further Browning machine gun on each side of the cargo bay.

• **Armoured Bulldozer** – This 'funny' was not a converted tank but a standard Caterpillar D8 Bulldozer equipped with armour protection for the driver and the engine. The vehicle's primary role

was to clear the invasion beaches of obstacles and to make roads accessible by clearing rubble and filling in bomb craters. Conversions were carried out by a Caterpillar importer: Jack Olding & Co Ltd of Hatfield, Hertfordshire.

• **Centaur Bulldozer** – An obsolescent Centaur tank with the turret removed and fitted with a simple, winch-operated, bulldozer blade, the Centaur

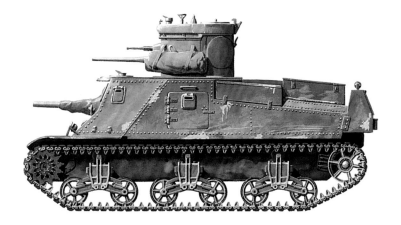

Specifications

Crew: 5	Speed: 42km/h (26mph)
Weight: 27.22 tonnes (26.7 tons) (estimated)	Range: 193km (120 miles)
Length: 5.64m (18ft 6in)	Armament: 1 x turret-mounted searchlight,
Width: 2.72m (8ft 11in)	1 x 75mm (2.9in) M2 or M3 gun, 1 x 7.92mm
Height: 3.12m (10ft 3in) (esimated)	(0.31in) Besa MG
Engine: 253.5kW (340hp) Continental R-975-	Radio: Wireless Set No. 19
EC2 radial petrol	

▲ **Grant Canal Defence Light (CDL)**

79th Armoured Division / 1st Tank Brigade / 11 RTR

The CDL was an ingenious device that suffered from excessive security – in effect, it was so secret that almost no one knew of it and so it was scarcely ever used. However, a detachment was used during the Rhine crossings, illuminating and destroying a number of floating mines launched against bridges and ferries.

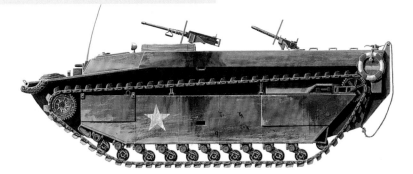

Specifications

Crew: 2 plus up 35 infantry	Engine: 186kW (250hp) Continental W670-9A
Weight: 12.42 tonnes (12.2 tons)	7-cylinder
Length: 7.95m (26ft 1in)	Speed: 32km/h (20mph)
Width: 3.25m (10ft 8in)	Range: 240km (150 miles)
Height: 2.46m (8ft 1in)	Armament: 1 x 12.7mm (0.5in) HMG,
	plus 2 x 7.62mm (0.3in) MGs

▲ **Landing Vehicle Tracked (LVT) 2 'Water Buffalo'**

79th Armoured Division / 33rd Armoured Brigade / 1st Northamptonshire Yeomanry

The Buffalo's 'main armament' of a 12.7mm (0.5in) heavy machine gun was frequently replaced with a 20mm (0.79in) cannon.

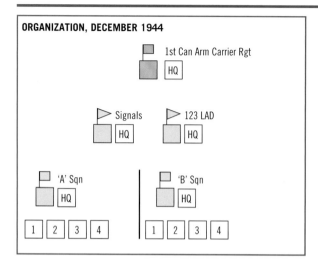

ORGANIZATION, DECEMBER 1944

1st Can Arm Carrier Rgt
HQ

Signals
HQ

123 LAD
HQ

'A' Sqn
HQ

1 2 3 4

'B' Sqn
HQ

1 2 3 4

Bulldozer was produced because of a need for a well-armoured, obstacle-clearing vehicle that, unlike a conventional bulldozer, was fast enough to keep up with tank formations. These vehicles were not used on D-Day but were issued to the 79th Armoured Division in Belgium during the latter part of 1944.

• **Grant Canal Defence Light (CDL)** – This was a powerful carbon-arc searchlight in a special turret fitted to a modified Grant. The device was given a deliberately misleading name for security reasons – its true purpose was to blind the defenders during night attacks. An ingenious optical design allowed the light to flood through a small slit in the armour, minimizing the risk of damage by enemy fire. The type was not used on D-Day, but was employed to create 'artificial moonlight' during the later attack on the Geilenkirchen Salient.

• **Kangaroos** – These armoured personnel carriers were devised by II Canadian Corps to minimize future infantry casualties after the heavy losses incurred in the early fighting to expand the Normandy beachheads. The first Kangaroos were converted from a batch of 102 surplus Priest self-propelled howitzers taken from artillery units that had re-equipped with 25pdr guns. At a field workshop (codenamed Kangaroo, hence the name), they were stripped of their howitzers, the gun mounting was plated over and bench seats for 12 infantrymen were fitted. They were first used in Operation *Totalize*, before being supplemented by further variants converted from Rams and Shermans which were widely used for the remainder of the war.

▲ **Better than marching**
A Ram Kangaroo carrying its infantry squad, autumn 1944.

▼ 1st Canadian Armoured Carrier Regiment, 'A' Squadron

Whilst several kinds of AFV were converted to Kangaroo APCs, the obsolescent Canadian Ram cruiser tank was the commonest base type. Ram Kangaroos had the advantage of similar levels of protection and mobility to the Shermans with which they most frequently operated, although their open-topped troop compartments were vulnerable to air-burst artillery fire. Initially they were operated by 1st Canadian Armoured Personnel Carrier Squadron, which was soon expanded to become 1st Canadian Armoured Carrier Regiment within 79th Armoured Division. By late 1944, it had been joined by the British 49th Armoured Personnel Carrier Regiment. Each unit fielded a total of 106 Ram Kangaroos and both were heavily committed to operations in support of Twenty-first Army Group until VE Day.

1 Troop

2 Troop

3 Troop

4 Troop

▲ Ram Kangaroo

79th Armoured Division / 31st Armoured Brigade / 1st Canadian Armoured Carrier Regiment

Several types of tanks and self-propelled guns, including Rams, Priests and Shermans, were converted to APCs (all of which were known as Kangaroos) by removing their main armament and fitting bench seats in the fighting compartment. The maximum number of passengers varied depending on the vehicle type, and armament varied wildly – all types mounted at least one machine gun, but extra pintle-mounted machine guns, heavy machine guns and 20mm (0.79in) cannon were 'acquired' whenever possible.

Specifications

Crew: 2 plus 10 infantry

Weight: 25.4 tonnes (25 tons)

Length: 5.79m (19ft)

Width: 2.77m (9ft 1in)

Height: 1.91m (6ft 3in)

Engine: 298kW (400hp) Continental R-975
9-cylinder radial petrol

Speed: 40km/h (25mph)

Range: 232km (144 miles)

Armament: 1 x 7.62mm (0.3in) MG in
sub-turret

Radio: Wireless Set No. 19

119

US armoured engineer AFVs
1944–45

US armoured engineering suffered from the lack of an equivalent of the 79th Armoured Division. Some work was carried out, particularly on mine-clearing devices and AFV-mounted flamethrowers, but most US formations came to rely on detachments of 'funnies' for armoured engineering tasks.

THE MAIN US MINE-EXPLODER device to see service, the T1E3, was named 'Aunt Jemima' after a popular pancake mix logo, as the big exploder wheels resembled gigantic pancakes. 'Jemima' comprised two massive steel rollers pushed in front of a Sherman, with one roller ahead of each tank track. Each roller was divided into five discs, each of which was about 10cm (3.9in) thick and 3m (10ft) in diameter. The whole device weighed in at almost 27,000kg (60,000lb), theoretically more than enough to detonate any mine.

Roller chains from the Sherman's sprockets drove the loosely mounted discs, and the T1E3 was found to work well in tests. In service, however, it was a different story – the device proved to be difficult to manoeuvre and its immense weight caused it to bog down repeatedly. As many as 70 'Jemimas' may have been issued, but US units heartily loathed them, much preferring to call on 79th Armoured Division's Sherman Crabs.

US Armoured Engineer Battalion	Strength
HQ Company:	
¼ ton truck	2
¾ ton truck	2
M3 halftracks	3
2½ ton truck	1
1 ton trailer	1
Company HQ:	
¼ ton truck	8
¾ ton truck	2
2½ ton truck	14
1 ton trailer	11
6 ton heavy wrecker	1
Motorised shop	1
Welding equipment trailer	1
Truck mounted compressor	1
3 ton bridge truck	3
water equipment trailer	4
M10 ammo trailer	2
Armoured Engineer Company:	
¼ ton truck	4
¾ ton truck	1
M3 halftrack	4
2½ ton truck	3
1 ton trailer	3
Truck mounted compressor	1
Tractor (bulldozer)	1
20 ton semi-trailer and tractor	1
6 ton bridge truck	1
2½ ton utility trailer	2
2½ ton dump truck	3

▲ **T15E1 Mine Resistant Vehicle**

Unidentified trials unit, continental USA

Whilst the idea of a mine resistant tank seemed attractive, it proved to be hopelessly impractical. Besides the difficulty of building a vehicle strong enough to cope with the repeated explosions of anti-tank mines, there was the problem of the 'unswept' strip of ground between the tracks.

Specifications

Crew: 5

Weight: 32.2 tonnes (31.6 tons)

Length: 5.9m (19ft 4in)

Width: 2.75m (9ft)

Height: 2.04m (6ft 8in)

Engine: 2 x 373kW (500hp) GeneralMotors 6-cylinder petrol

Speed: 48km/h (30mph)

Range: 270km (170 miles)

Radio: n/k

Flamethrowing tanks

US forces converted significant numbers of Stuarts and Shermans as armoured flamethrowers, but these were mainly deployed in the Pacific and South-East Asia. Four Shermans were converted (probably by 79th Armoured Division's workshops) to M4 Crocodiles, using standard Churchill Crocodile armoured fuel trailers but with an armoured fuel line running over the hull to a flame gun mounted next to the hull gunner's hatch. It is uncertain if any of these vehicles ever went into action, although they did serve with the US Ninth Army – in general, detachments of Churchill Crocodiles provided flamethrower support for US units.

▲ **Mine Exploder T1E3 (M1) 'Aunt Jemima'**

US Ninth Army / 739th Tank Battalion

The 'Aunt Jemima' was even trickier to manoeuvre than the Sherman Crab and was never popular with US armoured units.

Specifications

Crew: 5

Weight: 57 tonnes (56.1 tons) (estimated)

Length: 9.9m (32ft 6in) (estimated)

Width: 2.82m (9ft 3in) (estimated)

Height: 3m (9ft 10in)

Engine: 372.5kW (500hp) Ford GAA 8-cylinder petrol

Speed: 24km/h (15mph) (estimated)

Range: 110km (68.3 miles)

Armament: 1 x 75mm (2.9in) M3 gun,
   plus 1 x coaxial 7.62mm (0.3in) MG

Radio: SCR508

▲ **M4 Crocodile**

US Ninth Army / 739th Tank Battalion

The Sherman's thinner armour made it less well suited to the armoured flamethrower role than the Churchill. Only a single platoon of four M4 Crocodiles became operational with the 739th Tank Battalion from November 1944.

Specifications (tank alone)

Crew: 5

Weight: 30.3 tonnes (29.82 tons)

Length: 5.90m (19ft 4in)

Width: 2.62m (8ft 7in)

Height: 2.74m (8ft 11in)

Engine: 372.5kW (500hp) Ford GAA
   8-cylinder petrol

Speed: 42km/h (26mph)

Range: 210km (130 miles)

Armament: 1 x 75mm (2.9in) M3 gun,
   1 x flame gun by co-driver's hatch and
   2 x 7.62mm (0.3in) MGs (1 coaxial,
   1 ball-mounted in hull front)

Radio: SCR 508

Normandy to Arnhem

JUNE–SEPTEMBER 1944

The three and a half months between the Normandy landings and the end of Operation *Market Garden* were marked by grinding attritional warfare, followed by exhilarating pursuits and finally the frustration of a 'lost victory'. Throughout it all, Allied armour played a key role in countless actions, from great offensives to minor skirmishes.

IN THE MONTHS before the Normandy landings, reports from armoured units in Italy began to raise suspicions that the Sherman was rapidly becoming outclassed by the newer German AFVs such as the Panther and Jagdpanzer IV. American experts tended to ignore such concerns – the official US Army view was that updated versions of the Sherman with the

new 76mm (3in) gun would be quite capable of holding their own against any German tank. As a result, the enormous American tank production effort remained concentrated on improved versions of the Sherman until the last stages of the war in Europe, when it was belatedly accepted that new types were desperately needed to match the increasingly sophisticated German AFVs.

British designs were virtually a generation behind their German counterparts, but the first issues of tungsten-cored APDS (armour-piercing, discarding

▼ **Reinforcements**

Columns of Shermans and Churchills pass each other on a country road 'somewhere in France'.

sabot) ammunition for the 6pdr and 17pdr in the summer of 1944 marked a major advance in anti-tank technology. Fortunately, the new APDS round gave the 17pdr an anti-tank performance at least equal to all German AFV weapons, except for the rarely encountered 128mm (5in) of the Jagdtiger.

Producing the weapon was one thing, but finding suitable AFVs to mount it was quite another. Luckily, the 17pdr could be squeezed into a modified Sherman turret and that of the M10 tank destroyer, which were backed up by 650-plus Archers and a small number of Challengers. Unfortunately, there were

Specifications

Crew: 5	Speed: 42km/h (26mph)
Weight: 30.3 tonnes (29.82 tons)	Range: 210km (130 miles)
Length: 5.90m (19ft 4in)	Armament: 1 x 75mm (2.9in) M3 gun,
Width: 2.62m (8ft 7in)	plus 2 x 7.62mm (0.3in) MGs (1 coaxial,
Height: 2.74m (8ft 11in)	1 ball-mounted in hull front)
Engine: 372.5kW (500hp) Ford GAA	Radio: SCR508
8-cylinder petrol	

▲ M4A3 Sherman Medium Tank

US First Army / V Corps / 2nd Armored Division / 66th Armored Regiment

This Sherman's exhaust and air intakes are fitted with deep-wading trunking. Many vehicles had to be landed on the original invasion beaches long after D-Day and needed waterproofing or deep-wading equipment to minimize the risk of being swamped as they came ashore.

Specifications

Crew: 4	Speed: 56km/h (35mph)
Weight: 15.6 tonnes (15.45 tons)	Range: 210km (130 miles)
Length: 4.41m (14ft 6in)	Armament: 1 x 75mm (2.9in) M2 howitzer,
Width: 2.24m (7ft 4in)	plus 1 x 12.7mm (0.5in) AA HMG
Height: 2.32m (7ft 7in)	Radio: SCR508
Engine: 2 x 81.95kW (110hp) Cadillac Series	
42 V8 petrol	

▲ 75mm Howitzer Motor Carriage (HMC) M8

US First Army / V Corps / 2nd Armored Division / 24th Cavalry Reconnaissance Squadron

Based on the chassis of the M5 (Stuart), the M8 had an open-topped turret with a 75mm (2.9in) M2 or M3 howitzer. Most M8s were deployed to provide fire support to the M5s of reconnaissance squadrons. This vehicle is fitted with a 'Culin' hedgerow cutter for breaking through the thick hedges of the bocage.

▲ **Traffic control**

A Polish Sherman is directed through the ruins of Caen.

never enough AFVs capable of mounting the 17pdr, and those that were available had to be doled out in small numbers.

German armour

In the aftermath of the stunning German victories of 1940, France, Belgium and Holland became something of a backwater. By the end of 1941, when it became clear that there would be no quick ending

to the war in the East, the occupied territories of the West had come to be regarded as 'cushy' postings where German units could re-form and recuperate before returning to the Eastern Front.

Apart from training formations, very few armoured units were permanently stationed in these areas until the threat of invasion became acute in the spring of 1944. Despite the ever more urgent demands for Panzer units to stem the increasingly dangerous Soviet advances, elite formations, including 1st and 12th SS Panzer Divisions and *Panzer Lehr*, were moved to positions within striking distance of the likely invasion beaches on the Channel coast. Rommel, who had been appointed to command Army Group B covering those very beaches in December 1943, had drastically reinforced their defences.

Over two million mines were laid in the six months before D-Day, bringing the total to roughly four million, whilst 500,000 anti-tank and anti-glider obstacles blocked likely landing grounds. Rommel wanted to do more, planning to create a continuous minefield 1000m (1094 yards) deep along the whole Channel coast. This would be defended by all the available Panzer units, with the aim of destroying the invasion on the beaches. The Panzers would thus be close enough to attack when the Allies were

▲ **Tetrarch ICS**

6th Airborne Division / Airborne Armoured Reconnaissance Regiment

The Light Tank Mark VII entered production in 1940 and was adopted by the airborne forces in 1941 as it was light enough to be carried by the new Hamilcar glider. A small number were flown in to 6th Airborne Division's landing zones early on D-Day. They provided close fire support for the lightly equipped airborne infantry for a few days until relieved by armoured units advancing from the beaches. Most Tetrarchs were armed with the 2pdr; this example is one of a small number of Close Support (CS) variants that carried the 76mm (3in) CS howitzer.

Specifications

Crew: 3	Speed: 64km/h (40mph)
Weight: 7.62 tonnes (7.5 tons)	Range: 225km (140 miles)
Length: 4.11m (13ft 6in)	Armament: 1 x 76mm (3in) CS howitzer,
Width: 2.31m (7ft 7in)	plus 1 x coaxial 7.92mm (0.31in) Besa MG
Height: 2.12m (6ft 11.5in)	Radio: Wireless Set No. 19
Engine: 123kW (165hp) Meadows MAT	
12-cylinder petrol	

at their most vulnerable in the first few hours after landing, which would cut down the time the tanks were exposed to air attacks and naval gunfire. His ideas on Panzer deployment fell foul of his immediate superior, the Commander-in-Chief West, von Runstedt, who wanted to hold the tanks in reserve before launching them in a major counter-offensive once the main Allied attack had been slowed by the infantry divisions defending the Channel coast. This dispute was finally settled in a compromise – three of the six Panzer divisions were assigned to Rommel whilst the remainder, designated Panzer Group West, were held back under Hitler's control.

D-Day

British and American planners devised markedly different tactics for the use of armour on D-Day (6 June 1944). The US mistrust of the 'funnies' was such that they only deployed DD Shermans (many of which sank in the rough seas after being launched too far offshore). Their loss left the assault infantry and engineers to take heavy casualties from the defences, and they would have been horribly vulnerable if the Panzers had been close enough to intervene in the first crucial hours. In marked contrast, the British and Canadian landings were supported by all types of 'funnies', which

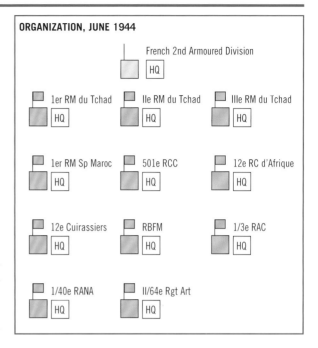

ORGANIZATION, JUNE 1944

French 2nd Armoured Division — HQ

1er RM du Tchad — HQ
IIe RM du Tchad — HQ
IIIe RM du Tchad — HQ

1er RM Sp Maroc — HQ
501e RCC — HQ
12e RC d'Afrique — HQ

12e Cuirassiers — HQ
RBFM — HQ
1/3e RAC — HQ

1/40e RANA — HQ
II/64e Rgt Art — HQ

undoubtedly saved many lives. They also made a major contribution to the rate of advance. By nightfall on D-Day, leading British and Canadian units were almost 10km (6 miles) inland, whilst US forces were no more than 5km (3 miles) inland and had sustained a far higher casualty rate.

▲ M4A2 Sherman Medium Tank

US Third Army / V Corps / French 2nd Armoured Division (2e Division Blindée, 2e DB) / 12e Regiment de Chasseurs d'Afrique

2e DB took part in the Allied breakout from Normandy, in which it served as a link between US and Canadian forces. It also played a key role in the virtual destruction of 9th Panzer Division in the fighting to eliminate the Falaise Pocket.

Specifications

Crew: 5	Speed: 48km/h (30mph)
Weight: 31.8 tonnes (31.29 tons)	Range: 240km (150 miles)
Length: 5.92m (19ft 5in)	Armament: 1 x 75mm (2.9in) M3 gun,
Width: 2.62m (8ft 7in)	plus 2 x 7.62mm (0.3in) MGs (1 coaxial,
Height: 2.74m (8ft 11in)	1 ball-mounted in hull front)
Engine: 305.45kW (410hp) General Motors	Radio: SCR508
6046 12-cylinder twin in-line diesel	

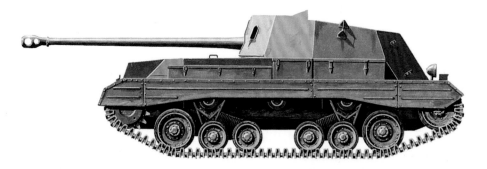

▲ **SP 17pdr, Valentine Mk I, Archer**

Twenty-first Army Group / Second Army / VIII Corps / 3rd Infantry Division /
20th Anti-Tank Regiment RA

The bulk and weight of the very effective 17pdr anti-tank gun were such that
the provision of self-propelled versions was a matter of priority. Rearming the
US-supplied M10 Wolverine tank destroyers provided a partial solution, but
there were never enough to meet demand. Fortunately, the Valentine was still
in production and it was decided to use its hull as the basis for a new vehicle,
designated Archer. The 17pdr was carried on a rearward-facing, limited-traverse
mount in an open-topped fighting compartment and the result was surprisingly
successful, having a low silhouette and good agility.

Specifications	
Crew: 4	
Weight: 18.79 tonnes (18.5 tons)	Speed: 24km/h (15mph)
Length: 6.68m (21ft 11in)	Range: 145km (90 miles)
Width: 2.64m (8ft 8in)	Armament: 1 x 76mm (3in) 17pdr OQF,
Height: 2.24m (7ft 4in)	plus 1 x 7.7mm (0.303in) Bren MG
Engine: 123kW (165hp) GMC M10 diesel	Radio: Wireless Set No. 18 CSL/126/14

Fortunately for the Allies, the German response to
the landings was fatally slowed by Rommel's absence
on leave and the need to get Hitler's permission
to move the reserves. As a result only 21st Panzer
Division was close enough to counterattack on
D-Day – by 20:00 several of its AFVs with a
Panzergrenadier company had managed to advance
as far as the coast between Sword and Juno Beaches.
Although it lacked the strength to do anything more
than impose a temporary delay on the British and
Canadian advance, the division showed what might
have been possible if Rommel had been allowed to
station all the available armour in readiness to launch
immediate counterattacks whilst the Allies were at
their most vulnerable.

The Allied invasion plans had assumed that Caen
and Bayeux would be taken on D-Day itself, with
all the beaches linked except for Utah, and that
the front line would be 10–16km (6–10 miles)
inland. Determined German resistance held the
Allied advance well short of most of its key objectives,
but the casualties had not been as heavy as some had
feared (around 10,000 compared with the 20,000
Churchill had estimated) and the bridgeheads had
withstood the expected counterattacks. The success
or failure of the landings now hung on the outcome
of the 'reinforcement race' – that is, whether Allied
reinforcements could be brought across the Channel
quickly enough to exceed the rate at which German
forces could be moved in to seal off and destroy the
beachheads.

Swings and roundabouts

Both sides faced severe problems – a prolonged
spell of bad weather could wreck the prefabricated
Mulberry Harbours, prevent resupply and ground
Allied aircraft, giving the Germans a superb
opportunity to attack unhindered by Allied air

▲ **Reconnaissance**

The crew of a US M8 armoured car observe a bombed-out building in
Normandy, July 1944.

supremacy. Meanwhile, 'on the other side of the hill', the Germans had to move formations over a road and rail system under constant attack from Resistance groups and the Allied air forces. Furthermore, there was always the threat of further landings to consider – Allied deception measures included a very convincing fake First US Army Group ('FUSAG'), supposedly preparing to invade the Pas de Calais. As a result, German units that might have had a major impact on the fighting in Normandy were held back to face this phantom threat.

Allied reinforcement measures were quick and effective. Once the beachhead had been established,

the components of two Mulberry Harbours were towed across the Channel. Both were assembled and operating by D+3 (9 June). The British Mulberry was set up at Arromanches, whilst its US counterpart was assembled at Omaha Beach. By 19 June, when severe storms delayed the landing of supplies for several days and destroyed the Omaha Mulberry, the British had

---

INSIGNIA

The badge of the French 2nd Armoured Division (*2e Division Blindée*) features the cross of Lorraine, emblem of the Free French, against a map of France.

▶ **M3A3 Light Tank**

US Third Army / V Corps / French 2nd Armoured Division (2e Division Blindée, 2e DB) / 1er Regiment de Marche de Spahis Marocains

General Leclerc's 2e DB scored its greatest triumph in the liberation of Paris on 24/25 August 1944. The M3s of the divisional reconnaissance unit were amongst the first French troops to enter the city.

Specifications

Crew: 4	Speed: 50km/h (31mph)
Weight: 14.7 tonnes (14.46 tons)	Range: 217km (135 miles)
Length: 5.02m (16ft 5in)	Armament: 1 x 37mm (1.5in) M6 gun,
Width: 2.52m (8ft 3in)	plus 2 x 7.62mm (0.3in) MGs (1 coaxial,
Height: 2.57m (8ft 5in)	1 ball-mounted in hull front)
Engine: 186.25kW (250hp) Continental	Radio: SCR508
W-670-9A 7-cylinder radial petrol	

▲ **M8 Armoured Car**

French First Army / HQ 1st Armoured Division (1re Division Blindée)

In 1944–45 the French Army's armoured formations were closely based on the US model and the vast majority of their equipment was of US origin.

Specifications

Crew: 4	Speed: 89km/h (55mph)
Weight: 8.12 tonnes (8 tons)	Range: 563km (350 miles)
Length: 5m (16ft 5in)	Armament: 1 x 37mm (1.5in) M6 gun,
Width: 2.54m (8ft 4in)	plus 1 x 12.7mm (0.5in) AA HMG and
Height: 2.25m (7ft 5in)	1 x coaxial 7.62mm (0.3in) MG
Engine: 82kW (110hp) Hercules JXD 6-cylinder petrol	Radio: SCR508

landed 314,547 men, 54,000 vehicles and 103,600 tonnes (102,000 tons) of supplies, and the Americans had put ashore 314,504 men, 41,000 vehicles and 117,850 tonnes (116,000 tons) of supplies. About 9100 tonnes (9000 tons) of stores were landed daily at the Arromanches Mulberry until the end of August, by which time the port of Cherbourg (captured on 27 June) was again fully operational.

In the vital first weeks of the Normandy campaign, the Germans were able to contain the Allied beachhead by matching their reinforcement rate. Their defence was greatly helped by the terrain – the infamous bocage with its thick, banked hedges and narrow lanes, dotted with villages that formed natural strongpoints. In this setting the German anti-tank guns and Panzerfausts were able to take a heavy

▲ M20 Armoured Utility Car

French First Army / HQ 1st Armoured Division (1re Division Blindée)

1re DB landed in Provence on 15 August 1944 as part of the Garbo Force under the command of General Jean de Lattre de Tassigny's French First Army. It took part in the liberation of Toulon and Marseilles and was the first Allied formation to reach the Rhone (25 August), the Rhine (19 November) and the Danube (21 April 1945).

Specifications

Crew: 4

Weight: 7 tonnes (6.89 tons) (estimated)

Length: 5m (16ft 5in)

Width: 2.54m (8ft 4in)

Height: 2m (6ft 7in) (estimated)

Engine: 82kW (110hp) Hercules JXD 6-cylinder petrol

Speed: 89km/h (55mph)

Range: 563km (350 miles)

Armament: 1 x 12.7mm (0.5in) AA HMG

Radio: SCR508

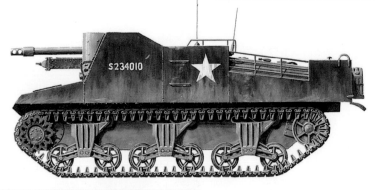

Specifications

Crew: 6

Weight: 25.9 tonnes (25.5 tons)

Length: 6.12m (20ft 1in)

Width: 2.71m (8ft 11in)

Height: 2.43m (8ft)

Engine: 298kW (400hp) Continental 9-cylinder radial petrol

Speed: 38km/h (24mph)

Range: 200km (125 miles)

Armament: 1 x 87.6mm (3.45in) 25pdr gun/ howitzer, plus 2 x 7.7mm (0.303in) Bren MGs

Radio: Wireless Set No. 19

▲ Sexton SP 25pdr

Twenty-first Army Group / Second Army / XXX Corps / 8th Armoured Brigade / 147th Field Regiment RA

The Sexton was a highly successful attempt to produce a British equivalent of the Priest self-propelled howitzer. For whilst the Priest was a very good AFV, its 105mm (4.1in) howitzer was not a standard British weapon and the necessity for special supply arrangements caused constant problems. The first of over 2000 Sextons were issued in 1943 and many remained in service until 1956.

Specifications

Crew: 5

Weight: 29.48 tonnes (29 tons)

Length: 5.79m (19ft)

Width: 2.77m (9ft 1in)

Height: 2.67m (8ft 9in)

Engine: 298kW (400hp) Continental R-975
9-cylinder radial petrol

Speed: 40km/h (25mph)

Range: 232km (144 miles)

Armament: 1 x 7.62mm (0.3in) MG
in sub-turret

Radio: 2 x Wireless Set No. 19

▲ Ram OP/Command Tank

Twenty-first Army Group / Second Army / XXX Corps / 8th Armoured Brigade / 147th Field Regiment RA

The Ram was a Canadian design based on the Sherman. Although it never saw combat service as a cruiser tank, 84 were converted to armoured observation posts for the Forward Observation Officers (FOOs) of Sexton self-propelled gun units. The main gun was replaced with a dummy 6pdr and two radios were fitted.

ORGANIZATION, JUNE 1944

7th Armoured Division — HQ

22nd Arm Bde — HQ

1 RTR — HQ | 5 RTR — HQ | 4th C Lon Yeo — HQ | 1st Rfl Bde — HQ

131st Bde — HQ

1/5th Queens — HQ | 1/6th Queens — HQ | 1/7th Queens — HQ | 2nd Devonshire — HQ | 9th DLI — HQ | Northumberland Fus — HQ

Divisional Troops — HQ | Royal Artillery — HQ

8th Hussars — HQ | 11th Hussars — HQ | 3rd RHA — HQ | 5th RHA — HQ | 15th Lt AA Rgt — HQ | 65th A-T Rgt — HQ

◀ **Pushing through the bocage**

A Churchill of 7 RTR, 31st Tank Brigade, moving up with infantry of 8th Royal Scots during Operation Epsom, 28 June 1944.

INSIGNIA

The 'Desert Rat' emblem was based on a design by the wife of 7th Armoured Ddivision's commander General Michael Creagh, giving rise to the legendary nickname.

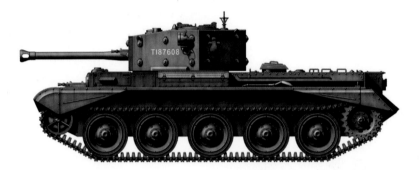

▲ **Cromwell Mark IV**

7th Armoured Division / 22nd Armoured Brigade / 1 RTR

By the time that it went into action in Normandy, the Cromwell had fallen a generation behind the latest German tanks – although roughly equivalent to contemporary versions of the Panzer IV, it was far outclassed by the Panther. Despite its thin armour, the design had some good points, especially its high speed and reliability, which were fully exploited after the breakout from the Normandy beachhead.

Specifications

Crew: 5

Weight: 27.94 tonnes (27.5 tons)

Length: 6.35m (20ft 10in)

Width: 2.9m (9ft 6in)

Height: 2.49m (8ft 2in)

Engine: 447kW (600hp) Rolls-Royce Meteor V12 petrol

Speed: 64km/h (40mph)

Range: 280km (174 miles)

Armament: 1 x 75mm (2.9in) OQF gun, plus 2 x 7.92mm (0.31in) Besa MGs (1 coaxial and 1 ball-mounted in hull front)

Radio: Wireless Set No. 19

▲ **Infantry Tank Mark IV, Churchill Mark III**

Twenty-first Army Group / Second Army / VIII Corps / 15th (Scottish) Infantry Division / 31st Tank Brigade / 7 RTR

By mid-1944, the earlier Churchills were steadily being replaced by the Churchill Mark VII, which was armed with the Ordnance Quick Firing (OQF) 75mm (2.9in) gun, essentially the 6pdr bored out to fire US 75mm (2.9in) ammunition. Although the new gun had a greatly improved performance when firing HE in the tank's infantry support role, its armour-piercing capability was far less than that of the 6pdr. This situation often had lethal consequences when facing the newer, more heavily armoured German AFVs, and some units retained a number of 6pdr-armed tanks to give anti-tank protection.

Specifications

Crew: 5

Weight: 39.62 tonnes (39 tons)

Length: 7.44m (24ft 5in)

Width: 2.74m (9ft)

Height: 3.25m (10ft 8in)

Engine: 261.1kW (350hp) Bedford 12-cylinder petrol

Speed: 25km/h (15.5mph)

Range: 193km (120 miles)

Armament: 1 x 57mm (2.24in) 6pdr OQF gun, plus 2 x 7.92mm (0.31in) Besa MGs (1 coaxial and 1 ball-mounted in hull front)

Radio: Wireless Set No. 19

Specifications

Crew: 4

Weight: 32.7 tonnes (32.18 tons)

Length: 7.85m (25ft 9in)

Width: 2.67m (8ft 9in)

Height: 2.74m (8ft 11in)

Engine: 316.6kW (425hp) Chrysler Multibank
A57 petrol

Speed: 40km/h (25mph)

Range: 161km (100 miles)

Armament: 1 x 76mm (3in) 17pdr OQF,
plus 1 x coaxial 7.62mm (0.3in) MG

Radio: Wireless Set No. 19

▲ **Sherman Firefly**

Twenty-first Army Group / Second Army / I Corps / 3rd Canadian Infantry
Division / 2nd Canadian Armoured Brigade / 1st Hussars

The Firefly was a brilliantly engineered conversion of the Sherman armed with the potent 17pdr gun. The first vehicles began to equip British and Canadian units shortly before D-Day, but were in short supply and initially had to be issued on the basis of one per troop, giving each troop one Firefly and three standard Shermans.

◀ **Ambush**

A Firefly lies in wait for a counterattack.

east of Caen with three armoured divisions, aimed at pinning down the Panzers and preventing their being transferred to counter the imminent American breakout from their western beachheads. Despite carpet-bombing (4500 Allied aircraft dropped 7100

toll of Allied armour. When either side attempted to attack in these conditions, it was liable to suffer crippling losses. An example was the mauling of 7th Armoured Division's advance guard at Villers-Bocage by four Tiger Is and a single Panzer IV of *Schwere SS-Panzer Abteilung* 101.

Epsom and Charnwood

The first British and Canadian offensives, Operations *Epsom* and *Charnwood*, made little progress against a determined German defence, although the ruins of Caen were finally taken on 10 July. Then on the 18th, Montgomery launched Operation *Goodwood* south-

ORGANIZATION, JUNE 1944

4th Armoured Brigade — HQ

R Scots Greys — HQ

3rd CLY — HQ

44 RTR — HQ

2nd King's R Rfls — HQ

4th RHA — HQ

5 Coy RASC — HQ

14th Lt Fld Amb — HQ

4th Wksp REME — HQ

4th Ord Wksp — HQ

271 Fwd Del Sqn — HQ

4th Signals — HQ

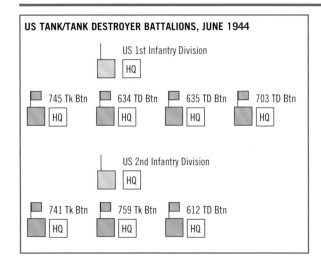

US TANK/TANK DESTROYER BATTALIONS, JUNE 1944

US 1st Infantry Division — HQ

745 Tk Btn — HQ
634 TD Btn — HQ
635 TD Btn — HQ
703 TD Btn — HQ

US 2nd Infantry Division — HQ

741 Tk Btn — HQ
759 Tk Btn — HQ
612 TD Btn — HQ

tonnes/7000 tons of bombs), three days of fierce fighting produced an advance of no more than 11km (7 miles) for the loss of almost 400 British and perhaps 60 German AFVs.

The US offensive, Operation *Cobra*, began on 25 July, and after 48 hours, broke through the weakened German lines, beginning one of the most dramatic advances of the war. By early August, Patton's armour was flooding south and east, threatening the rear of the German forces holding the line near Caen.

Four German divisions fielding 250 tanks counterattacked near Mortain on 7/8 August with the objective of cutting the American forces in two by driving through to the coast at Avranches. This desperate move was easily held and made the encirclement of the German Seventh Army and Fifth Panzer Army in the Falaise Pocket that much easier. When the pocket was finally overrun on 21 August, only 1300 Germans with 60 guns and 24 AFVs had escaped.

Limited supply

For a few weeks, it seemed as if the war in the West might be over – Paris was taken by the French 2nd Armoured Division (*2e Division Blindée, 2e DB*) on 25 August and Brussels was liberated by the Guards Armoured Division on 3 September. Then reality set in – on 4 September, supply shortages halted the Allied advance. Supply routes stretched back to the original invasion beaches and the nearby deep-water port of Cherbourg. Antwerp had been captured by Montgomery's Twenty-first Army Group, but its port facilities were unusable until German troops could be cleared from the approaches along the Scheldt estuary. Other Channel ports were either still under repair or, like Dunkirk, still in German hands. (The garrison of Dunkirk held out until May 1945.)

Frustratingly, although over-the-beach supply operations exceeded expectations and enough supplies were landed to support Allied operations,

▲ M10 Tank Destroyer
US Twelfth Army Group / First Army / VII Corps / 1st Infantry Division / 703rd Tank Destroyer Battalion

By the early stages of the Normandy campaign, the M10's 76mm (3in) gun was becoming less effective against the increasingly common up-armoured German AFVs. A further problem was the very slow traverse rate of its hand-cranked turret, which took about two minutes to rotate 360 degrees. These shortcomings led to the M10's replacement by the M36, with a much more potent 90mm (3.5in) gun.

Specifications

Crew: 5	Speed: 48km/h (30mph)
Weight: 29.05 tonnes (28.6 tons)	Range: 320km (200 miles)
Length: 5.82m (19ft 1in)	Armament: 1 x 76mm (3in) M7 gun,
Width: 3.05m (10ft)	plus 1 x 12.7mm (0.5in) HMG on AA mount
Height: 2.49m (8ft 2in)	Radio: SCR610
Engine: 305.45kW (410hp) General Motors	
6046 12-cylinder twin in-line diesel	

these could not be taken forward due to transport shortages. At the beginning of September, 71,000 tonnes (70,000 tons) of supplies were stockpiled at Cherbourg because there were no means of moving them. Railway services were non-existent for months whilst damage from pre-invasion bombing was repaired – very limited rail movement out of Normandy only resumed on 30 August. A final blow

to the hard-pressed supply services came when 1400 British 3-ton trucks were found to be useless because of faulty engine pistons — they could have moved 813 tonnes (800 tons) per day, enough to support two divisions.

These dire problems exacerbated disagreements amongst the senior Allied commanders – Montgomery and Patton's rivalry had remained fierce ever since

Specifications

Crew: 7

Weight: 26.01 tonnes (25.6 tons)

Length: 6.02m (19ft 9in)

Width: 2.88m (9ft 5in)

Height: 2.54m (8ft 4in)

Engine: 298kW (400hp) Continental R975 C1 radial petrol

Speed: 42km/h (26mph)

Range: 201km (125 miles)

Armament: 1 x 105mm (4.1in) M1A2 howitzer, plus 1 x 12.7mm (0.5in) HMG on 'pulpit' AA mount.

Radio: SCR608

▲ 105mm Howitzer Motor Carriage (HMC) M7 (Priest)

US First Army / V Corps / 2nd Armored Division / 14th Armored Field Artillery Battalion

Each US armoured division had three armoured field artillery battalions, each with 18 105mm (4.1in) M7s.

▲ 155mm Gun Motor Carriage (GMC) M12

US Twelfth Army Group / First Army / VII Corps / 4th Infantry Division / 630th Heavy Artillery Battalion

The M12 was a World War I-vintage 155mm (6.1in) gun mounted on a heavily modified M3 Lee medium tank. Only 100 vehicles were completed before production ended in 1943 and most were used for training or put into storage. A total of 74 were refurbished and issued to heavy artillery battalions taking part in the Normandy landings. The type proved to be highly successful and remained in service until the end of the war.

Specifications

Crew: 6

Weight: 29.46 tonnes (29 tons)

Length: 6.73m (22ft 1in)

Width: 2.67m (8ft 9in)

Height: 2.69m (8ft 10in)

Engine: 263kW (353hp) Continental R-975 radial petrol

Speed: 39km/h (24mph)

Range: 225km (140 miles)

Armament: 1 x 155mm (6.1in) M1918M1 gun

Radio: SCR608

the invasion of Sicily. Now both pressed claims that their forces alone could win the war with a single offensive deep into Germany, provided that they were given priority for the supplies that could be brought forward.

Operation *Market Garden*

Eventually it was agreed that Montgomery would be given just enough resources for his Operation *Market Garden*, a highly ambitious plan in which a major part of the First Allied Airborne Army would be

dropped to seize the bridges at Eindhoven, Nijmegen and Arnhem. The formations to be inserted were the British 1st Airborne Division, the US 82nd and 101st Airborne Divisions and the 1st Polish Parachute Brigade. The intention was to form a so-called 'airborne carpet' more than 100km (63 miles) long across the Rhine over which the British Second Army would advance into Germany.

The operation, which began on 17 September, was hastily and poorly planned. Errors included the selection of drop zones too far from the bridges and

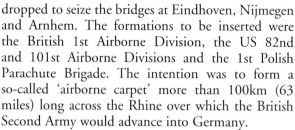

◀ Universal Carrier

Twenty-first Army Group / Second Army / VIII Corps / 15th (Scottish) Infantry Division / 8th Royal Scots

The Universal Carrier was subjected to a vast range of modifications by its users – this example has simply been rearmed with a captured MG42 machine gun in the fighting compartment. A Bren gun, fitted with the rarely used 100-round drum magazine, is carried on the AA mount.

Specifications	
Crew: 3	Engine: 63.4kW (85hp) Ford V8
Weight: 4.06 tonnes (4 tons)	8-cylinder petrol
Length: 3.76m (12ft 4in)	Speed: 52km/h (32mph)
Width: 2.11m (6ft 11in)	Range: 258km (160 miles)
Height: 1.63m (5ft 4in)	Armament: (Standard) 2 x 7.7mm (0.303in)
	Bren MGs

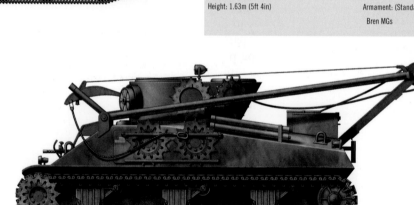

Specifications	
Crew: 6	Speed: 39km/h (24mph)
Weight: 29.2 tonnes (28.74 tons)	Range: 190km (120 miles)
Length: 5.89m (19ft 4in)	Armament: 1 x 81mm (3.19in) mortar, plus
Width: 2.62m (8ft 7in)	1 x 12.7mm (0.5in) AA HMG and 1 x 7.62mm
Height: 2.95m (9ft 8in)	(0.3in) MG ball-mounted in hull front
Engine: 298kW (400hp) Continental R975 C1	
9-cylinder radial petrol	

▲ Tank Recovery Vehicle M32

US First Army / V Corps / 2nd Armored Division / 66th Armored Regiment

The M32 was based on the chassis of the M4 medium tank with the turret replaced by a fixed superstructure. The vehicle was fitted with a 27,000kg (60,000lb) winch and a 5.5m (18ft) long pivoting A-frame jib. An 81mm (3.19in) mortar was mounted on the front of the hull and was primarily intended for firing white phosphorous smoke bombs to screen recovery work in front-line areas.

▲ 'Old Blood and Guts'

Lieutenant-General George S. Patton was an undoubted master of 'hot pursuit' operations. One of the most notable of these was Operation Cobra, in which his Third Army advanced 97km (60 miles) in two weeks.

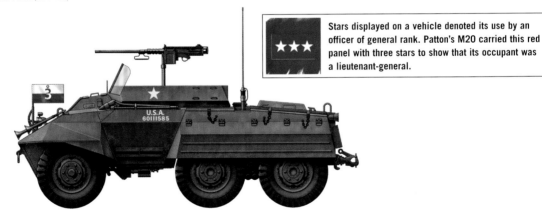

Stars displayed on a vehicle denoted its use by an officer of general rank. Patton's M20 carried this red panel with three stars to show that its occupant was a lieutenant-general.

▲ M20 Armoured Utility Car

US Twelfth Army Group / HQ Third Army

This modified M20 served as Patton's personal command vehicle.

Specifications

Crew: 4

Weight: 7 tonnes (6.89 tons) (estimated)

Length: 5m (16ft 5in)

Width: 2.54m (8ft 4in)

Height: 2m (6ft 7in) (estimated)

Engine: 82kW (110hp) Hercules JXD
6-cylinder petrol

Speed: 89km/h (55mph)

Range: 563km (350 miles)

Armament: 1 x 12.7mm (0.5in) AA HMG

Radio: SCR508

a disregard for intelligence that correctly identified two SS Panzer divisions refitting in the Arnhem area. In addition, the Guards Armoured Division, leading the ground forces' advance, was committed to attack along a single road, Highway 69.

There was literally no room for manoeuvre, since much of the road, which rapidly became known as 'Hell's Highway', ran along causeways above polder terrain, which was too soft to support tactical vehicle movement. In the circumstances, it was hardly surprising that the results fell far short of the optimists' hopes of winning the war before Christmas. Guards Armoured Division took continuous losses from the fire of small groups of German AFVs as it advanced along the horribly exposed Highway 69, and had to fight off repeated counterattacks aimed

▲ M3A1 Halftrack

US First Army / V Corps / 2nd Armored Division / 41st Armored
Infantry Regiment

Although its open-topped fighting compartment was vulnerable to air-burst artillery and grenades, the M3's high speed and mechanical reliability were invaluable during the rapid advances of Operation Cobra.

Specifications

Crew: 2 plus 11 passengers	Engine: 109.5kW (147hp) White 160AX
Weight: 9.3 tonnes (9.15 tons)	6-cylinder petrol
Length: 6.34m (20ft 10in)	Speed: 72km/h (45mph)
Width: 2.22m (7ft 3in)	Range: 320km (200 miles)
Height: 2.69m (8ft 10in)	Armament: 1 x 12.7mm (0.5in) HMG
	Radio: SCR508

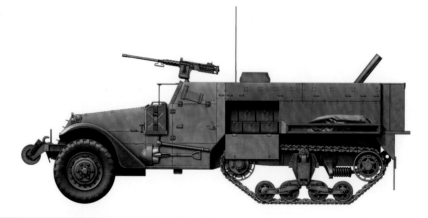

Specifications

Crew: 6	Speed: 72km/h (45mph)
Weight: 7.97 tonnes (7.84 tons)	Range: 320km (200 miles)
Length: 6.01m (19ft 9in)	Armament: 1 x 81mm (3.19in) M1 mortar,
Width: 1.96m (6ft 5in)	plus 1 x 12.7mm (0.5in) HMG
Height: 2.27m (7ft 5in)	Radio: SCR508
Engine: 109.5kW (147hp) White 160AX	
6-cylinder petrol	

▲ M4 Mortar Motor Carriage (MMC)

US First Army / V Corps / 2nd Armored Division / 41st Armored
Infantry Regiment

Each armoured infantry battalion had a mortar platoon with three M4s. These vehicles were later replaced by the M21 MMC, which mounted a forward-firing 81mm (3.19in) mortar.

at cutting the road. Although the division managed to link up with the US airborne force at Eindhoven and Nijmegen, it was held south of Arnhem by rapidly strengthening German forces. The remnants of the Allied airborne forces at Arnhem were evacuated on 25 September after holding out against overwhelming odds for nine days – more than twice as long as originally planned.

▲ Truck, 15cwt, GS, 4x2, Bedford MWD

Twenty-first Army Group / Second Army / XXX Corps / 7th Armoured Division /
22nd Armoured Brigade / 1st Rifle Brigade

The Bedford MWD was one of the best-known of the wartime 15cwts. It entered service just before the war, and Vauxhall Motors completed some 66,000 (not all of them GS trucks) by the time production ceased in 1945. In common with other 15cwts of the era, early models had an open cab and no tilt. They were initially issued on the basis of one per infantry platoon to carry the unit's ammunition, rations and kit. This example is finished in the so-called 'Mickey Mouse ear' camouflage widely used for British 'soft-skinned' support vehicles in 1944.

Specifications

Crew: 1	Engine: 53.7kW (72hp) Bedford OHV
Weight: 2.13 tonnes (2.09 tons)	6-cylinder petrol
Length: 4.38m (14ft 4.5in)	Speed: 80km/h (50mph) (estimated)
Width: 1.99m (6ft 6.5in)	Range: 270km (168 miles) (estimated)
Height: 2.29m (7ft 6in)	

Specifications

Crew: 1	Engine: 53.64kW (72hp) Bedford WD
Weight: 6.56 tonnes (6.46 tons)	6-cylinder petrol
Length: 6.22m (20ft 5in)	Speed: 80km/h (50mph) (estimated)
Width: 2.18m (7ft 2in)	Range: 450km (280 miles)
Height: 3.09m (10ft 2in)	

▲ Bedford 3-Ton Fuel Tanker

Twenty-first Army Group / Second Army / XXX Corps / 7th Armoured Division /
22nd Armoured Brigade / 5 RTR

Fuel was always a vital commodity and there never seemed to be enough tankers to meet demands. Conventional vehicles frequently had to make supplementary deliveries of thousands of jerricans of fuel to keep front-line units supplied.

Chapter 6

The Ardennes Offensive

In December 1944, it seemed as though the battered German forces were barely capable of effective defence. The accepted wisdom in Allied command circles was that the *Wehrmacht* would use the winter months to try to assemble some sort of strategic reserve to counter the offensives to be launched against the *Reich* in the spring of 1945. This was the logical military option, but most Allied commanders overlooked the fact that by this stage of the war German strategy was being shaped by Hitler's erratic intuition rather than by the highly professional officers of the German high command.

◄ **New kit**
US tank crews check their newly issued M24 Chaffee light tanks, December 1944.

Wacht am Rhein
16 DECEMBER 1944–24 JANUARY 1945

As early as August 1944, Hitler had directed that a force of at least 25 divisions should be made available for a major offensive in the West. By early December, this force had been assembled and was ready to be unleashed on a complacent and unsuspecting enemy.

IN THE AFTERMATH of Operation *Market Garden*, Allied forces closed up to the borders of the *Reich*, and the front from Switzerland to the North Sea seemed to settle into stalemate as winter closed in. This was partly due to increasingly effective resistance from German forces now holding shorter, more easily defensible lines. The other main factor was the seemingly interminable supply problem – which was alleviated but not solved by the opening of Antwerp in November 1944.

Hitler believed that this situation could be exploited by a major German offensive against one of the weak sectors of the long Allied front. Field-Marshals Walter Model and Gerd von Rundstedt favoured the so-called 'small solution' – a pincer attack near Aachen with the aim of trapping the US Third and Ninth Armies. Characteristically, Hitler rejected this plan in favour of a far more ambitious offensive through the Ardennes, with Antwerp as

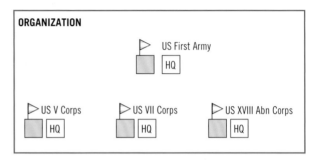

ORGANIZATION

US First Army — HQ

US V Corps — HQ
US VII Corps — HQ
US XVIII Abn Corps — HQ

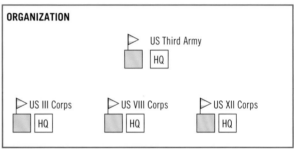

ORGANIZATION

US Third Army — HQ

US III Corps — HQ
US VIII Corps — HQ
US XII Corps — HQ

▲ **M4 Composite Medium Tank**

US Twelfth Army Group / Third Army / 6th Armored Division / 68th Armored Regiment

By 1944–45, it was rare to see such a pristine Sherman anywhere near the front-line. Almost all were festooned with spare track links, locally fitted appliqué armour plates and even sandbags in attempts to provide greater protection against the threat posed by Panzerfausts.

Specifications

Crew: 5

Weight: 31.8 tonnes (31.29 tons)

Length: 5.92m (19ft 5in)

Width: 2.62m (8ft 7in)

Height: 2.74m (8ft 11in)

Engine: 305.45kW (410hp) General Motors
6046 12-cylinder twin in-line diesel

Speed: 48km/h (30mph)

Range: 240km (150 miles)

Armament: 1 x 75mm (2.9in) M3 gun,
plus 2 x 7.62mm (0.3in) MGs (1 coaxial,
1 ball-mounted in hull front)

Radio: SCR508

the objective. If successful, it would split the US and British forces, retake Brussels and Antwerp and trap four Allied armies. This victory in the West would have immense propaganda value, besides allowing the transfer of the bulk of the Panzer force to meet the Soviet advances in Poland and the Balkans.

The commanders who had to try to transform Hitler's vision into reality were privately scathing in their reactions to the plan. Wily old Field-Marshal von Rundstedt was appalled at the news that Antwerp was the objective. 'Antwerp?' he snorted. 'If we reach the Meuse we should go down on our knees and thank God!'

The raw and the weary

Hitler's choice of the Ardennes may have been influenced by his ambition to repeat the stunning victories of 1940. German security measures were highly effective, helped by the widespread Allied assumption that the *Wehrmacht* was simply too badly battered to be capable of launching any major offensive. A few Allied planners predicted the coming attack, including the chief intelligence officers of the US First and Third Armies, whose warnings were ignored by the US Twelfth Army Group, which had overall responsibility for the Ardennes front.

This sector of the front-line was thinly held by a high proportion of raw troops (notably the US 99th and 106th Infantry Divisions). These were

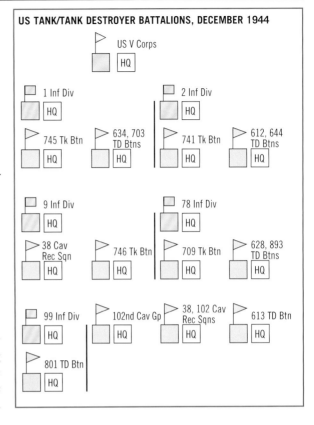

US TANK/TANK DESTROYER BATTALIONS, DECEMBER 1944

supplemented by exhausted veteran formations such as the US 2nd Infantry Division, which had been sent to this 'quiet area' to rest and refit. Each division

▲ M4A3E8 Sherman Medium Tank

US Twelfth Army Group / Third Army / 6th Armored Division / 68th Armored Regiment

The M4A3E8 'Easy Eight' introduced horizontal volute spring suspension (HVSS) and wider tracks, which considerably improved cross-country performance.

Specifications

Crew: 5	Speed: 42km/h (26mph)
Weight: 33.7 tonnes (33.16 tons)	Range: 161km (100 miles)
Length: 7.57m (24ft 10in)	Armament: 1 x 76mm (3in) M1A1 gun, plus 2
Width: 3m (9ft 10in)	x 7.62mm (0.3in) MGs (1 coaxial and 1 ball-
Height: 2.97m (9ft 9in)	mounted in hull front)
Engine: 372.5kw (500hp) Ford GAA 8-cylinder petrol	Radio: SCR508

AFV UNITS, US VII CORPS, DECEMBER 1944

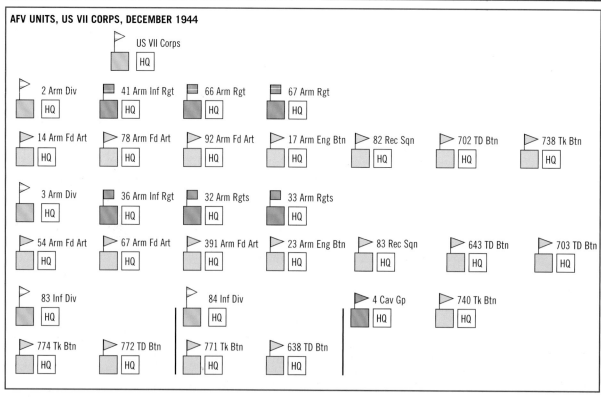

AFV UNITS, US XVIII CORPS, JANUARY 1944

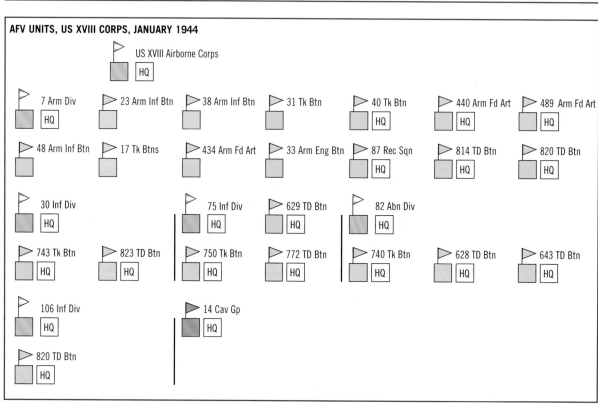

was badly overstretched, covering a front of roughly 45km (28 miles), three times the 'textbook figure'.

Offensive strength

The *Wehrmacht* and *Waffen*-SS forces assembling for the offensive were formidable but represented Germany's final strategic reserve. The main effort was to be made by Fifth Panzer Army, whose objective was Brussels, and Sixth SS Panzer Army, which was to take Antwerp. These two formations could field a total of 1500 AFVs, including some of the formidable Tiger II heavy tanks (which would prove to be dubious assets on the narrow, icy roads of the Ardennes).

The German forces also had to contend with serious problems – the success of the offensive was dependent on bad weather grounding the Allied air assets for long enough to allow the attacking forces to reach their objectives. This was risky enough, but dire fuel shortages meant that the Panzers would have to rely on captured stocks to cross the Meuse, let alone reach Brussels and Antwerp. In fact, the fuel crisis was so acute that the capture of Allied fuel dumps was added to the list of objectives.

The offensive began at 05:30 on 16 December 1944 with a massive artillery bombardment by

▲ **Waiting for the panzers**

Sherman crews keeping watch in the Ardennes, late December 1944.

2000 guns. By 08:00 three German armies were advancing through the Ardennes. In the northern sector SS General 'Sepp' Dietrich's Sixth SS Panzer Army assaulted the Losheim Gap and the Elsenborn Ridge in an attempt to break through to Liège. In the centre General Hasso von Manteuffel's Fifth Panzer Army attacked towards the key road junctions at Bastogne and St Vith. In the south General

▲ **M24 Chaffee Light Tank**

US Twelfth Army Group / Third Army / 82nd Airborne Division / 740th Tank Battalion

Only two M24s were issued to the 740th Tank Battalion in time to see action during the Ardennes Offensive.

Specifications

Crew: 5	Speed: 55km/h (34mph)
Weight: 18.28 tonnes (18 tons)	Range: 282km (175 miles)
Length: 5.49m (18ft)	Armament: 1 x 75mm (2.9in) M6 gun,
Width: 2.95m (9ft 8in)	plus 1 x 12.7mm (0.5in) HMG on AA mount
Height: 2.46m (8ft 1in)	and 2 x 7.62mm (0.3in) MGs (1 coaxial, 1
Engine: 2 x 82kW (110hp) Cadillac 44T24 V8	ball-mounted in hull front)
8-cylinder petrol	Radio: SCR508

Erich Brandenberger's Seventh Army began a limited offensive towards Luxembourg to protect the left flank of the advance from Allied counterattacks.

The attacks by Sixth SS Panzer Army's infantry bogged down in the face of unexpectedly fierce resistance by the US 2nd and 99th Infantry Divisions on the Elsenborn Ridge, which caused Dietrich to commit his Panzer forces earlier than planned in

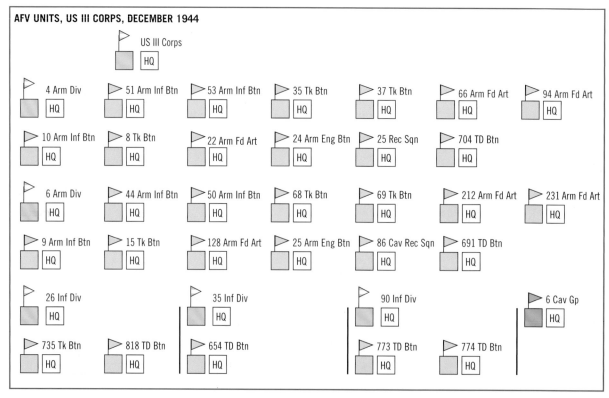

▲ 105mm Howitzer Motor Carriage (HMC) M7 (Priest)
US Twelfth Army Group / First Army / V Corps / 2nd Armored Division /
78th Armored Field Artillery Battalion

The M7 was the primary US self-propelled 105mm (4.1in) howitzer throughout the war. This example carries two pairs of logs for use as 'unditching beams'.

Specifications

Crew: 7	Speed: 42km/h (26mph)
Weight: 26.01 tonnes (25.6 tons)	Range: 201km (125 miles)
Length: 6.02m (19ft 9in)	Armament: 1 x 105mm (4.1in) M1A2 howitzer,
Width: 2.88m (9ft 5in)	plus 1 x 12.7mm (0.5in) HMG on 'pulpit' AA
Height: 2.54m (8ft 4in)	mount
Engine: 298kW (400hp) Continental R975 C1	Radio: SCR608

an attempt to achieve a breakthrough. This move was hampered by snow storms that rapidly created treacherous road conditions and inefficient traffic control that temporarily blocked several routes.

In the centre Fifth Panzer Army advanced on a 30km (19-mile) front, forcing the surrender of two regiments (more than 8000 men) of the US 106th Division. The advance soon threatened St Vith and

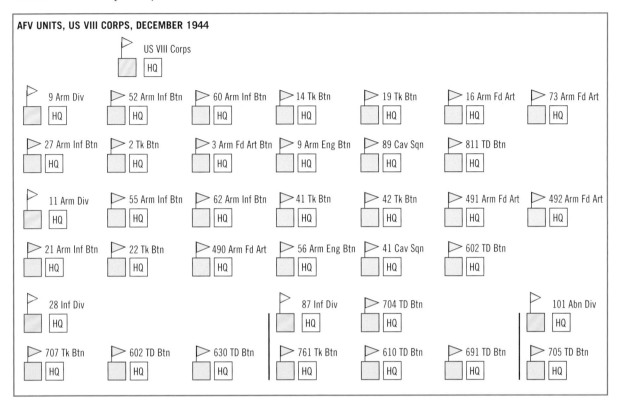

AFV UNITS, US VIII CORPS, DECEMBER 1944

US VIII Corps — HQ

| 9 Arm Div — HQ | 52 Arm Inf Btn — HQ | 60 Arm Inf Btn — HQ | 14 Tk Btn — HQ | 19 Tk Btn — HQ | 16 Arm Fd Art — HQ | 73 Arm Fd Art — HQ |

27 Arm Inf Btn — HQ | 2 Tk Btn — HQ | 3 Arm Fd Art Btn — HQ | 9 Arm Eng Btn — HQ | 89 Cav Sqn — HQ | 811 TD Btn — HQ

11 Arm Div — HQ | 55 Arm Inf Btn — HQ | 62 Arm Inf Btn — HQ | 41 Tk Btn — HQ | 42 Tk Btn — HQ | 491 Arm Fd Art — HQ | 492 Arm Fd Art — HQ

21 Arm Inf Btn — HQ | 22 Tk Btn — HQ | 490 Arm Fd Art — HQ | 56 Arm Eng Btn — HQ | 41 Cav Sqn — HQ | 602 TD Btn — HQ

28 Inf Div — HQ | | | 87 Inf Div — HQ | 704 TD Btn — HQ | | 101 Abn Div — HQ

707 Tk Btn — HQ | 602 TD Btn — HQ | 630 TD Btn — HQ | 761 Tk Btn — HQ | 610 TD Btn — HQ | 691 TD Btn — HQ | 705 TD Btn — HQ

▲ **M3 Halftrack**

US Twelfth Army Group / Third Army / III Corps / 4th Armored Division / 53rd Armored Infantry Battalion

With only a canvas tilt for protection against the elements, all variants of the M3 were cold vehicles to operate in the depths of winter.

Specifications

Crew: 2 plus 11 passengers

Weight: 9.3 tonnes (9.15 tons)

Length: 6.34m (20ft 10in)

Width: 2.22m (7ft 3in)

Height: 2.69m (8ft 10in)

Engine: 109.5kW (147hp) White 160AX
6-cylinder petrol

Speed: 72km/h (45mph)

Range: 320km (200 miles)

Armament: 1 x 12.7mm (0.5in) HMG

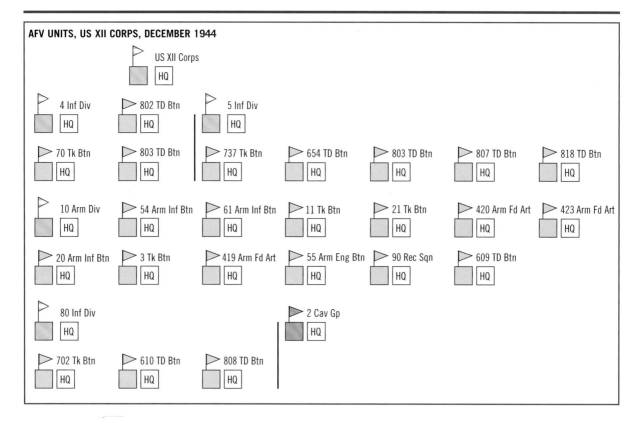

AFV UNITS, US XII CORPS, DECEMBER 1944

US XII Corps — HQ

4 Inf Div — HQ · 802 TD Btn — HQ · 5 Inf Div — HQ

70 Tk Btn — HQ · 803 TD Btn — HQ · 737 Tk Btn — HQ · 654 TD Btn — HQ · 803 TD Btn — HQ · 807 TD Btn — HQ · 818 TD Btn — HQ

10 Arm Div — HQ · 54 Arm Inf Btn — HQ · 61 Arm Inf Btn — HQ · 11 Tk Btn — HQ · 21 Tk Btn — HQ · 420 Arm Fd Art — HQ · 423 Arm Fd Art — HQ

20 Arm Inf Btn — HQ · 3 Tk Btn — HQ · 419 Arm Fd Art — HQ · 55 Arm Eng Btn — HQ · 90 Rec Sqn — HQ · 609 TD Btn — HQ

80 Inf Div — HQ · 2 Cav Gp — HQ

702 Tk Btn — HQ · 610 TD Btn — HQ · 808 TD Btn — HQ

Bastogne, whose defenders were reinforced by the US 82nd and 101st Airborne Divisions. German planners had counted on capturing St Vith by 17 December, but the town was only taken after its defenders withdrew on the 21st, having badly disrupted the German advance.

The 101st Airborne Division and Combat Command B of 10th Armored Division drove into Bastogne only hours before the town was encircled on 20 December. Four artillery battalions and the 705th Tank Destroyer Battalion also managed to reinforce the garrison, which was soon under attack by two Panzer and two infantry divisions from Fifth Panzer Army. 'Visualize the hole in a doughnut,' the 101st radioed Supreme Headquarters Allied Expeditionary Force (SHAEF) in Paris. 'That's us.' Bad weather grounded the Allied air forces, preventing air resupply or close air support, but the garrison held out, further slowing Fifth Panzer Army's advance by forcing it onto narrow minor roads. Despite this, its spearhead, 2nd Panzer Division, made the deepest penetration of the offensive, pushing to within 16km (10 miles) of the River Meuse on 24 December.

▶ **M3A1 Scout Car**

US Twelfth Army Group / Third Army / III Corps / HQ 4th Armored Division

Almost 21,000 M3A1s were produced between 1941 and 1944. Although partially superseded by the M8 and M20 armoured cars, large numbers remained in service throughout the war.

Specifications

Crew: 2 plus 6 passengers	Speed: 105km/h (65mph)
Weight: 5.61 tonnes (5.53 tons)	Range: 400km (250 miles)
Length: 5.62m (18ft 5in)	Armament: Up to 1 x 12.7mm (0.5in) HMG
Width: 2.03m (6ft 8in)	and 2 x 7.62mm (0.3in) MGs
Height: 2m (6ft 6in)	Radio: SCR608
Engine: 71kw (95hp) White Hercules JXD	
6-cylinder petrol	

▼ 703rd Tank Destroyer Battalion

By late 1944, the best-equipped tank destroyer battalions, such as the 703rd, were exceptionally effective anti-tank units. Their 90mm (3.5in) armed M36s had greater firepower than any other US AFVs until the first M26 Pershing heavy tanks began to reach front-line units in February 1945.

Battalion HQ (3 x M8 AC)

Reconnaissance Company   1 Platoon (3 x Jeeps, 1 x M8 AC)

2 Platoon (3 x Jeeps, 1 x M8 AC)

3 Platoon (3 x Jeeps, 1 x M8 AC)

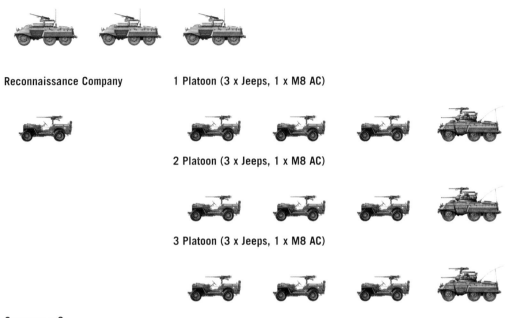

Company x 3
1 Platoon (1 x Jeep, 2 x M8 ACs, 4 x M36 tank destroyers)

2 Platoon (1 x Jeep, 2 x M8 ACs, 4 x M36 tank destroyers)

3 Platoon (1 x Jeep, 2 x M8 ACs, 4 x M36 tank destroyers)

Although good German security measures had ensured that the attacks achieved initial surprise, tenacious Allied defence of key points such as St Vith and Bastogne fatally slowed the tempo of the offensive. Whatever parallels Hitler may have drawn with the stunning victories won over the same ground in 1940 were misleading.

Conditions in 1944 were very different – the road network of the Ardennes had favoured the south-westerly axis of advance of the 1940 offensive, but *Wacht am Rhein* ('Watch on the Rhine', the codename for the 1944 operation) involved a north-westerly advance 'across the grain of the country'. Crucially, the Allied commanders of 1944 were

▲ Ambush

The commander of a well dug-in M36 scans the horizon for targets.

very different from those of 1940. Countermeasures were rapidly implemented as soon as it became clear that the operation was an all-out German offensive, rather than a limited spoiling attack. The US First Army and elements of Montgomery's Twenty-first Army Group to the north and west of the rapidly expanding German salient – the famous 'Bulge' – moved to protect the Meuse crossings. Away to the south, Patton swung the bulk of his US Third Army north to head for Bastogne. His progress was greatly aided by the failure of Brandenberger's Seventh Army to keep pace with the German advance to the north. This failure exposed Fifth Panzer Army's left flank to Patton's counterattack.

By 23 December, improving weather conditions allowed Allied air power to be brought into play

▲ M3 Halftrack

US Twelfth Army Group / Third Army / III Corps / 4th Armored Division / Medical Battalion

The versatile M3 was frequently employed as an armoured ambulance.

Specifications

Crew: 2 plus 11 passengers	Engine: 109.5kW (147hp) White 160AX
Weight: 9.3 tonnes (9.15 tons)	6-cylinder petrol
Length: 6.34m (20ft 10in)	Speed: 72km/h (45mph)
Width: 2.22m (7ft 3in)	Range: 320km (200 miles)
Height: 2.69m (8ft 10in)	

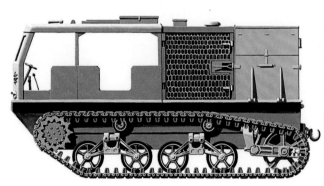

◀ M4 High-Speed Tractor

US Twelfth Army Group / Third Army / VIII Corps / 87th Infantry Division / 912th Field Artillery Battalion

The M4 was based on the automotive components of the M2 light tank and entered service in 1942. It was widely used for towing heavy AA guns and 155mm (6.1in) guns and howitzers. A total of 5500 were produced from 1942 to 1945.

Specifications

Crew: 1 plus 11 passengers	Engine: 156kW (210hp) Waukesha 145GZ
Weight: 14.28 tonnes (14.06 tons)	6-cylinder in-line petrol
Length: 5.23m (17ft 2in)	Speed: 53km/h (33mph)
Width: 2.46m (8ft 1in)	Range: 290km (180 miles)
Height: 2.51m (8ft 3in)	

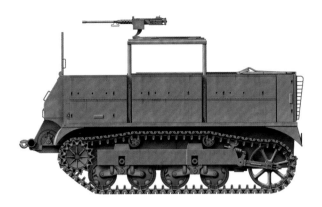

◀ M5 High-Speed Tractor

US Twelfth Army Group / Third Army / VIII Corps / 87th Infantry Division / 335th Field Artillery Battalion

The M5 was based on the tracks and suspension of the M3 light tank and was primarily used as a prime mover for 155mm (6.1in) howitzers.

Specifications

Crew: 1	Engine: 154kW (207hp) Continental R6572
Weight: 13.8 tonnes (13.58 tons)	6-cylinder petrol
Length: 5.03m (16ft 6in)	Speed: 48km/h (30 mph)
Width: 2.54m (8ft 4in)	Range: 290km (180 miles)
Height: 2.69m (8ft 10in)	

▶ Dodge WC51 Weapons Carrier

US Twelfth Army Group / Third Army / III Corps / 4th Armored Division / 126th Ordnance Maintenance Battalion

The WC51 had a very good cross-country performance and could carry three times the load of a jeep. It was often referred to as a 'beep' – 'big jeep'.

Specifications

Crew: 1	Engine: 68.54kW (92hp) Dodge T214
Weight: 3.3 tonnes (3.24 tons)	6-cylinder petrol
Length: 4.47m (14ft 8in)	Speed: 89km/h (55mph)
Width: 2.1m (6ft 10in)	Range: 384km (240 miles)
Height: 2.15m (7ft)	

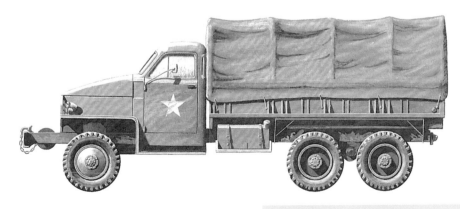

▲ Studebaker US6 2½-Ton Truck

US Twelfth Army Group / Third Army / III Corps / 4th Armored Division / 126th Ordnance Maintenance Battalion

The Studebaker and GMC 2½-ton trucks played an essential role in supplying US armoured formations.

Specifications

Crew: 1	Engine: 79kW (106hp) Hercules RXC
Weight: (loaded) 5.4 tonnes (5.3 tons)	6-cylinder petrol
Length: 6.82m (22ft 4.5in)	Speed: 64km/h (40mph)
Width: 2.44m (8ft)	Range: 255km (165 miles)
Height: 3.01m (9ft 10.5in)	

against the German advance, which was already faltering as fuel began to run out. (Some fuel had been seized, but the major US fuel dumps had either been destroyed before capture or were successfully defended.) As ever, air attacks against AFVs only had limited success, the real damage being inflicted on their 'soft-skinned' support vehicles, without which

the offensive was doomed. The effects of Allied air attacks were noted by Major-General Friedrich von Mellenthin, on his way to join 9th Panzer Division near Houffalize in the centre of the salient: 'The icebound roads glittered in the sunshine and I witnessed the uninterrupted air attacks on our traffic routes and supply dumps. Not a single German plane

Specifications

Crew: 5

Weight: 28.14 tonnes (27.7 tons)

Length: 6.15m (20ft 2in)

Width: 3.05m (10ft)

Height: 2.72m (8ft 11in)

Engine: 373kW (500hp) Ford GAA V8 petrol

Speed: 48km/h (30mph)

Range: 241km (150 miles)

Armament: 1 x 90mm (3.5in) M3 gun,
  plus 1 x 12.7mm (0.5in) AA HMG

Radio: SCR610

▲ 90mm Gun Motor Carriage (GMC) M36

US Twelfth Army Group / Third Army / VIII Corps / 82nd Airborne Division / 703rd Tank Destroyer Battalion

The M36 was rushed into service with tank destroyer battalions in late 1944. It was highly popular with its crews as its 90mm (3.5in) gun could destroy almost any German AFV at normal battlefield ranges.

Specifications

Crew: 5

Weight: 18.18 tonnes (17.9 tons)

Length: 6.66m (21ft 10in)

Width: 2.97m (9ft 9in)

Height: 2.57m (8ft 5in)

Engine: 298.5kW (400hp) Continental R-975
  9-cylinder radial petrol

Speed: 89km/h (55mph)

Range: 241km (150 miles)

Armament: 1 x 76mm (3in) M1 gun,
  plus 1 x 12.7mm (0.5in) AA HMG

Radio: SCR610

▲ 76mm Gun Motor Carriage (GMC) M18 'Hellcat'

US Twelfth Army Group / Third Army / VIII Corps / 101st Airborne Division / 705th Tank Destroyer Battalion

The 705th played an important role in the defence of Bastogne, destroying 43 German AFVs for the loss of six Hellcats.

was in the air and innumerable vehicles were shot up and their blackened wrecks littered the roads.'

Equally important, the improving weather allowed air resupply drops to the hard-pressed defenders of Bastogne from the morning of 23 December, after which a total of 1446 containers were parachuted into the perimeter. These containers were a crucial factor in the defence of the town, as artillery ammunition

▲ **Careful!**

A Sherman and infantry cautiously advance along a seemingly deserted street.

was almost exhausted – in many cases shells had to be rushed straight from the drop zones to the batteries.

Although much emphasis is rightly given to the importance of Allied air power, the battered *Luftwaffe* did its best to support the German offensive. Night

▲ **Sherman Firefly**

Twenty-first Army Group / Second Army / XXX Corps / 29th Armoured Brigade / 2nd Fife and Forfar Yeomanry

The 29th Armoured Brigade was rushed to Dinant to protect the Meuse crossings in late December 1944. By now British armoured units were well on the way to achieving a fifty-fifty mix of Fireflies and 75mm (2.9in) armed Shermans.

Specifications

Crew: 4	Speed: 40km/h (24.8mph)
Weight: 32.7 tonnes (32.18 tons)	Range: 161km (100 miles)
Length: 7.85m (25ft 9in)	Armament: 1 x 76mm (3in) 17pdr OQF,
Width: 2.67m (8ft 9in)	plus 1 x coaxial 7.62mm (0.3in) MG
Height: 2.74m (8ft 11in)	Radio: Wireless Set No. 19
Engine: 316.6kW (425hp) Chrysler Multibank	
A57 petrol	

▲ **Every little helps ...**
An M5 light tank, with unusual 'appliqué armour' of split logs on the glacis plate, moves up to the front.

ground-attack units equipped with a mixture of Fw 190s and Ju 87s attacked Allied AFVs, troops and supply lines on an almost nightly basis throughout the second half of December. These units were highly trained for this extremely demanding role and their aircraft were fitted with sophisticated 'blind-flying' equipment that allowed them to operate in weather conditions that grounded most other aircraft. In a typical sortie on the evening of 16 December, 50-plus Ju 87s attacked US positions around Monschau on the northern flank of the offensive, dropping flares before bombing and strafing the area.

Whenever possible, conventional ground-attack units also went into action, with their Fw 190s using the new 'Panzerblitz' anti-tank rockets against US armour around St Vith and Bastogne. However, the *Luftwaffe*'s efforts had only a limited impact, being crippled by fuel shortages and the overwhelming Allied numerical superiority.

On Christmas Day, a final German assault on Bastogne was beaten off and Patton's forces broke through to raise the siege the next day. Although it

would take almost another month to retake the entire Bulge, the relief of Bastogne marked the end of the real crisis. On 3 January 1945 the Allies went over to the offensive, and on the 16th units of the US First and Third Armies joined hands at Houffalize, eliminating the bulk of the salient. The offensive had inflicted 19,000 casualties on US Twelfth Army Group, and had taken 15,000 American prisoners. But the cost to the German Army had been 100,000 men killed or wounded and 800 AFVs destroyed – losses that could not be made up.

What went wrong?

In the wooded hills of the Ardennes, the Tigers and Panthers were unable to exploit their superior long-range firepower and were themselves vulnerable to anti-tank guns and bazooka teams lying in ambush. German attempts to manoeuvre were hampered by the terrain, which frequently limited advances to a single vehicle front. In these situations, a single well-positioned roadblock could halt an entire division.

Some reports indicate that a handful of 2nd Panzer Division's Panthers fitted with prototype infra-red (IR) searchlights and night sights were used for combat trials during the offensive. These may have been instrumental in defeating Task Force Harper (a tank battalion plus two armored infantry companies of the US 9th Armored Division) holding the crossroads at Fe'itsch on the approaches to Bastogne, where they were credited with the destruction of at least 10 Shermans in a single night attack. However, the handful of IR-equipped Panthers were too few to make a decisive impact on the outcome of the operation. Equally, the dire fuel shortages caused by Allied bombing meant that even when manoeuvres to by-pass Allied positions were possible, units could find themselves stranded with empty fuel tanks, often within a few kilometres of key objectives.

Sepp Dietrich, commanding Sixth SS Panzer Army, bluntly summed up the unrealistic thinking behind the planning of the offensive, remarking that 'All I had to do was to cross the river, capture Brussels, and then go on to take the port of Antwerp. The snow was waist deep and there wasn't room to deploy four tanks abreast, let alone six armoured divisions. It didn't get light until eight and it was dark again at four, and my tanks can't fight at night. And all this at Christmas time!'

Albert Speer, *Reichminister* for Armaments and War Production, wrote, 'The failure of the Ardennes Offensive meant that the war was over.'

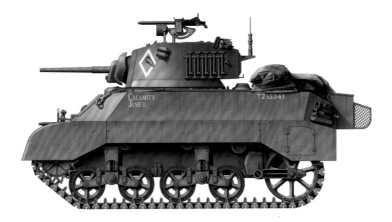

▲ M3A3 Stuart V Light Tank

Twenty-first Army Group / Second Army / XXX Corps / 29th Armoured Brigade / 23rd Hussars

Stuarts remained popular reconnaissance vehicles, but their relatively ineffective 37mm (1.5in) gun led to a significant number being converted to 'Stuart Recce' vehicles, with turrets removed and machine-gun pintle mounts fitted.

Specifications

Crew: 4	Speed: 50km/h (31mph)
Weight: 14.7 tonnes (14.46 tons)	Range: 217km (135 miles)
Length: 5.02m (16ft 5in)	Armament: 1 x 37mm (1.5in) M6 gun,
Width: 2.52m (8ft 3in)	plus 3 x 7.62mm (0.3in) MGs (1 AA, 1 coaxial,
Height: 2.57m (8ft 5in)	1 ball-mounted in hull front)
Engine: 186.25kW (250hp) Continental	Radio: Wireless Set No. 19
W-670-9A 7-cylinder radial petrol	

◄ Daimler Scout Car Mark II

Twenty-first Army Group / Second Army / XXX Corps / 29th Armoured Brigade / 23rd Hussars

This Daimler has been fitted with a 7.62mm (0.3in) Browning machine gun in place of the more usual Bren.

Specifications

Crew: 2	Engine: 41kW (55hp) Daimler 6-cylinder petrol
Weight: 3.22 tonnes (3.2 tons)	Speed: 89km/h (55mph)
Length: 3.23m (10ft 5in)	Range: 322km (200 miles)
Width: 1.72m (5ft 8in)	Armament: 1 x 7.62mm (0.3in) MG
Height: 1.5m (4ft 11in)	Radio: Wireless Set No. 19

Chapter 7

Invading the Reich

The Ardennes Offensive had fallen far short of its grandiose aims, but it had badly delayed and disrupted Allied preparations for the advance to the Rhine. As a result, the battles to reach the Rhine were fought in appalling conditions of alternating frost and thaw, which posed tremendous problems for armoured operations. Such natural hazards were compounded by the threat posed by a skilful and determined enemy. Although most panzer formations facing the Western Allies were now far below strength, even ad hoc groupings of three or four Panthers or Tigers could decimate an unwary British or US tank unit.

◀ Pershings at rest
US Army M26 Pershing heavy tanks are stopped beside a railway line in occupied Germany, April 1945. The first Pershings were issued in January of the same year and proved formidable in combat.

To the Rhine
JANUARY–MARCH 1945

By early 1945, victory was in sight, but the Ardennes Offensive had been a bloody reminder of the dangers of underestimating an enemy who showed no inclination to give in.

THE ALLIED OFFENSIVES of 1945 began with Operation *Blackcock*, which was launched by Second Army's XII Corps (7th Armoured Division, 43rd Wessex Division and 52nd Lowland Division) on 14 January. The objective was to clear the 'Roer Triangle', an area straddling the Dutch-German border, which included outlying defences of the Siegfried Line. Almost every farm and hamlet in the area had to be attacked, often with the support of detachments of Crocodile flamethrower tanks from 79th Armoured Division.

In a single action at Susteren, 1 RTR lost seven tanks to a combination of Panzerfaust teams and anti-tank guns. Total losses incurred in the operation were 43 tanks, 20 to enemy action and the remaining 23 to accidents and breakdowns. The area was finally cleared on 26 January and preparations began for the next offensive, Operation *Veritable*.

Operation *Veritable*

Veritable's objective was the Reichswald, a heavily forested area about 25km (16 miles) west of Nijmegen between the Waal and Maas Rivers. In the winter of 1944/45 the Germans opened the sluices on these

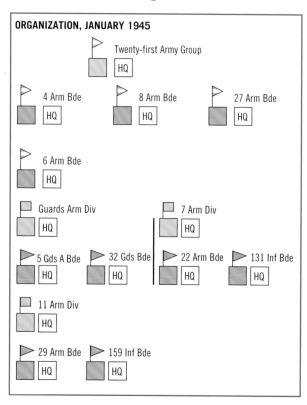

ORGANIZATION, JANUARY 1945

Twenty-first Army Group — HQ

4 Arm Bde — HQ
8 Arm Bde — HQ
27 Arm Bde — HQ

6 Arm Bde — HQ

Guards Arm Div — HQ
7 Arm Div — HQ

5 Gds A Bde — HQ
32 Gds Bde — HQ
22 Arm Bde — HQ
131 Inf Bde — HQ

11 Arm Div — HQ

29 Arm Bde — HQ
159 Inf Bde — HQ

▶ **M22 Locust Light Tank**

Twenty-first Army Group / 6th Airborne Division / Airborne Armoured Reconnaissance Regiment

This was the American equivalent of the Tetrarch but was never used in action by US airborne forces as they had no suitable gliders. A few were used by 6th Airborne Division alongside their Tetrarchs in the Rhine crossings.

Specifications

Crew: 3	Speed: 64km/h (40mph)
Weight: 7.41 tonnes (7.3 tons)	Range: 217km (135 miles)
Length: 3.94m (12ft 11in)	Armament: 1 x 37mm (1.5in) M6 gun,
Width: 2.24m (7ft 4in)	plus 1 x coaxial 7.62mm (0.3in) MG
Height: 1.73m (5ft 8in)	Radio: SCR510
Engine: 121kW (162hp) Lycoming	
0-435T 6-cylinder petrol	

rivers so that the areas north and south of the forest were flooded and impassable, forcing the Allies into a frontal attack on the area, which included sections of the Siegfried Line defences.

The operation was controlled by Twenty-first Army Group, which deployed elements of the First Canadian, Second British and Ninth US Armies. A two-pronged attack was planned: the northern prong would consist of XXX Corps under the command of First Canadian Army, and the southern prong would consist of formations of Ninth US Army, striking across the River Roer shortly after XXX Corps attacked. In the initial stages of its attack, XXX Corps deployed the following units and

formations: Guards Armoured Division; 15th, 43rd, 51st and 53rd Infantry Divisions plus 2nd and 3rd Canadian Infantry Divisions; 6th Guards Armoured Brigade plus 8th and 34th Armoured Brigades; 3rd, 4th, 5th, 9th and 2nd Canadian AGRAs (Army Groups Royal Artillery); as well as support units including two searchlight batteries, elements of 11 regiments of 79th Armoured Division and two Royal Engineers assault regiments.

The total strength of the corps was just over 200,000 all ranks. The offensive opened on 8 February, the attack preceded by an artillery barrage of over 6100 tonnes (6000 tons) of shells. Although roughly 500 Allied tanks were opposed by no more

▶ C15TA Armoured Truck

Twenty-first Army Group / Second Army / XII Corps / HQ 7th Armoured Division

The C15TA was developed by General Motors Canada based on the chassis of the Chevrolet C15 CMP truck. It was extensively used as an APC and armoured ambulance by British and Canadian units in 1944–45. A total of 3961 vehicles were produced in Canada between 1943 and 1945.

Specifications

Crew: 2 plus 8 passengers	Height: 2.31m (7ft 7in)
Weight: 4.5 tonnes (4.42 tons)	Engine: 74kW (100hp) GMC 6-cylinder petrol
Length: 4.75m (15ft 7in)	Speed: 65km/h (40mph)
Width: 2.34m (7ft 8in)	Range: 483km (300 miles)

▲ Sherman Firefly

Twenty-first Army Group / 7th Armoured Division / 22nd Armoured Brigade /
5th Royal Inniskilling Dragoon Guards

By early 1945 the 17pdr's anti-tank performance had significantly improved as APDS ammunition became more readily available.

Specifications

Crew: 4	Speed: 40km/h (24.8mph)
Weight: 32.7 tonnes (32.18 tons)	Range: 161km (100 miles)
Length: 7.85m (25ft 9in)	Armament: 1 x 76mm (3in) 17pdr OQF,
Width: 2.67m (8ft 9in)	plus 1 x coaxial 7.62mm (0.3in) MG
Height: 2.74m (8ft 11in)	Radio: Wireless Set No. 19
Engine: 316.6kW (425hp) Chrysler Multibank	
A57 petrol	

than 50 German tanks and 36 assault guns, the German armour included some Jagdpanthers plus six Sturmtigers armed with 380mm (14.9in) rocket launchers. Such opponents demanded respect – a single 350kg (770lb) rocket from a Sturmtiger was reported to have destroyed three US Shermans in January 1945.

The effectiveness of these small numbers of heavy German AFVs was enhanced by the terrain. Allied forces could not exploit their numerical superiority on the narrow front of less than 10km (6 miles), where dense forests and deep mud largely confined AFVs to roads and tracks. (Even the renowned cross-country ability of the Churchills was tested to the limit – several were lost after becoming hopelessly bogged down.) Besides the handful of powerful German AFVs, Allied armour also had to contend with repeated ambushes by infantry anti-tank teams armed with Panzershrecks and Panzerfausts, who exploited the ample cover to make killing shots from close range. Given the circumstances, it was understandable that it took until 21 February to clear the entire area.

The situation was not helped by the enforced delay in launching Operation *Grenade*, the southern prong of the offensive. As had been feared, the Germans had very efficiently sabotaged the Roer dams, flooding a large area and imposing a two-week delay on Ninth Army's attack, which finally seized crossings over the river on 23 February. The experience of combat in such a harsh environment prompted a special report by 9 RTR, which vividly summarizes the lessons of the battle (see below, Appendices).

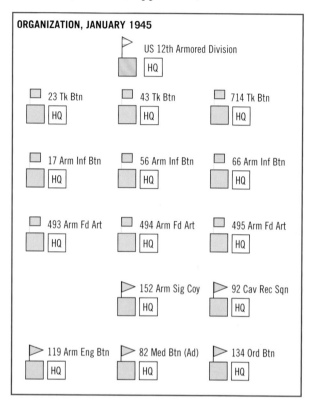

ORGANIZATION, JANUARY 1945

US 12th Armored Division · HQ

23 Tk Btn · HQ   43 Tk Btn · HQ   714 Tk Btn · HQ

17 Arm Inf Btn · HQ   56 Arm Inf Btn · HQ   66 Arm Inf Btn · HQ

493 Arm Fd Art · HQ   494 Arm Fd Art · HQ   495 Arm Fd Art · HQ

152 Arm Sig Coy · HQ   92 Cav Rec Sqn · HQ

119 Arm Eng Btn · HQ   82 Med Btn (Ad) · HQ   134 Ord Btn · HQ

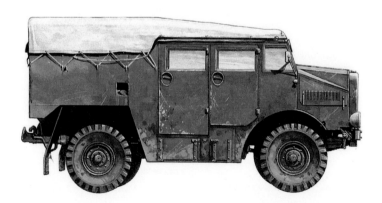

▲ **Tractor, Artillery, 4x4, Morris C8 Mark III**

Twenty-first Army Group / Second Army / XXX Corps / Guards Armoured Division / 55th Field Regiment RHA

The C8 Mark III entered service in 1944 as a dual-purpose vehicle, capable of towing both the 17pdr anti-tank gun and the 25pdr gun/howitzer.

Specifications

Crew: 1 plus 7 passengers	Height: 2.26m (7ft 5in)
Weight: 3.4 tonnes (3.34 tons)	Engine: 52.2kW (70hp) Morris 4-cylinder petrol
Length: 4.49m (14ft 9in)	Speed: 72km/h (45mph) (estimated)
Width: 2.21m (7ft 3in)	Range: 322km (200 miles) (estimated)

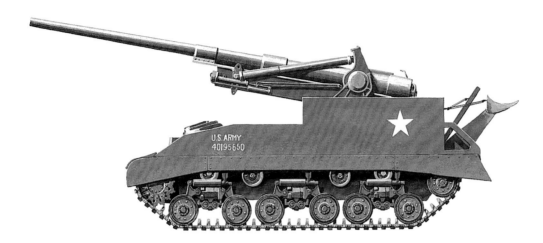

Specifications

Crew: 8
Weight: 40.64 tonnes (40 tons)
Length: 9.04m (29ft 9in)
Width: 3.15m (10ft 4in)
Height: 2.69m (8ft 10in)

Engine: 295kW (395hp) Continental 9-cylinder
  radial petrol
Speed: 39km/h (24mph)
Range: 161km (100 miles)
Armament: 1 x 155mm (6.1in) M1A1 gun
Radio: SCR608

▲ 155mm Gun Motor Carriage (GMC) M40
US Twelfth Army Group / First Army / 3rd Armored Division / 991st Field Artillery Battalion

The M40 comprised the 155mm (6.1in) M2 gun on a heavily modified hull of the M4A3 Sherman fitted with HVSS suspension. Only a single vehicle was issued for combat trials with 3rd Armored Division before the end of the war.

▲ M26 Pershing Heavy Tank
US Twelfth Army Group / Third Army / 9th Armored Division / 2nd Armored Regiment

A detachment of three Pershings attached to 9th Armored Division took part in the seizure of the Ludendorff Bridge across the Rhine at Remagen.

Specifications

Crew: 5
Weight: 41.86 tonnes (41.2 tons)
Length: 8.61m (28ft 3in)
Width: 3.51m (11ft 6in)
Height: 2.77m (9ft 1in)
Engine: 373kW (500hp) Ford GAF V8 petrol

Speed: 48km/h (30mph)
Range: 161km (100 miles)
Armament: 1 x 90mm (3.5in) M3 gun,
  plus 1 x 12.7mm (0.5in) AA HMG and
  2 x 7.62mm (0.3in) MGs (1 coaxial and
  1 ball-mounted in hull front)
Radio: SCR508/528

ORGANIZATION, 1944–45

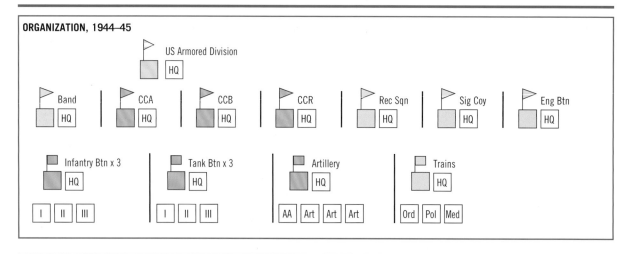

US Armored Division HQ

Band HQ | CCA HQ | CCB HQ | CCR HQ | Rec Sqn HQ | Sig Coy HQ | Eng Btn HQ

Infantry Btn x 3 HQ — I II III

Tank Btn x 3 HQ — I II III

Artillery HQ — AA Art Art Art

Trains HQ — Ord Pol Med

Principal Equipment, US Armored Division	Strength
Medium Tanks	186
Light Tanks	77
SP Howitzers 105mm (4.1in)	54
Carriers, Halftrack	501
MGs 7.62mm (0.3in)	465
MGs 12.7mm (0.5in)	404
Sub-machine Guns	2803
Carbines	5286
Rifles 7.62mm (0.3in)	2063

US Light Tank Company	Strength
Company HQ:	
¼-Ton Trucks	2
M5 Tanks	2
2½-Ton Trucks	1
1-Ton Trailers	1
M3 Halftracks	1
Light ARVs	1
Tank Platoons x 3:	
M5 Tanks	5

▲ **M24 Chaffee Light Tank**

US Twelfth Army Group / Third Army / 9th Armored Division / 14th Armored Regiment

The Chaffee was armed with a lightweight 75mm (2.9in) gun developed from a type used in the B-25H Mitchell bomber. The aircraft's gun was itself derived from the Sherman's M3 75mm (2.9in) and had the same ballistics, but used a thin-walled barrel and different recoil mechanism.

Specifications

Crew: 5

Weight: 18.28 tonnes (18 tons)

Length: 5.49m (18ft)

Width: 2.95m (9ft 8in)

Height: 2.46m (8ft 1in)

Engine: 2 x 82kW (110hp) Cadillac 44T24 V8 8-cylinder petrol

Speed: 55km/h (34mph)

Range: 282km (175 miles)

Armament: 1 x 75mm (2.9in) M6 gun, plus 1 x 12.7mm (0.5in) HMG on AA mount and 2 x 7.62mm (0.3in) MGs (1 coaxial, 1 ball-mounted in hull front)

Radio: SCR508

ORGANIZATION, 1944–45

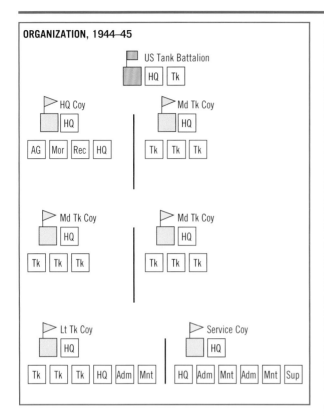

US Tank Battalion, Service Company	Strength
Company HQ:	
¾-Ton Trucks	1
2½-Ton Trucks	3
1-Ton Trailers	3
¼-Ton Trucks	1
Btn Maintenance Platoon:	
¼-Ton Trucks	1
¾-Ton Trucks	1
2½-Ton Trucks	2
1-Ton Trailers	2
M32 ARVs	2
Heavy Wreckers	2
Btn Supply & Transportation Platoon:	
¼-Ton Trucks	1
¾-Ton Trucks	1
2½-Ton Trucks	29
1-Ton Trailers	15
M10 Ammo Trailers	13

US Tank Battalion, HQ Company	Strength
Company HQ:	
¼-Ton Trucks	2
M3 Halftracks	2
2½-Ton Trucks	1
1-Ton Trailers	1
Battalion Recce Platoon:	
¼-Ton Trucks	5
M3 Halftracks	1
Mortar Platoon:	
M3 Halftracks	1
M21 81mm Mortar Carriers	3
Assault Gun Platoon:	
M3 Halftracks	2
M4 Tanks (105mm/4.1in Howitzer)	3
M10 Ammo Carriers	4

US Medium Tank Company	Strength
Company HQ:	
¼-Ton Trucks	2
M4 Tanks	2
M4 Tanks (105mm/4.1in Howitzer)	1
2½-Ton Trucks	1
1-Ton Trailers	1
M3 Halftracks	1
M32 ARVs	1
Tank Platoons x 3	
M4 Tanks	5

▶ **Amphibious operation**
A US Army DUKW amphibious vehicle is used to cross the Danube River alongside
a destroyed bridge, May 1945.

From the Rhine to victory

MARCH–MAY 1945

The Rhine was one of the last major natural obstacles to the Allied advance into the heart of the *Reich*. Remembering the failure of Operation *Market Garden*, Montgomery planned meticulous amphibious and airborne operations to secure bridgeheads across the river, but the first crossing was entirely unplanned, a matter of luck and daring.

ALLIED FORCES WERE now rapidly closing up to the Rhine, and on 7 March Combat Command B of the US 9th Armored Division reached Remagen, seizing the damaged but intact Ludendorff Bridge over the Rhine in one of the first combat operations involving the new M26 Pershing heavy tank. Despite heavy artillery bombardments and repeated *Luftwaffe* air raids against the bridge, three divisions crossed before the weakened structure collapsed on the 17th, by which time pontoon bridges had been completed to allow the offensive to continue.

Away to the north, Montgomery's Twenty-first Army Group was completing preparations for its own crossings of the Rhine. As heavy German resistance was expected, the crossings were to be made in overwhelming force on 23/24 March, with

the amphibious assault (Operation *Plunder*) being supplemented by major airborne landings (Operation *Varsity*). Defending German units were generally well understrength with very little armoured support, and many were understandably badly shaken by the preliminary bombardment of 5500 guns along the 35km (22-mile) front. The crossings were made with considerable support from the 'funnies' of 79th Armoured Division and quickly broke through the German defences. The only significant armoured counterattacks were made by 116th Panzer Division against the US Ninth Army's 30th Infantry Division, but these were rapidly broken up by the intervention of 8th Armored Division.

Once across the Rhine, the Allied armies fanned out to secure key objectives. The Ruhr was garrisoned

▲ **M19 Gun Motor Carriage (GMC)**

*US Twelfth Army Group / First Army / 639th AA Artillery Battalion**

The M19 was based on a lengthened M24 chassis. The engine was moved behind the driver's compartment and a new open-topped turret with twin 40mm (1.57in) Bofors guns was installed. A total of 342 rounds of 40mm (1.57in) ammunition was carried and there was provision for towing an M28 ammunition trailer with a further 320 rounds. *It is uncertain whether any M19s actually saw action before the end of the war. The type remained in service well into the 1950s and was extensively used in the Korean War in the infantry support role.

Specifications

Crew: 6	Engine: 163.9kw (220hp) Twin Cadillac 44T4
Weight: 18 tonnes (17.7 tons)	16-cylinder petrol
Length: 5.81m (19ft)	Speed: 56km/h (35mph)
Width: 2.93m (9ft 7in)	Range: 160km (100 miles)
Height: 2.96m (9ft 8.5in)	Armament: 2 x 40mm (1.57in) Bofors guns
	Radio: SCR508

by Model's Army Group B (21 divisions totalling 430,000 men) but had been largely isolated from the rest of the *Reich* by intensive Allied bombing, which had wrecked much of the region's road and rail network. The US First and Ninth Armies moved rapidly to encircle Army Group B on 4 April after fighting an especially fierce action against a force of 60 German AFVs crewed by the instructors and students of a *Waffen*-SS Panzer training centre at Paderborn. The sheer size of the newly formed Ruhr Pocket was daunting, and its defenders ranged from elderly *Volkssturm* 'Home Guards' to elite Panzer units (including the Jagdtiger-equipped *Panzerjäger Abteilung* 512).

Whilst many of the *Volkssturm* were only too glad to surrender, the regular units and fanatical Hitler Youth were another matter entirely. Ad hoc anti-tank teams of 12- to 15-year-olds stalked US armour with Panzerfausts whilst others sniped at tank commanders and command posts. At first, determined German units had little difficulty in breaking out as the Allied line ran for over 280km (175 miles) and was initially thinly held by armoured formations whose small infantry units could do little more than hold key points and patrol the perimeter. It was only when the infantry divisions caught up that a proper line could be established. Eventually a total of five infantry divisions, plus a cavalry group, held the line and preparations for the destruction of the pocket could begin.

It took until 12 April to cut Army Group B in two and, although the smaller eastern part of the pocket surrendered the next day, it was not until 21 April that the last units in the western sector finally gave in, bringing the total number of prisoners taken in the region to 325,000.

Mine menace

Montgomery's Twenty-first Army Group moved north-eastwards, with the main thrust directed at Hamburg. The experiences of 7th Armoured Division were typical of those of many other armoured

▼ **Left a little, steady, steady …**

A Challenger cruiser tank inches across a narrow temporary bridge somewhere in Holland. The Challenger was essentially an enlarged Cromwell mounting a 17pdr in a tall turret. Development was plagued by mechanical problems and it soon became clear that the Sherman Firefly was a much better vehicle. A limited production run of 200 vehicles was authorized, and these were issued on the basis of one per Cromwell troop.

formations in the last weeks of the war. Although by now the *Panzerwaffe* was reduced to a relative handful of skeleton units, its remaining AFVs were formidable opponents – as a contemporary British report noted: 'The enemy … has brought delaying actions by small bodies of infantry backed by SP guns to a fine art.' In addition to these threats, mines were a constant menace. The conventional anti-tank mines were bad enough, but these were now supplemented by a staggering variety of improvised devices using artillery shells, aircraft bombs and naval

mines. Many of these contained far more explosives than normal mines and were capable of inflicting devastating damage.

In one incident, a substantial roadblock was sealed by a large cylindrical concrete block that proved impervious to 75mm (2.9in) HE shellfire from a Sherman Crab. An AVRE was called up and destroyed the concrete obstacle with several rounds from its Petard mortar. As the Crab's flail drum was too wide for it to get through the breach, it was decided that the AVRE would go through and widen the gap from

▲ M8 Armoured Car

US Twelfth Army Group / Third Army / 9th Armored Division / 89th Cavalry Reconnaissance Squadron, Mechanized

Over 8500 M8s were built between 1942 and 1943 and the type proved to be a successful escort, patrol and reconnaissance vehicle.

Specifications

Crew: 4	Speed: 89km/h (55mph)
Weight: 8.12 tonnes (8 tons)	Range: 563km (350 miles)
Length: 5m (16ft 5in)	Armament: 1 x 37mm (1.5in) M6 gun, plus 1
Width: 2.54m (8ft 4in)	x 12.7mm (0.5in) AA HMG and 1 x coaxial
Height: 2.25m (7ft 5in)	7.62mm (0.3in) MG
Engine: 82kW (110hp) Hercules JXD 6-cylinder petrol	Radio: SCR508

▲ M3 Halftrack

US Twelfth Army Group / Third Army / 9th Armored Division / 52nd Armored Infantry Battalion

The M3 was deployed in huge numbers – each US armoured division had over 450 of these vehicles.

Specifications

Crew: 2 plus 11 passengers	Engine: 109.5kW (147hp) White 160AX
Weight: 9.3 tonnes (9.15 tons)	6-cylinder petrol
Length: 6.34m (20ft 10in)	Speed: 72km/h (45mph)
Width: 2.22m (7ft 3in)	Range: 320km (200 miles)
Height: 2.69m (8ft 10in)	Armament: 1 x 12.7mm (0.5in) HMG,
	plus 2 x 7.62mm (0.3in) MGs

the other side. It had just moved through the breach when it disintegrated in an enormous explosion. Subsequent investigations revealed that the AVRE had been the victim of a naval mine containing over 136kg (300lb) of high explosive, which had also detonated its Petard ammunition and demolition charges. Even when carefully flailing, Sherman Crabs were vulnerable to these devices due to their large blast radius.

On 29 March, the advance was delayed by four well-camouflaged anti-tank guns at Weseke, which had to be taken by an infantry assault using Kangaroos. At Sudlohn, another action had to be fought against a *Panzergrenadier* battlegroup, backed up by 88mm (3.5in) guns. Extensive bomb damage in the town itself held up the advance for some hours whilst 4th Field Squadron RE filled in the craters and strengthened the roads so that they could take the weight of the tanks.

On to Hamburg

The bombed-out ruins of the town of Stadtlohn, a few kilometres north of Sudlohn, had to be cleared of its garrison of two infantry battalions, after which a rickety wooden bridge across a stream was replaced by a Bailey Bridge. The momentum of the advance was maintained by night attacks, however, and by

▲ **All quiet?**

A patrolling M8 armoured car passes a destroyed Stug III assault gun.

1 April, the division had advanced almost 200km (125 miles) in a week.

Before 7th Armoured Division could reach Hamburg, it had to cross the Dortmund–Ems Canal and penetrate the difficult tank terrain of the Teutoburger Wald, a wooded area on an escarpment 40km (25 miles) long and over 1.5km (almost 1 mile) wide. This sector was defended by the cadets of the Hitler Youth Hanover Cadet School and their highly skilled instructors. By 2 April, the town of Ibbenburen at the north-east end of the Teutoburger

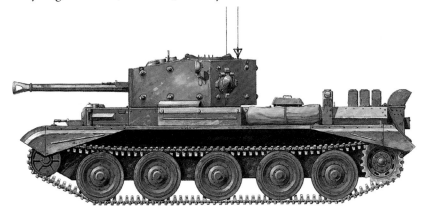

▲ **Cromwell Mark VII**

Twenty-first Army Group / Second Army / 7th Armoured Division / 22nd Armoured Brigade / 1 RTR

Later Cromwells such as the Mark VII had their frontal armour increased from 76mm (3in) to 101mm (4in) to improve battlefield survivability.

Specifications

Crew: 5	Speed: 64km/h (40mph)
Weight: 29 tonnes (28.54 tons) (estimated)	Range: 280km (174 miles)
Length: 6.35m (20ft 10in)	Armament: 1 x 75mm (2.9in) OQF gun,
Width: 2.9m (9ft 6in)	plus 2 x 7.92mm (0.31in) Besa MGs
Height: 2.49m (8ft 2in)	(1 coaxial and 1 ball-mounted in hull front)
Engine: 447kW (600hp) Rolls-Royce Meteor	Radio: Wireless Set No. 19
V12 petrol	

▶ AEC Armoured Car Mark III

Twenty-first Army Group / Second Army / XXX Corps / 51st Highland Division / 2nd Derbyshire Yeomanry

The AEC Mark III was the most powerful of all the British-designed armoured cars to see service during the war and equipped the heavy squadrons of armoured car regiments. Main armament was the 75mm (2.9in) OQF gun as fitted to the majority of contemporary Cromwell and Churchill tanks.

Specifications

Crew: 4

Weight: 12.9 tonnes (12.7 tons)

Length: 5.61m (18ft 5in)

Width: 2.69m (8ft 10in)

Height: 2.69m (8ft 10in)

Engine: 116kW (155hp) AEC 6-cylinder diesel

Speed: 66km/h (41mph)

Range: 402km (250 miles)

Armament: 1 x 75mm (2.95in) OQF gun,
plus 1 x coaxial 7.92mm (0.31in) Besa MG

Radio: Wireless Set No. 19

◀ Daimler Armoured Car

Twenty-first Army Group / Second Army / XXX Corps / 51st Highland Division / 2nd Derbyshire Yeomanry

A number of Daimlers were modified in 1944–45 by having their turrets removed and pintle-mounted machine guns fitted to produce 'heavy scout cars', which were widely known as 'SODs' – 'Sawn-Off Daimlers'.

Specifications

Crew: 3

Weight: 7.62 tonnes (7.5 tons)

Length: 3.96m (13ft)

Width: 2.44m (8ft)

Height: 2.24m (7ft 4in)

Engine: 71kW (95hp) Daimler 6-cylinder petrol

Speed: 80km/h (50mph)

Range: 330km (205 miles)

Armament: 1 x 40mm (1.57in) 2pdr OQF gun,
plus 1 x coaxial 7.92mm (0.31in) Besa MG

Radio: Wireless Set No. 19

Specifications

Crew: 1

Weight: 2.1 tonnes (2 tons)

Length: 6.2m (20ft 4in)

Width: 2.29m (7ft 6in)

Height: 3.05m (10ft)

Engine: 71kW (95hp) Ford V8 petrol

Speed: 80km/hr (50mph)

Range: 270km (168 miles)

▲ Chevrolet C60L

Twenty-first Army Group / Second Army / 7th Armoured Division / 22nd Armoured Brigade / 1st Rifle Brigade

Canadian Military Pattern (CMP) truck production was undertaken on a massive scale with over 900,000 vehicles built between 1940 and 1945. The C60 3-ton 4x4 was produced in the largest numbers, with over 209,000 examples completed.

US Medium Tank Company

By 1945, many US tank companies had been re-equipped with late-production M4A3E8 Shermans, armed with the 76mm (3in) M1 gun and fitted with the excellent Horizontal Volute Spring Suspension (HVSS). Whilst these tanks were still markedly inferior to the Panther and Tiger, they were a great improvement on earlier Shermans in terms of both firepower and protection.

Company HQ (2 x M4 Shermans, 1 x Sherman with 105mm/4.1in howitzer, 1 x jeep)

Admin, Mess & Supply Section (1 x 2½-ton truck)

Maintenance Section (1 x M3 halftrack, 1 x ARV, 1 x jeep)

1 Platoon (5 x M4 Shermans)

2 Platoon (5 x M4 Shermans)

3 Platoon (5 x M4 Shermans)

Wald was defended by seven companies from the school, who were formidable opponents. They worked in small, widely dispersed groups, showing a particular skill in sniping at tank commanders and platoon sergeants. They inflicted heavy casualties and many of them fought to the death, rather than surrender. After two days of fierce fighting, 7th Armoured Division was ordered to disengage and by-pass the area to continue the advance. It took another two days for the following 52nd and 53rd Infantry Divisions to overcome the cadets.

During the next stage of the advance, *Luftwaffe* fighter-bombers made one of their increasingly rare attacks and an Me 109 was shot down by an AA armoured car of the 11th Hussars. There was another fierce action, this time against the 20th SS Training Division as the advance neared Bremen, followed by a four-day battle against the 2nd Marine Division from Hamburg.

After a brief halt to rest and reorganize, the division moved on. On 16 April, the POW camp *Stalag* XI B, in the woods south-west of Fallingbostel, was liberated and 12,500 prisoners were freed. Soltau was heavily defended and had to be assaulted on the 17th with the assistance of Crocodile and Wasp flamethrower vehicles.

The advance continued to the Elbe on 20 April, with Wasp flamethrowers also playing a key role in the capture of the town of Daerstorf. By now the RHA Forward Observation Officers had reached the Elbe and were calling down fire on river shipping and rail traffic on the far bank. A night attack by a mixed force of SS, naval ratings, police and Hitler Youth was beaten off on 26 April, followed by further

▲ **Hold it!**

An M26 Pershing is carefully positioned on a raft before being ferried across a river 'somewhere in Germany'.

actions against other ad hoc forces that included ships' crews, stevedores, policemen and firemen from Hamburg, submarine crews, *Waffen*- SS, paratroops, *Wehrmacht* soldiers, Hitler Youth and *Volkssturm*

▲ **M24 Chaffee Light Tank**

US Twelfth Army Group / First Army / 3rd Armored Division / 33rd Armored Regiment

The Allied white star was frequently obscured or toned down by tank crews, who believed that it acted as a convenient aiming point for German gunners.

Specifications	
Crew: 5	Speed: 55km/h (34mph)
Weight: 18.28 tonnes (18 tons)	Range: 282km (175 miles)
Length: 5.49m (18ft)	Armament: 1 x 75mm (2.9in) M6 gun,
Width: 2.95m (9ft 8in)	plus 1 x 12.7mm (0.5in) HMG on AA mount
Height: 2.46m (8ft 1in)	and 2 x 7.62mm (0.3in) MGs (1 coaxial, 1
Engine: 2 x 82kW (110hp) Cadillac 44T24 V8	ball-mounted in hull front)
8-cylinder petrol	Radio: SCR508

'Home Guards'. These were supported by a powerful assortment of 88mm (3.5in) guns no longer needed for the air defence of Hamburg.

On 28 April, Hamburg itself was brought under artillery bombardment and the following day a deputation from the city came out to discuss surrender. Negotiations went on for some time, but the details were eventually agreed and the surrender was formally signed on 3 May. The division's long journey was not quite finished, though, and units pushed on as far as Kiel, which was occupied by VE Day (8 May 1945).

American advance

Whilst Twenty-first Army Group was completing its advance to the Baltic, US forces were making equally spectacular progress in the south. The First and Ninth Armies moved up to the Elbe, linking

▲ 105mm Howitzer Motor Carriage (HMC) M7 (Priest)

US Twelfth Army Group / First Army / 3rd Armored Division / 67th Field Artillery Battalion

All 3490 Priests were armed with 105mm (4.1in) M2A1 howitzers, firing a 14.97kg (33lb) shell to a maximum range of 11,430m (12,505 yards).

Specifications

Crew: 7	Speed: 42km/h (26mph)
Weight: 26.01 tonnes (25.6 tons)	Range: 201km (125 miles)
Length: 6.02m (19ft 9in)	Armament: 1 x 105mm (4.1in) M1A2 howitzer,
Width: 2.88m (9ft 5in)	plus 1 x 12.7mm (0.5in) HMG on 'pulpit'
Height: 2.54m (8ft 4in)	AA mount
Engine: 298kW (400hp) Continental R975 C1	Radio: SCR608
radial petrol	

▲ M3 Halftrack

US Twelfth Army Group / First Army / 3rd Armored Division / 36th Armored Infantry Regiment

Most M3s carried a 12.7mm (0.5in) Browning heavy machine gun and many added a 7.62mm (0.3in) machine gun on each side of the troop compartment.

Specifications

Crew: 2 plus 11 passengers	Engine: 109.5kW (147hp) White 160AX
Weight: 9.3 tonnes (9.15 tons)	6-cylinder petrol
Length: 6.34m (20ft 10in)	Speed: 72km/h (45mph)
Width: 2.22m (7ft 3in)	Range: 320km (200 miles)
Height: 2.69m (8ft 10in)	Armament: 1 x 12.7mm (0.5in) HMG,
	plus 2 x 7.62mm (0.3in) MGs

up with Soviet forces from Marshal Ivan Konev's 1st Ukrainian Front at Torgau on 25 April. Patton's Third Army fanned out into Czechoslovakia, Bavaria and northern Austria. The US Sixth Army Group skirted Switzerland, moving through Bavaria into Austria and northern Italy. The French First Army advanced through the Black Forest and Baden. The remnants of the German Army Group G fought delaying actions near Nuremberg and Munich but finally surrendered at Haar in Bavaria on 5 May.

The rapid advances of the last days of the war were typified by the experience of elements of the US 71st Infantry Division, which was moving through Bavaria and Austria. Just two days before Germany's final surrender, the 71st was ordered to make contact with elements of the Red Army advancing from Vienna.

On 6 May, the armoured cars of the 71st's cavalry reconnaissance unit were ordered on yet another mission in search of the Soviet forces. Although they failed to find a single Soviet soldier, they did find the headquarters of Army Group *Ostmark* (the former Army Group South), the largest organized field command remaining in

▶ M29 Weasel

US Twelfth Army Group / Ninth Army / 29th Infantry Division / 121st Engineer Battalion

The amphibious M29 Cargo Carrier 'Weasel' was used in a wide variety of roles including command, radio, ambulance, signal line laying and light cargo vehicle. Its wide tracks gave it exceptional mobility across the deep mud frequently encountered during the winter of 1944/45 which was impassable even by conventional tracked vehicles.

Specifications

Crew: 1 plus 3 passengers	Engine: 55.9kW (75hp) Studebaker Model
Weight: 2.19 tonnes (2.16 tons)	6-170 petrol
Length: 4.8m (15ft 9in)	Speed: 58km/h (36mph)
Width: 1.7m (5ft 7in)	Range: 265km (164 miles)
Height: 1.8m (5ft 11in)	

▲ M8 Armoured Car

US Twelfth Army Group / 2nd Armored Division / 82nd Armored Reconnaissance Battalion

The cramped fighting compartment of the M8 meant that much of the crew's kit had to be stowed externally.

Specifications

Crew: 4	Speed: 89km/h (55mph)
Weight: 8.12 tonnes (8 tons)	Range: 563km (350 miles)
Length: 5m (16ft 5in)	Armament: 1 x 37mm (1.5in) M6 gun,
Width: 2.54m (8ft 4in)	plus 1 x 12.7mm (0.5in) AA HMG and
Height: 2.25m (7ft 5in)	1 x coaxial 7.62mm (0.3in) MG
Engine: 82kW (110hp) Hercules JXD	Radio: SCR508
6-cylinder petrol	

the *Wehrmacht*. Its commander, General Lothar Rendulic, was understandably anxious to avoid capture by the rapidly advancing Red Army and surrendered his entire force of four field armies, each numbering around 200,000 men, to the division. As Allied forces celebrated VE Day, very few of them could have foreseen that the end of World War II in Europe marked the beginning of a new kind of war. Most would have been incredulous at the thought that British and US armoured formations would remain in Germany for almost another 50 years as a deterrent force in the Cold War.

Specifications

Crew: 5

Weight: 30.3 tonnes (29.82 tons)

Length: 5.90m (19ft 4in)

Width: 2.62m (8ft 7in)

Height: 2.74m (8ft 11in)

Engine: 372.5kW (500hp) Ford GAA
    8-cylinder petrol

Speed: 42km/h (26mph)

Range: 210km (130 miles)

Armament: 1 x 75mm (2.9in) M3 gun,
    plus 2 x 7.62mm (0.3in) MGs (1 coaxial,
    1 ball-mounted in hull front)

Radio: SCR508

▲ M4A3 Sherman Medium Tank

US Twelfth Army Group / 2nd Armored Division / 66th Armored Regiment

The M4's mechanical reliability was off-set by its tendency to burn readily when hit – some crews referred to them as 'Ronsons' after the contemporary cigarette lighter advertised as 'lighting every time'.

Specifications

Crew: 5

Weight: 18.28 tonnes (18 tons)

Length: 5.49m (18ft)

Width: 2.95m (9ft 8in)

Height: 2.46m (8ft 1in)

Engine: 2 x 82kW (110hp) Cadillac 44T24 V8
    8-cylinder petrol

Speed: 55km/h (34mph)

Range: 282km (175 miles)

Armament: 1 x 75mm (2.9in) M6 gun,
    plus 1 x 12.7mm (0.5in) HMG on AA mount
    and 2 x 7.62mm (0.3in) MGs (1 coaxial,
    1 ball-mounted in hull front)

▲ M24 Chaffee Light Tank

US Twelfth Army Group / 2nd Armored Division / 67th Armored Regiment

A total of 4731 Chaffees were produced during 1944/45 and the type was used as the basis for a wide variety of other vehicles including the M19 GMC, the M37 105mm (4.1in) HMC and the M41 155mm (6.1in) HMC.

▶ Ford WOA

Twenty-first Army Group / HQ Second Army

The Ford WOA was based on a militarized version of a contemporary civilian car chassis and was initially produced as a staff car with saloon bodywork. The type was also produced with a 'utility' body as the WOA2. Total production of both models was approximately 5000 vehicles.

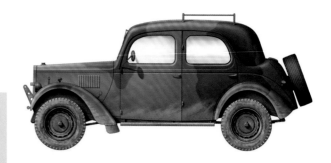

Specifications

Crew: 1

Weight: 2 tonnes (1.96 tons) (estimated)

Length: 4.39m (14ft 5in)

Width: 1.9m (6ft 3in)

Height: 1.78m (5ft 10in)

Engine: 63.32kW (85hp) Ford V8 petrol

Speed: 97km/h (60mph) (estimated)

Range: 280km (175 miles)

▶ Ford WOA2

Twenty-first Army Group / HQ Second Army

The Ford WOA2 entered service in May 1941 and was widely used by all three services as a staff and command car.

Specifications

Crew: 1

Weight: 2.17 tonnes (2.13 tons)

Length: 4.39m (14ft 5in)

Width: 1.9m (6ft 3in)

Height: 1.78m (5ft 10in)

Engine: 63.32kW (85hp) Ford V8 petrol

Speed: 97km/h (60mph) (estimated)

Range: 280km (175 miles)

▲ M26 Pershing Heavy Tank

US Twelfth Army Group / First Army / 3rd Armored Division /
32nd Armored Regiment

Whilst the M26 was appreciated for its protection and firepower, the poor power-to-weight ratio of its 373kW (500hp) Ford engine left it markedly underpowered.

Specifications

Crew: 5

Weight: 41.86 tonnes (41.2 tons)

Length: 8.61m (28ft 3in)

Width: 3.51m (11ft 6in)

Height: 2.77m (9ft 1in)

Engine: 373kW (500hp) Ford GAF V8 petrol

Speed: 48km/h (30mph)

Range: 161km (100 miles)

Armament: 1 x 90mm (3.5in) M3 gun,
plus 1 x 12.7mm (0.5in) AA HMG and
2 x 7.62mm (0.3in) MGs (1 coaxial and
1 ball-mounted in hull front)

Radio: SCR508/528

▲ **Cromwell Mark IV**

Twenty-first Army Group / 7th Armoured Division / 22nd Armoured Brigade / 5th Royal Inniskilling Dragoon Guards

The Cromwell's Christie suspension system and Meteor engine gave it an impressive turn of speed and great manoeuvrability. The engine's governor was frequently decommissioned by the crew to give a higher top speed.

Specifications

Crew: 5

Weight: 27.94 tonnes (27.5 tons)

Length: 6.35m (20ft 10in)

Width: 2.9m (9ft 6in)

Height: 2.49m (8ft 2in)

Engine: 447kW (600hp) Rolls-Royce Meteor V12 petrol

Speed: 64km/h (40mph)

Range: 280km (174 miles)

Armament: 1 x 75mm (2.9in) OQF gun, plus 2 x 7.92mm (0.31in) Besa MGs (1 coaxial and 1 ball-mounted in hull front)

Radio: Wireless Set No. 19

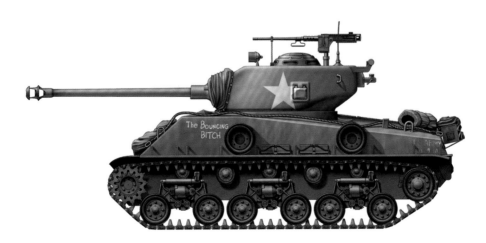

Specifications

Crew: 5

Weight: 33.7 tonnes (33.16 tons)

Length: 7.57m (24ft 10in)

Width: 3m (9ft 10in)

Height: 2.97m (9ft 9in)

Engine: 372.5kw (500hp) Ford GAA 8-cylinder petrol

Speed: 42km/h (26mph)

Range: 161km (100 miles)

Armament: 1 x 76mm (3in) M1A1 gun, plus 2 x 7.62mm MGs (1 coaxial and 1 ball-mounted in hull front)

Radio: SCR508

▲ **M4A3E8 Sherman Medium Tank**

US Twelfth Army Group / 2nd Armored Division / 67th Armored Regiment

Although the 76mm (3in) gun of late-model US Shermans had a markedly better anti-tank performance than the earlier 75mm (2.9in), it was outclassed by the 17pdr mounted by the Firefly.

US armour, 1918–1943

By 1918, the newly formed American Tank Corps was developing as a formidable force. Massive production of a wide range of AFVs was planned, including 4400 6-ton M1917 tanks (the US version of the Renault FT-17) and 1450 Mark VIII heavy tanks. Ford were to supplement these with 15,000 machine-gun carriers designated 'two-man tanks' and a further 1000 'three-man tanks' armed with a 37mm (1.5in) gun.

THE TANK CORPS was to have a number of brigades based on the contemporary British practice, each with two light battalions and a single heavy battalion, but by the end of the war, only three light battalions were operational. This ambitious programme was drastically cut back following the 1918 Armistice and only about 1000 M1917s, 100 Mark VIIIs and 15 Ford two-man tanks plus a single example of the Ford three-man tank were actually built. The National Defense Act of 1920 abolished the Tank Corps, bringing the remaining armoured units (four tank battalions) under the control of the Chief of Infantry, with their mission defined as being 'to facilitate the uninterrupted advance of the rifleman in the attack'. The first signs of change came after the US Secretary of War visited the British Experimental Mechanised Force manoeuvres in 1927 and ordered the formation of a similar force. In the following year this assembled at Fort Meade, Maryland, equipped with Mk VIIIs and M1917s.

So much unreliable, obsolete equipment caused dire problems and the force disbanded after three months, but re-formed at Fort Eustis, Virginia, in 1930 with its heavy tank battalion replaced by a second infantry battalion. This time it demonstrated the advantages of mechanization to the rest of the

US Army and won the support of its new chief of staff, General Douglas MacArthur. Although the Mechanized Force was officially disbanded in 1931, most of its units were transferred to Fort Knox, Kentucky, to form the nucleus of the 1st Cavalry Regiment (Mechanized) in 1932, but the unit remained incomplete until 1939 when it was finally brought up to its full strength of:

- Two mechanized cavalry regiments (totalling 112 light tanks).
- A motorized artillery regiment.

The Panzer victories in Poland and France prompted a massive expansion of US armour – in July 1940 the Armored Force was formed under Brigadier-General Adna Chaffee with an initial establishment of two armoured divisions and an independent tank battalion. Each division included:

- An armoured brigade of two light tank regiments (each of three battalions of M3 light tanks) plus a two-battalion medium tank regiment with M3 medium tanks.
- A two-battalion artillery regiment with self-propelled 105mm (4.1in) howitzers.
- A towed artillery battalion.
- A two-battalion motorized infantry regiment.

▶ M2A4 Light Tank

Desert Training Center, California-Arizona Maneuver Area (DTC-CAMA)

In 1941–42 the then Major-General George Patton commanded the newly established Desert Training Center, at which US armoured warfare doctrine was developed. This M2A4 served as Patton's personal tank at the DTC.

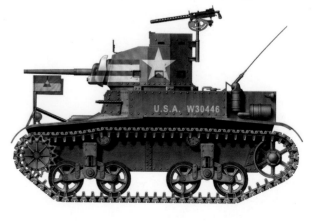

Specifications

Crew: 4	W-670-9A 7-cylinder petrol
Weight: 11.6 tonnes (11.4 tons)	Speed: 56km/h (36mph)
Length: 4.43m (14ft 6in)	Range: 110km (70 miles)
Width: 2.47m (8ft 1in)	Armament: 1 x 37mm (1.5in) M20 gun,
Height: 2.64m (8ft 8in)	plus 5 x 7.62mm (0.3in) MGs
Engine: 186.25kW (250hp) Continental	Radio: n/k

- A reconnaissance battalion.
- An engineer battalion.

Although each division officially had 381 tanks, there were only 44 serviceable tanks in the entire US Army and vast industrial resources were committed to AFV production to make up the required numbers. The total annual figures for the early 1940s were:

1940 – 330
1941 – 4052
1942 – 24,997
1943 – 29,487

Three more armoured divisions were raised before America entered the war in December 1941 and a further 11 followed by 1943. These divisions were extensively reorganized between 1941 and 1943 – the numbers of tanks were reduced whilst the infantry component was increased. The old brigade structure was abolished and replaced by two (and finally three) Combat Command HQs which came directly under the Divisional HQ and could be used to control any combination of armour, artillery and infantry as required. Thus, by 1943, the armoured divisions' components were:

- Combat Commands A, B and C (CCA, CCB and CCC).
- A reconnaissance battalion.
- Three tank battalions with a total of 219 tanks. (At first, many were equipped with M3 Mediums, but these were being replaced by M4 Mediums as they became available).

- Three armoured infantry battalions carried in M2 or M3 halftracks.
- Three artillery battalions equipped with self-propelled 105mm (4.1in) howitzers.
- An engineer battalion.

In addition to the armoured divisions, almost 50 additional tank battalions were deployed independently in the infantry support role by 1943.

Tank destroyer battalions

The Armored Force was supported by a separate Tank Destroyer (TD) Force which was raised in 1941 by Lieutenant-Colonel Andrew D. Bruce. The basic TD unit was the 36-gun battalion, although TD groups each of two battalions and TD brigades with two groups apiece were sometimes formed. At first, their equipment was basic, including the unarmoured 37mm Gun Motor Carriage (GMC) M6, a 37mm (1.5in) gun on a 15cwt truck, and the 75mm GMC M3, which was the old French 75mm (2.9in) field gun on the M3 halftrack. These were used in action in Tunisia, although by the end of the campaign, the much more formidable 76mm (3in) GMC M10 was entering service. Although the vast US industrial base could supply almost unlimited quantities of AFVs, in the end everything depended on just how quickly their inexperienced crews and commanders could learn to cope with the realities of armoured warfare.

▲ **M3 Halftrack**

Desert Training Center, California-Arizona Maneuver Area (DTC-CAMA)

This heavily modified M3 was fitted with an armoured roof and a radio for its role as Patton's armoured command vehicle at the Desert Training Center. Patton gained a reputation as a ruthlessly efficient trainer, insisting that 'A pint of sweat will save a gallon of blood'.

Specifications

Crew: 2, plus up to 11 passengers	6-cylinder petrol
Weight: 9.1 tonnes (8.95 tons)	Speed: 72km/h (45mph)
Length: 6.16m (20ft 3in)	Range: 320km (200 miles)
Width: 1.96m (6ft 5in)	Armament: 1 x 7.62mm (0.3in) MG
Height: 2.3m (7ft 6in)	*NB Data is given for standard early-
Engine: 109.51kW (147hp) White 160AX	production M3 halftrack

Combat trials – M26 Pershing heavy tank

In early 1945, the US Army finally recognised that there was a desperate need for a heavier tank than the Sherman, which still equipped the vast majority of US (and many British) armoured units.

The M26 Pershing heavy tank was the result of a programme to produce a successor to the M4 Sherman. In May 1942, the US Ordnance Department received orders to begin development of a new medium tank that would eliminate some of the shortcomings of the M4.

Although the experimental T26 (essentially the same design as the M26) could probably have entered production in late 1943 or early 1944, wrangling over the necessity for such a heavy tank delayed acceptance of the design until November 1944. There was still strong opposition to the whole heavy tank concept until the Ardennes Offensive, when German Tigers and Panthers inflicted severe losses on Sherman-equipped units.

This was the turning point and a batch of 20 M26 Pershings, including one of the two experimental M26A1E2 'Super Pershings' to be completed by the end of the war, were sent to Europe for combat trials. The M26A1E2 was armed with the 90 mm (3.5in) L/70 T15E1 high-velocity gun firing a 7.58kg (16.7lb) T44 HVAP round at 1,170 m/s (3,850 ft/s) and was capable of penetrating 220mm (8.5in) of rolled homogenous armour (RHA) at 30 degrees at 914m (1000 yards).

Pershings in action

The Pershings were issued in two batches of 10 vehicles each, one being assigned to 3rd Armored Division and the second to 9th Armored Division. Of these, a total of three were lost in action, two of them by 3rd Armored Division.

The best documented of these occurred on 6th March 1945 in an action at Niehl, north of Cologne, when a single shot from a Panzerjaeger Nashorn of *Panzer Jaeger Abteilung 93* penetrated the frontal armour of one of 3rd Amored Division's Pershings at a range of only 250m (273.4 yards). The American crew were incredibly lucky as the German round

struck the lower left frontal armour, passed between the driver's legs and under the turret basket where it started a fire. All the crew were able to bale out safely before the fire caused a major ammunition explosion.

The sole M26A1E2 was issued to 3rd Armored Division's 33rd Armored Regiment. It received extensive field modifications to improve its armour (master-minded by Lt. Belton Cooper) before it went into action on 4th April between the River Weser and Northheim. Lt. Cooper wrote that:

'Some of the German units that had fallen back from the bridgehead set up a few isolated strong points along our route. One such position on a wooded hill ... opened fire as the column passed. The Super M26, in the forward part of the column, immediately swung its turret to the right and fired an armor-piercing shot toward an object on the forward slope of a wooded hill about fifteen hundred yards away [over three-quarters of a mile]. A blinding flash of sparks accompanied a tremendous explosion as debris shot fifty feet into the air ... The unknown object was a tank or self-propelled gun; had it been a half-track or other vehicle, the flash would not have been as large ... The rest of the column let go with a deluge of tank and automatic weapons fire, and the Germans soon broke off the action ... we didn't know what the Super M26 hit ... no one was anxious to go over and check it out.'

Super Pershing versus Tiger II

The Super Pershing was next in action at Dessau on 21st April, commanded by SSgt Joe Maduri, a veteran of 10 months' continuous combat. The attack on Dessau was initially delayed by numerous concrete anti-tank obstacles which had to be laboriously cleared before the tanks could reach the city centre. Maduri's Super Pershing, accompanied by supporting infantry, reached a road junction and began to turn right when it came under fire at a range of roughly

550m (600 yards) from a Tiger II lying in ambush.

Fortunately for Maduri and his crew, the German gunner's aim was terrible and the 88mm (3.45in) shot missed. Maduri's gunner, Cpl John 'Jack' Irwin, only 18 years old, reacted almost instantly with an HE round that struck the Tiger's frontal armour and ricocheted skywards before exploding harmlessly. The Super Pershing had been loaded with an HE round only because Irwin had been expecting 'soft' urban targets, such as barricades, personnel and anti-tank guns. 'AP!' he shouted to his loader, to indicate that an armour-piercing round would be next.

Maduri and crew then felt a thud on the turret. It was never established if this shot came from the Tiger, or from some other anti-tank weapon, but no serious damage was done by the glancing blow. Irwin

quickly got in a second shot as the Tiger advanced over a pile of rubble, briefly exposing its thinly armoured underside. The 90mm (3.5in) AP round penetrated the Tiger's belly plates, detonating the ammunition in tremendous explosion which blew off the turret. The whole engagement took less than 30 seconds.

Maduri's crew spent the rest of the day fighting off the German infantry anti-tank teams who stalked their tank with panzerfausts. The next day, they were back in action, clearing the final German held areas of the city when they encountered a Panzer Mk V 'Panther', which they immobilised with a first round hit on a drive sprocket. Their second round penetrated the side armour, causing a massive ammunition explosion which wrecked the vehicle.

▲ **M26 Pershing prototype**

Although the Pershing's armament and armour were a welcome improvement to those of the Sherman, the early models were distinctly under-powered and prone to breakdowns.

US armoured divisions

All US armoured divisions used the same basic badge of a triangle divided into three with the top yellow, bottom left blue and bottom right red. The centre bore a stylized armoured vehicle track in black under a red lightning bolt. The sole distinction between badges was the divisional number in black on the yellow section.

1st Armored Division
(Nickname: *Old Ironsides*)

The division can trace its origins back to US experiments in mechanized warfare of the early 1930s utilizing the 7th Cavalry Brigade. On 15 July 1940, this formation was expanded to form the 1st Armored Division. As the US Army had no previous experience with armoured formations of this size, it took considerable time to develop a workable structure. (In the process, the division was subjected to a total of six separate reorganizations between 1940 and 1945!) After extensive training, the division deployed to the UK in May 1942 and prepared for Operation Torch, the invasion of north-west Africa. It landed near Oran in November 1942 and fought throughout the Tunisian campaign, gaining hard-won experience of the realities of armoured warfare at Kasserine Pass in February 1943. After reorganizing in Morocco, the division landed in Italy in October 1943, taking part in the assaults on the Winter Line, the Anzio landings and the liberation of Rome. It remained in Italy for the rest of the war, where it often had to fight on a 'single-tank front' over some of the world's most difficult terrain for armoured operations. In April 1945, the division took part in the final Allied offensive into the Po Valley, where it could once again operate as a complete formation. It took Milan on 30 April and had advanced 370 km (230 miles) in 19 days by the time that German forces in Italy surrendered on 2 May.

2nd Armored Division
(Nickname: *Hell on Wheels*)

The 2nd Armored Division was formed at Fort Benning, Georgia, on 15 July 1940. Although elements of the division took part in Operation Torch, it did not see action as a complete formation until the invasion of Sicily. It was then transferred to the UK to prepare for Operation Overlord and landed in Normandy on 9 June 1944, initially operating in the Cotentin Peninsula before taking part in Operation Cobra. In the autumn of 1944, the division broke through the Siegfried Line and advanced to the River Roer, but had to hastily redeploy to Belgium to help contain the Ardennes Offensive and regain the territory lost during the German attack. After crossing the Rhine in March 1945, 2nd Armored Division was the first US formation to reach the Elbe on 11 April, where it was ordered to halt. In July, it became the first US division to enter Berlin.

3rd Armored Division (Nicknames: *Spearhead Division* or the *Third Herd*)

The division was established on 15 April 1941 and deployed to the UK in September 1943 in preparation for Operation Overlord. After pre-invasion training, it landed in Normandy on 24 June 1944, taking part in the battle for St Lô and subsequently helping to trap the German Seventh Army in the Falaise Pocket.

By early September, the division had advanced into Belgium, cutting off 40,000 German troops at Mons. On 10 September, it claimed to fire the first US field artillery shell onto German soil and subsequently assaulted the Siegfried Line before participating in the Battle of Hürtgen Forest.

The 3rd Armored Division was heavily involved in the Allied counterattacks following the Ardennes Offensive, after which it resumed its advance into the Rhineland, taking Cologne and Paderborn before ending the war at Dessau.

4th Armored Division

The division was formed on 15 April 1941 based on a cadre drawn from the 1st Armored Division and deployed to the UK early in 1944. It landed in Normandy on 11 July and took part in Operation Cobra, advancing into Lorraine by September. In December, during the Ardennes Offensive, the division covered 240 km (150 miles) in 19 hours to raise the siege of Bastogne, subsequently closing up to the Rhine. After crossing the Rhine on 24/25 March 1945, the division rapidly advanced through south-eastern Germany, ending the war in Czechoslovakia.

5th Armored Division
(Nickname: *Victory*)

The 5th Armored Division was established on 10 October 1941 and deployed to the UK in February 1944. It landed in Normandy on 24 July, taking Le Mans on 8 August before advancing to Argentan to help form the Falaise Pocket.

It moved on to liberate Luxembourg City on 10 September, and on the following day, one of its reconnaissance patrols were the first Allied troops to cross the German frontier. After heavy fighting in the Hürtgen Forest, the division was temporarily placed in Twelfth Army Group reserve. In March 1945, the division closed up to the Rhine, crossing the river at Wesel on 30 March. By 12 April, it had reached the Elbe at Tangermünde and was only 72 km (45 miles) from Berlin. Unable to advance following Eisenhower's order to halt at the Elbe, the division took part in mopping-up operations in the Ninth Army's sector until VE Day.

6th Armored Division
(Nickname: *Super Sixth*)

The 6th Armored Division was formed on 15 February 1942 based on a cadre from 2nd Armored Division. It deployed to the UK in February 1944, landing in Normandy in July 1944 where it took part in Operation Cobra, before being sent to hold the siege lines around the German garrison in Lorient. In November, the division moved to the Saarland, reaching the German border on 6 December and setting up defensive positions around Saarbrücken.

The division was heavily engaged in the counterattacks around Bastogne following the Ardennes Offensive before closing up to the Rhine in March 1945. It crossed the river on 25 March and advanced to take Frankfurt and Mühlhausen.

On 11 April, the division liberated Buchenwald concentration camp and moved on to take Leipzig. By 15 April, it had advanced as far as the River Mulde, where it was ordered to halt and await the arrival of the Red Army.

7th Armored Division
(Nickname: *Lucky Seventh*)

The division was formed on 1 March 1942 and deployed to the UK in June 1944. It landed in Normandy in August, coming under the command of the US Third Army, and liberated Chartres, before advancing across the Seine to take Château-Thierry and Verdun.

It then became bogged down in fierce fighting around Metz before being transferred to the US Ninth Army on 25 September for operations to protect the right flank of the salient formed by Operation Market Garden.

In response to the Ardennes Offensive, the division was transferred to the US First Army and rushed to St Vith where it fought fierce delaying actions for almost a week before being ordered to evacuate the town on 23 December. It was then heavily engaged in the Allied counterattacks against the 'Bulge' created by the offensive, finally retaking St Vith on 23 January 1945.

In March 1945, 7th Armored Division crossed the Rhine and took part in the breakout from the Remagen bridgehead, helping to surround the Ruhr Pocket. It then played a key role in the destruction of the pocket, forcing the surrender of LIII Panzer Corps on 16 April, before being transferred to Twenty-first Army Group for operations on the Baltic coast in the final days of the war.

8th Armored Division (Nicknames: *Iron Snake, Thundering Herd, Tornado*)

The division was formed on 1 April 1942, deployed to the UK in November 1944 and moved to France in January 1945. Its first major actions were fought around the River Roer as part of Operation Grenade. It then advanced to the Rhine, fighting a fierce action against 130th Panzer Division near Rheinberg.

On 24 March, the division crossed the Rhine as part of Operation Plunder and advanced as far as Paderborn and Sennelager before being diverted to assist in the reduction of the Ruhr Pocket on 3 April. After 10 days of intensive combat, 8th Armored was ordered eastwards to clear the area around the Harz Mountains where it operated until the end of the war.

9th Armored Division
(Nickname: *Phantom Division*)

The division was formed on 15 July 1942 and deployed to the UK in September 1944 before landing in Normandy towards the end of the month. It was initially sent to a quiet sector of the front on the Luxembourg-German border, but was caught by the full weight of the Ardennes Offensive, with its units fighting in scattered groups at St Vith and Bastogne.

After a brief rest period, the division advanced to the Rhine, seizing the Ludendorff Bridge at Remagen on 7 March 1945 and establishing a bridgehead across the river before moving on to take Frankfurt and surround the Ruhr Pocket. During the following month, it advanced into eastern Germany, by-passing Leipzig and moving up to the River Mulde. As the war ended, the division was en route to reinforce US troops in Czechoslovakia.

10th Armored Division
(Nickname: *Tiger Division*)

The 10th Armored Division was formed on 15 July 1942, deploying to France in September 1944. It fought its first actions in the Metz area in November, before being caught up in the Ardennes Offensive, defending Bastogne, Noville and Bras. In February 1945, it cleared the Saar-Moselle Triangle before crossing the Rhine at Mannheim on 28 March and advancing into Bavaria. The 10th took Oberammergau and reached Innsbruck by VE Day.

11th Armored Division
(Nickname: *Thunderbolt*)

The division was established on 15 August 1942, deploying to France in December 1944. It was immediately involved in heavy fighting to contain the Ardennes Offensive and in the subsequent actions to regain the 'Bulge'. In March 1945, the division helped to clear the Saar-Moselle-Rhine Pocket, before crossing the Rhine and advancing into Bavaria. By 14 April, it had taken Coburg and Bayreuth and was moving on Linz, which was captured on 5 May. Elements of the division made contact with Soviet forces on 8 May, the day before the official end of the war in Europe.

12th Armored Division
(Nickname: *Hellcat Division*)

The division was formed on 15 September 1942 and deployed to France on 11 November 1944. After taking heavy losses in its first attacks against the German Rhine bridgehead at Herrlisheim, the 12th took part in the reduction of the Colmar Pocket. It was then engaged in operations to clear the Saar Palatinate before crossing the Rhine at Worms on 28 March. In the final month of the war the division swept across Bavaria and into Austria.

13th Armored Division
(Nickname: *The Black Cats*)

The division was formed on 15 October 1942, deploying to France at the end of January 1945. In April 1945, it took part in the reduction of the Ruhr Pocket before advancing into Bavaria and crossing the Danube. On 2 May, the division moved into Austria, taking Branau am Inn, and was preparing to advance further into Austria when the war in Europe ended.

14th Armored Division
(Nickname: *The Liberators*)

The division was formed on 15 November 1942 and deployed to France in October 1944. It advanced into Alsace and was on the point of breaking through the Siegfried Line when it was withdrawn in response to the Ardennes Offensive. The 14th was caught up in the subsidiary German offensive Operation Nordwind in January 1945 and suffered heavy tank losses in almost two weeks of fierce fighting.

In April, the division crossed the Rhine and moved into Bavaria, earning its nickname by accomplishing the liberation of approximately 200,000 Allied prisoners of war (POWs) from several camps including Stalag VII-A, Germany's largest POW camp. The 14th advanced as far as Mülhdorf am Inn and established bridgeheads across the River Inn, where it was ordered to halt, ending its combat operations on 2 May.

16th Armored Division
(Nickname: *Armadillo*)

The division was formed on 15 July 1943, deploying to France in February 1945. Its sole major combat actions were fought between 6 and 8 May 1945 when it advanced into Czechoslovakia to take the Skoda weapons factory complex in Pilsen.

20th Armored Division
(Nickname: *Armoraiders*)

The division was formed on 15 March 1943 and deployed to France in February 1945. On arrival, it was assessed as requiring substantial additional training before being committed to action. As a result, only its 27th Tank Battalion was involved in any significant combat (29–30 April) when it was detached to support the 42nd Infantry Division's attack on Munich.

British armoured divisions

British experience of armoured warfare dated back to 1916 and this, coupled with the tactics developed by the Experimental Mechanised Force in the inter-war years, gave the British Army a head start in developing effective armoured formations. Much of this advantage was lost as financial crises of the period drove successive governments to cut back defence spending until the risks of war became too obvious to ignore. Even then resources were poorly allocated and the lessons of the pre-war period had to be painfully relearned.

1st Armoured Division

The 1st Armoured Division was rushed to France in 1940 after the scale of the German offensive became apparent. The formation was 'robbed' of some of its units in a vain attempt to defend Calais and Boulogne and the remnants fought south of the Somme until evacuated on 16 June.

The division remained on anti-invasion duties in the UK until August 1941, when it was sent to North Africa, arriving in November. It fought in most of the major actions of the desert war, including both battles of El Alamein, before being transferred to Italy in May 1944. It took part in the assault on the Gothic Line before ceasing to be an operational unit in October 1944. It was finally disbanded on 1 January 1945.

2nd Armoured Division

The 2nd Armoured Division was formed in December 1939, but remained in the UK until early 1941, when it deployed to North Africa. Initially guarding the lines of communications in Cyrenaica, it lost its 1st Armoured Brigade which was sent to Greece in a vain attempt to halt the German invasion. Most of the division's remaining units were captured in April 1941, although some managed to escape and were evacuated from Tobruk. The division was disbanded on 10 May 1941 and was not re-formed.

6th Armoured Division

The 6th Armoured Division formed in the UK on 12 September 1940, but did not deploy abroad until November 1942 when it took part in Operation Torch. Operating under command of the British First Army in Tunisia, it spearheaded the final drive on Tunis.

Following the end of the North African campaign, the division was sent to Italy where it came under the command of the Eighth Army (and later the US Fifth Army), taking part in the fighting around Monte Cassino, the assaults on the Gothic Line and the final offensive in April 1945.

7th Armoured Division

The 7th Armoured Division began life as the Mobile Force at Mersa Matruh in Egypt in 1938. It was soon retitled the Mobile Division (Egypt) and came under the command of Major-General Percy Hobart, whose relentless training turned it into a formidable armoured force. In February 1940 it became the 7th Armoured Division and adopted the 'Desert Rat' insignia. A few months later it was in action against Italian forces, going on to fight in every major action in the desert war.

The division fought in the early stages of the Italian campaign, before returning to the UK to prepare for Operation Overlord. It landed in Normandy on the afternoon of D-Day, taking part in Operations Goodwood, Spring and Bluecoat before the breakout from the beachhead. It then moved up to the Seine before spearheading the advance into Belgium. In 1945, the division crossed the Rhine in Operation Plunder, capturing Hamburg and Kiel at the end of the war.

8th Armoured Division

The 8th Armoured Division was formed in November 1940 and eventually deployed to Egypt. Troop shortages meant that it never received its lorried infantry brigade, and although consideration was given to using its remaining elements in a deep penetration role in the pursuit after El Alamein, other units were used. The division was disbanded in Egypt on 1 January 1943.

9th Armoured Division

The 9th Armoured Division was raised on 1 December 1940 and served as a training and trials formation in the UK until disbanded on 31 July 1944.

10th Armoured Division

The 10th Armoured Division was raised in August 1941 from the 1st Cavalry Division which had been based in Palestine. It fought at Alam el Halfa and El Alamein, remaining in North Africa after the end of the desert war. It was disbanded in Egypt on 15 June 1944.

11th Armoured Division

The division formed in Yorkshire in March 1941 under the command of Major-General Percy Hobart who initiated an intensive training programme based on his experience with the 7th Armoured Division. The formation was engaged in training and home defence duties until July 1944 when it deployed to Normandy. It took part in Operations Epsom and Goodwood, before capturing Antwerp on 4 September. In March 1945, it crossed the Rhine, advancing deep into Germany and liberating Bergen-Belsen concentration camp on 15 April. The 11th took Lübeck on 2 May and spent the immediate post-war period administering the province of Schleswig Holstein until the division's disbandment in January 1946.

42nd Armoured Division

On 1 November 1941, the 42nd (East Lancashire) Infantry Division was formally converted to an armoured division, becoming the 42nd Armoured Division. It remained in the UK as a home defence/training formation until its disbandment in October 1943.

79th Armoured Division

In April 1943, 79th Armoured Division was formed from both Royal Engineers and Royal Armoured Corps units to provide specialised AFVs for dealing with the German fortifications of the 'Atlantic Wall' along the northern French coast. These specialized AFVs proved highly effective during the Normandy landings and the subsequent advance across Europe.

By 1945, the formation was the largest armoured division in the British Army – with 1,050 tracked vehicles, it was three times the size of a normal armoured division. The 79th Armoured Division was disbanded on 20th August 1945, but it had established the need for an armoured engineering capability and 32 Engineer Regiment continues to fulfil this role in the British Army, bearing the Bull's Head badge inherited from the division.

Guards Armoured Division

After its formation on 17 June 1941, the Guards Armoured Division was stationed in the UK on home defence and training duties. It deployed to Normandy on 26 June 1944, taking part in Operations Goodwood and Bluecoat.

After the breakout from Normandy, it liberated Brussels on 3 September. The division then spearheaded XXX Corps' attack during Operation Market Garden, linking up with US airborne forces at Eindhoven and Nijmegen, but failing to cut through strengthening German defences in time to relieve the 1st Airborne Division at Arnhem. During the Ardennes Offensive, the division was deployed to defend the line of the Meuse against a possible German breakthrough. In February/March 1945, it took part in Operation Veritable and the subsequent advance through northern Germany. In June 1945, the formation was re-formed as an infantry division, becoming the Guards Division.

Other Allied armoured divisions

The three Free French armoured divisions raised in 1943 were all organized on US lines, although their constituent units retained traditional titles (such as *12e Régiment de Chasseurs d'Afrique*). The Polish, Canadian and South African divisions all followed British organization.

French 1st Armoured Division
(*1re Division Blindée* – 1re DB)

The division formed at Mascara, Algeria, on 1 May 1943 under the command of Brigadier Jean Touzet de Vigier. In August 1944, it formed part of General de Lattre de Tassigny's French First Army for Operation Dragoon, the invasion of southern France. 1re DB took part in the liberation of Toulon and Marseilles, before advancing up the Rhone Valley to the Rhine. In 1945 it spearheaded French First Army's advance through southern Germany and was the first French formation to reach the River Danube.

French 2nd Armoured Division
(*2e Division Blindée* – 2e DB)

Initially known as the 2nd Light Division, 2e DB was formed in August 1943. It deployed to Normandy on 1 August 1944 under the command of Major-General Philippe Leclerc. It took part in Operation Cobra as part of Patton's Third Army, during which it largely destroyed 9th Panzer Division, before liberating Paris on 25 August. 2e DB then advanced into Lorraine and Alsace, destroying 112th Panzer Brigade and liberating Strasbourg on 23 November. In February 1945, the division was sent to assist in the reduction of the Royan Pocket on the French Channel coast, which surrendered on 18 April. The division was then redeployed to southern Germany where it operated against the remnants of Army Group G, ending the war in Berchtesgaden.

French 5th Armoured Division
(*5e Division Blindée* – 5e DB)

The original 2nd Armoured Division was formed on 1 May 1943, but was redesignated as the 5th Armoured Division on 16 July 1943 to allow 2nd Free French Division to become 2nd Armoured Division. Originally comprising a tank brigade and a support brigade, 5e DB was re-equipped and reorganized along US lines with three combat commands which were commonly detached to support French infantry divisions.

The division deployed to France in September 1944 and took part in the battles for Belfort and the reduction of the Colmar Pocket. It then went into reserve before supporting the French crossing of the Rhine in March and participating in the final campaign in Germany.

Polish 1st Armoured Division

The Polish 1st Armoured Division (1 Dywizja Pancerna) was formed in Scotland in February 1942 under the command of General Stanislaw Maczek. It deployed to Normandy at the end of July 1944 and played a key role in the Battle of Falaise, in which it sealed off the Falaise Pocket, trapping 80,000 German troops. Following the Allied breakout from Normandy, the division advanced along the Channel coast, liberating Ypres, Ghent, Passchendaele and Breda. In early 1945, it fought its way along the Dutch-German border, before advancing on the German naval base of Wilhemshaven, which was taken on 6 May.

4th Canadian Armoured Division

The division was formed in Canada early in 1942 and deployed to the UK later that year. It landed in Normandy at the end of July 1944, taking part in the Battle of Falaise. After the Allied breakout from Normandy, the division advanced rapidly, crossing the Seine and liberating St Omer on 5 September before crossing into Belgium. 4th Armoured Division was then committed to the long struggle to clear the Scheldt estuary to allow Allied supply convoys to use Antwerp docks, which dragged on until 8 November. After refitting during the winter of 1944/45, the division took part in Operation Veritable, taking Xanten after a fierce fight against 116th Panzer Division. Following the Rhine crossings, it operated in the eastern Netherlands before advancing into Germany, taking Oldenburg on 5 May.

5th Canadian Armoured Division
(Nickname: *The Mighty Maroon Machine*)

In 1941, the 1st Canadian Armoured Division was redesignated as the 5th Canadian Armoured Division and deployed to the UK in November of that year. In November 1943, it replaced the British 7th Armoured Division in Italy and took part in the breaching of the Hitler and Gothic Lines. In January 1945, the division was transferred to Belgium, joining First Canadian Army for operations in the eastern Netherlands and north-west Germany.

6th South African Armoured Division

This was the first ever South African armoured division, formed on 1 February 1943 from elements of the 1st and 2nd South African Infantry Divisions. After training in Egypt, the division deployed to Italy in April 1944, taking part in the capture of Florence on 4 August and the breaching of the Gothic Line, as well as the spring offensive of 1945.

French and British AFV production

The new generation of French AFVs included formidable designs such as the Somua and the Char B1 bis, but many of the factories building them were reliant on antiquated machinery and archaic working practices. (In the Hotchkiss factory, most components were hand-finished with files, as they had been in the nineteenth century.) Matters improved after the outbreak of war brought a greater sense of urgency, but many promising designs, such as the Renault G1 R heavy tank, were still at the prototype stage at the time of the French surrender.

In 1936, the total number of tanks held by the British Army was 375 (209 lights and 166 mediums) of which 304 were officially categorized as obsolete. The only 'modern' vehicles were the 69 Light Tanks Marks V and VI, plus two experimental medium tanks. Although a massive effort went into British tank production from the late 1930s, the types selected for production were often hopelessly inadequate as combat vehicles. It was only at the very end of the war that the first prototypes of a tank able to match German types, the Centurion, were completed.

FRENCH TANKS, MODEL	pre Sep '39	1939	1940	Total
Char 2C	10	–	–	10
Renault FT-17	1580	–	–	1580
NC27	36	–	–	36
Char D1	160	–	–	160
Char D2	50	–	50	100
R-35	1070	200	331	1601
FCM-36	100	–	–	100
Char B1	163	42	200	405
AMR-33	123	–	–	123
AMR-35	167	–	–	167
ZB	16	–	–	16
ZT2	–	–	10	10
ZT3	10	–	–	10
ZT4	–	–	40	40
AMC-34	12	–	–	12
AMC-35	22	23	5	50
Hotchkiss H-35	640	130	322	1092
Somua S-35	270	50	110	430
AMD White TBC	86	–	–	86
AMD Laffly 50	98	–	–	98
AMD Laffly 80	28	–	–	28
AMD Laffly S15 TOE	45	–	–	45
AMD Berliet VUDB	32	–	–	32
AMD Panhard 165/175	30	–	–	30
AMD Panhard 178	219	69	239	527
AMC Schneider P16	96	–	–	96
Total	5063	514	1307	6884

BRITISH TANKS, MODEL	Total
Mk I, Matilda I (A11)	140
Mk II, Matilda II (A12)	2987
Mk III, Valentine	8275
Mk IV, Churchill (A22)	–
Churchill Mk I	303
Churchill Mk II	1127
Churchill Mk III	675
Churchill Mk IV	1622
Churchill Mk V	241
Churchill Mk VI	200
Churchill Mk VII	1600
Churchill Mk VIII	1600
Mk VII, Tetrarch (A17)	177
Mk I, Cruiser Tank (A9)	125
Mk II, Cruiser Tank (A10)	175
Mk III, Cruiser Tank (A13)	65
Mk IV, Cruiser Tank (A13 Mk II)	665
Mk V, Cruiser Tank Covenanter (A13 Mk III)	1700
Mk VI, Cruiser Tank Crusader (A15)	5300
Mk VII, Cruiser Tank Cavalier (A24)	500
Mk VIII, Cruiser Tank Centaur (A27L)	950
Mk VIII, Cruiser Tank Cromwell (A27M)	3066
Mk VIII, Cruiser Tank Challenger (A30)	200
Comet I Cruiser Tank (A34)	1186
Centurion I Cruiser Tank (A41)	6
Total	32,885

US AFV production

Although the USA's pre-war tank-building facilities were limited, the country's huge automotive industry was able to quickly adapt. US factories were more modern than their European counterparts and American mass-production methods were well suited to wartime requirements.

Model	1940	1941	1942	1943	1944	1945	Total
Stuart Light Tank, M1	34	–	–	–	–	–	34
Stuart Light Tank, M2	325	40	10	–	–	–	375
Stuart Light Tank, M3	–	2551	7839	3469	–	–	13,859
Stuart Light Tank, M5 and M8 HMC	–	–	2825	4063	1963	–	8851
Light Tank, M22 Locust	–	–	–	680	150	–	830
Light Tank, M24 Chaffee	–	–	–	–	1930	2801	4731
Gun Motor Carriage, M18 Hellcat	–	–	–	812	1695	–	2507
Medium Tank, M2A1	6	88	–	–	–	–	94
Medium Tank, M3 Lee/Grant	–	1342	4916	–	–	–	6258
Medium Tank, M4 Sherman (75)	–	–	8017	21,231	3504	651	33,403
Medium Tank, M4 Sherman (76)	–	–	–	–	7135	3748	10,883
Medium Tank, M4 Sherman (105)	–	–	–	–	2286	2394	4680
Gun Motor Carriage, M10	–	–	639	6067	–	–	6706
Gun Motor Carriage, M36	–	–	–	–	1400	924	2324
Howitzer Motor Carriage, M7	–	–	2028	786	1164	338	4316
Gun Motor Carriage, M12	–	–	60	40	–	–	100
Cargo Carrier, M30	–	–	60	40	–	–	100
Heavy Tank, M26 Pershing	–	–	–	–	40	2162	2202

Allied/Axis AFV losses by battle/campaign

Battle	Date	Allied	Axis
Arras Counterattack	21 May 1940	57	30
Sidi Barrani	9–12 December 1940	–	73
Bardia/First Battle of Tobruk	3–22 January 1941	–	210
Beda Fomm	5–7 February 1941	less than 12	100
Operation Crusader	18 November – 7 December 1941	278	300
First Battle of El Alamein	1–27 July 1941	193	100
Dieppe Raid	19 August 1942	28	–
Alam el Halfa	30 August – 2 September 1942	68	49
Second Battle of El Alamein	23 October – 4 November 1942	500	500
Medinine	6 March 1943	–	50
Falaise Pocket	13–21 August 1944	n/k	724
Ardennes Offensive	16 December 1944 – 16 January 1945	800	800

Tank armaments

British

Size	Type of Gun	Calibre	Type of Round	Muzzle Velocity f.p.s.	Projectile Weight lbs/oz	Penetration at 30° range in yards						Effective Range in yards		
						100	500	1000	1500	2000	2500	HE	Smoke	Shot
2pdr 40mm 1.575"	OQF 2pr Gun Mks IX and X	50	AP	2800	2–6	–	–	40	–	–	–	–	–	–
			APCBC	2600	2–11	–	53	49	44	40	–	2000	–	–
			SV	4200	1–0	–	88	72	60	48	–	–	–	–
3pdr 47mm 1.85"	OQF 3pr 2cwt Gun Mk II	40	APHE	1840	3–4	–	–	25	–	–	–	–	–	2000
6pdr 57mm 2.24"	OQF 6pr 7cwt Gun Mk 3 or 5	50	APCBC	2630	7–2	–	87	80	73	67	–	5500	–	2000
			APDS	4000		–	131	117	103	90	–			
75mm 2.95"	OQF 75mm Gun Mk V	36.5	APC	2030	14–4	–	68	61	54	47	–	10000	4500	2000
			APCBC	2650		–	103	94	86	78	–			
76.2mm 3"	OQF 77mm Gun Mk 2	50	APCBC	2575	17	–	120	110	100	90	–	7000	2000	2000
			APDS	3675	7–11	–	182	165	148	130	–	–	–	1500
17pdr 76.2mm 3"	OQF 17pdr Gun Mk 2	55	APCBC	2900	17	–	125	118	110	98	–	12000	–	2500
			APDS	3950	7–11	–	187	170	153	135	–	–	–	1800
95mm 3.74"	OQF 95mm Tank Howitzer Mk I	20	HEAT	1650	14–13	110	110	110	110	110	110			
			HE	1050	25	–	–	–	–	–	–	6000	3400	–

United States

Size	Type of Gun	Calibre	Type of Round	Muzzle Velocity f.p.s.	Projectile Weight lbs	Penetration at 30° range in yards						Effective Range in yards		
						100	500	1000	1500	2000	2500	HE	Smoke	Shot
37mm 1.46"	37mm M6 Gun	57	APC	2900	1.92	–	46	42	40	37	–	3000	–	1000
75mm 2.95"	75mm M2 Gun 75mm M3 Gun	31 40	APCBC	1930	14.4	–	–	62	48	40	–	13300	1500	3500
			APC	2030	14.96	–	70	59	55	50	–	14000		
76.2mm 3"	76mm Gun M1A1 and M1A2	55	APCBC	2600	15.44	–	94	89	81	76	–	14200	2000	3500
			HVAP	3400	9.4	–	158	134	117	99	–			
90mm	90mm M3 Gun	53	APCBC	2650	24.1	–	126	120	114	105	–	19600	–	3500
			HVAP	3350	16.8	–	221	200	177	154	–			
105mm	105mm M4 Howitzer	25	HEAT	1250	29.2	100	100	100	100	100	100	12000	4800	–

KEY:

AP – Armour-Piercing

APC – Armour-Piercing Capped

APCBC – Armour-Piercing Capped, Ballistic Capped

APDS – Armour-Piercing, Discarding Sabot

APHE – Armour-Piercing High Explosive

HE – High Explosive

HEAT – High Explosive Anti-Tank

HVAP – High Velocity Armour Piercing

SV – Super Velocity

Report by 9 RTR: Aspects of close support to infantry in Forest Fighting

AUTHOR NOTE: After the actions in the Reichswald in February 1945 34 Armoured Brigade commander asked 9 RTR to prepare a report on their experiences and the lessons they had learnt during those actions. This report, a summary of which is reproduced below, was used as the basis for a Brigade Conference on the matter of forest fighting.

General

1. An operation fought by tanks and infantry in close co-operation in forest country should not be looked upon as an entirely different type of warfare to an operation fought in normal European country. The same principles and rules apply, though they must, in many cases, be adapted to suit the unusual conditions of limited visibility and restricted manoeuvre. These two factors, as well as imposing many restrictions and difficulties on the actual fighting troops, make it extremely difficult for a commander to influence the battle, once he has launched his troops into an attack.

Training

2. For an operation in this type of country to be successfully conducted, it is imperative that co-operative training in forest country be carried out by the troops taking part. This Regiment had approximately one week's training in forest country prior to the action in the Reichswald. This was the absolute minimum required, and when possible a period of a fortnight should be made available.

Types of Forest

3. This Regiment has now fought in woods of many varieties. As a result of this experience it is considered that it is practicable for tanks to support infantry in forests where the trees are more than 12 feet high and 3 feet apart. It is not practicable, however, for tanks to support infantry in young plantations where visibility is nil. In such plantations it is impossible for tanks to keep in touch with the infantry, except in the rides, and tanks are unable to defend themselves against bazooka teams.

4. A coniferous forest presents less difficulty to the passage of tanks than does a deciduous forest. A Churchill tank will knock down a coniferous tree of 2 feet diameter, and a "Honey" a tree of 1 foot diameter. The tree is normally broken off at the base, though sometimes, and more particularly by 'Honeys' it is uprooted. The reason for this is that the 'Honey' tank tends to ride up the tree before pushing it over, while the 'Churchill' with a flat forward plate produces a more horizontal push. A deciduous tree is invariably uprooted, and the type of soil will have considerable effect on the size of the tree that can be pushed over. In the Reichswald it was found that a Churchill tank would push over a beech tree of 9 inches diameter but failed to push over a tree of 1 foot diameter. Crashing through trees at high speed is not feasible, as the shock of the impact breaks off the tops of the trees which fall on the commander's head.

Co-operation with Infantry

5. In view of the blindness of tanks in forests, it is essential that in all advances, both by day and night, deployed infantry should precede the tanks, irrespective of whether the tanks are advancing down the rides or through the forest. In order to avoid falling trees hitting the infantry, they must be approximately 30 yards ahead of the tanks. To ensure this, advances at night must be by bounds and movement light must be used. The infantry must carry some easily seen mark on their backs, and infantry and tank commanders must be close together. In one case, infantry carrying white mugs on their backs advanced 80 yards at a time, signalling back with red lights to the tanks behind them each time they halted. This system worked satisfactorily. Flank as well as frontal protection must be provided.

6. At night great difficulty was experienced by troop commanders in recognizing the company which they were supporting. It is recommended that each company should wear some distinguishing mark, which would render them easily recognizable.

Tank Formations

7. The value of tanks in forest country is more moral than material. It is, therefore, essential that the element of surprise should be maintained as long as possible. To do this, formations and tactics must be varied as much as conditions allow, always remembering that close contact with the infantry must be maintained and that tanks must be in visual contact. As a generalization it is reasonable to say that at night tanks within a troop should move in line ahead in close forest, and can only deploy in fairly open forest in daylight. Squadrons have, however, advanced successfully four troops up through the forest at night.

The following formations in the attack were adopted and proved satisfactory by one squadron:

(a) Four troops up; tanks in line ahead, advanced through the trees.

(b) A track used as a Centre Line with one troop deployed on either side. Two other troops followed after 10 minutes in same formation on a parallel ride. Deployment only possible in daylight.

(c) Two troops up; deployed in the forest, using two tracks as Centre Lines; one troop following close behind and another troop in reserve. Deployment only possible in daylight.

8. Although it is possible for tanks to deploy into and move through a forest it must be remembered that moving through this type of country imposes very severe strain on tanks and therefore, if contact is unlikely, tanks should move along tracks and rides, always ensuring that an infantry screen to front and flanks is maintained, and that on straight rides crests and crossings are carefully reconnoitred before being crossed.

Communications & Control

9(a) The squadron commander should travel well up behind his leading troops.

(b) The Recce Officer must travel in a Churchill tank.

(c) The No. 19 set gives adequate communications within the Regiment.

(d) Close liaison between flanking sub-units, units etc. must be maintained, or there is great danger of firing into one's own troops.

Artillery

10(a) SP Anti-tank artillery must be maintained well forward and be able to get into position quickly on an objective being gained.

(b) An FOO travelling with squadrons is most valuable and should always be provided when possible.

Night Leaguers

11. It is essential that as soon as an objective has been reached at night, tanks be withdrawn at least 20 yards from the foremost infantry positions and placed where they are adequately protected by the infantry. If possible it is highly desirable that tanks should be rallied by squadrons near the infantry battalion HQ (one squadron of tanks in support of an infantry battalion). The tanks must also have their own guards, armed with Sten guns at the ready. No movement of any kind within company positions should be allowed, and any person walking about must be shot without being challenged. In the Reichswald a German was able to penetrate a company position, and, on being challenged by a tank commander from his turret, shot him through the head. On another occasion a tank was hit by a bazooka at night while supposedly protected by the infantry dispositions.

Firing

12. During the night advances Besas were loaded with belts cleared of tracer and fired into the tops of the trees above the heads of the advancing infantry. It is considered that this has a useful horrific value.

During the attack it is of definite value to maintain Besa fire into the forest even when no more enemy are visible as it is found that those moving back out of sight become casualties.

13. In order to avoid inflicting casualties on one's own infantry, HE should normally be fired only in clearings.

14. The consumption of Besa ammunition is much in excess of all other types.

Recovery

15. ARVs should travel where they can give early assistance to bogged tanks. A liberal support of bulldozers well forward is most essential to clear trees off tracks and enable essential wheeled vehicles to go forward.

Supplies

16. Getting supplies forward presented great difficulty. The following methods were tried:-

(a) Churchills towing sledges. Sledges were too heavy to tow over heavy ground. Tanks could only tow in bottom gear with difficulty and eventually got bogged, but the sledges with wheels were much more satisfactory.

(b) RHQ tanks, carrying supplies forward. A certain but slow and laborious method. As these tanks obviously cannot be made available for this duty for long periods, it can only be looked upon as an emergency measure.

(c) Using two RHQ tanks (2IC and HQ Troop Commander's tanks) to tow forward two 3-tonners each. This is a feasible method and the majority of the supplies were taken forward in the Reichswald by this method.

(d) Recce Troop tanks used to carry supplies forward. This is the quickest and most efficient method, but special racks should be fitted to the tanks to increase their carrying capacity. In the Reichswald operation Recce Troop were unfortunately frozen by Traffic Control authorities while employed on this duty.

Volume Two: Soviet Tank Units

Introduction

In 1941 the Red Army was little more than a collection of
raw conscripts whose officers' authority was undermined
by fanatical but militarily incompetent political commissars.
Despite this, it survived the German invasion and four
years of bloody combat to become one of the world's
most formidable armies by 1945. This book provides
an introduction to the key vehicles that made that
transformation possible, setting the scene with a summary
of the pre-war Red Army's equipment. There is detailed
coverage of the war years, including the little-known
'August Storm' Offensive against the Japanese forces in
Manchuria in 1945. Whilst the emphasis is on the Soviet and
Lend-Lease armoured fighting vehicles (AFVs)
of the period, there is also coverage of their essential
support vehicles, including 'Katyusha' rocket launchers,
artillery tractors and transport.

◀ Tank attack

'Tank riders' (tankodesantniki) cluster on an SU-76 self-propelled gun as they
advance through northern Europe, late 1944. Even in 1945, most Soviet assault
infantry were still carried on tanks, where they formed a concentrated target for
MG and artillery fire.

THE RED ARMY OF WORLD WAR II might well be described in Churchill's phrase about Russia itself: 'It is a riddle, wrapped in a mystery, inside an enigma…'

While the riddle has become slightly less puzzling with the release of vast amounts of previously classified or censored material since the collapse of the former Soviet Union, there are still many problems. An astonishing number of sources disagree about key dates and statistics, and all too few Soviet documents are available in translation to resolve the discrepancies. It would take a far longer book than this volume to treat exhaustively such a huge subject as the tanks and vehicles of the wartime Red Army, but hopefully this introduction to the subject will encourage readers to delve more deeply into this fascinating topic. From its foundation in 1918 until the early 1930s, the Red Army was little more than a vast conscript force of infantry, cavalry and artillery, with few motor vehicles and even fewer Armoured Fighting Vehicles (AFVs). The handful of tanks and armoured cars in service were largely ageing vehicles

captured from the White Russian armies during the Civil War.

Reorganization

The situation was to undergo a dramatic change from 1931, when Marshal Tukhachevsky effectively took charge of the army's training and equipment. Within a few years, the commitment of massive resources was creating an ultra-modern, well-equipped armoured force far more powerful than that of any other nation. All this progress was swept away by Stalin's paranoia, when in 1937 he turned on the leadership of the Red Army, fearing that it might stage a military coup. The self-inflicted wound of the purges was very nearly fatal for the Red Army and the Soviet Union itself. The fiasco of the Winter War against Finland in 1939–40 gave warning of just how bad the situation was, and reforms began to restore combat capability, but the process was slow and much remained to be done by the time of the German invasion.

Operation *Barbarossa* came terrifyingly close to success – the mere survival of the Red Army was a

▲ **Winter offensive**

Whitewashed T-34/76 Model 1943 tanks of the 1st Ukrainian Front wait by the roadside near Kiev, December 1943. The wide tracks of the T-34 made them ideal for operations in the snow and mud of a Russian winter.

▲ **Capture of Berlin**
Soviet infantry ride on the back of an SU-100 self-propelled gun following the
capture of Berlin, May 1945.

victory in itself. This victory allowed it to exploit
its inherent resilience and adaptability, raising small
armoured units to give largely untrained officers the
chance to learn essential command skills. The powers
of the political commissars were gradually reduced so
that front-line officers were not constantly in fear of
denunciation by fanatical but militarily incompetent
'Party hacks'.

Although command skills dramatically improved
as the war went on, the level of unit effectiveness
remained low. This was largely because the most able
officers were rapidly promoted, leaving a mixture of
inept 'old hands' and new recruits at unit level. (The
situation was worsened by the lack of a professional
cadre of NCOs to handle basic training.)

Leadership problems were a major factor
contributing to the horrendous Soviet casualties
sustained throughout the war. The Red Army is
estimated to have lost 10,000,000 dead: its victory in
1945 was truly hard-won.

KEY TO TACTICAL SYMBOLS USED IN ORGANIZATION CHARTS

Symbol for division
or larger

Symbol for regiment or
brigade-sized formation

Symbol for battalion

| HQ | HQ units |

| Lt | Light tank unit (battalion or company) |

| Med | Medium tank unit |

| Hv | Heavy tank unit |

| AC | Armoured car unit |

| MC | Motorcycle unit |

| Sig | Signals |

| Pio | Pioneer unit |

| Sup | Support unit |

| Inf | Infantry unit |

| Bat | Battery |

| Mn | Maintenance unit |

| Flm | Flamethrower unit |

| Btn | Battalion |

| Br | Bridge-building unit |

| AA | Anti-aircraft unit |

Chapter 8

The Pre-War Years

In the 15 years following its victory in the Russian Civil War, the Red Army developed equipment and operational concepts that were as advanced as any in the world. It created the world's largest armoured force and the doctrine of 'deep operations', which was formally adopted in 1936. Stalin's paranoid fear of a military *coup d'etat* drove him to launch the murderous purges of the late 1930s, which destroyed much of this sophisticated military structure. Possibly 50 per cent of the Soviet officer corps was executed or imprisoned and innovative military thought was brutally suppressed. The effects of the purges were still all too evident in 1941 and were instrumental in bringing the Red Army to the very brink of total defeat.

◀ **Propaganda weapons**

A unit of British-made Mark V 'male' tanks captured from the White forces during the Russian Civil War in 1920–21 parades across Red Square on May Day 1930. The number '3' denotes the battalion and the encircled numbers the company and the number of the individual tank.

Pre-war development
1914–39

The Imperial Russian Army began developing armoured forces from the beginning of World War I, but the first foreign supplied tanks went into action only in the Russian Civil War (1918–21).

IN THE 10 YEARS leading up to the outbreak of World War I, the Imperial Russian army began an ambitious modernization programme. The first Russian AFVs were eight French-designed Nakashidze-Charron armoured cars, which entered service in 1908 and underwent prolonged troop trials. By 1913, the results were so promising that even the conservative Imperial Artillery Commission was forced to authorize orders for a variety of armoured cars from Russian and foreign sources.

Automobile Corps

Deliveries had only just started at the beginning of the war, but the first unit of the newly formed Automobile Corps – 15 machine-gun (MG) armed Russo-Balt light armoured cars and three Putilov-Garford armoured lorries with 76mm (3in) guns – was in action against Austro-Hungarian forces as early as October 1914. Its effectiveness prompted increased orders for AFVs and throughout 1915 and 1916 new units were formed as fast as vehicles could be obtained. These were:

■ Detachments – each with two MG-armed light armoured cars and a single gun-equipped heavy.

■ Companies – each with 12 lights and three heavies.

Development of tanks was much slower and only a single example of the tiny *Vezdekhod* light tank was built. A prototype of the gigantic Tsar 'tank' was also completed in 1915; this was a 36-tonne (40-ton) wheeled vehicle with two main wheels 10m (32ft 10in) in diameter and triple trail wheels perhaps a fifth of that size. Each main wheel was powered by a 186kW (250hp) Sunbeam engine and it was planned to fit turret and sponson-mounted MGs.

Trials rapidly showed just how impractical the machine was, and future efforts were concentrated on obtaining British and French tanks, but none had arrived by the time of the collapse of the Tsarist regime in 1917.

First actions

The first 'Russian' tanks to go into action were small numbers of Medium Mark Vs, Whippets and Renault FTs supplied to the anti-Bolshevik White forces during the Russian Civil War of 1918–21. Many of these were taken over by the Red Army after the war and formed virtually its entire tank

▲ **GAZ-AA 4x2 1½-ton truck**
The GAZ-AA 4x2 1½-ton truck was the workhorse of the pre-war Red Army. A licence-built copy of the Ford AA-Model 1929, it provided essential logistic support for Soviet experiments in armoured warfare during the 1930s. Over 150,000 vehicles were delivered by 1941.

Specifications

Crew: 1 driver (plus 15 troops)	Height: 1.97m (6ft 6in)
Weight: 1.55 tonnes (1.5 tons)	Engine: 29.8kW (40hp) 4-cylinder SV petrol
Length: 5.33m (17ft 6in)	Speed: 70km/h (43.5mph)
Width: 2.1m (7ft)	

▶ **Comrades-in-arms**

Lenin and Stalin, 1922. By 1945, Stalin's ruthlessness had transformed Lenin's ragged Red Army into one of the world's most powerful armoured forces.

strength until 1929, when Soviet tank production reached levels that allowed large-scale experiments with armoured units. An experimental Mechanized Brigade was formed during the summer of 1929 comprising a tank regiment, a motor rifle regiment, an artillery battalion and support units. By 1931, the lessons learned were being applied in the formation of a new tank 'regiment' that included:

- A Scout Group of two tankette battalions, an armoured car detachment, a lorried MG battalion and an artillery battery.
- An Attack Group with two tank battalions and two batteries of SU-12 76mm (3in) lorry-mounted self-propelled (SP) guns.
- A Support Group based on a motor rifle battalion.
- An Artillery Group with three batteries (76mm/3in and 122mm/4.8in guns) plus an anti-aircraft (AA) battery.

▶ **D-8 armoured car**

The D-8 armoured car was produced in small numbers from 1932 until 1934. Late production versions such as the vehicle seen here were fully enclosed and armed with two side-mounted 7.62mm (0.3in) MGs.

Specifications

Crew: 2	Engine: 31.3kW (42hp) GAZ-A 4-cylinder petrol
Weight: 1.58 tonnes (1.55 tons)	Speed: 85km/h (53mph)
Length: 2.63m (8ft 7in)	Range: 225km (140 miles)
Width: 1.7m (5ft 6in)	Armament: 2 x 7.62mm (0.3in) DT MGs
Height: 1.8m (5ft 10in)	

▶ **T-26A Model 1931 light tank**

The twin-turreted T-26 Model 1931, fitted with a single 7.62mm (0.3in) DT MG in each turret.

Specifications

Crew: 3	Engine: 68kW (91hp) GAZ T-26 8-cylinder
Weight: 9.3 tonnes (9.2 tons)	petrol
Length: 4.8m (15ft 8in)	Speed: 28km/h (17mph)
Width: 2.39m (7ft 10in)	Range: 200km (124 miles)
Height: 2.33m (7ft 8in)	Radio: N/A
	Armament: 2 x 7.62mm (0.3in) DT MGs

▶ **T-26TU Model 1931 command tank**

The T-26TU Model 1931 command tank, with prominent 'clothes line' radio aerial.
These vehicles were armed with a 37mm (1.5in) gun in the right hand turret and
a 7.62mm (0.3in) DT MG in the left.

Specifications

Crew: 3	Speed: 28km/h (17mph)
Weight: 9.3 tonnes (9.2 tons)	Range: 200km (124 miles)
Length: 4.8m (15ft 8in)	Radio: RSMK
Width: 2.39m (7ft 10in)	Armament: 1 x 45mm (1.8in) tank gun Model
Height: 2.33m (7ft 8in)	1932, 1 x coaxial 7.62mm (0.3in) DT MG
Engine: 68kW (91hp) GAZ T-26 8-cylinder petrol	

Development and expansion

During the 1930s, Soviet tank designers began producing faster and more powerful combat vehicles, despite the depradations of Stalin's purges.

OVER THE NEXT few years, annual tank production figures soared, which allowed the creation of two larger armoured units in the form of mechanized corps. Each included two mechanized brigades totalling 430 tanks and 215 armoured cars, plus a lorried infantry brigade and support units.

This expansion was matched by a flood of written theories of armoured warfare and ever-larger annual manoeuvres, which culminated in the huge 1935 exercises held in the Kiev Military District. Western observers at these manoeuvres were staggered to see the hundreds of AFVs deployed and would have been even more amazed had it been known that the Soviets had more tank units (and indeed more AFVs)

than the rest of the world's armies combined. Many of these AFVs were highly advanced – the T-26 Model 1933 light tank had a high-velocity 45mm (1.8in) gun in contrast to the MG armament of its Western counterparts, while the BT-5 fast tank's 298kW (400hp) engine and Christie suspension gave it a top speed of 72km/h (45mph).

A new generation of commanders provided the driving force for such developments, and of these generals the most influential was Mikhail Tukhachevsky, a former lieutenant in the Tsarist army who had made his name during the Russian Civil War commanding Red Army units opposing the forces of Admiral Kolchak. Ironically, it was

◀ **T-26 Model 1933 light tank**

The small twin turrets of the T-26 Model 1931 severely limited attempts at up-gunning the design. The much larger single turret of the Model 1933 allowed the installation of the powerful new 45mm (1.8in) tank gun Model 1932.

Specifications

Crew: 3	Speed: 28km/h (17mph)
Weight: 10.4 tonnes (10.3 tons)	Range: 200km (124 miles)
Length: 4.8m (15ft 8in)	Radio: N/A
Width: 2.39m (7ft 10in)	Armament: 1 x 45mm (1.8in) AT gun;
Height: 2.33m (7ft 8in)	1 x 7.62mm (0.3in) DT MG
Engine: 68kW (91hp) GAZ T-26 8-cylinder petrol	

▶ **Mikhail Nikolayevich Tukhachevsky (1893–1937)**
Marshal Tukhachevsky was the driving force of Red Army modernization in the
1930s. Tried for espionage, he became one of the most prominent victims of
Stalin's purges and was executed in 1937.

Tukhachevsky's very ability that was to prove fatal,
as Stalin came to see him as a threat to his power, a
view that may have been influenced by information
planted by German intelligence. Stalin began a
series of bloody purges of the Communist Party in
1936 and turned his attention to the Red Army in
the following year.

Show trials

On 9 June 1937, Tukhachevsky and his most
prominent supporters were suddenly arrested on
treason charges, tried by a special military court
on 11 June and shot at dawn the next day. Over
the next year or so, the total of those executed or
imprisoned rose to three of the five Marshals of the
Soviet Union plus 14 of the 16 army commanders,
60 of 67 corps commanders, 136 of 199 divisional
commanders and 221 of 397 brigade commanders.

Thousands of more junior officers were also shot
or imprisoned and the wave of terror spread out
to include the heads of the defence industries and
even weapons design teams. Their successors were
appointed more because they were politically 'safe'
than for their military abilities and were, in any case,
understandably terrified of Stalin's secret police,
the NKVD.

The result of this terror was the stagnation of
Soviet military thought – at one stage, armoured
warfare was officially condemned as 'bourgeois,
reactionary and unworthy of Marxist society'.

▶ **T-37 Model 1934 amphibious light tank**
The T-37 Model 1934 amphibious light tank equipped many reconnaissance units
during the Winter War against Finland and was still in service at the time
of the German invasion. An estimated 1200 vehicles were produced between 1933
and 1936.

Specifications	
Crew: 2	Engine: 30kW (40hp) GAZ-AA petrol
Weight: 3.2 tonnes (3 tons)	Speed: 35km/h (22mph)
Length: 3.75m (12ft 4in)	Range: 185km (115 miles)
Width: 2.10m (6ft 10in)	Radio: N/A
Height: 1.82m (6ft)	Armament: 1 x 7.62mm (0.3in) DT MG

Specifications

Crew: 11	Speed: 30km/h (18.5mph)
Weight: 45 tonnes (44.3 tons)	Range: 150km (93miles)
Length: 9.72m (31ft 10in)	Radio: RSMK
Width: 3.20m (10ft 6in)	Armament: 1 x 76mm (3in) gun Model
Height: 3.43m (11ft 4in)	27/32 (main gun); 2 x 37mm (1.5in) guns
Engine: 370kW (500hp) Mikulin M-17M	(secondary turrents); 5 or 6 x 7.62mm
12-cylinder petrol	(0.3in) DT MGs

▲ **T-35 Model 1932**

5th Independent Heavy Tank Brigade, Moscow 1935

The T-35 Model 1932 was the first of a family of 'land battleships' all bearing the T-35 designation. It was armed with a 76mm (3in) howitzer in the main turret, flanked by four sub-turrets, two with 37mm (1.5in) guns and the other two with 7.62mm (0.3in) machine-guns. Only 10 examples of the Model 1932 were completed before production switched to the Model 1935, in which the 37mm (1.5in) guns were replaced with the more potent 45mm (1.8in) weapons.

Khalkhyn Gol
1939

By the late 1930s, Japan had established control of Manchuria (renamed Manchukuo) in northern China. This move brought it into conflict with the neigbouring Soviet satellite state of Mongolia.

THE JAPANESE CLAIMED that the Khalkhyn Gol (Khalkha River) formed the border between Manchukuo and Mongolia, while the Mongolians and Soviets maintained that it ran 16km (10 miles) east of the river, just east of Nomonhan village.

The Kwantung Army formed the main Japanese force in Manchukuo, and it included some of the best Japanese units. However, the western region of Manchukuo was garrisoned by the newly raised 23rd Division at Hailar, together with various Manchukuoan army and border guard units. On the other side of the frontier, the Red Army's LVII Special Corps, deployed from the Trans-Baikal Military District, was responsible for the defence of the border between Siberia and Manchuria.

Small border skirmishes in May 1939 gradually escalated, leading to the destruction of a regiment of the Kwantung Army's 64th Division at the end of

the month. Large-scale Japanese air attacks the following month raised the tension still further as the Kwantung Army prepared an offensive to 'expel the invaders'.

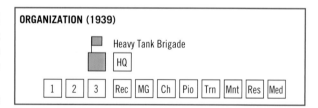

ORGANIZATION (1939)

Heavy Tank Brigade

HQ

| 1 | 2 | 3 | Rec | MG | Ch | Pio | Trn | Mnt | Res | Med |

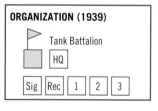

ORGANIZATION (1939)

Tank Battalion

HQ

| Sig | Rec | 1 | 2 | 3 |

This was to be a pincer movement by elements of the 23rd Division and the Yashuoka Detachment to encircle and destroy Soviet and Mongolian forces along the Khalkhyn Gol. (The Yasuoka Detachment was one of the few sizeable Japanese armoured formations, with almost 100 AFVs.)

While preparations for the offensive were under way, Georgi Zhukov, the most promising general to survive Stalin's purges, was appointed to command the Soviet forces. He quickly recognized the need for massive transport resources to support the powerful armoured force needed to inflict a decisive defeat on Japanese – initially 1000 fuel tankers and over 1600 cargo trucks were deployed over the 750km (466-mile) route from his supply bases to the front-line, later supplemented by a further 1625 vehicles from European Russia. This logistic support allowed him to assemble a striking force of as many as 550 tanks (mainly T-26s and BT-7s), plus 450 armoured cars.

The Japanese offensive opened on 2 July, in which the Yasuoka Detachment lost more than half its tanks

to Soviet anti-tank (AT) guns, while perhaps 120 Soviet AFVs were destroyed. Despite these losses, Zhukov still had overwhelming armoured strength totalling nearly 500 tanks and 350 armoured cars to spearhead a devastating counter-offensive, launched on 20 August. Within five days, this achieved a classic double envelopment of the Japanese 23rd Division, which was effectively destroyed by 31 August.

Zhukov had proved himself a capable commander of armoured forces, and his decisive actions had effectively ended the power of the 'Strike North' group within the Japanese High Command, which sought to expand into Soviet Central Asia and Siberia. After almost two years of uneasy peace, the Soviet-Japanese Neutrality Pact of April 1941 finally removed the lingering threat to Stalin's eastern frontiers.

▶ BA-20 armoured car

The command version of the BA-20, which was the standard light armoured car of Soviet reconnaissance units at the time of the invasion of Poland.

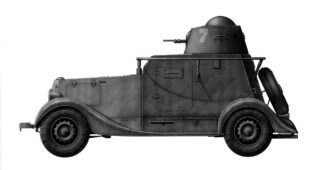

Specifications

Crew: 3	Engine: 37kW (50hp) GAZ-M1 petrol
Weight: 2.5 tonnes (2.46 tons)	Speed: 85km/h (53mph)
Length: 4.31m (14ft 2in)	Range: 450km (280 miles)
Width: 1.75m (5ft 8in)	Radio: RSMK
Height: 2.13m (7ft)	Armament: 1 x 7.62mm (0.3in) DT MG

Specifications

Crew: 6	Speed (road): 37km/h (23mph)
Weight: 28 tonnes (27.4 tons)	Range: 220km (137 miles)
Length: 7.44m (24ft 5in)	Radio: N/A
Width: 2.87m (9ft 5in)	Armament: 1 x 76mm (3in) L-10 L/26 gun; 4 x
Height: 2.82m (9ft 3in)	7.62mm (0.3in) DT MGs
Engine: 373kW (500hp) Mikulin M-17	

▲ T-28 Model 1938 medium tank

The 76mm (3in) L/16.5 Model 1927/32 gun of the T-28 Model 1934 was a low-velocity weapon, optimized for firing high-explosive (HE) in the infantry support role. In the Model 1938, it was replaced by the higher-velocity 76mm (3in) L-10 L/26 gun, which had markedly better armour-piercing performance.

▲ BT-2 fast tank

A 1932 vintage BT-2 in markings typical of those used during the opening phases
of Barbarossa, summer 1941.

Specifications

Crew: 3

Weight: 10.2 tonnes (9.8 tons)

Length: 5.58m (18ft 3in)

Width: 2.23m (7ft 3in)

Height: 2.20m (7ft 2in)

Engine: 298kW (400hp) Liberty

Speed: 100km/h (62mph)

Range: 300km (186 miles)

Radio: N/A

Armament: 1 x 37mm (1.5in) Model 1931 gun;
1 x 7.62mm (0.3in) coaxial DT MG

Heavy Tank Brigade (1939)	BA-20	BTs	T-28
Brigade HQ	–	–	2
HQ Company	5	–	–
Reconnaissance Company	10	6	–
Signal Platoon	5	3	–
Reconnaissance Platoon	3	–	–
Heavy Tank Company x 3	5	3	10

▼ Heavy Tank Company (1939)

Three of these companies formed the main strike force of each heavy tank battalion. (Each heavy tank brigade had three such battalions.) Even by the standards of
1939, the T-28 was inadequately armoured for its role and proved to be vulnerable to Finnish 37mm (1.5in) anti-tank guns during the Winter War. A number of vehicles
were rebuilt, with frontal armour increased from 30mm to 80mm (1.2in to 3.1in), but the extra weight impaired speed, range and agility.

Heavy Tank Company (10 x T-28s) and signals platoon (5 x BA-20s, 3 x BTs)

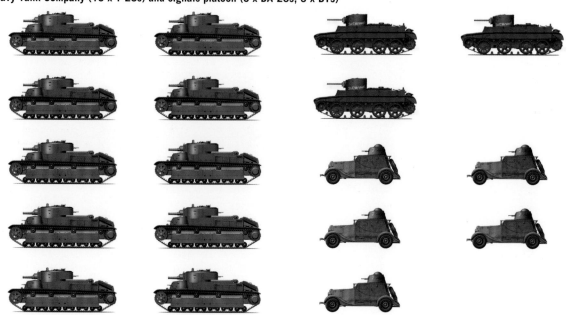

▶ **T-26TU Model 1936 command tank**

The T-26TU Model 1936 command tank, fitted with a distinctive turret-mounted 'horse shoe' radio aerial.

Specifications

Crew: 3

Weight: 10.4 tonnes (10.3 tons)

Length: 4.8m (15ft 8in)

Width: 2.39m (7ft 10in)

Height: 2.33m (7ft 8in)

Engine: 68kW (91hp) GAZ T-26
  8-cylinder petrol

Speed: 28km/h (17mph)

Range: 200km (124 miles)

Radio: RSMK

Armament: 1 x 45mm (1.8in) AT gun;
  1 x 7.62mm (0.3in) DT MG; additional
  7.62mm (0.3in) DT MG ball-mounted into
  turret rear

Spanish Civil War
1936–39

Stalin's reign of terror also contributed to the wrong lessons being drawn from the Spanish Civil War, in which General Pavlov commanded a sizeable Soviet armoured contingent in support of the Republicans. This force included 300 T-26s and 50 BT-5s.

WHILE THERE WERE no large-scale tank battles, a number of actions proved that these machines were technically far superior to the Panzer Is and Italian tankettes fielded by the Nationalist forces.

The first such action took place on 29 October 1936 in and around the small town of Sesena about 40km (25 miles) south of Madrid. Sesena had just been taken by Nationalist cavalry spearheading a force of eight infantry brigades supported by 23 artillery batteries and a single Italian tank company with CV 33/35s – a 15,000-strong force that posed a clear threat to the capital.

Although the first Soviet-equipped Republican tank units were still forming, the situation was so serious that ad hoc combat teams were rushed to the front, including one with 15 T-26s commanded by an able Russian tank officer, Major Paul Arman, who was serving under the code-name 'Greisser'. His force led a counterattack by two Republican infantry brigades to recapture Sesena, but almost immediately three tanks were disabled by mines and the remainder lost contact with their infantry. The Nationalist cavalry holding the town were supported by two Italian 65mm (2.5in) howitzer batteries that now opened fire, destroying one T-26 and immobilizing

another (it continued to return fire for 40 minutes before it was knocked out by a newly arrived Spanish 75mm/2.9in field gun). Arman's 10 surviving tanks pushed on into Sesena, shooting up targets of opportunity, but their lack of infantry meant that they could not hold the positions they had overrun. This situation made them vulnerable to attack by the determined Nationalist troopers, who destroyed another T-26 with improvised petrol bombs, soon to become famous as 'Molotov Cocktails'. The rest of the unit broke out of the town and headed east in a raid on the Nationalist rear areas.

They destroyed a field gun battery, then encountered three CV 33/35s. Two tankettes were knocked out and the T-26s went on to destroy nearby military stores and 20–30 lorries before returning to the Republican lines. By November

Soviet Tanks Delivered to Spain		
Date of arrival	T-26	BT-5
12 Oct 36	50	–
25 Nov 36	37	–
30 Nov 36	19	–
6 Mar 37	60	–
8 Mar 37	40	–
7 May 37	50	–
10 Aug 37	–	50
13 Mar 38	25	–

1936, Nationalist forces were closing in on Madrid and had begun to receive German tanks and AT guns. The Panzer Is were hopelessly out-gunned by the T-26s, although the Soviet tanks' thin armour was vulnerable to armour-piercing MG rounds at ranges up to 100m (328ft). In practice, this wasn't much help as the T-26s' 45mm (1.8in) guns could wreck the little Panzer I or the CV 33/35 at ranges of more than 1000m (3280ft), which forced the Nationalists to attach up to five 37mm (1.5in) or 47mm (1.9in) AT guns per tank company to provide additional protection. Other measures included fitting a few Panzer Is with 20mm (0.79in) gun, the first experimental use of the Condor Legion's 88mm (3.5in) Flak guns in the AT role and even the offer of cash rewards for every T-26 captured in running order. These moves, coupled with increasingly effective Nationalist air attacks, helped the situation, but the Republican tanks kept their technical edge throughout the war.

In early 1937, the Nationalists attempted a further attack on Madrid, this time from the north-east. The first stage was an offensive by four Italian divisions aimed at Guadalajara and Alcala, and it opened in foul weather on 8 March. Heavy snow reduced visibility to a few metres and prevented the planned massive Nationalist air support, while Republican aircraft could operate freely thanks to good weather over their bases. At times, over 100 Soviet-supplied fighters were committed to ground-attack missions in which their MG and cannon fire destroyed many of the Italian supply vehicles and even knocked out a few of the CV 33/35s. (The single battalion of these tankettes allocated to spearhead the attack was no match for the 60 T-26s deployed by General Pavlov to stiffen the Republican defences.) After two days, the Italian advance was halted and the Republicans were able to counterattack. On the 13th, T-26s destroyed five CV 33/35s and damaged two more without loss to themselves, and five days later, they

▶ T-26 Model 1936 light tank

A former Republican T-26 Model 1936 pressed into Nationalist service sports a non-standard camouflage finish. This vehicle carries additional armament comprising a 7.62mm (0.3in) DT MG in the turret rear and a similar weapon on a P-40 AA mounting.

Specifications

Crew: 3	Speed: 28km/h (17mph)
Weight: 10.4 tonnes (10.3 tons)	Range: 200km (124 miles)
Length: 4.8m (15ft 8in)	Armament: 1 x 45mm (1.8in) tank gun
Width: 2.39m (7ft 10in)	Model 1932; 1 x coaxial 7.62mm (0.3in)
Height: 2.33m (7ft 8in)	DT MG; 2 x additional 7.62mm (0.3in) DT
Engine: 68kW (91hp) GAZ T-26	MGs, one ball-mounted in turret rear and
8-cylinder petrol	one on P-40 AA mount

▶ T-26 Model 1935 light tank

A captured Republican T-26 Model 1935 in Spanish Nationalist service. The prominent red/yellow/red recognition markings were applied in an attempt to minimize the risk from 'friendly fire'.

Specifications

Crew: 3	Speed: 28km/h (17mph)
Weight: 10.4 tonnes (10.3 tons)	Range: 200km (124 miles)
Length: 4.8m (15ft 8in)	Radio: N/A
Width: 2.39m (7ft 10in)	Armament: 1 x 45mm (1.8in) AT gun;
Height: 2.33m (7ft 8in)	1 x 7.62mm (0.3in) DT MG; additional
Engine: 68kW (91hp) GAZ T-26 8-cylinder	7.62mm (0.3in) DT MG ball-mounted into
petrol	turret rear

led a further counterattack that routed several Italian units and secured the approaches to Guadalajara. By this time, breakdowns, artillery and AT guns had reduced Pavlov's force to only nine operational tanks, ruling out any chance of a decisive victory.

Fuentes de Ebro was the only major action fought by the Republican International Tank Regiment, which was equipped with 48 of the BT-5s shipped to Spain in August 1937. Besides a cadre of Soviet 'volunteers', their crews included Spaniards and International Brigade personnel who had trained at

the Red Army's Gorkiy Tank School. On 13 October 1937, the formation was committed to a hastily planned attack on the town of Fuentes de Ebro, an attack intended to open the road to Saragossa. In fact, it would be fairer to say that the operation was improvised rather than planned – it was scheduled for noon on the 13th, but the tank crews received their orders only at 2300 hours the previous day and then had a 50km (31-mile) road march to the assembly area. Barely two hours before the attack was due to start, the formation was told that it would

▲ **BT-5 fast tank**

A Republican BT-5 captured by Nationalist forces on the Ebro Front, 1938.

Specifications

Crew: 3	Speed: 72km/h (44mph)
Weight: 11.5 tonnes (11 tons)	Range: 200km (124 miles)
Length: 5.58m (18ft 3in)	Radio: N/A
Width: 2.23m (7ft 3in)	Armament: 1 x 45mm (1.8in) Model 1932 gun;
Height: 2.25m (7ft 5in)	1 x 7.62mm (0.3in) coaxial DT MG
Engine: 298kW (400hp) Model M-5	

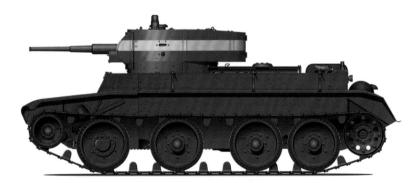

▲ **BT-5 fast tank**

A captured BT-5 in full Nationalist markings. (In this case, the recognition stripes run right around the turret.)

Specifications

Crew: 3	Speed: 72km/h (44mph)
Weight: 11.5 tonnes (11 tons)	Range: 200km (124 miles)
Length: 5.58m (18ft 3in)	Radio: N/A
Width: 2.23m (7ft 3in)	Armament: 1 x 45mm (1.8in) Model 1932 gun;
Height: 2.25m (7ft 5in)	1 x 7.62mm (0.3in) coaxial DT MG
Engine: 298kW (400hp) Model M-5	

be carrying infantry from the 15th International Brigade into action on its tanks, despite the fact that neither unit had any training for this role. The harassed crews were then told that there was no time to carry out any battlefield reconnaissance and that the Republican commanders could not give any information about the terrain or enemy AT defences, which they regarded as trivial matters.

In the circumstances, it was hardly surprising that things went wrong from the beginning of the operation – the BTs fired a single salvo before racing off with the infantry clinging to their sides. Many fell off as the tanks bucked and bounced across country, while others became casualties when startled front-line Republican infantry (who had not been warned of the attack), opened fire as the BTs came roaring over their positions. After clearing this unexpected hazard, the attackers found that the plain in front of the Nationalist defences consisted mainly of sugar cane fields, criss-crossed with irrigation ditches. As the tanks attempted to force their way through, they came under increasingly effective fire from enemy artillery and AT guns hidden in farm buildings. The

handful of infantry who remained with the tanks were too few to neutralize the Nationalist guns or hold the ground that had been gained, and the operation was finally abandoned with the loss of 19 tanks plus several more damaged.

Limited impact

Despite the technological superiority of Soviet tanks, their operations were crippled by poor communications and a lack of properly integrated infantry and artillery. Even if these problems could have been solved, it is hardly likely that the limited Soviet armoured force committed to Spain could have prevented the ultimate Nationalist victory in March 1939. It seems likely that Pavlov and his staff appreciated that these problems affected the Red Army as much as the Spanish Republican forces, but this was the era of Stalin's most savage purges and no-one was safe from the NKVD. In the circumstances, it is hardly surprising that official reports tended to play down serious problems, blaming them on poorly trained Spanish troops rather than failings in Soviet doctrine or equipment.

▲ **Training exercise**

A BT-7 advances with infantry – the lack of any camouflage or extra kit stowed on the tank and the remarkably evenly spaced shell bursts would suggest that this is a pre-war exercise rather than a true combat photograph.

Poland

SEPTEMBER 1939

On 17 September 1939, Soviet forces invaded Poland, which had been desperately fighting against the German invasion for over two weeks.

THE RED ARMY deployed over 3000 AFVs against Polish forces, but took unnecessary losses in a number of actions through over-confidence and tactical ineptitude. At Grodno on 20 September, the XV Tank Corps attempted a frontal assault on the city with minimal infantry support, and was beaten off with the loss of 19 tanks and four armoured cars. On 28 September, a scratch Polish force comprising elements of the Border Defence Corps and the Independent Operational Group *Polesie* ambushed the 52nd Rifle Division and its supporting T-26 brigade near Szack, inflicting roughly 2000 casualties and destroying or capturing 40 tanks.

These setbacks were no more than pin-pricks, as Soviet forces were deployed in overwhelming strength, but the warning signs were ignored by Stalin and his cronies. In November 1939, the four Tank Corps (which had replaced the former Mechanized Corps barely a year earlier) were broken up to form motorized divisions. These had roughly 275 tanks apiece and were intended to operate in conjunction with horsed cavalry. Independent tank brigades were to be more closely integrated with infantry and cavalry, while it was planned to increase the armoured component of rifle divisions from a tank battalion to a tank brigade.

Belarus (9/1939)	T-37	T-26	BT	T-28	Arm Car
XV Tank Corps	–	–	461	–	122
6th Tank Bde	–	–	248	–	–
21st Tank Bde	–	–	29	105	19
22nd Tank Bde	–	219	–	–	3
25th Tank Bde	–	251	–	–	27
29th Tank Bde	–	188	–	–	3
32nd Tank Bde	–	220	–	–	5

Ukraine (9/1939)	T-37	T-26	BT	T-28	Arm Car
XXV Tank Corps	–	27	435	–	74
10th Tank Bde	–	10	30	98	19
23rd Tank Bde	–	8	209	–	5
24th Tank Bde	–	8	205	–	28
26th Tank Bde	–	228	–	–	22
36th Tank Bde	–	301	–	–	24
38th Tank Bde	4	141	–	–	4

▲ **BT-5 fast tank**

Byelorussian Front / XV Tank Corps / 27th Light Tank Brigade

A BT-5 of the Soviet Belorussian Front during the invasion of Poland, 1939.

Specifications

Crew: 3

Weight: 11.5 tonnes (11 tons)

Length: 5.58m (18ft 3in)

Width: 2.23m (7ft 3in)

Height: 2.25m (7ft 5in)

Engine: 298kW (400hp) Model M-5

Speed: 72km/h (44mph)

Range: 200km (124 miles)

Armament: 1 x 45mm (1.8in) Model 1932 gun;
1 x 7.62mm (0.3in) coaxial DT MG

▲ BT-7A 'artillery tank'

Specifications

Crew: 3

Weight: 14.5 tonnes (13.8 tons)

Length: 5.66m (18ft 6in)

Width: 2.29m (7ft 6in)

Height: 2.52m (8ft 1in)

Engine: 373kW (500hp) Model M-17T

Speed: 86km/h (53mph)

Range: 250km (155 miles)

Radio: N/A

Armament: 1 x 76mm (3in) KT-28 Model

1927/32 howitzer; 3 x 7.62mm (0.3in) DT MGs

(coaxial, rear turret, hatch)

Byelorussian Front / XV Tank Corps / 27th Light Tank Brigade

A BT-7A 'artillery tank', armed with a 76mm (3in) howitzer for the close support role. The 76mm (3in) HE shell was far more effective against AT guns or field defences than the rounds fired by the 45mm (1.8in) guns of the standard BT tanks.

▼ Heavy Tank Brigade, Reconnaissance Company (September 1939, Poland)

As befitted its role, the reconnaissance company was a fast-moving unit, hampered only by the differing mobility of its BTs and armoured cars. While the latter could outpace the tanks on roads, they had very limited off-road capability and were apt to become bogged down when attempting cross-country moves.

6 x BTs plus 10 x BA-20s

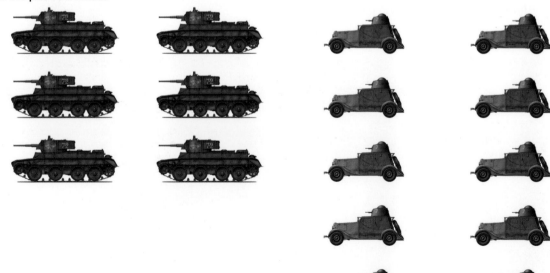

◀ *Komsomolyets* artillery transporter

Over 4000 of these partially armoured artillery tractors were produced between 1937 and 1941. They were mainly used as prime movers for the 45mm (1.8in) anti-tank gun.

Specifications

Crew: 2 (plus 6 seats for gun crew)	Engine: 37kW (50hp) GAZ-M 4-cylinder petrol
Weight: 3.5 tonnes (3.44 tons)	Speed: 50km/h (31mph)
Length: 3.45m (11ft 4in)	Range: 250km (155miles)
Width: 1.86m (6ft 1in)	Armament: 1 x 7.62mm (0.3in) DT MG
Height: 1.58m (5ft 1in)	

Humiliation in Finland
NOVEMBER 1939 – MARCH 1940

The extent of the self-inflicted damage to the combat capability of the Red Army was shown in the bloody fiasco of Russia's Winter War against Finland, which began on 30 November 1939.

IN KARELIA, THE INITIAL Soviet assaults by the Seventh Army against the fortifications of the Mannerheim Line were repulsed with heavy losses, despite the support of the three tank brigades of X Tank Corps and four artillery regiments. At least 180,000 troops, 900 guns and 1400 AFVs were committed against roughly 133,000 Finnish defenders who were woefully short of artillery and armour – the most critical shortage being AT guns, only 67 of which were available.

Before being overwhelmed, the Finns graphically demonstrated the shortcomings of contemporary Soviet armoured warfare practice. The Red Army's

Armoured Units (Finland 1939)	Battalions
Seventh Army (Karelian Isthmus)	
10th Tank Bde	1st, 4th, 6th, 8th, 9th, 15th, 19th
20th Tank Bde	90th, 91st, 95th
35th Tank Bde	105th, 108th, 112th
40th Tank Bde	155th, 157th, 160th, 161st
Eighth Army (Ladoga)	
34th Tank Div	76th, 82nd, 83rd
Ninth Army (mid Finland)	97th, 100th, 312th, 365th
Fourteenth Army (Northern Lapland)	349th, 411th

▶ T-26 Model 1938 light tank

Seventh Army / 10th Tank Brigade / 15th Tank Battalion

The T-26 Model 1938 was fitted with a new turret that used sloped armour to improve protection. Despite this, it proved vulnerable to even light AT weapons during the Winter War against Finland.

Specifications

Crew: 3	Speed: 28km/h (17mph)
Weight: 10.4 tonnes (10.3 tons)	Range: 200km (124 miles)
Length: 4.8m (15ft 8in)	Armament: 1 x 45mm (1.8in) tank gun
Width: 2.39m (7ft 10in)	Model 1932; 1 x coaxial 7.62mm (0.3in)
Height: 2.33m (7ft 8in)	DT MG; 2 x additional 7.62mm (0.3in) DT
Engine: 68kW (91hp) GAZ T-26	MGs, one ball-mounted in turret rear and
8-cylinder petrol	one on P-40 AA mount

tanks were frequently committed to assaults without adequate reconnaissance and with abysmal levels of artillery and infantry support. These failings made them horribly vulnerable to well-camouflaged Finnish AT guns, and infantry AT teams that scored numerous kills with Molotov Cocktail incendiaries and demolition charges. While most AT guns opened fire at ranges of 400–600m (1312–1968ft), an unofficial record was set by a 37mm (1.5in) Bofors gun of the 7th Anti-Tank Detachment, which destroyed a T-37 on the ice of Lake Ladoga at a range of 1700m (5577ft).

It seems likely that as many as 6000 Soviet AFVs were deployed against Finland during the three-and-a-half months of the war and that losses from all causes may have exceeded 3500 vehicles. Finnish forces captured or destroyed roughly 1600 of these, besides inflicting an estimated 250,000 casualties, highlighting the inadequacies of the Red Army.

Light Tank Brigade (1940)	Arm Car	T-37	T-26
Signal Company	5	–	–
Armoured Car Company	16	–	–
Light Tank Company	–	16	–
Battalion HQ	–	–	3
Reconnaissance Platoon x 3	1	1	–
Tank Company x 3	–	–	17
Reserve Tank Company	–	–	8

▼ Light Tank Brigade, Tank Battalion (January 1940, Karelian Front)

By the standards of 1939/1940, these tank battalions were powerful units, but their potential was never fully realized due to poor training, coupled with abysmal command and control.

Battalion HQ (3 x T-26s)

Tank Company x 3 (17 x T-26s)

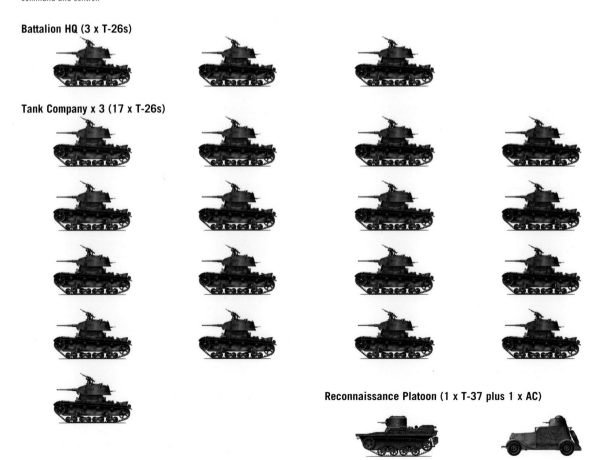

Reconnaissance Platoon (1 x T-37 plus 1 x AC)

Specifications

Crew: 1 driver

Weight: 3.52 tonnes (3.46 tons)

Length: 5.34m (17ft 6in)

Width: 2.36m (7ft 9in)

Height: 2.1m (6ft 11in)

Engine: 37kW (50hp) GAZ-M 4-cylinder

Speed: 35km/h (21.75mph)

▲ GAZ-AAA 6x4 truck

The GAZ-AAA was the first Soviet 6x4 truck and was a familiar sight in Red Army supply columns from the mid-1930s until 1945. Total production ran to roughly 37,000 vehicles.

▲ GAZ-60 cargo halftrack

A GAZ-60 cargo halftrack, as used in Finland during the Winter War of 1939–40. Almost 900 vehicles were delivered to the Red Army in 1939–40, based on the GAZ-AAA truck and the French Citroën-Kegresse halftrack suspension.

Specifications

Crew: 1 driver

Weight: 3.52 tonnes (3.46 tons)

Length: 5.34m (17ft 6in)

Width: 2.36m (7ft 9in)

Height: 2.1m (6ft 11in)

Engine: 37kW (50hp) GAZ-M 4-cylinder

Speed: 35km/h (21.75mph)

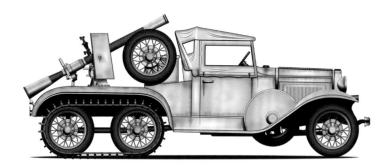

Specifications

Crew: 2

Weight: 1.5 tonnes (1.47 tons)

Length: 4.4m (14ft 5in)

Width: 1.7m (5ft 7in)

Height: 1.6m (5ft 3in)

Engine: 31.3Kw (42hp) GAZ-A 4-cylinder petrol

Speed: 63km/h (39.15mph)

Armament: 1 x 76mm (3in) recoilless gun

▲ GAZ-TK 76mm recoilless gun

A total of 23 experimental GAZ-TK 76mm self-propelled recoilless guns were produced in the mid-1930s. Two of these were lost undergoing combat trials during the Winter War and it seems likely that the remainder succumbed to mechanical failure during the first weeks of Operation Barbarossa.

Calm before the storm

JANUARY–MAY 1941

Even Stalin was finally forced to face reality in the aftermath of the German victory in France, and the mechanized corps underwent reform from June 1940 onwards. By the time of the German invasion in June 1941, no less than 30 corps had been raised.

ALTHOUGH FRANTIC EFFORTS were made, these corps were far from being effective combat units when they were thrown into action a year later, despite the massive numbers of AFVs then available (see table opposite).

Even these holdings were inadequate to meet the needs of so many massive formations – over 6000 more tanks were required. The situation was even worse than the totals would suggest, as there were far too few modern vehicles – 3000 more KVs and almost 11,000 more T-34s should have been available.

Equally seriously, the emphasis on producing new tanks rather than spare parts led to appalling serviceability – it seems likely that only 27 per cent of Soviet tanks were fully operational at the time of the German invasion.

Mechanized Equipment, RKKA (May 1941)	Strength
Tanks:	
T-27	400
T-37	2400
T-38	1200
T-40	222
T-18M	400
T-26	11,000
BT	6000
T-28	500
T-34	967
T-35	40
KV	508
Armoured cars:	4819
Tractors:	
STZ-3	3658
STZ-5	7170
Komsomolyets	4041
Komintern	1017
Voroshilovyets	228
Kommunar	504
Other motor vehicles (trucks/cars/etc):	272,600

▼ KV-1 Model 1940 heavy tank

Special Western Military District / Tenth Army / VI Mechanized Corps

The KV-1 was the outcome of a 1938 requirement for a heavy tank to replace the obsolescent T-35. Initial designs were the very similar twin-turreted SMK and T-100, both of which underwent combat trials in the Winter War, together with a single-turreted version of the SMK, designated the KV (Klimenti Voroshilov). These trials indicated the clear superiority of the KV, which entered production as the KV-1 in early 1940.

Specifications

Crew: 5

Weight: 45 tonnes (44.3 tons)

Length: 6.75m (22ft 2in)

Width: 3.32m (10ft 10in)

Height: 2.71m (8ft 9in)

Engine: 450kW (600hp) 12-cylinder diesel Model V-2

Speed: 35km/h (22mph)

Range: 335km (208 miles)

Radio: N/A

Armament: 1 x 76mm (3in) F-32 gun;
   3 x 7.62mm (0.3in) DT MGs

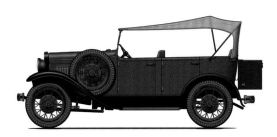

◀ GAZ-A staff car

Special Western Military District / Third Army / XI Mechanized Corps

The GAZ-A was developed from a licence-built copy of the 1927 Ford Model A - approximately 42,000 vehicles were produced between 1932 and 1936. Its simplicity and ability to withstand harsh operating conditions ensured that surviving examples remained in service throughout the war.

Specifications

Crew: 1 driver	Height: 1.8m (5ft 10in)
Weight: 1.08 tonnes (1.06 tons)	Engine: 31.3kW (42hp) GAZ-A 4-cylinder petrol
Length: 3.87m (12ft 7in)	Speed: 90km/h (60mph) on paved road
Width: 1.7m (5ft 6in)	

▶ BA-10 armoured car

Odessa Military District / Twelfth Army / XV Mechanized Corps

It seems likely that as many as 1200 BA-10 heavy armoured cars were produced between 1938 and 1940. Large numbers were captured in the opening stages of Barbarossa and were subsequently taken into German service for anti-partisan duties as the Panzerspahwagen BAF 203(r).

Specifications

Crew: 4	Engine: 37kW (50hp) GAZ-MM
Weight: 5.14 tonnes (5.05 tons)	Speed: 53km/h (33mph)
Length: 4.65m (15ft 3in)	Range: 300km (186miles)
Width: 2m (6ft 6in)	Armament: 45mm (1.8in) gun 20-K plus
Height: 2.20m (7ft 2in)	2 x 7.62 (0.3in) DT MGs

Specifications

Crew: 5	Speed: 26km/h (17mph)
Weight: 52 tonnes (51.1 tons)	Range: 140km (87 miles)
Length: 6.79m (22ft 3in)	Radio: N/A
Width: 3.32m (10ft 10in)	Armament: 1 x M-10 152mm (5.9in) howitzer;
Height: 3.65m (12ft)	1 x 7.62mm (0.3in) DT MG
Engine: 410kW (550hp) Model V-2	
12-cylinder diesel	

▲ KV-2 heavy tank

The horrendous Soviet casualties incurred in assaulting Finnish defences during the Winter War led to demands for a heavy tank with a large-calibre 'bunker-busting' weapon. The hull of the KV-1 was fitted with a massive slab-sided turret mounting a 152mm (5.9in) howitzer, which proved highly effective in trials against captured Finnish bunkers. However, the design was totally unsuitable for the fast-moving armoured warfare of 1941 and most of the 334 examples completed were lost in the opening stages of Barbarossa.

Chapter 9

Defending the Motherland

The Soviet-German Non-Aggression Pact of
August 1939 shocked governments across the world.
They could not have imagined such fierce enemies making a
lasting treaty. Yet from the beginning, both Stalin and Hitler
were trying to twist its provisions for their own advantage.
In less than a year, Stalin seized a great arc of territory to
protect his western frontiers, including eastern Poland,
eastern Finland, the Rumanian provinces of
northern Bukhovina and Bessarabia, Lithuania, Latvia and
Estonia. Hitler had temporarily removed any threat of a war
on two fronts and was able to concentrate his forces for the
campaigns in Norway and France. Significantly, it was in July
1940 that Hitler ordered the first studies for the invasion
that finally evolved into Operation *Barbarossa*, which was
intended to be launched by a total of
152 divisions on 15 May 1941.

◀ **Raising the banner**
A Soviet tank crewman raises a regimental flag on his KV-1 heavy tank during the defence of Moscow,
31 December 1941.

Operation *Barbarossa*
22 JUNE 1941

The overall objective of *Barbarossa* was to trap and destroy the bulk of the Red Army in a series of encirclements in western Russia before finally securing a line from Archangel to Astrakhan.

THREE MAIN ARMY GROUPS would be used in the invasion. Army Group North was to advance from East Prussia through the Baltic states and join with the Finns to take Leningrad. Army Group Centre's initial operations from its concentration areas around Warsaw were intended to clear the invasion route to Moscow as far as Smolensk before swinging north to help the attack on Leningrad. After the city was taken, the advance on Moscow would be resumed. Army Group South, including Rumanian and Hungarian divisions, was tasked with taking the rich agricultural lands of the Ukraine. The invasion's chances of success depended on the 19 Panzer divisions concentrated in four *Panzergruppen*, which

also incorporated the 14 motorized divisions. These had the daunting task of cutting through the massive forces that the Red Army could deploy in European Russia, which totalled perhaps 170 divisions, including up to 60 tank divisions and at least 13 motorized divisions.

The bulk of the Soviet units were deployed close to the frontier, and for almost 50 years the accepted explanation for this was Stalin's obsession with securing his newly conquered territories. German wartime claims that they invaded to pre-empt a Soviet attack have almost always been dismissed as crude propaganda, but this traditional view has been challenged in recent years as new material has

▲ **T-34 company**

A column of T-34 Model 1941 tanks in an assembly area, southern Ukraine, autumn 1941. By this time, the *Luftwaffe* had complete air superiority and such formations were prime targets for devastating dive-bomber attacks.

emerged from Soviet archives. One of the most significant of these documents is the plan formulated by Zhukov in May 1941 on his appointment as Chief of the Soviet General Staff. The introduction to the draft plan stated: 'In view of the fact that Germany at present keeps its army fully mobilized with its rear services deployed, it has the capacity of deploying ahead of us and striking a sudden blow. To prevent this I consider it important not to leave the operational initiative to the German command in any circumstances, but to anticipate the enemy and attack the German army at the moment when it is in the process of deploying...'

This plan proposed a pre-emptive strike by 152 Red Army divisions (including 76 tank divisions and 44 mechanized divisions) against the Axis forces assembling in German-occupied Poland. While this may have been no more than a contingency plan, it is at least possible that Stalin really was intending to make just such an attack.

The attack begins

The German offensive achieved almost complete surprise when it opened on 22 June 1941. The *Panzergruppen* quickly broke through the Soviet lines; General Hoepner's *Panzergruppe* IV played a key role in the destruction of the Soviet III and XII Mechanized Corps before driving through the Baltic states as the spearhead of Army Group North's advance on Leningrad, which was besieged by 8 September. *Panzergruppen* II (Guderian) and

III (Hoth) leading Army Group Centre's advance pulled off a spectacular encirclement east of Minsk, which trapped about 30 Soviet divisions (including six mechanized corps) barely a week after the invasion began. These units were destroyed by the following German infantry divisions over the next three weeks whilst Guderian and Hoth raced on to trap a further 21 Red Army divisions around Smolensk in mid-July.

Kleist's *Panzergruppe* I, forming the main armoured strength of Army Group South, had thrust deep into Ukraine, advancing to within 20km (12.4 miles) of Kiev by 11 July after decimating desperate counterattacks launched by the five mechanized corps of the Kiev Special Military District.

AFV Strength (22 June 1941)	Required	Actual
KV heavy tanks	3528	508
T-34 medium tanks	11,760	967
T-28 tanks (obsolete)	–	500
BT light tanks	7840	6000
T-26 light tanks	5880	11,000
T-37/38/40 scout tanks	476	4222
Total Tanks	29,484	23,197
Armoured cars	7448	4819

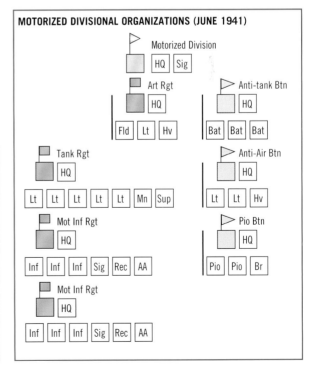

TANK DIVISIONAL ORGANIZATIONS (JUNE 1941)

MOTORIZED DIVISIONAL ORGANIZATIONS (JUNE 1941)

Facing Army Group Centre

By mid-July 1941, Soviet losses were staggering, totalling perhaps 5700 AFVs, 4500 guns and 610,000 prisoners, while the Soviet Air Force had been virtually wiped out, losing almost 6000 aircraft.

COMPLETE GERMAN AIR superiority allowed the *Luftwaffe* to mount unopposed reconnaissance and bombing sorties that disrupted many Soviet counterattacks before they got under way. Those that were delivered were usually badly mishandled, often being made by armour without any proper infantry or artillery support. Soviet armour was generally decimated by German AT units screening the flanks of the advance before the Panzers mopped up the remnants.

On the technical level, the majority of Soviet AFVs were far outclassed by their German counterparts – very few Red Army vehicles had radios, a fact that reinforced their crews' tendency to stick rigidly to detailed orders regardless of rapidly changing battlefield conditions. By contrast, the radio-controlled Panzers could concentrate quickly to defeat the clumsy counterattacks. (The hapless Red Army tank crews soon found that the signal flags on which they were supposed to rely were

▶ **T-40 Model 1940 amphibious light tank**

XI Mechanized Corps / 29th Tank Division

The T-40 was the last Soviet amphibious light tank to enter service before the German invasion. Probably no more than 230 were delivered during 1940/41 before wartime priorities forced production to switch a simpler version, the non-amphibious T-60.

Specifications

Crew: 3	Speed: 45km/h (28mph)
Weight: 5.6 tonnes (5.5 tons)	Range: 350km (215 miles)
Length: 4.43m (13ft 6in)	Radio: 71-TK-3 (when fitted)
Width: 2.51m (8ft 3in)	Armament: 1 x 12.7mm (0.5in) DShK HMG plus
Height: 2.12m (6ft 11in)	1 x coaxal 7.62mm (0.3in) DT MG
Engine: 70kW (52hp) GAZ-202 petrol	

SPECIAL WESTERN MILITARY DISTRICT					
	Tank Div	Mot Div	Commander (Maj-Gen)	Staging Area	Strength
6 MK	4, 7 TD	29 MD	MG Khatskilevich	Bialystok	1000
11 MK	29, 33 TD	204 MD	DK Mostovenko	Grodno	204
13 MK	27, 31 TD	4 MD	PN Akhlyustan	Belsk	300
14 MK	22, 30 TD	205 MD	SI Oborin	Brest	508
17 MK	25, 54 TD	103 MD	MA Petrov	Baranovichi	300
20 MK	26,38 TD	210 MD	N Vedeneyev	Minsk	300

MOSCOW MILITARY DISTRICT					
	Tank Div	Mot Div	Commander (Maj-Gen)	Staging Area	Strength
7 MK	14, 18 TD	1 MD	VI Vinogradov	Vitebsk-Kaluga	1000
21 MK	42, 46 TD	185 MD	DD Lelyushenko	Opochka	98

▾ Reconnaissance Battalion (June 1941)

In common with all Red Army armoured units of the time, the reconnaissance battalion's effectiveness was troubled by the very limited number of radio-equipped AFVs. It was also handicapped by the differing levels of mobility of its three companies – the light tanks had difficulty keeping up with the armoured cars and motorcycles during road moves, but had far better cross-country performance.

Armoured Car Company (15 x BA-10s)

Light Tank Company (17 x T-40s)

Motorcycle Company (12 x motorcycles with 3 mortars)

almost impossible to read accurately under combat conditions.) The thinly armoured BTs and T-26s that formed a high proportion of the total Red Army tank strength at the beginning of the campaign were vulnerable to almost all German tank and AT guns at normal battle ranges. In contrast, the Soviet 45mm (1.8in) could penetrate the up-armoured Panzer IIIH/J and Panzer IVE/F only at point-blank range. Moreover, the three-man turrets of the Panzer III and IV allowed the commander to concentrate on command duties, which gave them a distinct edge in tank-versus-tank actions against most Red Army AFVs – in his two-man turret, the Soviet commander was distracted by having also to act as gunner or loader.

The run of German victories provoked drastic action from Stalin, who had General Pavlov, the commander of the Western Front facing Army Group Centre, arrested and shot on 22 July, together with his Chief of Staff and chief signals officer. This warning was reinforced by the 'dual command' principle, under which a political commissar shared authority with each CO. All too often, the effect was simply to saddle hard-pressed COs with political officers whose fanaticism was matched only by their military incompetence. Corps Commissar Vashugin, for example, while commanding a counterattack by a reinforced tank division from IV Mechanized Corps, actually directed it into a swamp, losing the entire formation in the fiasco.

▶ **T-26 Model 1938 light tank**

XXII Mechanized Corps / 41st Tank Division

The T-26 formed the bulk of the Soviet tank fleet in June 1941, with an estimated 11,000 vehicles in service. Huge numbers were lost during the early stages of Barbarossa and in the winter battles of 1941/42.

Specifications

Crew: 3	Speed: 28km/h (17mph)
Weight: 10.4 tonnes (10.3 tons)	Range: 200km (124 miles)
Length: 4.8m (15ft 8in)	Radio: N/A
Width: 2.39m (7ft 10in)	Armament: 1 x 45mm (1.8in) AT gun;
Height: 2.33m (7ft 8in)	3 x 7.62mm (0.3in) DT MG (coaxial, rear
Engine: 68kW (91hp) GAZ T-26 8-cylinder	turret, turent hatch)
petrol	

▲ **BT-5 Model 1935 fast tank**

IV Mechanized Corps / 32nd Tank Division

This BT-5 is operating in the wheeled mode with the tracks stowed. Almost all the BT series had this capability, but removing and refitting tracks was a lengthy business and was avoided whenever possible.

Specifications

Crew: 3	Speed: 72km/h (44mph)
Weight: 11.5 tonnes (11 tons)	Range: 200km (124 miles)
Length: 5.58m (18ft 3in)	Radio: N/A
Width: 2.23m (7ft 3in)	Armament: 1 x 45mm (1.8in) Model 1932 gun;
Height: 2.25m (7ft 5in)	1 x 7.62mm (0.3in) coaxal DT MG
Engine: 298 kW (400hp) Model M-5	

▶ **T-60 Model 1941 light tank**

I Guards Special Rifle Corps / 4th Tank Brigade

The T-60 Model 1941 was about to enter service at the time of the German invasion. Over 6000 vehicles, including the up-armoured T-60 Model 1942, were produced before the design was superseded by the T-70 in September 1942.

Specifications

Crew: 2	Speed: 45km/h (28mph)
Weight: 5.8 tonnes (5.7 tons)	Range: 450km (280 miles)
Length: 4.1m (13ft 5in)	Radio: N/A
Width: 2.46m (8ft 1in)	Armament: 1 x 20mm (0.79in) TNSh gun;
Height: 1.89m (6ft 2in)	1 x 7.62mm (0.3in) coaxial DT MG
Engine: 2 x GAZ-202 52+52kW (70+70hp)	

Defence of the North

The general picture of Panzer superiority was marred only by the relatively few encounters with T-34s and KVs, both of which were formidable opponents.

APART FROM THE FEW Panzer IIIs armed with the 50mm (2in) L/60 gun, the T-34's sloped armour was almost invulnerable to all German AFV weapons except at point-blank range, whilst the KVs were only effectively countered by 88mm (3.5in) Flak guns or medium artillery.

The KVs had the greatest psychological impact as even single vehicles could impose significant delays on the German advance. On 23/24 June, a single KV-2 of III Mechanized Corps cut the supply route to 6th Panzer Division's bridgeheads across the Dubissa River in Lithuania for over 24 hours. It

▲ **KV-1 Model 1940 heavy tank**

I Mechanized Corps / 1st Tank Division

Lieutenant Kolobanov's tank, one of five KV-1s that mauled the 8th Panzer Division on 14 August 1941 during its advance on Leningrad. The KV-1 was fitted with a 71-TK-2 radio (although even by 1945, not all Soviet AFVs had radios).

Specifications

Crew: 5	Speed: 35km/h (22mph)
Weight: 45 tonnes (44.3 tons)	Range: 335km (208 miles)
Length: 6.75m (22ft 2in)	Radio: 71-TK-2
Width: 3.32m (10ft 10in)	Armament: 1 x coaxial 7.62mm (0.3in) DT
Height: 2.71m (8ft 9in)	MG; 2 x additional 7.62mm (0.3in) DT MGs,
Engine: 450kW (600hp) model V-2	1 ball-mounted in turret rear and 1 ball-
12-cylinder diesel	mounted in hull front

LENINGRAD MILITARY DISTRICT					
	Tank Div	Mot Div	Commander (Maj-Gen)	Staging Area	Strength
1 MK	1, 3 TD	163 MD	ML Chernyavskiy	Pskov	163
10 MK	21, 24 TD	198 MD	Lavrionovich	N of Leningrad	–

SPECIAL BALTIC MILITARY DISTRICT					
	Tank Div	Mot Div	Commander (Maj-Gen)	Staging Area	Strength
3 MK	2, 5 TD	84 MD	AV Kurkin	Vilno	460
12 MK	23, 28 TD	202 MD	NM Shestpalov	Shauliya	690

▼ Heavy Tank Battalion (1941)

When fully up to strength, the heavy tank battalions were the world's most powerful armoured units of their size in 1941. However, only a small number of these battalions were fully operational at the time of the German invasion, as the Red Army had only 508 of the 3528 KVs it required to equip all its units.

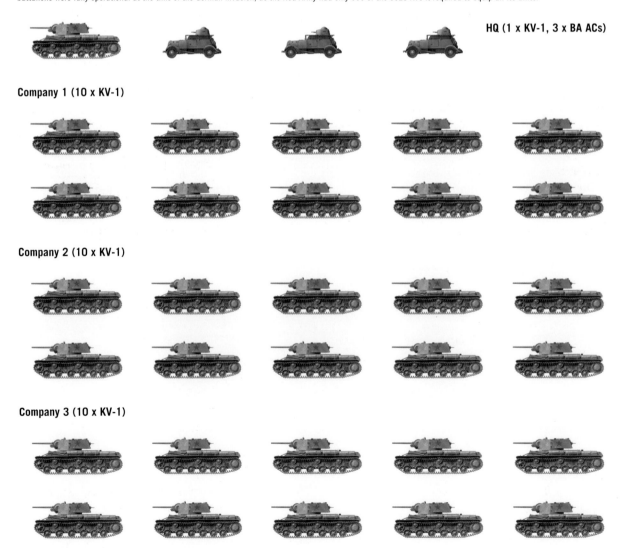

HQ (1 x KV-1, 3 x BA ACs)

Company 1 (10 x KV-1)

Company 2 (10 x KV-1)

Company 3 (10 x KV-1)

proved invulnerable to fire from German tanks and was only destroyed by an '88' brought up to close range while a Panzer platoon acted as a decoy.

In another incident, the leading elements of the 8th Panzer Division were badly mauled on 14 August by five well-camouflaged KV-1s dug in at Krasnogvardeysk near Leningrad. The Soviet commander, Lieutenant Zinoviy Kolobanov, had carefully selected the position to cover the region's only road at the point where it crossed a swamp. Each KV-1 was loaded with some extra ammunition and Kolobanov issued his instructions that the other tanks should hold fire until ordered, to conceal the strength of the detachment.

KV defence

As the 8th Panzer Division's vanguard approached, Kolobanov's KV knocked out the lead tank with its first shot. The Germans assumed that an AT mine was responsible and halted the column, giving Kolobanov the opportunity to destroy the second tank. Only then did the Germans realize that they were under attack. At this point, Kolobanov knocked out the rear German tank, trapping the entire column, which began firing blindly.

Kolobanov's tank was subjected to heavy fire, but German tanks moving off the road bogged down in the swampy ground and became easy targets. A total of 22 German tanks and two towed artillery pieces fell victim to Kolobanov's KV before it ran out

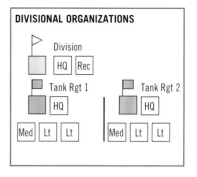

of ammunition. He then called up another KV-1, and 21 other German tanks and AFVs were destroyed before the half-hour battle ended. After the battle, Kolobanov's crew counted a total of 135 hits on their tank, none of which had penetrated the armour.

The short L/30.5 76mm (3in) gun of the early T-34s and KV-Is was soon replaced by a 76mm (3in) L/41.2 with a significantly improved armour-piercing performance. Fortunately for the Germans, many T-34s and KVs had been destroyed in air raids or captured on their rail transporters while moving up to the front and others had been abandoned after breakdowns or had run out of fuel.

Soviet AFV camouflage was generally very simple, with most vehicles finished in dark green (top). A small number of tanks were finished in a variety of disruptive patterns, using random brown or black bands or patches over the standard dark-green finish (lower). Given the devastating effects of the *Luftwaffe*'s air superiority, tank crews soon came to appreciate the benefits of using natural foliage to conceal their vehicles whenever possible.

▲ Improvised Tank Destroyer

Leningrad Garrison, autumn 1941

Shortly after the '900-day siege' of Leningrad began in September 1941, the city's factories began production of a bewildering variety of improvised AFVs. The vehicle illustrated is a tank destroyer based on a partially armoured ZiS-5 lorry armed with a 45mm (1.8in) Model 1937 AT gun and a 7.62mm (0.3in) MG.

Specifications

Crew: 4/5

Weight: (Estimated) 6.1tonnes (6 tons)

Length: 6.06m (19ft 10in)

Width: 2.24m (7ft 4in)

Height: (Estimated) 2.76m (9ft 1in)

Engine: carburettor liquid-cooled

73hp/2300rpm (from I 1944 - 76hp/2400rpme

Radio: N/A

Armament: 1 x 45mm (1.8in) Model 1937

antitank gun; 1 x 7.62mm (0.3in) DT MG

▶ T-30B light tank

I Mechanized Corps / 3rd Tank Division

The T-30B light tank was designed as a simpler, non-amphibious version of the T-40, with thicker armour and an improved armament of a 20mm (0.79in) ShVAK gun and a coaxial MG. Only a small number of vehicles were completed before production switched to the improved T-60 in mid 1941.

Specifications

Crew: 2	Speed: 45km/h (28mph)
Weight: 5.8 tonnes (5.7 tons)	Range: 450km (280 miles)
Length: 4.1m (13ft 5in)	Radio: 71-TK-3 (when fitted)
Width: 2.46m (8ft 1in)	Armament: 1 x 20mm (0.79in) gun;
Height: 1.89m (6ft 2in)	1 x 7.62mm (0.3in) coaxial DT MG
Engine: 2 x GAZ-202 52+52 kW (70+70 hp)	

Retreat from Byelorussia

Theoretically, General Pavlov's Western Front was a match for Army Group Centre since it had 700,000 men, over 2000 tanks (including 383 T-34s and KVs) plus 1900 aircraft, but events were to turn out very differently.

ARMY GROUP CENTRE'S initial offensive into Byelorussia achieved almost complete surprise. Its progress was greatly assisted by *Luftflotte* II's thousand or so aircraft, which effectively destroyed the VVS (Red Air Force) units assigned to the Western Front within a matter of days. Elements of the garrison of the border fortress of Brest-Litovsk,

which included fanatical NKVD units, held out for almost a month, but most of the Western Front's formations were swept away by the speed of the German advance.

Pavlov's initial reaction was to order an immediate counterattack by the Tenth Army, which was concentrated around Bialystok – this predictably

Specifications

Crew: 3	Speed: 86km/h (53mph)
Weight: 14 tonnes (13.2 tons)	Range: 250km (155 miles)
Length: 5.66m (18ft 6in)	Radio: N/A
Width: 2.29m (7ft 6in)	Armament: 1 x 45mm (1.8in) Model 1932 gun;
Height: 2.42m (7ft 10in)	1 x 7.62mm (0.3in) coaxal DT MG
Engine: 373kW (500hp) Model M-17T	

▲ BT-7 Model 1937 fast tank

XIV Mechanized Corps / 205th Motorized Division

A BT-7 Model 1937 in markings typical of the opening stages of Operation Barbarossa. BTs and T-26s formed the bulk of the Red Army's tank strength during the first few months of the campaign.

failed and simply ensured that the Tenth Army would be the first major Soviet formation to be encircled and destroyed when the German Third and Fourth Armies sealed off the Bialystok pocket on 25 June. A further counterattack by VI and XI Mechanized Corps, plus VI Cavalry Corps, was ordered against the flank of *Panzergruppe* III, which was making rapid progress towards Vilnius. The operation was harried by constant air attacks and finally collapsed when the Soviet forces hit a strong German AT screen supported by infantry.

On 28 June, *Panzergruppen* II and III linked up east of Minsk, the Byelorussian capital, which was captured 24 hours later. In six days, they had advanced over 320km (199 miles), covering a third of the distance to Moscow. It was undoubtedly a spectacular achievement – when the remnants of the Soviet Third, Fourth, Tenth and Thirteenth Armies finally surrendered, the Red Army had lost roughly 420,000 men (including 290,000 prisoners) plus 2500 tanks and 1500 guns. However, the Panzers had far out-run their supporting infantry divisions, which were essential for effectively sealing the pocket, and a large number of Soviet troops (possibly as many as 250,000) were able to break out after abandoning their heavy equipment. Nonetheless, it seemed as though the road to Moscow was open.

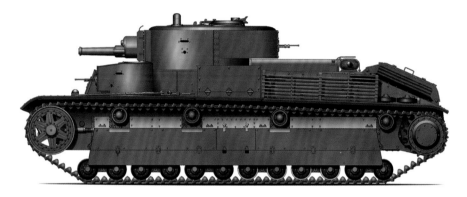

Specifications

Crew: 6	Speed (road): 37km/h (23mph)
Weight: 28 tonnes (27.4 tons)	Range: 220km (137 miles)
Length: 7.44m (24ft 5in)	Radio: N/A
Width: 2.87m (9ft 5in)	Armament: 1 x 76mm (3in) L-10 L/26 gun;
Height: 2.82m (9ft 3in)	4 x 7.62mm (0.3in) DT MGs
Engine: 373kW (500hp) Mikulin M-17 12-cylinder	

▲ T-28 Model 1938 medium tank
XIII Mechanized Corps / 27th Tank Division

One of the 500 T-28s in service during the summer of 1941. By the end of the year, the Soviet armies may well have lost as many as 20,000 of the 22,500 tanks which they held just before the war.

▲ SU-12 76mm (3in) self-propelled gun
XX Mechanized Corps / 26th Tank Division

The SU-12 was the first Soviet SP gun to enter service in the 1930s. It was a simple conversion of the 6x4 GAZ-AAA truck mounting the 76mm (3in) Model 1927 regimental gun, which remained in service until 1945.

Specifications

Note: for Gaz-AAA chassis	Width: 2.36m (7ft 9in)
Crew: 1 driver	Height: 2.1m (6ft 11in)
Weight: 3.52 tonnes (3.46 tons)	Engine: 37kW (50hp) GAZ-M 4-cylinder
Length: 5.34m (17ft 6in)	Speed: 35km/h (21.75mph)

RVGK (HIGH COMMAND RESERVE)					
	Tank Div	Mot Div	Commander (Maj-Gen)	Staging Area	Strength
5 MK	13, 17 TD	109 MD	IP Alekseyenko	Vinista	700
23 MK	44, 48 TD	220 MD	–	–	–
25 MK	50, 55 TD	219 MD	SM Krivoshein	Kharkov	–

▲ GAZ-AAA 6x4 truck

XIII Mechanized Corps / 4th Motorized Division

The 6x4 GAZ-AAA was produced in vast numbers – over 37,000 vehicles were delivered between 1934 and 1943. One of its many roles was that of air defence when armed with the 4M system, which consisted of quadruple 7.62mm (0.3in) MGs on a pedestal AA mounting.

Specifications

Crew: 1 driver, plus 2/3 gun crew

Weight: 3.52 tonnes (3.46 tons)

Length: 5.34m (17ft 6in)

Width: 2.36m (7ft 9in)

Height: 2.1m (6ft 11in)

Engine: 37kW (50hp) GAZ-M 4 cylinder,

Speed: 35km/h (21.75mph)

Armament: quadruple 7.62mm (0.3in) MGs on a pedestal AA mounting

▲ ZiS-6 BM-13-16 'Katyusha' salvo rocket launcher

NKVD Independent Artillery Battery

The ZiS-6 6x4 truck was the first vehicle to mount the 132mm (5.2in) 'Katyusha' salvo rocket launcher. The operational debut of the first seven vehicle batteries was a bombardment of the key Orsha rail junction in July 1941.

Specifications

Crew: 1 (rocket crew in separate vehicle)

Weight: 4.23 tonnes (4.66 tons)

Length: 4.44m (14.57ft)

Width: 0m (0ft)

Height: 2.16m (8.5ft)

Engine: 54kW (73hp) 6-cylinder

Speed: 55km/h (34mph)

Rocket Range: 8.5km (5.28 miles)

Armament: 16 x 132mm (5.2in) M-13 rockets

TRANSBAIKAL MILITARY DISTRICT					
	Tank Div	Mot Div	Commander (Maj-Gen)	Staging Area	Strength
30 MK	58, 60 TD	239 MD	–	–	–

FAR EASTERN FORCE					
	Tank Div	Mot Div	Commander (Maj-Gen)	Staging Area	Strength
26 MK	–	12 MD	–	–	–
27 MK	–	–	–	–	–
29 MK	–	–	–	–	–

▲ **Multi-turreted monster**
A knocked-out T-35 Model 1935, autumn 1941. The vehicle appears to have suffered internal explosions that have blown off both the front MG sub-turret and the rear 45mm (1.8in) sub-turret.

Disaster in the Ukraine

German Army Group South had the largest area of operations in the opening phases of *Barbarossa*, but spearheaded by Kliest's *Panzegruppe* I, were able to cover vast tracts of territory.

THESE SAME VICTORIES led to Hitler's increasing interference in all aspects of operations, with devastating consequences for Germany's chances of victory. Despite Army Group South's success at Uman in early August, where 20 Red Army divisions were surrounded and destroyed, he ordered the suspension of the advance on Moscow so that

Guderian's *Panzergruppe* II was freed to turn south to help complete the conquest of the Ukraine.

Kleist's *Panzergruppe* I was ordered to strike north-eastwards to link up with Guderian and encircle Kiev. These moves caught the Soviets entirely by surprise and their frantic efforts to reinforce Kiev only increased the losses when the city's defenders were finally surrounded on 16 September. Over the next two weeks, they were subjected to constant air and ground attacks before the final collapse.

As a result of this victory, Army Group South was able to complete the occupation of the Black Sea coast as far east as the Crimea and the Sea of Azov, although the heavily fortified naval base of Sevastopol was to hold out until the summer of 1942.

Saving the Soviet tank industry

The Axis advance rapidly threatened the tank factories that were concentrated around Kharkov and Leningrad. Fortunately for the Red Army, pre-war industrialization of the Urals and central Asia had provided a measure of reserve capacity well beyond the reach of the invading German forces.

The trains that brought troops to the front were used to evacuate key factories to safe areas such as the Urals, Siberia and Kazakhstan far from the front-lines. Such evacuations often had to carried out at breakneck speed – the Zaporozhstal steelworks in the Ukraine was stripped bare in 19 days (19 August–5 September), during which time 16,000 railway wagons were loaded with vital machinery, including the especially valuable rolling-mill equipment.

Between July and November 1941, no fewer than 1523 industrial enterprises, including 1360 large war production, plants had been moved to the east. The equipment evacuated amounted to a one and a half million railway wagon-loads. The massive evacuation programme put 300 armament factories temporarily

Tank Divisional Strength (Autumn 1941)	Strength
Reconnaissance battalion:	
T-40	10
Armoured cars	26
Motorcycle company	12
Tank regiments x 2:	
Armoured cars	3
Quad anti-aircraft machine guns	3
KV	10
T-34	20
T-26	60

out of production, but draconian measures quickly restored output. Beria, the head of the NKVD state security apparatus, was appointed to the State Defence Committee (GKO) with responsibility for armament production, and ruthlessly used the millions of prisoners in the Gulag as slave labour.

In addition to running the Gulag, the NKVD played a key role in 'supporting' Soviet scientific research and arms development. Many researchers and engineers who had been convicted for political crimes were held in privileged prisons colloquially known as *sharashkas* (which were much more comfortable than the Gulag), where they continued their work under extremely close NKVD supervision. After their release, some went on to become world leaders in science and technology, notably the aircraft designer Andrei Tupolev, who would produce numerous post-war civil and military

▶ NI Tank

Odessa Garrison, September 1941

The huge losses of Soviet tanks suffered in the initial stages of Operation Barbarossa led to a plethora of improvised AFVs reminiscent of those produced by the Home Guard in 1940. Workshops in the besieged port of Odessa built 68 of these NI Tanks (Na Ispug: Terror Tanks) in August/September 1941 based on the hulls of STZ-5 tractors, which were fitted with boiler plate 'armour' and MG turrets from T-26 Model 1931 tanks.

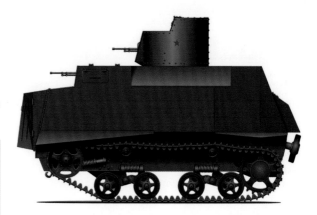

Specifications

Crew: 3

Length: 4.15m (13ft 6in)

Width: 1.86m (6ft 1in)

Height: 0m (0ft)

Engine: 39kW (52hp) 4-cylinder petrol-kerosene

Armament: 2 x 1 x 7.62mm (0.3in) DT MGs, one turret mouted, one in hull

ODESSA MILITARY DISTRICT					
	Tank Div	Mot Div	Commander (Maj-Gen)	Staging Area	Strength
2 MK	11, 16 TD	15 MD	YuV Novoselskiy	Lipkany	350
18 MK	36, 47 TD	209 MD	–	–	350

▶ T-26 M1938 light tank

South-Western Front / Fifth Army / IX Mechanized Corps / 20th Tank Division

At the time of the German invasion, IX Mechanized Corps was entirely equipped with older vehicles such as this T-26.

Specifications

Crew: 3

Weight: 10.4 tonnes (10.3 tons)

Length: 4.8m (15ft 8in)

Width: 2.39m (7ft 10in)

Height: 2.33m (7ft 8in)

Engine: 68kW (91hp) GAZ T-26 8-cylinder petrol engine

Speed: 28km/h (17mph)

Range: 200km (124 miles)

Radio: N/A

Armament: 1 x 45mm (1.8in) AT gun; 1 x 7.62mm (0.3in) DT MG; additional 7.62mm (0.3in) DT MG ball-mounted into turret rear

▶ STZ-3 artillery tractor

47th Tank Division / 47th Motorized Artillery Regiment

The STZ-3 artillery tractor entered production in 1937 and was a standard prime mover for medium and heavy artillery throughout the war.

Specifications

Crew: 1

Weight: 5.1 tonnes (5.02tons)

Length: 3.70m (12 1½in)

Width: 1.86m (6 1 ½in)

Height: 2.21m (7 3in)

Engine: 52hp/1250rpm, straight 4-cylinder petrol start kerosene working OHV, 7461c

Speed: 8km/h (4.97mph)

60km (37.28 miles)

▶ KhTZ tank destroyer

Kharkov Garrison, October 1941

Following the German invasion, the Kharkov Tractor Works produced roughly 60 KhTZ tank destroyers based on the STZ-3 hull and armed with a 45mm (1.8in) gun and coaxial MG in a limited traverse mounting.

Specifications

Crew: 2

Weight (estimated): 7 tonnes (6.89 tons)

Length: 3.70m (12ft 1½in)

Width: 1.86m (6ft 1 ½in)

Height: 2.21m (7ft 3in)

Engine: (52hp) 4-cylinder petrol

Speed: 8km/h (4.97mph)

Range: 50km (31.07 miles)

Armament: 1 x 45mm (1.8in) tank gun Model 1932; 1 x coaxial 7.62mm (0.3in) DT MG

▼ Light Tank Battalion (June 1941)

Five of these battalions were intended to form the tank regiment of each motorized division. By the standards of 1941, such regiments would have been powerful and highly mobile forces, well suited for exploiting breakthroughs made by the more heavily armoured AFVs of the tank divisions. Very few were at full strength in the summer of 1941 and all lacked the training to carry out heir roles effectively.

HQ (3 x BT-5)

Company 1 (17 x BT-5)

Company 2 (17 x BT-5)

Company 3 (17 x BT-5)

Fall of Kiev

September 1941

Operation *Barbarossa*'s most demanding tasks were assigned to Field Marshal von Rundstedt's Army Group South. He had only Kleist's *Panzergruppe* I to provide the armoured punch for a motley collection of forces, including ill-equipped Rumanian, Hungarian and Italian formations.

THESE FACED GENERAL KIRPONOS' South-Western Front, the best-equipped Soviet Front (see table right for units and numbers). The initial Soviet response to the invasion was to activate the Zhukov pre-emptive strike plan. All eight mechanized corps were to destroy *Panzergruppe* I before launching an offensive across the frontier into German-occupied Poland to seize Lublin. Unfortunately for Kirponos, some of his forces had to cover 400km (248.5 miles) to intercept Kleist, a recipe for disaster given *Luftwaffe* air superiority.

Untrained and underequipped

Even worse, most of the mechanized corps were far from being fully trained and equipped formations. At the time, the future Marshal Rokossovsky commanded IX Mechanized Corps, and in his memoirs, he recalled: 'Up to the beginning of the war our corps was up to half of its establishment for personnel, but had not received basic equipment: tanks and motor transport. Here, the stocks were no more than 30 percent of the authorized strength.... Put simply, the corps was unready for military operations as a mechanized unit in any form. There was no way that the Kiev Special Military District (KOVO) headquarters and the General Staff did not know this.'

The five-pointed red star of the Soviet Union was used as a national identification symbol throughout the war on both AFVs and support vehicles. Usually, it would be placed on the turret, hull or glacis plate.

South-Western Front (June 1941)	AFVs (total)	T-34s/KVs
IV Mechanized Corps	979	460
VIII Mechanized Corps	899	170
IX Mechanized Corps	316	–
XV Mechanized Corps	749	133
XVI Mechanized Corps	478	–
XIX Mechanized Corps	453	2
XXII Mechanized Corps	712	31
XXIV Mechanized Corps	222	–

Kirponos initially planned to halt (and hopefully destroy) *Panzergruppe* I with flank attacks by six mechanized corps – a total of 3700 tanks. The concentration of the corps was chaotic – air attacks and mechanical breakdowns took a steady toll of tanks and support vehicles long before they encountered Kleist's Panzers. The Soviet formations were committed to action piecemeal and suffered accordingly. On 26 June, the counterattack was finally made in the Brody-Dubno area. Elements

SPECIAL KIEV MILITARY DISTRICT					
	Tank Div	Mot Div	Commander (Maj-Gen)	Staging Area	Strength
4 MK	8, 32 TD	81 MD	AA Vlasov	Lvov	860
8 MK	12, 34 TD	7 MD	DI Ryabyshev	Dubno	600
9 MK	20, 35 TD	131 MD	KK Rokossovskiy	Zytomierz	700
15 MK	10, 37 TD	212 MD	II Karpezo	Zytomierz	915
16 MK	15, 39 TD	240 MD	AD Sokolov	Ksmenets-Podolskiy	–
19 MK	40, 43 TD	213 MD	NV Feklenko	Zytomierz	160
22 MK	19, 41 TD	215 MD	SM Kondrusev	Rovno-Dubno	–
24 MK	45, 49 TD	216 MD	VI Christyakov	Proskurov	–

of VII, IX, XV and XIX Mechanized Corps were sent against Kleist's flanks, with the aim of cutting the *Panzergruppe* in two. Although the 16th Panzer Division took significant casualties and the *Panzergruppe*'s advance was delayed for several days, by the beginning of July all four mechanized corps had been comprehensively defeated. South-Western Front had sustained over 173,000 casualties,

▶ **GAZ M-1 command car**

XXII Mechanized Corps / 19th Tank Division / HQ

The GAZ M-1 was based on the 1933 US Ford V8-40 and no less than 63,000 vehicles were produced from 1936 until 1941. It was the principal staff car in the early war years and was widely used by Red Army commanders, but its 4x2 configuration was a major drawback under operational conditions.

Specifications

Crew: 1	Height: 1.78m (5ft 10in)
Weight: 1.37 tonnes (1.35 tons)	Engine: 37kW (50hp) 4-cylinder
Length: 4.62m (15ft 2in)	Speed: 100km/h (62.1mph)
Width: 1.77m (5ft 10in)	

▶ **GAZ-61-40 staff car**

XXII Mechanized Corps / 41st Tank Division / HQ

The GAZ-61-40 was the first Soviet 4x4 staff car to enter service, proving far more versatile than earlier 4x2 vehicles.

Specifications

Crew: 1	Height: 1.9m (6ft 3in)
Weight: 1.54 tonnes (1.52 tons)	Engine: 63kW (85hp) 6-cylinder
Length: 4.67m (15ft 3in)	Speed: 100km/h (62.1mph)
Width: 1.75m (5ft 9in)	

Specifications

Crew: 1	Height: 1.97m (6ft 6in)
Weight: 3.46 tonnes (3.41 tons)	Engine: 37kW (50hp) 4-cylinder
Length: 5.33m (17ft 6in)	Speed: 70km/h (43.5mph)
Width: 2.04m (6ft 8in)	

▲ **GAZ-MM 1½-ton truck**

XIX Mechanized Corps / 43rd Tank Division / Transport Battalion

The GAZ-MM was essentially a simplified version of the GAZ-AA, with a more powerful engine and modified cargo platform.

terrifying numbers compounded by the loss of an estimated 4381 tanks and 1218 aircraft.

As Army Group Centre's advance approached Smolensk in mid-July, Hitler became concerned at the potential threat to its southern flank posed by the still substantial Soviet forces in the Ukraine. By late August, he was convinced that Army Group South needed reinforcement to eliminate this threat and ordered Guderian's *Panzergruppe* II into the Ukraine. Guderian made rapid progress, linking up with Kleist on 16 September and trapping the South-Western Front in the vast Kiev pocket, which surrendered 10 days later, with the loss of approximately 665,000 men, 880 tanks and 3700 guns.

▲ GAZ-55 Ambulance

XX Mechanized Corps / 41st Tank Division / Medical Battalion

The GAZ-55 equipped the medical battalions of most tank divisions in 1941.

Specifications

Crew: 2 (10 capacity)	Height: 2.34m (7ft 8in)
Weight: 2.37 tonnes (2.33 tons)	Engine: 4 cylinder, carb., 4-stroke, sv;
Lengt: 5.43m (17ft 1in)	50hp @ 2800 rpm
Width: 2.04m (6ft 8in)	Speed: 70km/h (43.5mph)

▲ ZiS-6 Parm 1b 6x4 mobile workshop

XX Mechanised Corps / 41st Tank Division / Maintenance Battalion

Many Soviet tank losses were due to breakdowns caused by inadequate holdings of spare parts and poor maintenance. The situation was worsened by the destruction of many support vehicles in the opening stages of *Barbarossa*.

Specifications

Crew: 1	Height: (Estimated) 2.74m (9ft)
Weight: (Estimated) 6.73 tonnes (6.62 tons)	Engine: ZiS-5, 6 cylinder, 54Kw (73hp)
Length: 6.06m (19ft 11in)	Speed: 55km/h (34mph)
Width: 2.24m (7ft 4in)	

Defence of Moscow
SEPTEMBER–DECEMBER 1941

As it became clear that the Kiev pocket was doomed, Hitler ordered that Leningrad was not to be stormed, but blockaded and starved into surrender in order to free resources for a renewed attack on Moscow.

T O GIVE THE NEW OFFENSIVE a reasonable chance of success before it became bogged down by the autumn rains, both Army Group North and Army Group South had to be stripped of most of their Panzer units. Guderian's command was re-designated Second Panzer Army and launched the drive on Moscow (code-named Operation *Typhoon*) on 30 September while the other two *Panzergruppen* began their attacks two days later.

Both sides were now feeling the effects of three months of fierce combat – the Red Army's massive losses had forced the disbandment of the Mechanized Corps as early as mid-July and in August most of the surviving armour was concentrated in tank brigades with a nominal strength of 93 tanks in a single tank regiment plus a motor rifle battalion. The tank

▶ **Mobile repairs**

AFV maintenance in the depths of a Russian winter posed major problems for both sides. Here the turret is lifted from a BT-5 in a field workshop during the winter of 1941/42.

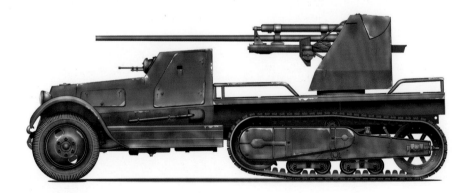

▲ **ZiS-41 tank destroyer**

Trials Unit, Moscow

The ZiS-2 57mm (2.2in) AT gun was mounted on an armoured ZiS 22M halftrack to produce the experimental ZiS-41 tank destroyer. Although the vehicle underwent trials in November 1941, it did not get beyond the prototype stage.

Specifications

Crew: 1/2, plus gun crew of 4/5	Height: 1.97m (6ft 6in)
Weight: 2.54 tonnes (2.5 tonnes)	Armament: ZiS 57mm (2.2in) AT gun; 1 x
Length: 5.33m (17ft 6in)	7.62mm (0.3in) DT MG
Width: 2.1m (7ft)	

Tank Regiment – Personnel Strength (November 1941)	Officers	NCOs	Other
Headquarters	14	5	4
Heavy Tank Company	7	19	–
Medium Tank Company	13	30	–
Light Tank Company x 2, each	7	16	–
Train Elements	5	12	47

Tank Regiment – Vehicle Strength (November 1941)	Strength
Headquarters:	
T-34	1
Motorcycle	2
Truck	1
Heavy Tank Company:	
KV tank	5
Medium Tank Company:	
T-34 tank	10
Light Tank Company:	2
T-40	10
Train Elements:	
Motorcycle	1
Car	1
Cargo truck	22
Shop truck	6
Tractor	4

regiment had a heavy company with KVs, a company of T-34s and a third company equipped with whatever light tanks were available. By September, combat casualties had forced a reduction in the paper strength of these units to 67 tanks, although very few had that many.

On the other side of the lines, the Panzer divisions were in better shape, but their tanks and other vehicles were in need of major overhauls after covering thousands of kilometres across country or over appalling dirt roads. The infantry divisions (which had virtually no motor vehicles) were exhausted by the epic marches needed to keep up with the rapidly advancing Panzers, but all were buoyed up by the sheer scale of their victories and the thought that Moscow was now within reach.

The *Panzergruppen* quickly broke through the Soviet lines and by 9 October had pulled off two more major encirclements, one between Smolensk and Vyazma and the other around Bryansk. These netted a total of 657,000 prisoners, 1241 AFVs plus 5396 guns and effectively opened the road to Moscow. As early as 6 October, a new factor began to help the Red Army's defence of the capital – the first snows fell. At first these rapidly melted, turning the roads to thick, clinging mud that slowed the momentum of the German advance and increased

the already alarming rate of breakdowns. (Hard-pressed *Luftwaffe* transport units were diverted to drop tow-ropes to supply columns floundering along mud-clogged roads.)

Winter halt

Despite the logistical and mechanical problems they faced, Hoth's *Panzergruppe* IV had captured Kalinin by 14 October, cutting the Moscow–Leningrad highway and the main north–south railway. This unwelcome development for the Soviets sparked off a temporary panic in the capital and it was lucky for

▶ **T-40 BM-8-24 'Katyusha' salvo rocket launcher**
9th 'Dzerzhinsky' NKVD Division / Artillery Regiment
One of the 44 T-40 light tanks that were converted to mount BM-8-24 'Katyusha' salvo rocket launchers in the autumn of 1941.

Specifications
Crew: 3

Weight: 5.6 tonnes (5.5 tons)

Length: 4.43m (13ft 6in)

Width: 2.51m (8ft 3in)

Height: 2.12m (6ft 11in)

Engine: 70kW (52hp) GAZ-202 petrol

Speed: 45km/h (28mph)

Range: 350km (215 miles)

Stalin that the German airborne forces were unable to exploit the situation after their heavy losses in the assault on Crete.

By mid-November, sharp frosts had frozen the thick mud solid and restored the Panzers' mobility, which allowed them to make a renewed drive on Moscow. During the next two weeks, the Germans came tantalizingly close to taking the city – *Panzerguppen* III and IV swung north of Moscow, breaching the Volga Canal defence line on 28 November, while away to the south, Guderian's Second Panzer Army had taken Stalinogorsk and cut the capital's main railway link with the south. It looked as it a German victory was in the making.

By 4 December, leading German units were within 45km (28 miles) of Moscow when plummeting temperatures finally brought the advance to a halt. It was so cold that guns could not be fired because oiled parts froze solid. Fires had to be lit under vehicles at night to prevent their engines freezing. Very few German units had proper winter clothing and cases of severe frostbite soared, rapidly exceeding

Snow camouflage tended to be simple and was usually just an overall coat of water-soluble white paint, although once again a minority of tanks sported disruptive camouflage, with the white paint applied in irregular bands or patches. A few vehicles had small red stars on the turret sides and quite a number had various patriotic slogans painted or chalked on hull or turret sides. The slogan on this turret translates as 'For the Homeland!'.

the number of battlefield casualties. Red Army equipment was far less severely affected by the intense cold and deep snow, the virtue of long experience dealing with Arctic-grade winters. The T-34 was fitted with a compressed air starting system that could operate even in the temperatures of -28°C (-19°F) which were not uncommon that winter. The wide tracks of the KV-1 and T-34 resulted in low ground pressure, which allowed them to operate far more easily in powdery, deep snow than German AFVs with their narrower tracks and consequent higher ground pressure.

▲ **Infantry support**

The dire shortages of KV-1s and T-34s during the winter of 1941/42 compelled the Red Army to use even thinly armoured T-40 Model 1940 amphibious light tanks in the infantry support role.

▶ **T-26 Model 1933 light tank**

Western Front / Fifth Army / 20th Tank Brigade

The T-26s, especially older versions such as this, were vulnerable to even the lightest German AT weapons and suffered heavy losses.

Specifications

Crew: 2	Speed: 45km/h (28mph)
Weight: 5.8 tonnes (5.7 tons)	Range: 360km (224 miles)
Length: 4.29m (14ft 1in)	Radio: N/A
Width: 2.32m (7ft 7in)	Armament: 1 x 45mm (1.8in) Model 38 gun;
Height: 2.04m (6ft 7in)	1 x 7.62mm (0.3in) coaxial DT MG
Engine: 2 x GAZ-202 52+52kW (70+70hp)	

▲ **ZiS-30 tank destroyer**

9th 'Dzerzhinsky' NKVD Division / Anti-tank Battery

Roughly 100 Komsomolyets artillery tractors were converted to ZiS 30 tank destroyers in 1941 by the installation of the powerful ZiS-2 57mm anti-tank gun on a shielded limited traverse mounting. These vehicles equipped the anti-tank batteries of tank brigades taking part in the defence of Moscow in 1941/42, but very few survived these winter battles.

Specifications

Crew: 5	Width: 1.86m (6ft)
Weight (estimated): 4.5 tonnes (4.43 tons)	Engine: 37kW (50hp) GAZ-M 4-cylinder
Height (estimated): 2.44m (8ft)	Speed: 47km/h (29mph)
Length: 3.45m (11ft ½in)	Range: 250km (155miles)

▶ **T-26 Model 1938 light tank**

Fifth Army / 20th Tank Brigade

T-26s that survived the summer battles played an important role in the defence of Moscow.

Specifications

Crew: 3	Speed: 28km/h (17mph)
Weight: 10.4 tonnes (10.3 tons)	Range: 200km (124 miles)
Length: 4.8m (15ft 8in)	Radio: N/A
Width: 2.39m (7ft 10in)	Armament: 1 x 45mm (1.8in) AT gun;
Height: 2.33m (7ft 8in)	1 x 7.62mm (0.3in) DT MG; additional
Engine: 68kW (91hp) GAZ T-26	7.62mm (0.3in) DT MG ball-mounted into
8-cylinder petrol	turret rear

▼ Medium Tank Battalion (October 1941)

The Red Army's inability to handle the massive mechanized corps effectively became clear in the opening stages of Barbarossa. As an initial step, all remaining tanks were concentrated in smaller tank divisions, each with two tank regiments. Each regiment fielded a small HQ, together with a single medium tank battalion and two light tank battalions.

HQ (3 x BA ACs, 1 x T-34)

Heavy Tank Company 1 (10 x KV-1)

Medium Tank Company 2 (10 x T-34)

Medium Tank Company 3 (10 x T-34)

Losses

The overall losses on both sides were staggering. The German casualties may well have totalled 800,000 plus 2300 AFVs. These figures were dwarfed by the enormous Soviet losses – roughly 3,000,000 prisoners, 20,000 AFVs and 25,000 guns. Operation *Barbarossa* was failing, and Germany was now trapped into fighting a war on several fronts. The situation was worsened by Hitler who, on hearing of the Japanese attack on Pearl Harbor, chose to declare war on the United States, adding its enormous potential strength to Germany's existing enemies.

 Individual vehicle and unit tactical markings were generally applied in white or yellow to the standard dark green summer camouflage scheme. In winter, they were normally replaced with red markings.

▲ **T-34 Model 1941 medium tank**

Forty-Third Army / 24th Tank Brigade

A T-34 Model 1941 in winter camouflage. The Model 1941 was a marked advance on the Model 1940 – mechanical reliability, armament and armour were all significantly improved.

Specifications

Crew: 4
Weight: 26.5 tonnes (26.2 tons)
Length: 5.92m (19ft 5in)
Width: 3.00m (9ft 8in)
Height: 2.44m (8ft)
Engine: 373kW (500hp) V-2-34 V-12 cylinder diesel
Speed (road): 53km/h (33mph)
Range: 400km (250 miles)
Radio: N/A
Armament: 1 x 76mm (3in) F-34 gun;
2 x 7.62mm (0.3in) DT MGs (bow and coaxial)

Specifications

Crew: 5
Weight: 45 tonnes (44.3 tons)
Length: 6.75m (22ft 2in)
Width: 3.32m (10ft 10in)
Height: 2.71m (8ft 9in)
Engine: 450kW (600hp) V-2 12-cylinder diesel
Speed: 35km/h (22mph)
Range: 335km (208 miles)
Radio: N/A
Armament: 1 x 76mm (3in) F-32 gun;
3 x 7.62mm (0.3in) DT MGs

▲ **KV-1 Model 1940**

Sixteenth Army / 4th Tank Brigade

A KV-1 Model 1940 – with armour up to 75mm (2.9in) thick, it proved almost impervious to German tank and AT guns in the first few months of Barbarossa – 88mm (3.5in) Flak guns or medium artillery frequently had to be deployed to guarantee a kill at anything other than suicidally short ranges.

The Moscow counter-offensives
DECEMBER 1941 – MARCH 1942

As the German advance ground to a halt in early December, the Soviet war machine was beginning to show signs of recovery.

DESPITE MASSIVE SOVIET casualties, a ruthless mobilization programme had brought the Red Army's strength up to 4,196,000 men. However, this measure resulted in a further reduction in industrial manpower, which had already been hit by the loss of population (35,000,000) in territories overrun by Axis forces. Coupled with the disruption caused by the evacuation of war industries, the newly raised and sketchily trained military forces suffered from a dire shortage of all types of weaponry, ranging from tanks to small arms.

In this crisis, there was no chance to rebuild the grandiose mechanized corps with their official tank strengths of over 1000 tanks apiece – the tanks simply did not exist and most surviving commanders were too inexperienced to cope with anything other than the simplest units. The small tank brigades that had replaced all larger formations from August 1941 shrank steadily – in December, they were reduced to 46 tanks apiece, with a further reduction to 42 in January 1942 and a final cut to 27 tanks in February 1942. (These were all 'official strengths' – in practice, many brigades were significantly weaker.)

Winter attack

By 5 December 1941, average temperatures around Moscow had dropped to -12°C (-10°F) and the *Wehrmacht* lay horribly exposed at the end of tenuous

▲ **First winter offensive**
Whitewashed T-34/76 Model 1941 tanks move through the town of Izyum near Kharkov, January 1942.

supply lines, with frostbite casualties climbing to 100,000 during the month. It was the ideal time for a Soviet counterattack and the Red Army had managed to assemble a force totalling 8 tank brigades, 15 rifle divisions and 3 cavalry divisions, many of which had been transferred from the Far East. Stalin was prepared to risk weakening his forces in Siberia and Mongolia as intelligence reports indicated that Japanese attention was indeed focused on South-East Asia and the Pacific.

His innate caution, however, led him to keep substantial formations in the Far East, including roughly 2000 of the 4500 operational AFVs left in the Red Army.

Shortages

Shortages of tanks and artillery, combined with sheer inexperience, led to heavy Soviet casualties, but the initial counterattacks succeeded in pushing back Army Group Centre and eliminating the immediate threat to Moscow. Buoyed up by this success, Stalin started to become over-confident. On 17 December, he ordered more attacks:

- The Leningrad, Volkhov and North-West Fronts were to break the siege of Leningrad.
- An offensive by Fourth Shock Army was to split Army Groups North and Centre and then retake Smolensk.

▲ **T-40 Model 1940 Amphibious Light Tank**

Western Front / Sixteenth Army / 4th Tank Brigade

Despite steadily declining numbers of combat-worthy Soviet AFVs in the winter of 1941/42, Stalin threw the bulk of the Red Army's surviving tanks into a series of offensives. T-40s were highly vulnerable to even the lightest German AT weapons and suffered heavy losses in these actions.

Specifications

Crew: 3	Speed: 45km/h (28mph)
Weight: 5.6 tonnes (5.5 tons)	Range: 350km (215 miles)
Length: 4.43m (13ft 6in)	Radio: N/A
Width: 2.51m (8ft 3in)	Armament: 1 x 12.7mm (0.5in) DShK MG plus
Height: 2.12m (6ft 11in)	1 x 7.62mm (0.3in) DT MG
Engine: 70kW (52hp) GAZ-202 petrol engine	

Specifications

Crew: 3	Speed: 72km/h (44mph)
Weight: 11.5 tonnes (11 tons)	Range: 200km (124 miles)
Length: 5.58m (18ft 3in)	Radio: 71-TK-1
Width: 2.23m (7ft 3in)	Armament: 1 x 45mm (1.8in) Model 1932 gun;
Height: 2.25m (7ft 5in)	1 x 7.62mm (0.3in) coaxial DT MG
Engine: 298kW (400hp) Model M-5	

▲ **BT-5TU Model 1934 Fast Tank**

Western Front / Thirtieth Army / 21st Tank Brigade

A BT-5TU command tank with its prominent 'clothes line' radio aerial that made such vehicles a prime target for German AT guns.

ARMIES, KALININ FRONT	Tank and Mechanized Units
Twenty-Ninth	8 Tank Bde
Thirtieth	58 Tank Div
	107 Motorized Rgt
	21 Tank Bde
	2, 11 Motorcycle Rgt
Front HQ	46 Motorcycle Rgt

ARMIES, WESTERN FRONT	Tank and Mechanized Units
Fifth	18, 19, 20, 22, 25 Tank Bde,
	27 STB, 36 Motorcycle Rgt
Sixteenth	4, 27, 28 Tank Bde
	22 Armoured Train Btn
Thirty-Third	5 Tank Bde
Forty-Third	9, 17, 24 Tank Bde
	31 STB
Front HQ	23, 26 Tank Bde

ARMIES, BRYANSK FRONT	Tank and Mechanized Units
Third	42, 121, 133 Tank Bde
Thirteenth	141, 150 Tank Bde
	38 Motorcycle Rgt
Fiftieth	108 Tank Div
5, 11, 32 Tank Bdes	

Jan 1942	TD	Bgde	Rifle	Mtcl	STB	Train
Kalinin Front	1	2	1	3	–	–
Western Front	–	14	–	1	2	1
Bryansky Front	1	7	–	1	–	–

Soviet High Command) that the current operations were to be supplemented by a general offensive from the Baltic to the Black Sea with the objectives of decisively defeating Army Group North, destroying Army Group Centre, recapturing the Donbass and the Crimea. Zhukov protested that the necessary resources were not there, but he was overruled.

Throughout the rest of January and February, the offensive was maintained at the cost of appalling casualties, pushing Axis forces back between 80km (50 miles) and 300km (186 miles), despite hopelessly inadequate numbers of tanks (including the first Lend-Lease Matildas and Valentines.)

■ An amphibious operation to seize the Kerch Peninsula in the Crimea as a prelude to raising the Axis siege of Sevastopol.

To say the least, these were highly ambitious objectives, but on 5 January Stalin went further, announcing to a horrified meeting of *Stavka* (the

▲ **KV-1 Model 1941**

Kalinin Front / Third Shock Army / 146th Tank Battalion

By the beginning of 1942, the Red Army's tank strength had fallen to dangerously low levels – even the official establishment of the tank brigade had dropped to five KV-1s. This one has had winter camouflage applied.

Specifications

Crew: 5

Weight: 45 tonnes (44.3 tons)

Length: 6.75m (22ft 2in)

Width: 3.32m (10ft 10in)

Height: 2.71m (8ft 9in)

Engine: 450kW (600hp) V-2 12-cylinder diesel

Speed: 35km/h (22mph)

Range: 335km (208 miles)

Radio: N/A

Armament: 1 x 76mm (3in) F-32 gun;

3 x 7.62mm (0.3in) DT MGs

Rzhev–Vyaz'ma offensive
JANUARY–APRIL 1942

The Rzhev-Vyaz'ma offensive was intended to be the blow that would destroy Army Group Centre, building on earlier Soviet progress in gaining ground towards Rzhev.

THE MAIN OPERATION was launched on 8 January with pincer attacks by the Western and Kalinin Fronts, and threatened the Warsaw–Moscow highway within a few days. This was one of the few all-weather roads in the region and was vital since it formed the Fourth Panzer Army's *Rollbahn* (main supply route). By 19 January, Soviet forces had cut this route and were preparing for the next stage in the operation.

While the Western and Kalinin Fronts were pushing their armoured forces to the limit, it was clear, even to Stalin, that these were not strong enough to achieve decisive results. It was decided to drop a full parachute corps – IV Airborne Corps – south of Vyaz'ma to link up with Soviet partisans

▶ **Zhukov with staff**

Marshal Georgi Zhukov (1896–1974) was the archetypal Red Army commander, who rose from serving as a trooper in a Tsarist cavalry regiment in World War I to become a Marshal of the Soviet Union. One of the great commanders of World War II, he was one of the most decorated heroes in the history of both Russia and the Soviet Union.

▲ **BT-5 Model 1934 Fast Tank**

Western Front / Sixteenth Army / 33rd Tank Brigade

Large numbers of thinly armoured BT-5s were among the obsolescent AFVs committed to the Soviet offensives in January and February 1942.

Specifications

Crew: 3	Speed: 72km/h (44mph)
Weight: 11.5 tonnes (11 tons)	Range: 200km (124 miles)
Length: 5.58m (18ft 3in)	Radio: N/A
Width: 2.23m (7ft 3in)	Armament: 1 x 45mm (1.8in) Model 1932 gun;
Height: 2.25m (7ft 5in)	1 x 7.62mm (0.3in) coaxial DT MG
Engine: 298kW (400hp) Model M-5	

and seal off the Rzhev–Vyaz'ma salient, trapping the German Ninth Army and Fourth Panzer Army.

Such airborne operations were always highly risky, even with the benefit of complete air superiority, and in early 1942 it was the *Luftwaffe* that ruled the skies, threatening to massacre the slow, unwieldy Soviet transport aircraft.

Airborne operations

Two battalions from 21st Parachute Brigade and 250th Air Assault Regiment formed the first wave of this part of the operation, but had to be dropped over a period of several days (18–22 January). After I Guards Cavalry Corps cut the Warsaw-Moscow

highway on 27 January, the most that could be done was to drop 8th Airborne Brigade in support – only a third of the intended force. Ironically this was not due to the *Luftwaffe,* but to the diversion of Soviet aircraft to supply Red Army formations, notably Thirty-Ninth Army, which had been cut off by German counter-attacks.

The limited airborne forces that could be deployed were too weak to be effective – immense efforts reopened supply routes to Ninth Army and Fourth Panzer Army. Well-executed German counter-attacks were able to turn the tables, eliminating the threat from 8th Airborne Brigade and trapping a number of other Soviet formations (the final tally included the

Battalion HQ (1 x T-34, 2 x motorcycles, 1 x truck)

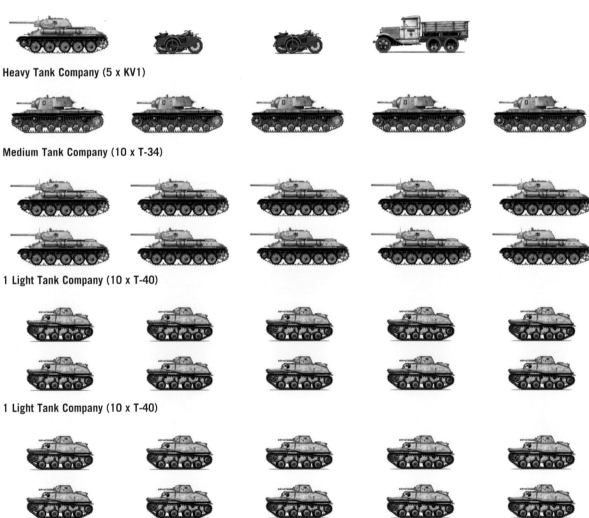

Heavy Tank Company (5 x KV1)

Medium Tank Company (10 x T-34)

1 Light Tank Company (10 x T-40)

1 Light Tank Company (10 x T-40)

Twenty-Second, Twenty-Ninth and Thirty-Ninth Armies) until the front became a complex mass of isolated pockets separated by wide gaps that neither side had the strength to exploit. (The encircled Red Army forces were not finally eliminated until July 1942, when Army Group Centre was able to launch a new offensive, Operation Seydlitz, which netted 50,000 prisoners in addition to capturing 230 tanks and 760 guns.)

Results

As the Soviet operation wound down, it was possible to make some assessment of the results. Army Group Centre had been mauled and had been pushed back by between 80km (50 miles) and 250km (150 miles), but had inflicted over 750,000 casualties, three to four times its own losses. Soviet forces had also lost 957 tanks, almost 7300 guns and 550 aircraft.

Several factors contributed to the Red Army's failure to achieve a decisive victory, including the dire equipment shortages following the loss of so much materiel in the summer and autumn battle, the crisis in weapons production caused by the evacuation of much of the Soviet arms industry to the Urals, and the inexperience – coupled with poor, sometimes non-existent training – which led to units launching costly and unneccessary frontal attacks on well-fortified German positions.

Train (1 x motorcycle, 1 x car, 22 x cargo trucks, 6 x workshop vehicles, 4 x tractors)

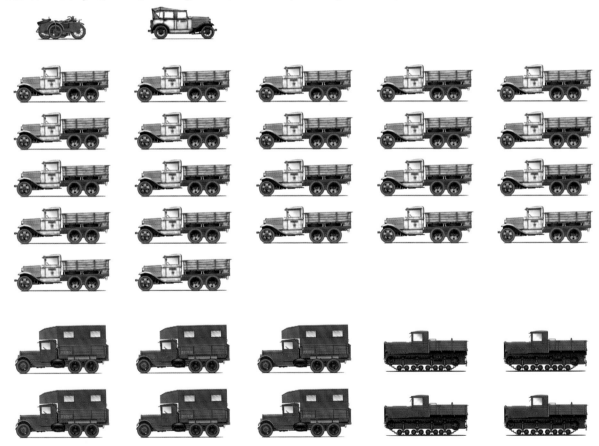

▲ Separate Tank Battalion (1942)

Separate tank battalions (STBs) began to be formed in late 1941, and 100 such units were raised within a few months. They were intended to operate in the infantry support role, freeing the tank brigades for breakthrough and exploitation operations. In practice, logistical support proved difficult due to the mix of tank types, while operational planning was complicated by their differing mobility.

▶ M3A5 medium tank (early production model)

Bryansk Front / XXIII Tank Corps / 114th Tank Brigade

The first M3 Lee medium tanks were delivered to the Red Army in late 1941. They were unpopular due to their high silhouette and vulnerability – their seven-man crews soon dubbed them 'Coffins for Seven Brothers'.

Specifications

Crew: 7

Weight: 29.1 tonnes (32.1tons)

Length: 5.64m (18.5ft)

Width: 2.72m (8.9ft)

Height: 3.12m (10.24ft)

Engine: 253kW (340hp) General Motors 6046 12-cylinder diesel

Speed: 29km/h (18mph)

Radio: N/A

Armour: 57–12mm (2.24–0.47in)

Armament: 1 x 75mm (2.9in) main gun; 1 x 37mm (1.5in) gun; 3 x 7.62mm (0.3in) MGs

Specifications

Crew: 1

Weight: 3.1 tonnes (3.42 tons)

Length: 6.1m (20ft)

Width: 2.25m (7ft 4.5°in)

Height: 2.16m (7ft 1in)

Engine: 54/57kW (73/76hp) ZIS-5/ZIS-5M

Speed: 60km/h (37.3mph)

▲ ZiS-5V 4x2 3-ton truck

Bryansk Front / Twenty-First Army / 10th Tank Brigade / AA Battery

In common with many other Soviet trucks, the ZiS-5 was modified soon after the German invasion to simplify production, the most obvious change being the adoption of a wooden cab. This vehicle serving with an AA battery has been fitted with a 12.7mm (0.5in) DShK HMG.

▶ STZ-5 Medium Tractor

Bryansk Front / Twenty-First Army / 1st Motorized Rifle Brigade / Artillery Battalion

More than 10,000 STZ-5 medium tractors were produced for the Red Army. The type was one of the few tracked artillery tractors specifically designed for the role – the vast majority of were modified agricultural machines.

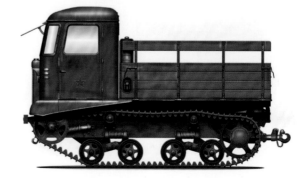

Specifications

Crew: 1

Weight: 5.84 tonnes (5.75 tons)

Length: 4.15m (13ft 7in)

Height: 2.36m (8ft 9in)

Engine: 69.68Kw (52hp) 1MA 4-cylinder petrol

Range: not known

Radio: n/a

▶ M3 light tank

Bryansk Front / XXIV Tank Corps / 130th Tank Brigade

A small number of US M3 light tanks were dispatched from British stocks to the Red Army in 1941. Most of these were lost in the abortive 'Timoshenko Offensive' and the subsequent German advances in the summer of 1942.

Specifications

Crew: 4	Engine: 185kW (250hp) Continental W-670
Weight: 14.7 tonnes (14.4 tons)	7-cylinder radial petrol
Length: 4.45m (14ft 10in)	Speed: 58km/h (36mph)
Width: 2.22m (7ft 4in)	Range: 113km (70miles)
Height: 2.30m (7ft 7in)	Armament: 1 x 37mm (1.5in) gun;
	2 x 7.62mm (0.3in) Browning MGs

◀ T-60 BM-8-24 'Katyusha' salvo rocket launcher

Bryansk Front / XIII Tank Corps / 309th Guards / Mortar Battalion

As the supply of T-34s improved, they began to supplant the ineffective T-60s in tank battalions. Many surplus T-60 hulls were then converted to launchers for 82mm (3.22in) M-8 rockets.

Specifications

Crew: 2	Engine: 2 x GAZ-202 52+52kW (70+70hp)
Weight: 5.8 tonnes (5.7 tons)	Speed: 45km/h (28mph)
Length: 4.1m (13ft 5in)	Range: 450km (280 miles)
Width: 2.46m (8ft 1in)	Radio: N/A
Height: 2.0m (6ft 6in)	Armament: 1 x 82mm (3.22in) rocket launcher

▲ KV-1 Model 1941

South-Western Front / Twenty-Eighth Army / 90th Tank Brigade

As large-scale production began in tank factories evacuated from Western Russia in 1941, the strength of tank formations began to rise. In March 1942, new tank corps began to form, each with an official strength of 20 KV-1s.

Specifications

Crew: 5	Speed: 35km/h (22mph)
Weight: 45 tonnes (44.3 tons)	Range: 335km (208 miles)
Length: 6.75m (22ft 2in)	Radio: N/A
Width: 3.32m (10ft 10in)	Armament: 1 x 76mm (3in) F-32 gun;
Height: 2.71m (8ft 9in)	3 x 7.62mm (0.3in) DT MGs
Engine: 450kW (600hp) V-2 12-cyliinder diesel	

Disaster at Kharkov
MAY 1942

The spring thaws of 1942 gave both sides a chance to take stock and plan their summer campaigns. Stalin turned his attention to the south and ordered Marshal Timoshenko to prepare an attack to recapture Kharkov and disrupt German preparations for their own offensive.

THESE OBJECTIVES were ambitious enough, but Timonshenko was soon expanding them to include the recapture of a great swathe of territory as far west as the Dnieper – a total advance of roughly 250km (155 miles). German intelligence was aware of the build-up of Soviet forces, coming up with an accurate estimate of 620,000 men, 1300 AFVs, 10,000 guns and mortars, supported by 926 aircraft. (The majority of the tanks were concentrated in new tank corps, each with 20 KV-1s, 40 T-34s and

Ninth Army (May 1942)	KV-1	T-34	T-60	Pz III
12th Tank Battalion	2	8	0	0
15th Tank Battalion	1	2	5	0
121st Tank Battalion	3	8	20	3

40 light tanks of various types. Shortly before the offensive, many of these corps were strengthened and grouped into tank armies, which were supposed to have 200–300 tanks each.)

▲ **Matildas at Kharkov**
While the British Matilda was out-classed by later Soviet tanks, surviving vehicles remained in service in the infantry support role until 1944–45.

The Soviet offensive opened on 12 May, with a thrust by South-Western Front from Volchansk to the north of Kharkov, while the Southern Front attacked from the Barvenkovo Salient to the south of the city. The operation was spearheaded by 15 of the Red Army's 20 operational tank brigades, whose initial objective was to envelop Kharkov before driving westwards to the Dnieper. Timoshenko achieved initial successes by sheer weight of numbers, but after making advances averaging 25km (15.5 miles) in the first 48 hours, he was unable to maintain the tempo of the offensive.

One factor in delaying the Soviet progress was a plethora of local counterattacks by Axis forces, backed up by repeated *Luftwaffe* air strikes. However, the Red Army's poor logistical support and planning also played a part, as was apparent on 15 May, when an opportunity to achieve a decisive breakthrough was missed because XXI and XXIII Tank Corps were 25km (15.5 miles) behind the frontline.

They took a further 48 hours to assemble and move up, by which time German reinforcements had arrived to stabilize the threatened sector and the opportunity was lost.

▲ **Infantry Tank Mark II 'Matilda'**

South-Western Front / Thirty-Eighth Army / XXII Tank Corps / 13th Tank Brigade

Matildas were among the first British tanks to be sent to Russia in 1941 under the Lend-Lease programme. A total of 1084 Matildas were shipped, of which 252 were lost in transit on the Arctic convoys.

Specifications

Crew: 4	Engine: Two petrol 6-cylinder AEC engines,
Weight: 26.9 tonnes (29.7 tons)	64.8kW (87bhp)
Length: 5.61m (18ft 5in)	Speed: 24km/h (15mph)
Width: 2.59m (8ft 6in)	Range: 257km (160 miles)
Height: 2.5m (8ft 3in)	Armament: 1 x 40mm (1.57in) gun;
	1 x 7.92mm (0.31in) Besa MG

▶ **Universal Carrier Mark I**

Bryansk Front / XVI Tank Corps / 107th Tank Brigade

An initial consignment of 330 Universal Carriers arrived in Soviet ports during the autumn of 1941, with deliveries totalling over 2500 vehicles by 1945. This example retains its Boys AT rifle, although the Bren Gun in the rear compartment has been replaced with a DP MG.

Specifications

Crew: 2/3	Speed: 48km/h (30mph)
Weight: 3.81 tonnes (3.75 tons)	Range: 250km (150miles)
Length: 3.65m (12ft)	Radio: N/A
Width: 1.92m (6ft 4in)	Armament: 1 x Boys AT rifle, plus 1 x 7.62mm
Height: 1.57m (5ft 2in)	(0.3in) Degtyarev DP MG
Engine: 85kW (85hp) Ford V-8 petrol	

Nonetheless, Timoshenko's forces were still advancing on 17 May when Kleist's Army Group A (First Panzer Army and Seventeenth Army) launched a devastating counter-offensive against the southern flank of the Barvenkovo Salient. Over the next few days, Stalin rejected increasingly urgent requests from Timoshenko to call off the offensive and a bizarre situation developed as Soviet armour continued to advance westwards as Kleist's Panzers were cutting through the neck of the salient.

By the time that Timoshenko received belated authorization to retreat, it was too late – the salient was sealed off on 23 May and during the next six days the bulk of the trapped units were virtually wiped out. Red Army losses probably totalled 208,000 men – 22 rifle divisions, 7 cavalry divisions and 15 tank brigades were destroyed. Equipment losses were equally severe – some 1200 tanks, 1600 guns, 3200 mortars and 540 aircraft.

Inexperience and fear

The disaster at Kharkov vividly demonstrated the fragility of the Red Army at this stage of the war. Its ranks were full of barely trained conscripts and the officer corps, emasculated by the purges, was struggling to learn the basics of armoured warfare while campaigning against a sophisticated enemy.

All ranks went in fear of the NKVD – whose malign influence was personified by Lev Mekhlis, the *Stavka* representative to the Crimean Front, who was also Head of the Main Political Administration of the Red Army. He was an arrogant bully who quarrelled with General Kozlov, the Front commander, and engineered the dismissal of his highly competent chief of staff, the future Marshal Tolbukhin.

Mekhlis was largely responsible for the Soviet failure to attack von Manstein's force besieging Sevastopol when it was at its most vulnerable in early 1942 and, when the Germans counter-attacked on

▶ **T-60 Model 1941**

South-Western Front / Twenty-Eighth Army / 90th Tank Brigade, Kharkov,
May 1942

This immobilized and abandoned T-60 has distinctive air recognition markings on the turret hatch. Such markings were temporarily applied for specific operations to minimize the risk from friendly fire.

Specifications

Crew: 2	Speed: 45km/h (28mph)
Weight: 5.8 tonnes (5.7 tons)	Range: 450km (280 miles)
Length: 4.1m (13ft 5in)	Radio: N/A
Width: 2.46m (8ft 1in)	Armament: 1 x 20mm (0.79in) TNSh gun;
Height: 1.89m (6ft 2in)	1 x 7.62mm (0.3in) coaxial DT MG
Engine: 2 x GAZ-202 52+52kW (70+70hp)	

▶ **T-60 Model 1942**

South-Western Front / Fifth Army / I Tank Corps

The T-60 Model 1942 was up-armoured in an attempt to improve its battlefield survivability. Disc pattern road wheels replaced the spoked type fitted to the Model 1941.

Specifications

Crew: 2	Speed: 45km/h (28mph)
Weight: 5.8 tonnes (5.7 tons)	Range: 450km (280 miles)
Length: 4.1m (13ft 5in)	Radio: N/A
Width: 2.46m (8ft 1in)	Armament: 1 x 20mm (0.79in) TNSh gun;
Height: 1.89m (6ft 2in)	1 x 7.62mm (0.3in) coaxial DT MG
Engine: 2 x GAZ-202 52+52kW (70+70hp)	

8 May, his incompetence contributed to the destruction of the Crimean Front in barely 10 days.

Uncoordinated response

As at Kharkov, there was little coordination between the Soviet tank brigades, whose 350 AFVs were committed to action piecemeal, negating their numerical superiority over the sole German armoured formation, the under-strength 22nd Panzer Division, which was largely equipped with obsolescent Panzer 38(t)s.

Once again, Soviet losses were staggering – three armies (Forty-Fourth, Forty-Seventh and Fifty-First) totalling 21 divisions had been broken and von Manstein's forces had taken 170,000 prisoners, as well as capturing 258 tanks and over 1100 guns.

▲ **KV-1 Model 1941**

South-Western Front / Twenty-First Army / 10th Tank Brigade

Although Soviet tank production dramatically increased in the first half of 1942, this was not matched by comparable improvements in strategic or tactical skill. A high proportion of the new Red Army armoured formations were destroyed in Timoshenko's over-ambitious Kharkov offensive in May 1942.

Specifications

Crew: 5	Speed: 35km/h (22mph)
Weight: 45 tonnes (44.3 tons)	Range: 335km (208 miles)
Length: 6.75m (22ft 2in)	Radio: N/A
Width: 3.32m (10ft 10in)	Armament: 1 x 76mm (3in) F-32 gun;
Height: 2.71m (8ft 9in)	3 x 7.62mm (0.3in) DT MGs
Engine: 450kW (600hp) 12-cylinder V-2 diesel	

Specifications

Crew: 4	GMC 6004 diesel
Weight: 16 tonnes (17.6 tonnes)	Speed: 24km/h (15mph)
Length: 5.4m (17ft 9in)	Range: 145km (90 miles)
Width: 2.6m (8ft 8in)	Armament: 1 x 40mm (1.57in) gun;
Height: 2.2m (7ft 6in)	1 x 7.92mm (0.31in) Besa MG
Engine: 131–210hp (97–157kW)	

▲ **Infantry Tank Mark III, Valentine Mark V**

South-Western Front / Sixth Army / XXI Tank Corps / 64th Tank Brigade

The Valentine was regarded by the Red Army as the best British tank supplied under Lend-Lease. A total of 3782 Valentines of all Marks were shipped to Soviet Russia between 1941 and 1945, of which 320 were lost en route.

Retreat to the Don

In April 1942, Hitler had chosen to make his main effort in the south with the aim of taking Stalingrad and driving deep into the Caucasus to seize the oilfields of Maikop, Grozny and Baku.

TIMOSHENKO'S OFFENSIVE at Kharkov had disrupted preparations for the offensive, but the sheer scale of the Soviet disaster (almost 75 per cent of the Red Army's tanks were destroyed) meant that there was very little left to oppose the Panzers as they struck deep into southern Russia on 28 June.

By 5 July, Hoth's Fourth Panzer Army had taken Voronezh, reinforcing Stalin's instinctive belief that Moscow was still the primary German objective. While *Stavka* concentrated on directing reserves to counter the illusory threat to Moscow, von Paulus' Sixth Army was making for Stalingrad and Kleist's First Panzer Army was well on its way to the oilfields of the Caucasus.

The psychological impact of these events was sharpened by the first indications that the *Panzerwaffe* was regaining lost ground in the gun/armour race. After the triumphant advances of 1941 ground to a halt in the winter snows, German planners realized that radical measures were needed to meet the threat of the T-34 and KV-1. As a first step, production of the 50mm (2in) L/60 and its tungsten-cored ammunition was stepped up to ensure that the Panzer III stood some chance against these opponents. Frantic efforts also went into replacing the 75mm (2.9in) L/24 of the Panzer IV with a long-barrelled

SW FRONT					
Tank Brigades	**KV1**	**T-34**	**M3 Light**	**T-60**	**Total**
6th Gds	5	7	–	16	28
65th	24	–	–	23	47
90th	7	3	15	15	40
Total	36	10	15	54	115

NINTH ARMY						
Tank Brigades	**T-34**	**BT5/T-26**	**T-60**	**Matilda**	**Valentine**	**Total**
12th	2	–	–	–	–	2
71st STB	–	20	24	2	5	51
132nd STB	3	–	3	1	4	11
Total	5	20	27	3	9	64

L/43 version, but this took time and it was mid-1942 before the first deliveries were made to front-line units. At the same time, work was in hand to rearm the StuG III with the L/43 and up-gunned versions were produced alongside the new Panzer IVs.

New armoured tactics

At the end of June, General Fedorenko, the head of the Red Army's armoured force, issued a directive on the principles for its future employment. Whilst

▶ **M3A5 medium tank (late production vehicle)**

Voronezh Front / Thirty-Eighth Army / 192nd Tank Brigade

This late production M3A5 has a long-barrelled M3 75mm (2.9in) gun. Both the gun and the turret armament have early stabilization systems fitted to improve accuracy when firing on the move.

Specifications

Crew: 7

Weight: 29.1 tonnes
   (32.1 tons)

Length: 5.64m (18.5ft)

Width: 2.72m (8.9ft)

Height: 3.12m (10.24ft)

Engine: 254kW (340hp) General
   Motors 6046 12-cylinder diesel

Speed: 29km/h (18mph)

Range: 193km (120 miles)

Armour: 57–12mm (2.2–0.47in)

Armament: 1 x 75mm (2.9in)
   main gun; 1 x 37mm (1.5in)
   gun; 3 x 7.62mm (0.3in) MGs

hardly original, they represented a willingness to learn from German practice, calling for the use of armour *en masse* against strategic targets. There was a new emphasis on the importance of surprise, the exploitation of favourable terrain and a call for logistical support capable of sustaining prolonged advances. For the time being, these were little more than hopes for the future – the pressing issue was whether the Red Army could survive long enough to put them into practice.

As the Germans advanced, a few of the remaining Soviet tank units fought effective delaying actions, such as that at the River Resseta in July, where the 11th and 19th Panzer Divisions had to tackle well dug-in AT guns while fending off repeated counterattacks directed against their flanks by small groups of T-34s.

However, across most of the vast front, the impression was one of the Red Army almost on the point of collapse. The First Tank Army and Sixty-Second Army were pinned against the Don in a classic double envelopment by Paulus' Sixth Army. Both the Stalingrad Front and the Southern Front temporarily collapsed, with the loss of 350,000 men and over 2000 AFVs.

Premature triumphalism

On 20 July, Hitler joyously announced 'The Russian is finished!' and even the commander

Thirty-Eighth Army (April 1942)						
Tank Brigades	KV1	T-34	T-60	Matilda	Valentine	Total
3rd	1	2	4	0	0	7
13th	0	0	0	0	1	1
36th	5	1	13	1	9	29
133rd	0	0	0	0	0	0
156th	2	0	0	0	0	2
159th	0	0	20	0	28	48
168th	3	10	17	0	0	30
92nd STB	7	0	7	0	0	14
Total	18	13	61	1	38	131

of the *Oberkommando des Heeres* (Army High Command; OKH), the cautious, scholarly General Halder, agreed. 'I must admit, it looks like it.' Such impressions were not confined to the high command – a Panzer NCO commented that the situation on the ground was different than in 1941. 'It's more like Poland. The Russians aren't nearly so thick on the ground. They fire their guns like madmen, but they don't hurt us.'

Order 227

Stalin was certainly conscious that the string of defeats and a seemingly unstoppable German advance had seriously affected morale – on 28 July, he issued Order No. 227, which instructed commanders to

▲ **ZiS-6-BZ Fuel Tanker**

Voronezh Front / XVIII Tank Corps / 180th Tank Brigade / Transport Company

The Red Army's supply columns suffered heavy losses throughout much of 1942, both from air attacks and the rapid German advances to the Don and the Caucasus.

Specifications

Crew: 1

Weight: 4.23 tonnes (4.66 tons)

Length: 6.06m (19.9ft)

Width: 2.23m (7.33ft)

Height: 2.16m (7ft 1in)

Engine: 54kW (73hp) 6-cylinder

Speed: 55km/h (34mph)

'decisively eradicate retreat attitude in the troops' and to 'remove from office and send to *Stavka* for court-martial those army commanders who allowed their troops to retreat without authorization'.

Each Front was instructed to form penal battalions and companies for the punishment of offenders and create well-armed guard units (*zagradotryads*), deploying them in the rear of unreliable divisions with power to execute 'panic-mongers and cowards' on the spot. An estimated 13,500 Soviet troops were executed in the three months following Stalin's order, while the number of penal companies grew until there were 1049 in the Red Army as a whole. The overall total of those sentenced to often fatal service in penal units throughout the war may well have exceeded 400,000.

▲ **KV-1 Model 1942**

Voronezh Front / XVIII Tank Corps / 180th Tank Brigade

Following the loss of 1200 tanks in the abortive Kharkov offensive, Soviet armour was in no condition to do more than fight delaying actions in the summer and autumn of 1942.

Specifications

Crew: 5	Speed: 35km/h (22mph)
Weight: 45 tonnes (44.3 tons)	Range: 335km (208 miles)
Length: 6.75m (22ft 2in)	Radio: N/A
Width: 3.32m (10ft 10in)	Armament: 1 x 76mm (3in) F-32 gun;
Height: 2.71m (8ft 9in)	3 x 7.62mm (0.3in) DT MGs
Engine: 450kW (600hp) 12-cylinder diesel Model V-2	

Specifications

Crew: 4	Speed (road): 53km/h (33mph)
Weight: 26.5 tonnes (26.2 tons)	Range: 400km (250 miles)
Length: 5.92m (19ft 5in)	Radio: N/A
Width: 3.0m (9ft 8in)	Armament: 1 x 76mm (3in) F-34 gun;
Height: 2.44m (8ft)	2 x 7.62mm (0.3in) DT MGs (bow and coaxial)
Engine: 373kW (500hp) V-2-34 V-12 diesel	

▲ **T-34 Model 1942**

Voronezh Front / XVIII Tank Corps / 181st Tank Brigade

The T-34 Model 1942 was essentially the same as the Model 1941, but incorporated numerous small changes to simplify production.

Specifications

Crew: 1

Weight: 5.25 tonnes (5.79 tons)

Length: 6.09m (20ft)

Width: 2.36m (7.74ft)

Height: 2.17m (7.12ft)

Engine: 57kW (76hp) ZiS-5m 6-cylinder

Speed: 45km/h (28mph)

Range: 500km (311miles)

▲ **ZiS-42M 2½-ton cargo halftrack**

Voronezh Front / Thirty-Eighth Army / 192nd Tank Brigade / Supply Company

Roughly 5000 ZiS-42M halftracks were produced between 1942 and 1945, although Lend-Lease US halftracks were much preferred for their armour protection and the superior cross-country capability conferred by their powered front axles.

Defending Stalingrad and Caucasus
JUNE–NOVEMBER 1942

Despite Stalin's orders forbidding retreat and surrender, the Germans continued their advance as the *Fall Blau* (Case Blue) offensive ground its way towards south-east Russia.

THE SHEER SCALE of the advance soon began to cause problems for the Germans as the Panzers outran their supply lines. Hitler's interference had also delayed the advance. The Fourth Panzer Army had been temporarily diverted from its assigned role of spearheading the advance on Stalingrad to 'assist the early passage of the lower Don'.

Logistical problems were causing far more delay to the First Panzer Army than the shaky Soviet defence, and these were compounded by the arrival of the Fourth Panzer Army, which created a monumental traffic jam at the Don crossings. In Hoth's absence, the advance on Stalingrad slowed, allowing the Soviets just enough time to reinforce the city's garrison before the Germans arrived in August. The Sixty-Second Army defending Stalingrad had 54,000 men, 900 guns and 110 tanks. Thus, instead of taking a largely undefended city, more and more

German forces were sucked into fierce street fighting, in which their rate of advance slowed to no more than a few hundred metres a day.

As the German Sixth Army and Fourth Panzer Army became ever more deeply committed to fighting in Stalingrad itself, responsibility for protection of their long, vulnerable flanks had to be assigned to comparatively weak and ill-equipped satellite armies. The Eighth Italian Army and Third Rumanian Army held a long sector of front north-west of the city,

XXII TANK CORPS (July 1942)				
	T-34	T-60	T-70	Total
173rd TK Bde	32	13	21	66
176th TK Bde	32	0	16	48
182nd TK Bde	32	13	21	66
Total	96	26	58	180

SOUTH-EASTERN FRONT – operational tanks (Aug 1942)				
Sixty-Fourth Army, XIII Tank Corps	Registered	Operable	In Repair	Lost
6th Gd Bde				
T-34	44	13	17	14
13th Tank Bde				
T-34	44	11	12	21
254th Tank Bde				
T-34	32	6	15	11
T-70	16	4	7	5
133rd Tank Bde				
KV-1	40	38	2	0
Total Corps	136	34	51	51

Tank Brigade (July 1942)	Men	T-34	T-60/70
Brigade HQ and Company	24	1	–
Medium Tank Battalion:	151	–	–
Battalion HQ and Platoon	23	1	–
Medium Tank Company x 3	132	30	–
Supply and Trains Group	39	–	–
Light Tank Battalion:	146	–	–
Battalion HQ and Platoon	–	–	1
Light Tank Company x 2	–	–	20
Supply and Trains Group	–	–	–

whilst the Fourth Rumanian Army held the line south of Stalingrad.

At first, Kleist's drive into the Caucasus achieved spectacular results – the First Panzer Army took the first of the oilfields at Maikop on 9 August and pushed on towards Grozny and Baku. Stalin was conscious of the potentially disastrous political implications of the German advance – Turkey might well join the Axis and launch an attack that would almost certainly destroy the hard-pressed Trans-Caucasus Front. There was also the possibility of a revolt against Soviet rule throughout the region, which was taken so seriously that Beria was sent there to supervise an urgent programme of repression.

However, the dire consequences of Hitler's decision to advance on Stalingrad and the Caucasus simultaneously rapidly became apparent. Essential supplies could only be brought up by continual improvisation – harassed quartermasters resorted to a motley collection of pack animals to transport vital supplies. Distances in this region were so vast that in many areas there were no conventional front-lines. Armoured patrols from both sides roamed the Kalmyk Steppe, the Soviets seeking Kleist's vulnerable supply lines, while the Germans attacked targets such as the Baku–Astrakhan railway. Ultimately, so many resources were diverted to Stalingrad that Kleist was robbed of any chance of taking the remaining oilfields.

▲ **KV-1S heavy tank**

South-Eastern Front / Front HQ / 133rd Independent Tank Brigade

The KV-1S (Skorostniy: Speedy) was a final attempt to update the KV-1, which was rapidly becoming out-classed by improved German AFVs and AT guns. The turret layout was re-arranged and the transmission up-rated to improve road speed and cross-country performance.

Specifications

Crew: 5

Weight: 42.5 tonnes (41.8 tons)

Length: 6.75m (22ft 2in)

Width: 3.32m (10ft 10in)

Height: 2.71m (8ft 9in)

Engine: 450kW (600hp) Model V-2
12-cylinder diesel

Speed: 45km/h (28mph)

Range: 250km (155 miles)

Radio: N/A

Armament: 1 x 76mm (3in) ZIS-5 gun;
3 x 7.62mm (0.3in) DT MGs

Specifications

Crew: 4

Weight: 30.9 tonnes (30 tons)

Length: 5.92m (19ft 5in)

Width: 3.00m (9ft 8in)

Height: 2.44m (8ft)

Engine: 373kW (500hp) V-2-34 V-12 cylinder diesel

Speed (road): 53km/h (33mph)

Range: 465km (290 miles)

Radio: N/A

Armament: 1 x 76mm (3in) L-40 gun;

    2 x 7.62mm (0.3in) DT MGs (bow and coaxial)

▲ T-34 Model 1943

South-Eastern Front / Sixty-Fourth Army / XIII Tank Corps

Despite its designation, the T-34 Model 1943 actually entered service in 1942. The most obvious change from earlier versions was the enlarged turret, which gave welcome extra space for the crew. This T-34 has all-metal road wheels, a result of the dire shortage of rubber that affected Soviet war industries for much of 1942.

▲ T-34 Model 1943

South-Eastern Front / Sixty-Second Army / XXIII Tank Corps / 6th Tank Brigade

The use of all-metal road wheels was soon found to create harmonic vibrations when the T-34 was running at high speed, which loosened parts and caused engine damage. Rubber-rimmed road wheels had to be reinstated in the first and fifth positions to solve the problem.

Specifications

Crew: 4

Weight: 30.9 tonnes (30 tons)

Length: 5.92m (19ft 5in)

Width: 3.00m (9ft 8in)

Height: 2.44m (8ft)

Engine: 373kW (500hp) V-2-34 V-12 diesel

Speed (road): 53km/h (33mph)

Range: 465km (290 miles)

Radio: N/A

Armament: 1 x 76mm (3in) L-40 gun;

    2 x 7.62mm (0.3in) DT MGs (bow and coaxial)

▶ Harley-Davidson 42WLA motorcycle

Stalingrad Front / Sixty-Fourth Army / HQ XIII Tank Corps

The Red Army greatly appreciated the reliability of the WLA and received a total of 26,000 machines by 1945.

Specifications

Crew: 1/2

Weight: 191kg (512lb)

Engine: 17kW (23hp) V-2

Speed: 105km/h (65.2mph)

Range: 201km (125miles)

STALINGRAD FRONT (Oct 1942)	Operable	Inoperable
62 Army, 6 Gds Tk Bde:		
T-34	9	5
T-60	–	2
T-70	4	1
64 Army, XIII TK Corps, 13 Tk Bde:		
T-34	11	2
T-60	–	–
T-70	2	1
64 Army, XIII Corps, 56 Tk Bde:		
T-34	4	2
T-60	1	1
T-70	4	1
Total XIII Corps:		
T-34	15	4
T-60	1	1
T-70	6	2
51 Army, 254 Tk Bde:		
T-34	1	–
T-60	9	–
T-70	–	–
57 Army, 155 Tk Bde:		
T-34	3	–
T-60	9	–
T-70	–	–
Total for four armies:		
T-34	28	9
T-60	19	3
T-70	10	2

▲ **Appliqué armour**

T-34 Model 1941s with appliqué armour fitted to the hull front and driver's hatch in response to the threat posed by increasing numbers of German towed and SP 75mm (2.9in) AT guns.

▶ **Light Tank Mark VII 'Tetrarch'**

North Caucasus Front / Forty-Fifth Army / 151st Tank Brigade

A consignment of 20 Tetrarchs from British Army stocks were supplied to the Red Army via Iran in 1941. They were deployed in the Caucasus, where their cross-country agility could be put to good use and there was little threat from heavier Axis AFVs.

Specifications

Crew: 3
Weight: 7.5 tonnes (7.4t)
Length: 4.04m (13ft 3in)
Width: 2.31m (7ft 7in)
Height: 2.12m (6ft 11in)
Engine: 123kW (165hp) Meadows 12-cylinder petrol

Speed: 42km/h (28mph) off-road
Range: 224km (140miles)
Radio: N/A
Armament: 1 x 40mm (1.57in);
 1 x 7.92mm (0.3in) Besa MG

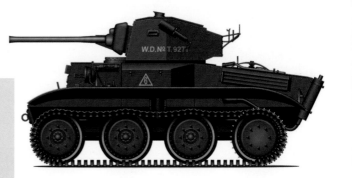

▼ Tank Brigade (July 1942)

At this stage of the war, there were still insufficient T-34s and light tanks had to be used to make up numbers. Tactical handling of the brigade was hampered by a shortage of radios, which were normally issued only to platoon commanders and above, leaving two-thirds of all tanks without radios. In addition to the tanks illustrated, each tank brigade included a 400-strong motorized rifle battalion, an AT battery and a mortar company.

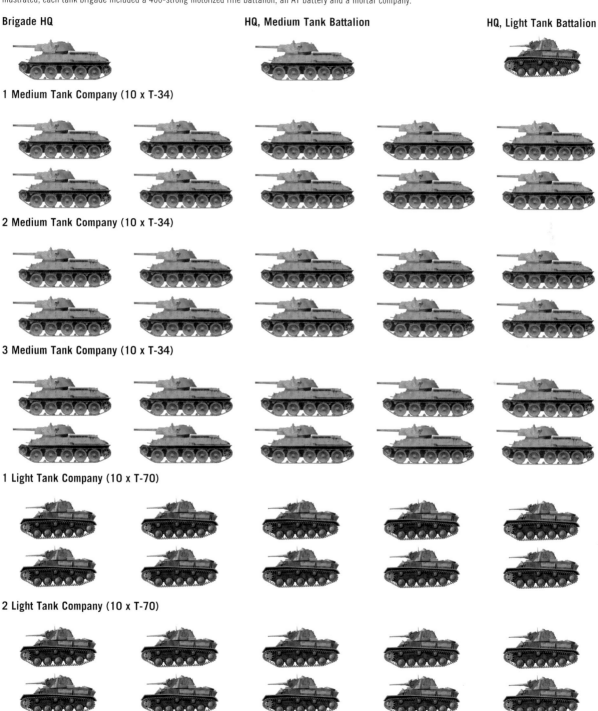

Brigade HQ

HQ, Medium Tank Battalion

HQ, Light Tank Battalion

1 Medium Tank Company (10 x T-34)

2 Medium Tank Company (10 x T-34)

3 Medium Tank Company (10 x T-34)

1 Light Tank Company (10 x T-70)

2 Light Tank Company (10 x T-70)

▶ T-70 Model 1942 light tank

Stalingrad Front / Sixty-Second Army / XIII Tank Corps / 56th Tank Brigade

The T-70 was the final Soviet light tank to enter service in quantity during the war. While the 45mm (1.8in) gun and thicker armour were welcome advances on earlier designs, the retention of a one-man turret severely limited the type's battlefield performance.

Specifications

Crew: 2

Weight: 5.8 tonnes (5.7 tons)

Length: 4.29m (14ft 1in)

Width: 2.32m (7ft 7in)

Height: 2.04m (6ft 7in)

Engine: 2 x GAZ-202 52+52kW (70+70hp)

Speed: 45km/h (28mph)

Range: 360km (224 miles)

Radio: N/A

Armament: 1 x 45mm (1.8in) Model 38 gun;
　　　　　 1 x 7.62mm (0.3in) coaxial DT MG

▶ Harley-Davidson 42WLA motorcycle with M72 side car

South-Eastern Front / Sixty-Second Army / XXIII Tank Corps / 13th Tank Brigade / Motorized Rifle Battalion / Mortar Company

Most of the Red Army's WLAs were fitted with M72 sidecars and a proportion of these combinations were modified to mount the standard 82mm (3.2in) mortar.

Specifications

Crew: 3

Engine: 17kW (23hp) V-2 cylinder 750cc (45ci)

Speed: 0km/h (0mph)

Armament: 1 x 82mm (3.2in) mortar;
　　　　　 1 x 7.62mm (0.3in) DP MG

Operation *Uranus*
NOVEMBER 1942

In September 1942, Stalin approved plans for Operation *Uranus*, an ambitious counter-offensive intended to punch through the Third and Fourth Rumanian armies, before enveloping the German Sixth Army and Fourth Panzer Army around Stalingrad.

THROUGHOUT THE autumn of 1942, the Red Army built up reserves around Stalingrad while feeding in just enough reinforcements to prevent any decisive German breakthrough. General Chuikov's Sixty-Second Army held the city itself, steadily wearing down the attacks of the Sixth Army and Fourth Panzer Army in an expert campaign of attrition. At the same time, Zhukov steadily assembled his forces, including 894 tanks and 13,500 guns, to strike at the Rumanians both north and south of Stalingrad.

When the South-West Front launched its attack on the Third Rumanian Army on 19 November, the 80-minute Soviet barrage by at least 3000 guns could be heard 50km (31 miles) away. A 12km (8-mile) gap was ripped in the Rumanian defences, which was rapidly exploited by the Fifth Tank Army. Twenty-four hours later, the Stalingrad Front's offensive hit the Fourth Rumanian Army, tearing a 30km (20-mile) hole in its line before launching IV Mechanized Corps and IV Cavalry Corps into the breach to link up with Fifth Tank Army.

Surprised and unprepared

Most German planners had simply not believed that the Red Army had the resources or the skill to conduct an offensive on this scale. Soviet armour

▲ Winter offensive

Infantry of the South-West Front's Twenty-First Army advance past a knocked-out T-70 light tank on the banks of the Don at Kalach, November 1942. It was here that the Fifth Tank Army broke through the Fourth Panzer Army's defences to link up with the Fourth Mechanized Corps and trap the Sixth Army in Stalingrad. (The transport and spectators on the bridge make it highly likely that this is a staged propaganda photograph.)

Specifications

Crew: 4

Weight: 26.5 tonnes (26.2 tons)

Length: 5.92m (19ft 5in)

Width: 3.00m (9ft 8in)

Height: 2.44m (8ft)

Engine: 373kW (500h) V-2-34 V-12 diesel

Speed (road): 53km/h (33mph)

Range: 400km (250 miles)

Radio: N/A

Armament: 1 x 76mm (3in) F-34 gun;
  2 x 7.62mm (0.3in) DT MGs (bow and coaxial)

▲ T-34 Model 1942

South-Western Front / Fifth Tank Army / XXVI Tank Corps

On 23 November, IV and XXVI Tank Corps linked up with IV Mechanized Corps to complete the encirclement of Stalingrad. The two tank corps had covered 130km (81 miles) since crossing the start line four days earlier.

Tank Corps – vehicle strength (late 1942)	Weapons
HQ:	
Medium tank	3
Tank Brigade x 3:	
Light tank	21
Medium tank	32
LMG	18
MG	4
ATR	6
82mm (3.22in) mortar	6
76mm (3in) guns	4
Motorized Rifle Brigade:	
LMG	110
MG	18
HMG	3
ATR	54
82mm (3.2in) mortar	30
120mm (4.7in) mortar	4
45mm (1.8in) AT	12
37mm (1.5in) AA	12
76mm (3in) guns	12
Reconnaissance Battalion:	
Armoured car	20
Rocket Launcher Battalion:	
Rocket launcher	8

Tank Corps – personnel/small arms strength (late 1942)	Officers	NCOs	Other	SMGs	Rifles
HQ	56	38	36	5	27
Brigade x 3	229	423	464	490	225
Mot Rifle	390	1187	1960	1364	1396
Recon	41	146	21	50	56
Rocket Lch	30	56	164	5	104
Pioneer Mine	9	20	77	36	60
Fuel Trans	8	9	58	0	51
Maintenance Coy x 2	9	13	53	10	20
NKVD	11	6	32	10	20
Total	1250	2757	3846	2068	3126

was now being employed – and most effectively – in accordance with the principles laid down by General Fedorenko earlier in the year.

In contrast, the German response was clumsy and ineffective. XLVIII Panzer Corps had been assigned to act as an armoured reserve for the Third Rumanian Army, but it was an exceptionally weak formation, comprising the 22nd Panzer Division with only 45 operational tanks and the 1st Rumanian Tank Division with 40 R-2 tanks (obsolete Panzer 35(t) s). Despite being massively outnumbered by Soviet armour, these two divisions managed to break out to the West. The under-strength elements of the Fourth Panzer Army that attempted to block the Fifth Tank Army's advance at the Don crossings near Kalach were not so fortunate. They were inadequately briefed and committed to an understandably rushed deployment with low fuel and ammunition. Although they reached Kalach just ahead of Soviet forces, their small combat teams lacked infantry support to hold vital ground and were quickly overrun by Soviet armour operating *en masse*.

On 23 November, the Red Army pincers closed at Sovietskiy, 20km (12.4 miles) south-east of Kalach, trapping an estimated 300,000 Axis troops in Stalingrad. The tables had been decisively turned.

◀ **Tank crews**
Tank crewmen of the South-West Front relax after completing the encirclement of the Sixth Army in Stalingrad. At this stage of the war, many Soviet tank crews went into action with as little as 72 hours classroom training, a deficiency that contributed to their high casualty rates.

▲ **T-34 platoon**

November 1942 – a platoon of T-34 Model 1943 tanks awaits orders to move up to the front. Access to the enlarged turret of the T-34 Model 1943 was improved by the installation of twin hatches instead of the clumsy single hatch of previous models.

Specifications

Crew: 1 driver

Weight: 1.55 tonnes (1.5 tons)

Length: 5.33m (17ft 6in)

Width: 2.1m (7ft)

Height: 1.97m (6ft 6in)

Engine: 29.8kW (40hp) 4-cylinder
SV petrol

Speed: 70km/h (43.5mph)

▼ **ZIS-6 BM-8-48**

Stalingrad Front / Sixty-Second Army / XXVI Tank Corps / Rocket Launcher Battalion

The ZiS-6 was the first type of truck to be converted to carry the various versions of the 'Katyusha' salvo rocket launcher. Although largely superseded in this role by Lend-Lease trucks, surviving vehicles remained in service throughout the war.

▲ **GAZ-65 1½-ton halftrack**

South-Western Front / Fifth Tank Army / XXVI Tank Corps / Supply Battalion

The GAZ-65 was a conversion to allow the GAZ-AA truck to operate as a halftrack whenever required. The tracks were readily removable and the small roadwheels could be raised so that the truck could be used in the conventional wheeled mode.

Specifications

Crew: 1

Weight: 4.31 tonnes (4.756 tons)

Length: 6.06m (19.9ft)

Width: 2.23m (7.33ft)

Height: 2.16m (7ft 1in)

Engine: 54kW (73hp) 6-cylinder

Speed: 55km/h (34mph)

Armament: 48 x 82mm M-8 rockets with a maximum
range of 5.9 km (3.66 miles)

Chapter 10

False Dawn: Kharkov to Kursk

During much of the winter of 1942–43, it seemed
that the Red Army was on the verge of achieving a decisive
victory. Hitler had characteristically refused to allow the
Sixth Army to break out from Stalingrad and insisted that
Kleist's Army Group A should remain in the Caucasus.
Even von Manstein's genius could not compensate for this
folly – his attempt to relieve Stalingrad was beaten back and
the last remnants of the garrison surrendered on
2 February 1943. The Soviet advance threatened to cut off
Army Group A, which was forced to retreat to the Taman
Peninsula. Within a week of the surrender at Stalingrad,
the Voronezh and South-Western Fronts had retaken Kursk
and Belgorod. Kharkov fell on 14 February and
Soviet armour was threatening the Dnieper
crossings at Zaporozhe.

◄ Transient victory

A T-34 Model 1943 of the Voronezh Front enters Kharkov, 16th February 1943. Manstein's masterly
counter-offensive re-took the city on 15 March.

Reverse at Kharkov

FEBRUARY–MARCH 1943
The seemingly irresistible Red Army offensive was pushed too far, out-running its supply lines and providing an opportunity for a devastating German counterattack.

B Y MID-FEBRUARY, there was very little time left before the mud of the spring thaw made major operations impossible, but von Manstein showed just what could be achieved in the most threatening situation. By getting a shaken Hitler to authorize a mobile defence and release the necessary resources

(the SS Panzer Corps, five *Wehrmacht* Panzer divisions and the elite *Grossdeutschland* Division), he was able to shorten his front and concentrate the Panzers to take advantage of Soviet overconfidence. This overconfidence was understandable – Soviet armour had advanced as much as 300km (186 miles) in a month and seemed poised to re-conquer the entire Ukraine. Such spectacular successes brought their own problems as the tanks outran their supply lines and had to struggle forward with totally inadequate reserves of fuel and ammunition. By this time, Lieutenant-General Popov's 'mobile group' of four tank corps spearheading the advance had been reduced to 53 serviceable tanks.

On 20 February, von Manstein unleashed four Panzer corps supported by a 'maximum effort' from the *Luftwaffe*, which rapidly established air

◀ **Objective Kharkov**

T-34s of the Voronezh Front advance on Kharkov in the depths of the winter of 1942/43. The T-34's wide tracks gave it good mobility across snow and ice.

▲ **T-34 Model 1943**

South-Western Front / Lieutenant-General Popov's Mobile Group

This T-34 was one of only 53 operational tanks left in all four tank corps comprising Popov's Mobile Group when it was destroyed by Manstein's counter-offensive in February 1943.

Specifications	
Crew: 4	Engine: 373kW (500hp) V-2-34 V-12
Weight: 30.9 tonnes (30 tons)	cylinder diesel
Length: 5.92m (19ft 5in)	Speed (road): 53km/h (33mph)
Width: 3.00m (9ft 8in)	Range: 465km (290 miles)
Height: 2.44m (8ft)	Armament: 1 x 76mm (3in) L-40 gun; 2 x
	7.62mm (0.3in) DT MGs (bow and coaxial)

superiority over the battlefield, flying up to 1000 sorties per day. The concentrated Panzer thrusts achieved massive local superiority over the scattered and depleted Red Army armoured forces, rapidly defeating each in detail. The SS Panzer Corps recaptured Kharkov on 15 March, going on to take Belgorod three days later before the thaw and the exhaustion of the German forces combined to end the counter-offensive.

After coming tantalizingly close to winning a major victory, the Red Army had been badly mauled – the South-Western Front had lost 23,000 men, 615 AFVs and 354 guns, whilst the Voronezh Front's casualties were even worse, totalling 40,000 men, 600 tanks and 500 guns. German forces once again held much of the territory lost during the winter except for a large salient centred on the small provincial city of Kursk.

▲ SU-12 self-propelled gun

North Caucasus Front / 1448th Artillery Regiment

Initially designated the SU-12, the first model of the SU-76 was an early attempt to produce a light self-propelled gun by mounting the 76.2mm (3in) ZiS-3 gun on a lengthened T-70 chassis. The power-train was nearly identical to that of the early T-70 light tank, with two commercial GAZ-202 engines each powering one track through separate, unsynchronized transmissions. Unsurprisingly, this proved to be a mechanical nightmare and was a major factor in cancelling production in March 1943 after only 360 units had been completed.

Specifications

Crew: 4	Engine: 2 x GAZ 6-cylinder petrol 52+52kW
Weight: 10.8 tonnes (11.9 tons)	(70+70hp)
Length: 4.88m (16ft)	Speed (road): 45km/h (28mph)
Width: 2.73m (8ft 11.5in)	Range: 450km (280miles)
Height: 2.17m (7ft 1.4in)	Armament: one 76mm (3in) gun and one
	7.62mm (0.3in) MG

▲ T-38 light tank

Southern Front / HQ 28th Army / Reconnaissance Company

A total of 1340 T-38s were produced between 1936 and 1939 and were widely used by reconnaissance units. Some of these vehicles were fitted with a 20mm (0.79in) ShVAK cannon in place of the usual DT MG, but few survived the first months of the war.

Specifications

Crew: 2	Engine: 30 kW (40hp) GAZ-AA
Weight: 3.3 tonnes (3.25 tons)	Speed: 40 km/h (24.86mph)
Length: 3.78m (12ft 5in)	Range: 170km
Width: 3.33m (10ft 11in)	Radio: N/a
Height: 1.63m (5ft 4in)	Armament: 1 x 7.62mm (0.3in) DT MG

Specifications

Crew: 1 driver	Engine: 54.39 kW (73hp) 6 cylinder
Weight: 4.66 tonnes (4.59 tons)	ZiS-5 petrol
Length: 6m (19ft 8in)	Speed: 36 km/h (22.37mph)
Width: 2.4m (7ft 10in)	Range: 300km (186.4 miles)
Height: 2.23m (7ft 4in)	Radio: N/A

▲ **ZiS-22(M) halftrack**

Voronezh Front / HQ Forty-Sixth Army / Supply Battalion

In common with many other Soviet-produced halftracks, the front wheels of this ZiS-22(M) have been fitted with wooden 'skis' to improve its performance while moving across snow.

Kursk: the last *Blitzkrieg*
JULY 1943

From the German perspective, the Kursk salient was an obvious target for a summer offensive in 1943 – unfortunately for them, it was just as obvious to the Red Army.

A N ATTACK TO 'PINCH OUT' the Kursk salient would shorten the German front by 250km (155 miles), freeing up to 20 divisions for use elsewhere, besides destroying what was seen as a 'gateway for the invasion of the Ukraine'. Typically, von Manstein proposed a radical alternative, a new offensive on the same principles as his recent operations that had led to the recapture of Kharkov and Belgorod. He intended to tempt the Southern and South-Western Fronts into attacks against the newly reconstituted Sixth Army, drawing them into eastern Ukraine. A counter-offensive would then be launched from the Kharkov area towards Rostov, to trap most of the two Fronts against the Sea of Azov.

Predictably, this 'Manstein plan' was vetoed by Hitler, who ordered an offensive against the Kursk

▶ **BA-64B Model 1943 light armoured car**

Voronezh Front / Fifth Guards Tank Army / XVIII Tank Corps

The BA-64B gradually replaced pre-war types of armoured cars in reconnaissance units from 1943. It first saw action during the Kursk offensive.

Specifications

Crew: 2	Engine: 37kW (50hp) GAZ-64 4-cylinder
Weight: 2.3 tonnes (2.54 tons)	Speed: 80km/h (50mph)
Length: 3.66m (12ft)	Range: 540km (869 miles)
Width: 1.53m (5ft)	Armament: 7.62mm (0.3in) DT MGn
Height: 1.90m (6ft 3in)	

salient, which seemed to invite the sort of Panzer-led pincer attack that had been so successful in the past. This was equally obvious to the Soviets, who were busily fortifying the area, and Hitler was urged to strike quickly before the odds became too great.

New technology

Fortunately for the Red Army, Hitler was convinced that only the new *Elefants* and Panthers could guarantee to break the strengthening Soviet defences and imposed delay after delay until he felt that the

SOVIET TANK ARMIES, KURSK (July 1943)		
Front	Army	Corps
Central	Second Tank	III Tank
		XVI Tank
Voronezh	First Tank	VI Tank
		XXXI Tank
		III Mechanized
Steppe	Fifth Guards Tank	V Guards Mechanized
		XXIX Guards Tank

▲ T-34 Model 1943

Voronezh Front / Fifth Guards Tank Army / XXIX Tank Corps

This T-34 Model 1943 incorporates the final updates applied to the type, notably the commander's 360-degree vision cupola and 'drum type' long-range fuel tanks.

Specifications

Crew: 4

Weight: 30.9 tonnes (30 tons)

Length: 5.92m (19ft 5in)

Width: 3.00m (9ft 8in)

Height: 2.44m (8ft)

Engine: 373kW (500hp) V-2-34 V-12 diesel

Speed (road): 53km/h (33mph)

Range: 465km (290 miles)

Armament: 1 x 76mm (3in) L-40 gun; 2 x 7.62mm (0.3in) DT MGs (bow and coaxial)

Specifications

Crew: 5

Weight: 50.16 tonnes (45.5 tons)

Length: 8.95m (29ft 4in)

Width: 3.25m (10ft 7in)

Height: 2.45m (8 ft)

Engine: 450kW (600hp) 12-cylinder V-2K diesel

Speed: 43 km/h (27mph)

Range: 330km (205miles)

Armament: 152mm (5.9in) ML-20S gun-howitzer

▲ SU-152 heavy self-propelled gun

Voronezh Front / Fifth Guards Tank Army / XXIX Tank Corps

The SU-152 was developed under a crash programme to produce a heavy tank destroyer on the KV-1S chassis. In the type's first actions at Kursk, the 152mm (5.9in) ML-20's 48.7kg (107lb) armour-piercing rounds proved capable of dealing with even the latest German AFVs at normal battle ranges.

commanders were appalled at the prospect of a head-on attack against the deep belts of minefields and *Pakfronts* – the massed AT gun batteries – which showed up all too clearly in air reconnaissance photographs. They were also well aware of the security risks that grew with each successive delay. (In fact, the so-called Red Orchestra spy ring was

busily sending Moscow complete details of the German plans).

German attack

On 5 July, the German attack, code-named *Zitadelle* ('Citadel') went in against the flanks of the salient. Model's Ninth Army struck south to meet Hoth's

Specifications	
Crew: 5	Engine: 1450kW (600hp) Model V-2
Weight: 45 tonnes (44.3 tons)	2-cylinder diesel
Length: 6.75m (22ft 2in)	Speed: 35km/h (22mph)
Width: 3.32m (10ft 10in)	Range: 335km (208 miles)
Height: 2.71m (8ft 9in)	Armament: 1 x 76mm (3in) F-32 gun;
	3 x 7.62mm (0.3in) DT MGs

▲ KV-1A heavy tank
Voronezh Front / First Tank Army / III Mechanized Corps / 203rd Separate Heavy Tank Regiment

By mid-1943, it was clear that the KV-1 was being overtaken by newer German AFVs such as the Tiger and Panther. Soviet design teams began work on a successor, the JS-2, which finally entered service in the spring of 1944.

Specifications	
Crew: 4	Engine: 223.5 kW (300hp) 12 cylinder Maybach
Weight: 23.9 tonnes (23.52 tons)	HL120 TRM petrol
Length: 6.77m (22ft 2in)	Speed: 40km/h (24.86mph)
Width: 2.95m (9ft 8in)	Range: 155km (96.32 miles)
Height: 2.38m (7ft 10in)	Radio: 9R (when fitted)
	Armament: 1 x 76.2mm (3in) ZiS-3 gun

▲ SU-76i assault gun
Voronezh Front / Fifth Guards Tank Army / 1902nd Self-Propelled Artillery Regiment

The SU-76i was brought into service in 1943 to provide an interim assault gun pending the arrival of the SU-76M. Just over 200 were produced, using captured Panzer III and Stug III hulls fitted with a 76mm (3in) F-34 or ZiS-5 tank gun in a limited traverse mounting.

▲ **Loading up**

T34/76 tanks of the Sixth Guards Tank Army of the Voronezh Front prepare to move out, July 1943. These are older model T-34s, with the single-turret hatch.

Specifications

Crew: 4	Engine:373kW (500hp) V-2-34 V-12 diesel
Weight: 30.9 tonnes (30 tons)	Speed (road): 53km/h (33mph)
Length: 5.92m (19ft 5in)	Range: 465km (290 miles)
Width: 3.0m (9ft 8in)	Armament: 1 x 76mm (3in) L-40 gun; 2 x
Height: 2.44m (8ft)	7.62mm (0.3in) DT MGs (bow and coaxial)

▲ **T-34 Model 1943**

Voronezh Front / First Tank Army / VI Tank Corps / 22nd Tank Brigade

Almost 35,000 T-34s were built between 1940 and 1944, when production tapered off in favour of the T-34/85. This example has a combination of all-steel and rubber-rimmed road wheels, as rubber supplies were still limited in 1943.

Fourth Panzer Army moving north on Kursk. A total of 16 Panzer and *Panzergrenadier* divisions with 2700 AFVs were fielded with the support of 10,000 guns and 2000 aircraft. Despite these numbers, the offensive soon ran into trouble – the first attacks quickly bogged down in massive minefields averaging over 3000 mines per kilometre,

which were swept by the fire of up to 100 guns and mortars per kilometre.

The attackers frequently used the *Panzerkeil*, or armoured wedge, a formation in which *Elefants* or Tigers formed the point of the wedge and were followed by the lighter AFVs. Even this formation was only partially successful in the face

▲ **Dodge T-110 L-5 D-60L 3-ton truck**
Voronezh Front / Forty-Eighth Army / HQ / Supply Battalion
A total of 1700 of these Canadian vehicles were shipped to Soviet forces via Iran.

Specifications

Crew: 1	Engine: six cylinder 70.84kW (95hp) engine
Weight: not known	Speed: 70km/h (43mph)
Length: 6.55m (21ft 6in)	Range: not known
Width: 2.286m (7ft 7in)	Armament: none
Height: 3.15m (10ft 4in)	

Specifications

Crew: 1 driver + 3 MG crew	Engine: 6 cylinder 73.82kW (99hp) petrol
Weight: not known	engine
Length: (wheel base): 4.064m (13ft 4in)	Speed: 70km/h (43mph)
Width: not known	Range: not known
Height: not known	Armament: Quadruple 7.62mm (0.3in) Maxim
	Maxim anti-aircraft MG

▲ **Dodge WF-32 4x2 1½-ton Truck (Maxim 4M AA MG Mount)**
Voronezh Front / Fifth Guards Tank Army / XXIX Tank Corps / AA Company
Roughly 9500 of these trucks were sent to Soviet Russia in 1942/43 to replace the massive losses suffered by transport units during the German offensives. In common with many other Lend-Lease trucks, a proportion of these vehicles were issued to AA units.

▶ **Surrender**

Red Army tank crew surrender to a Waffen-SS soldier during the bloody battle of
Kursk in 1943.

of such massive Soviet defences – the Tigers and
Elefants might well get through, but all too often
the lighter vehicles and infantry were destroyed as
they attempted to follow. This left the 'heavies'
unsupported and horribly vulnerable to Soviet
infantry AT teams using demolition charges
or flamethrowers.

Soviet counterattack

Rokossovsky's Central Front holding the north of
the salient launched a counterattack by the Second
Tank Army on 6 July, which broke down after taking
heavy losses (in part from Soviet minefields, which
had been strengthened by German engineers). In
contrast, General Vatutin's Voronezh Front in the
south did not commit major armoured formations
against the initial German attacks, relying on the
minefields and *Pakfronts*.

Although Model's advance was halted after little
more than 15km (9.3 miles) – far short of Kursk –
Hoth managed to penetrate rather deeper, beating
off all counterattacks and threatening to make a
decisive breakthrough.

▲ **Tank column**

T-34s advance through the Ukraine in the wake of the successful counter-offensive at Kursk, summer 1943.

▼ Soviet Tank Brigade (November 1943)

By late 1943, Soviet tank brigades had evolved into powerful formations. The vulnerable light tanks had now been replaced by T-34s and battlefield communications were improved by the increasing numbers of radio-equipped tanks.

Brigade HQ, Staff Section (2 x T-34)

Brigade HQ, Reconnaissance Section (3 x ACs)

Battalion 1, HQ (1 x T-34)

Battalion 2, HQ (1 x T-34)

Reconnaissance Platoon (3 x APCs)

Reconnaissance Platoon (3 x APCs)

Company 1, HQ (1 x T-34)

Company 1, HQ (1 x T-34)

Medium Tank Platoon 1 (3 x T-34)

Medium Tank Platoon 1 (3 x T-34)

Medium Tank Platoon 2 (3 x T-34)

Medium Tank Platoon 2 (3 x T-34)

Medium Tank Platoon 3 (3 x T-34)

Medium Tank Platoon 3 (3 x T-34)

Company 2, HQ (1 x T-34)

Company 2, HQ (1 x T-34)

Medium Tank Platoon 1 (3 x T-34)

Medium Tank Platoon 1 (3 x T-34)

Medium Tank Platoon 2 (3 x T-34)

Medium Tank Platoon 2 (3 x T-34)

Medium Tank Platoon 3 (3 x T-34)

Medium Tank Platoon 3 (3 x T-34)

SOVIET TANK BRIGADE (1943)

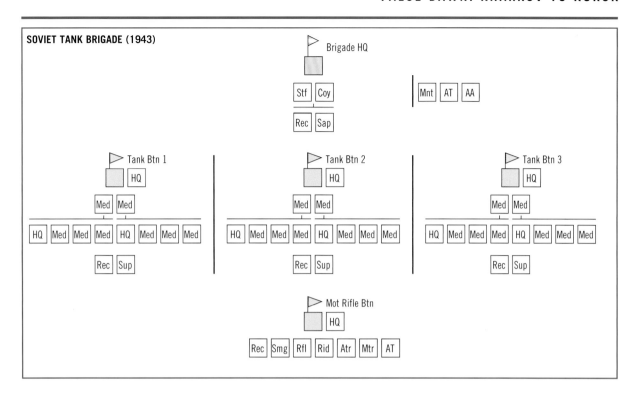

Battalion 3, HQ (1 x T-34)

Reconnaissance Platoon (3 x APCs)

Company 1, HQ (1 x T-34)

Company 2, HQ (1 x T-34)

Medium Tank Platoon 1 (3 x T-34)

Medium Tank Platoon 1 (3 x T-34)

Medium Tank Platoon 2 (3 x T-34)

Medium Tank Platoon 2 (3 x T-34)

Medium Tank Platoon 3 (3 x T-34)

Medium Tank Platoon 3 (3 x T-34)

 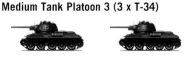

Prokhorovka
12–13 JULY 1943

Despite halting the German advance from the north of the Kursk salient, Hoth's attack from the south was making steady progress and desperate measures were called for.

BY 11 JULY, HOTH'S FOURTH PANZER ARMY was threatening to capture Prokhorovka and secure a bridgehead over the River Psel, the last natural barrier between the Panzers and Kursk. The German attack

was led by Hausser's II SS Panzer Corps, which had begun the offensive with over 300 tanks.

Vatutin believed that the situation was critical and committed the 650 tanks of Rotmistrov's 5th Guards

▲ **Infantry Tank Mark IV, Churchill Mark III**

Voronezh Front / Fifth Guards Tank Army / 36th Independent Guards Breakthrough Heavy Tank Regiment

Almost 250 Churchills were issued to Soviet tank units, including Fifth Guards Tank Army, which took part in the action at Prokhorovka.

Specifications

Crew: 5	Engine: 261kW (350hp) Bedford Twin Six
Weight: 38.5 tonnes (42 tons)	12-cylinder liquid-cooled petrol
Length: 7.3m (24ft 5in)	Speed: 24km/h (15mph)
Width: 3.0m (10ft 8in)	Range: 140km (88 miles)
Height: 2.8m (8ft 2in)	Armament: 1 x 57mm (2.2in) gun;
	1 or 2 x 7.92mm (0.31in) MG

Specifications

Crew: 5	Engine: 350hp (261kW)
Weight: 38.5 tonnes (42 tons)	Bedford twin-six petrol
Length: 7.3m (24ft 5in)	Speed (road): 24km/h (15mph)
Width: 3m (10ft 8in)	Range: 90km (56 miles)
Height: 2.8m (8ft 2in)	Armament: 1 x 75mm (2.9in) or 94mm (3.7in)
	gun; 2 x Besa 7.92mm (0.31in) MGs

▲ **Infantry Tank Mark IV, Churchill Mark IV**

Voronezh Front / Fifth Guards Tank Army / 49th Guards Heavy Tank Regiment

The Churchill was never popular with the Red Army, who compared it unfavourably with the KV-1.

▲ **Advance from Prokhorovka**

Churchill Mk.IV of the Fifth Guards Tank Army, 49th Guards Heavy Tank Regiment passes a destroyed German SdKfz 232 armoured car, Kursk area, July 1943.

Tank Army, which had been intended to spearhead the Soviet 'post-Kursk' offensive, Operation *Rumyantsev*. On 11 July, the Fifth Guards Tank Army arrived in the Prokhorovka area, after a four-day march from assembly areas 300km (186 miles) to the east. It was reinforced by II Tank Corps and II Guards Tank Corps, increasing its strength to about 850 tanks, 500 of which were T-34s.

These forces were opposed by 211 operational German tanks, including only 15 Tigers, when the battle opened on 12 July with massed Soviet tank attacks from Prokharovka. Waves of 40–50 T-34s and T-70s carrying infantry were launched in frontal charges against the German armour, which were broken up with heavy losses. The Germans resumed their advance on Prokharovka and were engaged by Rotmistrov's reserves, including the 181st Tank Regiment, which was virtually wiped out when it attempted to charge a handful of Tigers of the 1st SS Panzer Regiment. It was only late in the day that the intervention of the Soviet V Mechanized Corps finally stabilized the situation.

The first day's fighting had resulted in massive Soviet casualties – almost 650 tanks were destroyed, while II SS Panzer Corps' losses totalled 70 AFVs, of which 22 were repaired and serviceable on the

▶ **Universal Carrier Mark I with AT rifle**

Voronezh Front / Fifth Guards Tank Army / 12th Guards Mechanized Brigade / Reconnaissance Company

Many of the Red Army's 2000-plus Universal Carriers were issued to reconnaissance units, sometimes, as here, retaining their original armament of a Boys AT rifle and a Bren Gun.

Specifications

Crew: 2/4	Engine: 63.4 kW (85hp) 8-cylinder Ford V8
Weight: 4.06 tonnes (4 tons)	Speed: 52km/h (32 mph)
Length: 3.76m (12ft 4in)	Range: 258km (160 miles)
Width: 2.11m (6ft 11in)	Armament: 1 x 14mm (0.55in) Boys AT rifle,
Height: 1.63m (5ft 4in)	1 x 7.7mm (0.303in) Bren Gun

following day. When combat resumed on 13 July, the Fifth Guards Tank Army was reduced to 150–200 operational tanks and was incapable of effective offensive action. Hausser's forces continued to attack, but were unable to make a decisive breakthrough. There was still a chance of a German victory – von Manstein urged Hitler to commit the three experienced Panzer divisions of 24th Panzer Corps, which he believed could destroy the Fifth Guards and take Kursk itself. Despite these forceful arguments, Hitler called off the operation to free units for Italy,

as the Allied landings in Sicily were on the point of causing the collapse of Mussolini's regime.

Although the Kursk offensive had failed, it demonstrated that the Red Army was in danger of losing the technological battle – the T-34 and KV were out-gunned by the Tiger and Panther, and their 76mm (3in) armament was ineffective against both German types, except at suicidally short ranges. The new SU-152 had proved to be a highly effective tank destroyer, but was, at best, only a partial solution to the problem.

Counterattack
JULY–AUGUST 1943

Soviet forces in the north of the Kursk salient recovered quickly from the German attack and launched their own offensive – Operation _Kutuzov_ – against Orel on 12 July.

OREL WAS STRONGLY DEFENDED – only falling on 3/4 August after the Third Guards Tank Army and 4th Tank Army had been committed to the assault. Further south, the battering that Hoth's highly capable Fourth Panzer Army had inflicted meant that Operation _Rumyantsev_, the Soviet attack directed towards Belgorod and Kharkov, could not begin until 3 August. Belgorod fell on 5 August, but

Kharkov was far more strongly defended, its garrison reinforced by the 2nd SS Panzer Division _Das Reich_, with 96 Panthers, 32 Tigers and 25 assault guns. When Rotmistrov's newly re-equipped Fifth Guards attacked in an attempt to encircle the city, its initial assaults were beaten off with the loss of 420 tanks. It was only on 22 August that the defenders withdrew to avoid being cut off.

▲ Infantry Tank Mark III, Valentine Mark IV
Central Front / HQ Second Tank Army
The Red Army greatly appreciated the Valentine's reliability and large numbers remained in service throughout the war. The cranelike structure on the turret here is the Lakeman AA mount for a Bren Gun. The whole assembly could be folded away – the Bren Gun was normally stowed in the turret.

Specifications

Crew: 3

Weight: 17.69 tonnes (19.5 tons)

Length: 5.41m (17ft 9in)

Width: 2.63m (8ft 7.5in)

Height: 2.27m (7ft 5.5in)

Engine: 103kW (138bhp) GMC diesel

Speed (road): 24km/h (15mph)

Range: 145km (90 miles)

Armament: 1 x 40mm (1.57in) gun;
1 x 7.92mm (0.31in) Besa MG

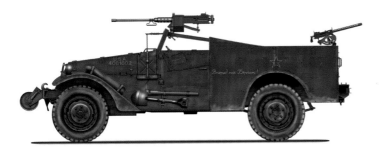

▲ Scout Car M3A1

Voronezh Front / HQ Fifth Guards Tank Army

The speed and light armour of the M3A1 made it popular as a command vehicle. This example was used by General Rotmistrov, commander of the Fifth Guards Tank Army.

Specifications

Crew: 2, plus up to 6 passengers
Weight: 5.618 tonnes (5.53 tons)
Length: 5.62m (18ft 5in)
Width: 2.03m (6ft 8in)
Height: 2m (6ft 6in)
Engine: 71 kW (95hp) 6-cylinder White Hercules
    JXD petrol
Speed: 105 km/h (65 mph)
Range 400km (250 miles)
Armament: 1 x 12.7mm (0.5in) Browning HMG,
    1 x 7.62mm (0.3in) Browning MG

▲ M4A2 Sherman medium tank (early production)

Central Front / Forty-Eighth Army / 229th Independent Tank Regiment

Shermans began to appear in significant numbers in Red Army units during 1943. Initially they were mainly issued to Independent Tank Regiments to ease the logistic support burden.

Specifications

Crew: 5
Weight: 32.28 tonnes (35.58 tons)
Length: 5.92m (19ft 5in)
Width: 2.62m (8ft 7in)
Height: 2.74m (9ft)
Engine: 280kW (375hp) General Motors 6046
    12-cylinder diesel
Speed: 48km/h (30mph)
Range: 240km (150 miles)
Armament: 1 x 75mm (2.9in) M3 L/40 gun;
    1 x 12.7mm (0.5in) I Browning M2HB MG

▲ M4A2 Sherman medium tank

Central Front / Forty-Eighth Army / 229th Independent Tank Regiment

Although not as well suited to Russian conditions as the T-34, the Sherman's mechanical reliability was greatly appreciated.

Specifications

Crew: 5
Weight: 32.28 tonnes (35.58 tons)
Length: 5.92m (19ft 5in)
Width: 2.62m (8ft 7in)
Height: 2.74m (9ft)
Engine: 280kW (375hp) General Motors 6046
    12-cylinder diesel
Speed: 48km/h (30mph)
Range: 240km (150miles)
Armament: 1 x 75mm (2.9in) M3 L/40 gun;
    1 x 12.7mm (0.5in) I Browning M2HB MG,
    1 x turret mounted 12.7mm 0.50 cal MG

▲ **M31B2 (T48) armoured recovery vehicle (ARV)**

Voronezh Front / 245th Tank Regiment

One-hundred-and-twenty Lend-Lease M31s were the only purpose-built ARVs issued to Soviet tank units during the war years.

West to the Dnieper and beyond

AUGUST–DECEMBER 1943

The Red Army now held the strategic initiative, but its advances were to be costly affairs as German forces fought a series of highly effective rearguard actions.

IN THE AFTERMATH of the Red Army's capture of Orel and Kharkov, even Hitler recognized that there was little chance of holding any line east of the Dnieper. Orders to construct the Dnieper defence line, which formed part of the Panther-Wotan Line or the Eastern Wall, had been issued as early as 11 August 1943 and work began immediately. In theory, fortifications were to be erected along the length of the Dnieper, but the resources did not exist to undertake such a massive project and defence works were concentrated in sectors where Soviet assault crossings were most likely to be attempted, especially Kremenchug, Zaporozhe and Nikopol.

On 15 September 1943, Hitler finally authorized Army Group South to fall back to the Dnieper

defence line and a deadly race ensued, with the Red Army attempting to beat the German retreat. *Stavka* assigned the Third Tank Army to spearhead the drive to the river, which it reached on the night of 21/ 22 September. Small bridgeheads were secured, but were very vulnerable and it was decided to expand them by an airborne operation using the 1st, 3rd and 5th Guards Airborne Brigades. The operation on the night of 24/25 September was rushed and ill-planned, with transport aircraft taking off as they were ready, rather than in properly organized formations. This was a major factor in scattering the 10,000 paratroops over a wide area on the west bank of the Dnieper. Most of the 5th Guards Airborne Brigade was slaughtered when it was dropped on

▲ **KV-85 Heavy Tank**

1st Ukrainian Front / Twenty-Eighth Army / 34th Guards Heavy Tank Breakthrough Regiment

Only 130 KV-85s were produced because the type was essentially an interim design to provide an up-dated heavy tank pending the introduction of the Josef Stalin (JS) series. The hull of the KV-1S was fitted with the turret of the JS-1, armed with an 85mm (3.3in) gun.

Specifications	
Crew: 4/5	Engine: 450kW (600hp) Model V-2
Weight: 46 tonnes (45.3 tons)	12-cylinder diesel
Length: 8.6m (28ft 2in)	Speed: 42km/h (26mph)
Width: 3.25m (10ft 8in)	Range: 330km (205 miles)
Height: 2.8m (9ft 2in)	Armament: 1 x 85mm (3.3in) D-5T gun;
	2 x 7.62mm (0.3in) DT MGs

▲ **SU-76M self-propelled Gun**

1st Ukrainian Front / Third Guards Tank Army / IX Mechanised Corps

The SU-76M was a re-designed SU-76. A revised power-train dramatically improved the type's mechanical reliability and the replacement of the SU-76's enclosed fighting compartment by an open-topped design cured the problems with engine and gun fumes. It was more frequently used as an assault gun than for long-range artillery fire.

Specifications	
Crew: 4	Engine: 2 x GAZ-203 6-cylinder petrol,
Weight: 10.2 tonnes (11.2 tons)	103kW (138bhp)
Length: 5m (16ft 5in)	Speed: 45km/h (28mph)
Width: 2.7m (8ft 10in)	Range: 320km (199 miles)
Height: 2.1m (6ft 11in)	Armament: 1 x 76mm (3in) ZiS-3 L/41 gun

the 19th Panzer Division, which was moving up to reinforce the Dnieper defences. While the operation was a disaster, German efforts to eliminate the scattered pockets of airborne forces did distract attention from the build-up of Soviet forces for a decisive breakthrough on the Panther-Wotan Line.

The handful of initial bridgeheads were slowly enlarged and new ones secured until by the end of September, there were no less than 23, some of them 10km (6.2 miles) wide and 2km (1.2 miles) deep. All these attracted fierce German counterattacks, but managed to hold out with massive fire support from Soviet artillery on the east bank of the river.

By mid-October, the forces assembled in the bridgeheads were strong enough to go over to the offensive, coupled with diversionary attacks in the

MECHANIZED BRIGADE (1943)				
AFVs	Arm Truck	AC	Lt Tk	Med Tk
Reconnaissance Coy	10	7	–	–
Tank Rgt	–	3	7	32

Mechanized Brigade (light veh)	Mot cycl	Field Car	Truck
Brigade HQ	–	2	4
HQ Coy	6	–	5
Reconnaissance Coy	6	–	4
Tank Rgt	4	2	70
Motorized Rifle Btn x3	1	1	26
Submachine-Gun Coy	1	–	1
Anti-Tank Rifle Coy	–	–	–
Mortar Btn	–	–	20
Artillery Btn	–	1	25
Anti-Aircraft MG Coy	–	–	12
Pioneer Mine Coy	–	–	6
Trains Coy	1	–	31
Medical Platoon	–	–	5

Mechanized Brigade (personnel)	Officers	NCOs	Other
Brigade HQ	39	15	26
HQ Coy	5	17	51
Reconnaissance Coy	7	72	62
Tank Rgt	89	194	187
Motorized Rifle Btn x3	48	212	389
Submachine Gun Coy	4	22	68
Anti-Tank Rifle Coy	4	20	45
Mortar Btn	23	47	127
Artillery Btn	24	67	123
Anti-Aircraft MG Coy	4	23	21
Pioneer Mine Coy	8	23	90
Trains Coy	6	28	38
Medical Platoon	8	5	19

▶ **Crowded target**

A heavily laden T-34 advances through Kiev shortly after its liberation in
November 1943. Crowded onto a tank's decks with few secure hand-holds,
tank riders ran a high risk of accidental death or injury, as well as being highly
vulnerable to enemy fire.

Mechanized Brigade	Sub MG	Carbines	Aut-rifles	Light MG	Med MG	Heavy MG	Anti-Tank	82mm	120mm	45mm AT	76mm Fld
Brigade HQ	3	8	19	2	–	–	–	–	–	–	–
HQ Coy	0	60	–	–	–	–	–	–	–	–	–
Reconnaissance Coy	79	14	–	–	–	–	–	–	–	–	–
Tank Rgt	143	95	57	2	–	–	–	–	–	–	–
Motorized Rifle Btn x3	273	99	138	36	15	–	18	6	–	4	–
Submachine Gun Coy	88	5	–	–	–	–	–	–	–	–	–
Anti-Tank Rifle Coy	37	–	–	–	–	–	27	–	–	–	–
Mortar Btn	2	–	147	–	–	–	–	12	6	–	–
Artillery Btn	60	100	9	–	–	–	–	–	–	–	12
Anti-Aircraft MG Coy	–	32	–	–	–	9	–	–	–	–	–
Pioneer Mine Coy	53	10	50	–	–	–	–	–	–	–	–
Trains Coy	1	43	–	–	–	–	–	–	–	–	–
Medical Platoon	–	9	–	–	–	–	–	–	–	–	–

south to draw German forces away from Kiev. At the end of the offensive, the Red Army controlled a bridgehead 300km (186 miles) wide and up to 80km (50 miles) deep, while in the far south, Army Group A was now cut off in the Crimea.

German tactical expertise could still impose serious delays – throughout much of October 1943, Vatutin's forces were penned into the 'Bukrin Bend' of the Dnieper and had to be redeployed northwards to the tiny bridgehead across the Dnieper at Lyutlezh,

just upstream of Kiev. By 3 November, the move was complete and VII Artillery Breakthrough Corps unleashed a bombardment by 2000 guns, mortars and rocket launchers before the Third Tank Army went in to the attack. The German forces screening the bridgehead were smashed, and Kiev was liberated on 6 November.

Fourth Panzer Army attempted to halt the Soviet advance, but Vatutin's newly re-designated 1st Ukrainian Front took Zhitomir and Korosten,

Specifications

Crew: 3

Weight: 18.6 tonnes (20.5 tons)

Length: 5.4m (17ft 9in)

Width: 2.6m (8 ft 8in)

Height: 2.2m (7ft 6in)

Engine: 97–157kW (131–210hp) GMC 6004 diesel

Speed: 24km/h (15mph)

Range: 145km (90miles)

Armament: 1 x 57mm (2.2in) gun

▲ Infantry Tank Mark III, Valentine Mark IX

2nd Ukrainian Front / 27th Guards Tank Brigade

The Valentine's popularity with the Red Army was such that production was continued into 1944 solely to meet its requirements.

▲ SU-152 heavy self-propelled gun

1st Ukrainian Front / Eighteenth Army / 5th Guards Tank Brigade

The SU-152 was highly valued for its effectiveness both as a tank destroyer and assault gun. Over 700 vehicles were completed during 1943 before production switched to the JSU-152.

Specifications

Crew: 5

Weight 45.5 tonnes (44.78 tons)

Length: 8.95m (29ft 4in)

Width: 3.35m (10ft 8in)

Height: 2.45m (8ft)

Engine: 372.5kW (500hp) V-2 12-cylinder diesel

Speed: 43km/h (26.72mph)

Range: 330km (205 miles)

Radio: 9R (when fitted.)

Armament: 1 x 152mm (5.98in) ML-20S howitzer

cutting the rail link between Army Groups Centre and South.

At this critical point, von Manstein counterattacked with LVIII Panzer Corps (1st, 7th, 19th and 25th Panzer Divisions, plus 1st SS Panzer Division and elements of the 2nd SS Panzer Division.) This force recaptured Zhitomir, fighting a fierce battle with the VII Guards Tank Corps before the deep mud created by the autumn rains temporarily halted operations. Both sides took advantage of the enforced lull to refit, but LVIII Panzer Corps took the initiative. As soon as the ground froze in early December, it launched an attack north of Zhitomir with the aim of encircling the Sixtieth Army, which hurriedly withdrew from Korosten. The situation was so critical that *Stavka* transferred

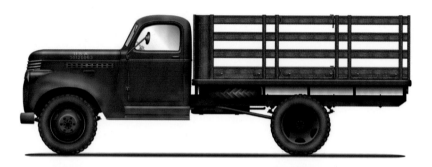

▲ **Chevrolet 3116, 1½-ton, 4x2 Truck, with stake-and-platform body**

4th Ukrainian Front / Fifty-First Army / Supply Battalion

Lend-Lease transport vehicles rarely lasted long in Red Army service. Apart from the risks of enemy action, they were commonly overloaded, fuelled with very low octane petrol and driven for thousands of kilometres over appalling terrain.

Specifications

Crew: 1 driver	Engine: 6 cylinder 63.38kW (85hp) 4F1R
Weight: not known	petrol engine
Length: 5.69m (18ft 7in)	Speed: 70km/h (43mph)
Width: 2.18m (7ft 2in)	Range: not known
Height: 2m (6ft 6in)	Radio: none

TANK BRIGADE (1943)	Mot cycl	Field Car	Trucks	Men	Arm Car	Med Tank
Brigade HQ	3	–	1	54	–	2
HQ Company	9	–	10	164	3	–
Tank Battalion x 3	–	1	12	148	–	21
Mot Submachine Gun Btl	–	–	30	507	–	–
Anti-Air Machine Gun Coy	–	–	9	48	–	–
Trains Coy	–	1	58	123	–	–
Medical Pltn	–	–	2	14	–	–

Tank Brigade	Sub MG	Rifle/Carbine	Light MG	Medium MG	Heavy MG	AT Rifle	82mm Mort	45mm AT
Brigade HQ	–	8	–	–	–	–	–	–
HQ Company	41	97	4	–	–	–	–	–
Tank Battalion x3	30	43	0	–	–	–	–	–
Mot Submachine Gun Btl	280	50	18	4	–	18	6	4
Anti-Air Machine Gun Coy	1	37	–	–	9	–	–	–
Trains Coy	10	113	–	–	–	–	–	–
Medical Pltn	–	14	–	–	–	–	–	–

▶ **Tank train**

Winter 1943/44 – a trainload of T-34 Model 1943 tanks en route to the front. The Soviet rail network was vitally important for all strategic movements of armoured forces.

the First Tank Army and the Eighteenth Army to the 1st Ukrainian Front. These reinforcements allowed Vatutin to halt the German attack and return to the offensive – by mid-December, it seemed that both sides were exhausted and LCVIII Panzer Corps was withdrawn to rest and refit. However, Vatutin was determined to exploit his numerical superiority and renewed his attacks on 24 December – these made good progress and as the year ended, his forward units were approaching the 1939 Polish frontier.

Soviet AFV production totalled just under 20,000 vehicles in 1943 compared to almost 6000 in Germany. However, this did not give the Red Army the overwhelming numerical superiority that might have been expected, as the Germans destroyed 22,400 Soviet tanks in the course of the year – approximately four times their own losses.

▶ **Light Tank M3A1 'Stuart', early production series**

Central Front / Forty-Eighth Army / 45th Separate Tank Regiment

Over 1600 Lend-Lease Stuarts were shipped to the Red Army. This vehicle has the riveted hull of early production runs and has been fitted with two auxiliary fuel tanks, which virtually doubled its operating range.

Specifications

Crew: 4	Engine: Continental W-970-9A 7-cylinder
Weight: 14.7 tonnes (32,400lb)	radial petrol
Length: 4.54m (14ft 10.75in)	Speed (road): 58km/h (36mph)
Width: 2.24m (7ft 4in)	Range: 112.6km (70miles)
Height: 2.30m (7ft 6.5in)	Armament: 37mm (1.5in) M6 L/56 gun; 3 x
	7.62mm (0.3in) Browning M1919A4 MGs

▶ **Light Tank M3A1'Stuart', standard production series**

Central Front / Forty-Eighth Army / 45th Separate Tank Regiment

This M3A1 from a late production batch has an all-welded hull. Although Soviet tank crews disliked the tank's high silhouette, the Stuart's two-man turret was far superior to the one-man turret of the T-70.

Specifications

Crew: 4	Engine: Continental W-970-9A 7-cylinder
Weight: 14.7 tonnes (32,400lb)	radial petrol
Length: 4.54m (14ft 10.75in)	Speed (road): 58km/h (36mph)
Width: 2.24m (7ft 4in)	Range: 112.6km (70miles)
Height: 2.30m (7ft 6.5in)	Armament: 37mm (1.5in) M6 gun; 3 x 7.62mm
	(0.3in) Browning M1919A4 MGs

▲ SU-57 tank destroyer

1st Ukrainian Front / Third Guards Tank Army / 16th Tank Destroyer Brigade

A total of over 600 US T-48 tank destroyers – M3 halftracks armed with the 57mm (2.2in) M1 AT gun – were supplied to the Red Army, which knew it as the SU-57. These were concentrated in tank destroyer brigades, each with 60–65 SU-57s.

Specifications

Crew: 5	Engine: 109.5kW (147hp) White 160AX
Weight: 8.6 tonnes (8,46 tons)	6- cylinder in-line petrol
Length: 6.42m (21ft)	Speed: 72km/h (45mph)
Width: 1.962m (6ft 5in)	Range: 320km (200 miles)
Height: 2.3m (7ft 6in)	Armament: 1 x 57mm (2.24in) M1 gun

▲ M2 halftrack

4th Ukrainian Front / Twenty-Eighth Army / HQ

The 342 M2 halftracks received by the Red Army were used mainly as command vehicles.

Specifications

Crew: 2, plus up to 8 passengers	Engine: 109.5kW (147hp) White 160AX
Weight: 8.7 tonnes (8.56 tons)	6- cylinder in-line petrol
Length: 5.96m (19ft 6in)	Speed: 72km/h (45mph)
Width: 1.962m (6ft 5in)	Range: 320km (200 miles)
Height: 2.3m (7ft 6in)	Armament: 1 x 12.7mm (0.5in) Browning HMG,
	plus 1 x 7.62mm (03in) Browning MG

▶ Willys MB 'Jeep'

3rd Ukrainian Front / HQ

At least 50,000 Lend-Lease jeeps were issued to Red Army units between 1942 and 1945.

Specifications

Crew: 1 driver	Engine: 44.7kW (60hp) 4-cylinder petrol
Weight: 1.04 tonnes (1.02 tons)	Speed: 88.5km/h (55mph)
Length: 3.33m (10ft 11in)	Range: not known
Width: 1.575m (5ft 2in)	Radio: N/A
Height: 1.83m (6ft)	

▼ GAZ-MM 4x2 1½-ton Truck Model 1943 with 25mm (1in) 72-K Model 1940 AA Gun

4th Ukrainian Front / Twenty-Eighth Army / 1693rd AA Regiment

The increasing threat from Luftwaffe armoured ground-attack aircraft such as the Henschel HS129B, which were largely invulnerable to MG fire, prompted the development of these more powerful self-propelled AA guns.

Specifications

Crew: 1 driver, 4 gun crew

Weight: 18.1 tonnes (19.96 tons) (without gun)

Length (hull): 5.35m (17ft 6in)

Width: 2.04m (6ft 8in)

Height: 1.97m (6ft 51/2in)

Engine: 37kW (50hp) Gaz-MM 4-cylinder

Speed: 70km/h (43.5mph)

Armament: 1 x 25mm (1in) 72-K Model 1940 AA gun

Motorized Rifle Battalion, personnel/weapons (1943)				
	Officers	NCOs	Other	Main Weapons
Battalion HQ	13	3	5	–
SMG Coy x2	5	22	74	9 LMG, 2 MG
SMG Coy	4	10	81	–
Mortar Coy	3	13	26	6 82mm Mortars
AT Rifle Coy	–	–	–	18 AT Rifles
AT Battery	4	15	25	4 45mm AT
Trains Ptn	2	14	29	–
Medical Det	1	1	3	–

Specifications

Crew: 1 driver

Weight: 1.53 tonnes (1.5 tons)

Length: 5.69m (18ft 7in)

Width: 2.28m (7ft 6in)

Height: 2.64m (8ft 8in)

Engine: 69.3kW (93hp) 6 cylinder 4F1R petrol engine

Speed: not known

Range: not known

Armament: none

▲ Chevrolet G-7117 4x4 1½-ton truck with PARM-1 Type B field repair workshop

4th Ukrainian Front / HQ / Maintenance Battalion

Substantial numbers of Lend-Lease trucks were converted to fulfil a range of specialist functions. A proportion of those allocated to maintenance units were fitted with field repair workshop bodies.

Chapter 11

The Destruction of the *Wehrmacht*

As 1944 began, the balance of power on the Eastern Front swung more strongly in favour of the Red Army. Five Tank Armies, each comprising two tank and one mechanized corps, were already in existence and a sixth was forming. A uniquely Soviet addition to the more conventional forces was the cavalry mechanized group (KMG), a combination of a cavalry corps and a mechanized corps. This formation proved to be ideal for 'deep-penetration' missions to exploit breakthroughs across thickly forested areas or swamps, which were marginal terrain for tanks. The *Luftwaffe*'s demonstration of effective close air support operations in 1941–43 led to increased resources being devoted to the Red Air Force. An expansion and re-equipment programme provided each Front with its own air army of 700–800 fighters and ground-attack aircraft.

◀ New Year, new victories
A column of T-34 Models 1943 and their tank riders advance across the Ukraine in early 1944.

Korsun Pocket
DECEMBER 1943 – FEBRUARY 1944

By 24 December 1943, the 4th Ukrainian Front had sealed off 150,000 German and Rumanian troops in the Crimea. As the New Year began, cavalry of the 1st Ukrainian Front crossed the 1939 Polish frontier and turned southwards in an attempt to trap the German forces in the Dneiper bend south of Kiev.

THE BULK OF these forces (elements of 11 divisions of the Eighth Army) held a salient centred on Korsun, west of Cherkassy. *Stavka* quickly appreciated the salient's vulnerability, assigning Vatutin's 1st Ukrainian Front and Konev's 2nd Ukrainian Front to strike at its flanks. By this stage of the war, both the Fronts were powerful formations, with each fielding three tank armies, plus three to four other armies.

Konev's Fifth Guards Tank Army and Sixth Tank Army sealed off the salient on 3 February 1944 despite appalling weather conditions (intense cold spells broken by brief thaws that turned the region's dirt roads to thick, clinging mud.) Approximately 60,000 men under General Stemmermann (*Gruppe Stemmermann*) were trapped in this newly formed Korsun Pocket. A rescue attempt was made by the

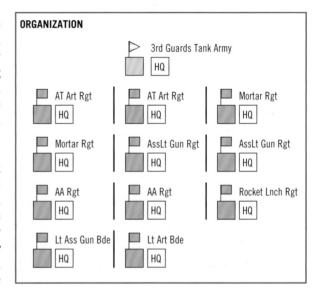

ORGANIZATION

▲ **KV-85 heavy tank**

1st Ukrainian Front / Thirty-Eighth Army / 7th Independent Guards Heavy Tank Regiment

The KV-85 was produced by fitting the hull of the KV-1S with the turret of the JS-1, armed with an 85mm (3.3in) gun. Only 130 KV-85s were produced, as the type was essentially an interim design to provide an up-dated heavy tank pending the introduction of the Josef Stalin (JS) series.

Specifications

Crew: 4/5	Engine: 450kW (600hp) Model V-2
Weight: 46 tonnes (45.3 tons)	12-cylinder diesel
Length: 8.6m (28ft 2in)	Speed: 42km/h (26mph)
Width: 3.25m (10ft 8in)	Range: 330km (205 miles)
Height: 2.8m (9ft 2in)	Armament: 1 x 85mm (3.3in) D-5T gun;
	2 x 7.62mm (0.3in) DT MGs

First Panzer Army, which managed to seize small bridgeheads across the River Gniloy Tikich on 11 February, but was unable to break through to the pocket 30km (19 miles) away to the east. During the next few days, the First Panzer Army was locked in fierce combat with the Sixth Tank Army, but the relief force could do no more than hold its ground in the face of such strong opposition.

By 15 February, it was clear that the trapped forces would have to attempt a breakout. They had already edged closer to the stalled relief force and launched their main effort on the night of 16/17

Tank Corps (January 1944)	Strength
Personnel	12,010
Armour:	
T-60 light tank	–
T-70 light tank	–
T-34 medium tank	208
KV heavy tank	1
SU-76	21
SU-85	16
SU-152/ISU-152	12
Guns and Mortars:	
82mm (3.2in) mortars	52
120mm (4.7in) mortars	42
45mm (1.8in) AT guns	12
57mm (2.2in) AT guns	16
37mm (1.5in) AA guns	18
76mm (3in) guns	12
M-13 rocket launchers	8

Mechanized Corps (January 1944)	Strength
Personnel	16,370
Armoured Vehicles:	
Light tanks	21
Medium tanks	176
Heavy tanks	–
Light assault guns	21
Medium assault guns	16
Heavy assault guns	12
Guns and Mortars:	
82mm (3.2in) mortars	100
120mm (4.7in) mortars	54
45mm (1.8in) AT guns	36
57mm (2.2in) AT guns	8
37mm (1.5in) AA guns	18
76mm (3in) guns	36
BM-13 rocket launchers	8

▲ **T-34/85 Medium Tank**

2nd Ukrainian Front / Fifth Guards Tank Army

The T-34/85's 85mm (3.3in) gun was a major factor in restoring the technological balance between Soviet and German armoured forces. Although it was not as effective as the guns of the Panther or the Tiger, its armour-piercing performance was almost twice as good as the 76.2mm weapons of earlier T-34s.

Specifications

Crew: 5

Weight: 32 tonnes (31.5 tons)

Length: 6m (19ft 7in)

Width: 3m (9ft 9in)

Height: 2.60m (8ft 6in)

Engine: 1 x V-2 V-12 cylinder 372 kW (493hp) diesel engine

Speed (road): 55km/h (33mph)

Range: 360km (223 miles)

Radio: 9R (When fitted)

Armament: 1 x 85mm (3.4in) ZiS-S-53 cannon; 2 x 7.62mm (0.3in) DT MGs (bow and coaxial)

▲ **Tank riders**
Soviet infantry hitch a lift on a T-34 as troops from the 1st Ukrainian Front push through the Ukraine, spring 1944.

February. Elements of three Soviet tank armies lay between *Gruppe* Stemmermann and the forward elements of the First Panzer Army only 12km (7.5 miles) away.

Konev furious

Konev reacted furiously to the German breakout attempts – he had rashly promised Stalin a second Stalingrad – and threw in all available units, including the new JS-2s of XX Tank Corps. Lacking infantry support, Soviet tanks initially stood off, firing into the escaping units from a distance, but as it became obvious that there were very few AT weapons to oppose them, the T-34s charged into the German columns. Although as many as 35,000 German troops eventually fought their way clear after abandoning all their artillery and heavy equipment, the Eighth Army had been badly mauled and the First Panzer Army had lost large numbers of AFVs, which were increasingly difficult to replace.

Headquarters

▼ **Light Assault Gun Regiment**
Light assault gun regiments were generally used in the infantry support role and suffered particularly heavy losses, as their thinly armoured, open-topped SU-76Ms were highly vulnerable to even light AT weapons.

Battery 1 **Battery 2** **Battery 3** **Battery 4**

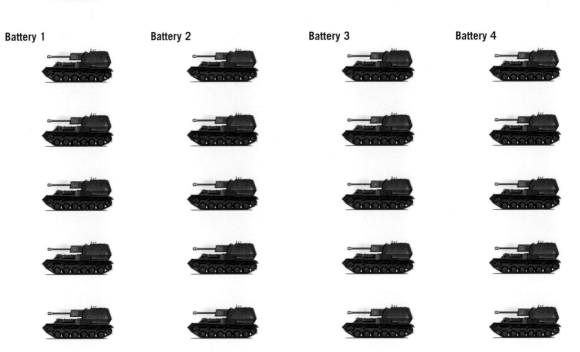

Specifications

Crew: 4

Weight: 10.8 tonnes (11.9 tons)

Length: 4.88m (16ft)

Width: 2.73m (8ft 11.5in)

Height: 2.17m (7ft 1.4in)

Engine: 2 x GAZ 6-cylinder petrol 52+52kW
(70+70hp)

Speed (road): 45km/h (28mph)

Range: 450km (280miles)

Armament: one 76mm (3in) gun and one
7.62mm (0.3in) MG

▲ SU-76M SP assault gun

2nd Ukrainian Front / Fifth Guards Tank Army / 1223rd Light Self-Propelled Artillery Regiment

When operating in the indirect-fire role, the SU-76M's ZiS-3 76mm (3in) gun had a maximum range of over 13,000m (42,650ft).

Operation *Bagration*
22 JUNE – 19 AUGUST 1944

Throughout April and May 1944, *Stavka* planned Operation *Bagration*, a massive offensive intended to destroy Army Group Centre and drive German forces from Soviet territory.

ELABORATE DECEPTION measures were employed to convince the Germans that the forthcoming offensive would exploit earlier Soviet advances in the south by retaking the remaining occupied areas of the Ukraine and driving into the Balkans to knock Rumania out of the war.

These measures were highly successful and the offensive achieved complete surprise when it opened on 22 June, the third anniversary of the start of Operation *Barbarossa*. The balance of forces was very much in favour of the Red Army (see table opposite for figures).

By this stage of the war, the Soviet Air Force had gained air superiority and flew 153,000 combat sorties in support of the offensive. Almost 1000 aircraft of Soviet Long Range Aviation based in southern Russia supplemented these operations with

Operation *Bagration*	Soviet Forces	Army Group Centre
Troops	2,400,000	1,200,000
AFVs	5200	900
Artillery and mortars	36,400	9500
Aircraft	5300	1350

Operation *Bagration*	Armies employed
1st Baltic Front	4th Shock, 6th Guards, 43rd
3rd Byelorussian Front	11th Guards, 5th, 39th, 31st, 5th Guards Tank
2nd Byelorussian Front	33rd, 49th, 50th, 4th Air
1st Byelorussian Front	3rd, 28th, 48th, 65th

bombing raids on targets such as German HQs and *Luftwaffe* airfields. In crucial sectors of the front, the Soviets had local numerical superiority of up to 10:1 and quickly broke through the German defences. Within days, the three tank armies assigned to the operation were able to exploit the breakthroughs and advance deep into the German rear areas, while a KMG moved through the Pripet Marshes to cut off the German Ninth Army's line of retreat.

Encirclement operations

On 25 June, Vitebsk was surrounded by a second KMG and Soviet forces pressed on, cutting off Mogilev, Bobruisk and Minsk by 3 July. In each case, large German forces were trapped, the haul increased by Hitler's refusal to authorize timely retreats. By this time, Army Group Centre had lost 25 of its 63 divisions (including the bulk of the Ninth Army) and the Soviet offensive was still far from over.

The second stage of Operation *Bagration* began on 5 July. The German pocket around Minsk was

▶ Marshall Rokossovsky
Rokossovsky survived imprisonment and torture during Stalin's purges to become a Marshal of the Soviet Union in recognition of his victories during Operation Bagration.

▲ JS-2m heavy tank
1st Ukrainian Front / First Guards Tank Army / 72nd Independent Guards Heavy Tank Regiment

By late 1944, a total of at least 34 independent heavy tank regiments had been formed, each with 21 JS-2s.

Specifications

Crew: 4	Speed: 37km/h (23mph)
Weight: (46 tonnes) 45.27 tons	Range: 240km (149miles)
Length: 9.9m (32ft 6in)	Armament: 1 x 122mm (4.8in) D-25T gun,
Width: 3.09m (10ft 2in)	3 x 7.72mm (0.3in) DT MGs (1 coaxial, 1 fixed
Height: 2.73m (8ft 11in)	in bow, 1 ball-mounted in turret rear)
Engine: 383kW (513hp) V-2 12-cylinder diesel	

destroyed between 5 and 11 July, before the advance resumed, taking Vilnius on 13 July. Throughout this period, the tank armies and the KMGs formed the spearhead of the advance, frequently out-running their artillery support.

For the first time, the Red Air Force proved capable of providing effective close air support to these formations and resupplying them. (During the operation, it delivered 1182 tonnes/1163 tons of fuel, 1240 tonnes/1220 tons of ammunition and around 1000 tonnes/984 tons of equipment and spare parts to forward units.)

Soviet progress was, in fact, so rapid that the German front-line entirely disintegrated – so many defensive pockets were formed that there was no chance of any organized relief efforts. In fact, there were insufficient reserves to re-establish any proper front-line and the isolated units were left to their

▲ **SU-122 SP gun**

Voronezh Front / Fifth Guards Tank Army / 1446th Self-Propelled Gun Regiment
The SU-122 was the first successful assault gun design based on the T-34 and was armed with the 122mm (4.7in) M-30 howitzer in a fully enclosed fighting compartment. Medium SP gun regiments, each with 16 SU-122s, began to enter service early in 1943. (A total of 638 vehicles were completed before production ended in November 1943.)

Specifications

Crew: 5	Speed: 55km/h (34.18mph)
Weight: 30.9 tonnes (11.02 tons)	Range: 300km (186.4miles)
Length: 6.95m (22ft 9in)	Radio: 9R (When fitted – even by
Width: 3m (9ft 8in)	1945, not all Soviet AFVs had radios.)
Height: 2.32m (7ft 7in)	Armament: 122mm (4.8in) M30-S howitzer
Engine: 373kW (500hp) V-2 diesel	

▲ **M10 'Wolverine' tank destroyer**

3rd Byelorussian Front / Fifth Guards Tank Army / 29th Tank Corps / 1223rd Self-Propelled Artillery Regiment
The Red Army received no more than 52 Lend-Lease M10s, which seem to have seen action only with Fifth Guards Tank Army during 1944.

Specifications

Crew: 5	Engine: 277.89kW (375hp) General Motors
Weight: 29.6 tonnes (29.13 tons)	6046; 12 cylinder, twin in-line diesel
Length: 5.82m (19ft 1in)	Speed: 48km/h (30mph)
Width: 3.05m (10ft)	Range: 320km (200miles)
Height: 2.49m (8ft 2in)	Armament: 1 x 76mm M7 gun, plus 1 x pintle-mounted 12.7mm (0.5in) Browning HMG

▼ Tank Brigade (June 1944)

By 1944, Soviet tank brigades were far more effective formations than they had been earlier in the war. Increasing standardization of vehicle types eased maintenance and support problems, while the more widespread issue of radios greatly improved operational command and control.

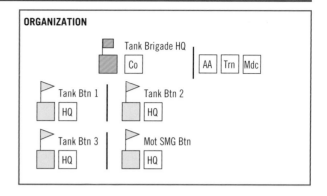

ORGANIZATION

Brigade HQ (3 x MCs, 1 x truck, 2 x T-34/85s)

HQ Company (3 x ACs, 9 x MCs, 10 x trucks)

Tank Battalion 1 (1 x staff car, 21 x T-34/85s, 12 x trucks)

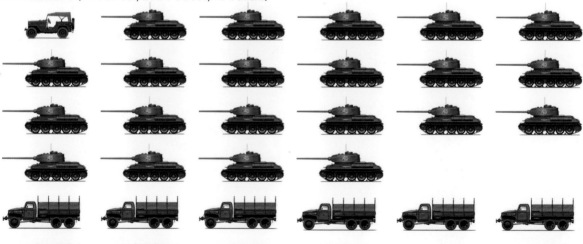

own devices. A minority managed to break out to the west, but most were destroyed by the Red Army or partisan bands.

Inevitably, supply problems and sheer exhaustion took their toll as the advance continued, but by the time that the offensive finally wound down in the third week of August, Soviet forces had crossed the frontier of East Prussia, were on the point of reaching the Baltic and had advanced to the gates of Warsaw. German forces were in a state of utter chaos, with on-paper units and formations bearing little resemblance to the forces on the ground.

Army Group Centre had, indeed, been practically annihilated, with 2000 AFVs and 57,000 other

Tank Battalion 2 (1 x staff car, 21 x T-34/85s, 12 x trucks)

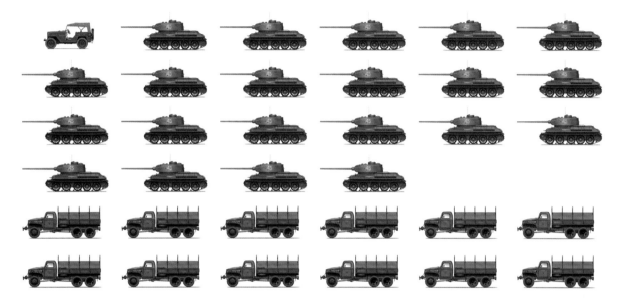

Tank Battalion 3 (1 x staff car, 21 x T-34/85s, 12 x trucks)

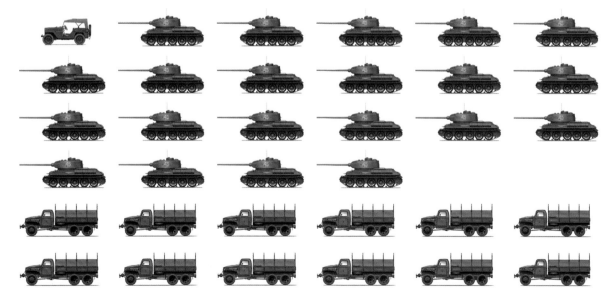

▲ **Crushing Army Group Centre**

Summer 1944 – a JS-2 of the 1st Ukrainian Front operating in the infantry support role during Operation Bagration.

Operation *Bagration* Losses	German	Soviet
Tanks	2000	2957
Other Vehicles	57,000	–
Artillery Pieces	–	2447
Aircraft	–	822
Dead	300,000	60,000
Wounded	250,000	110,000
Captured	120,000	–
Missing	–	8000
Overall Casualties	670,000	–

vehicles destroyed or captured. German casualties may well have been as high as 300,000 dead, 250,000 wounded and about 120,000 prisoners. The *Wehrmacht* simply could not afford casualties on this scale – experienced NCOs were vital in restoring the effectiveness of units that had to absorb large numbers of replacement personnel and their loss gradually reduced the tactical superiority that German units had previously taken for granted.

Red Army losses were also high, with 60,000 killed, 110,000 wounded and about 8000 missing. In terms of equipment, Soviet forces lost 2957 tanks, 2447 guns and 822 aircraft, but Soviet war production and Lend-Lease supplies meant that these losses could readily be replaced.

Specifications

Crew: 1 driver

Weight: 2.6 tonnes (5750lb) fully laden

Length: 4.72m (15ft 6in)

Width: 2m (6ft 6in)

Height: 2.03m (6ft 7in)

Engine: 6 cylinder 68.6kW (92hp) petrol engine

Speed: not known

Range: not known

Armament: none

▲ **WC-53 Truck, ¾-ton 4x4 Dodge Carryall**

HQ 1st Belorussian Front

Roughly 200 Lend-Lease WC-53s were supplied to the Red Army. Their six-seat capacity and 4x4 configuration made them ideal staff cars.

Lvov–Sandomir Offensive
13 JULY – 29 AUGUST 1944

This offensive towards Lvov was intended to ensure the success of Operation *Bagration* by preventing the Germans from reinforcing Army Group Centre.

THE OPERATION WAS assigned to Konev's 1st Ukrainian Front, which could deploy over 1,200,000 troops, 2050 tanks, about 16,000 guns and mortars and over 3250 aircraft of the Second Air Army. They were opposed by General Harpe's Army Group North Ukraine, totalling roughly 370,000 men with 420 AFVs.

The 1st Ukrainian Front's offensive was launched on two axes. Three armies were to attack towards Rava-Ruska, whilst a further four advanced on Lvov. The attacks were to be made on a front of only 26km (16 miles). The attack towards Rava-Ruska began on 13 July 1944 and by nightfall the Thirteenth Army had advanced 20km (12.4 miles). On the following day, the advance on Lvov began, which left the German XIII Corps in a dangerously exposed salient around Brody.

The southern arm of the Soviet offensive achieved a decisive breakthrough on a front of only 3–4km (1.8–2.5 miles; the Koltiv Corridor) between XIII Corps and XLVIII Panzer Corps. Fierce German counterattacks on the corridor were beaten off, and on 16 July Konev took the risk of committing the Third Guards Tank Army to an attack through the Corridor, which was still under heavy bombardment from German artillery. By 18 July, 45,000 men of XIII Corps were trapped around Brody, and a 200km (124-mile) breach had been created in the German front. The Brody pocket was destroyed on 22 July and Lvov was captured four days later, completing the reconquest of Ukraine.

The second stage of the offensive opened on 29 July, aimed at a seizing a bridgehead across the Vistula and taking Sandomierz in southern Poland. The bridgehead was taken, but Sandomierz did not fall until 18 August.

The badge is the Piast eagle, the symbol of the *Ludowe Wojsko Polskie* (LWP) – the People's Army of Poland, which was adopted as the unit insignia of the 1st Polish Armoured Brigade.

▲ **PT-34 engineer tank**

1st Byelorussian Front / Polish First Army / 1st Armoured Brigade

This late-production T-34 Model 1943 was converted to a PT-34 by the installation of a Mugalev mine-clearing roller, which could withstand between eight and 10 detonations of AT mines before requiring replacement. The system equipped seven Red Army Engineer Tank Regiments from 1943 onwards.

Specifications

Crew: 5

Weight: 3.90 tonnes (30.41 tons) (without roller)

Length: 6.75m (22ft 1in) (without roller)

Width: 3m (9ft 8in) (without roller)

Height: 2.45m (8ft 0in)

Engine: 373kW (500hp) V-2 diesel

Speed: 55km/h (34.2mph)

Range: (road) 465km (289 miles);
 (terrain) 365km (227miles)

Radio: 9R (When fitted)

Armament: Main: 76.2mm (3in) F-34 gun,
 Secondary: 2 x 7.62mm (0.3in) DT machine
 guns (coaxial and bow)

◀ Into Poland

A GAZ-MM truck passes a column of SU-152s in Lvov, July 1944. Despite the introduction of the JSU-152, surviving SU-152s remained in service throughout the war. These vehicles are heavily laden with spare fuel drums to extend their range.

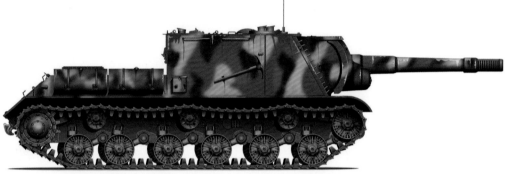

Specifications

Crew: 5

Weight: 46 tonnes (45.27 tons)

Length: 9.2m (30ft 1in)

Width: 3.07m (10ft 1in)

Height: 2.48m (8ft 1in)

Engine: 447kW (600hp) V-2 diesel

Speed: 37km/h (23mph)

Range: (Road) 220km (136.7miles);

(Terrain) 80km (49.7miles)

Radio: 10RF (When fitted)

Armament: 152mm (5.9in) ML-20S howitzer

▲ JSU-152 heavy SP gun

1st Ukrainian Front / Third Guards Tank Army / Independent Heavy Self-Propelled Artillery Regiment

The SU-152 was a highly effective assault gun, but as production of the KV series was scheduled to end in late 1943, the design had to be adapted to fit the hull of the JS-2. The new JSU-152, which entered service in 1944, had an enlarged fighting compartment and thicker armour.

▲ T-34 Model 1943

1st Ukrainian Front / Fourth Tank Army / XI Tank Corps

This unusual four-tone camouflage pattern, applied to some Red Army AFVs during the Lvov–Sandomir operation of July–August 1944, is in striking contrast to the far more common overall dark-green finish.

Specifications

Crew: 4

Weight: 30.9 tonnes (30 tons)

Length: 5.92m (19ft 5in)

Width: 3.00m (9ft 8in)

Height: 2.44m (8ft)

Engine: 373kW (500hp) V-2-34 V-12 cylinder diesel

Speed (road): 53km/h (33mph)

Range: 465km (290 miles)

Armament: 1 x 76mm (3in) L-40 gun; 2 x 7.62mm (0.3in) DT MGs (bow and coaxial)

▼ Tank Regiment (1944)

By 1944, these tank regiments were powerful units, especially when equipped with the new T-34/85 with its greatly improved protection and firepower. Such units provided close support for infantry formations, freeing the tank armies for deep-penetration operations.

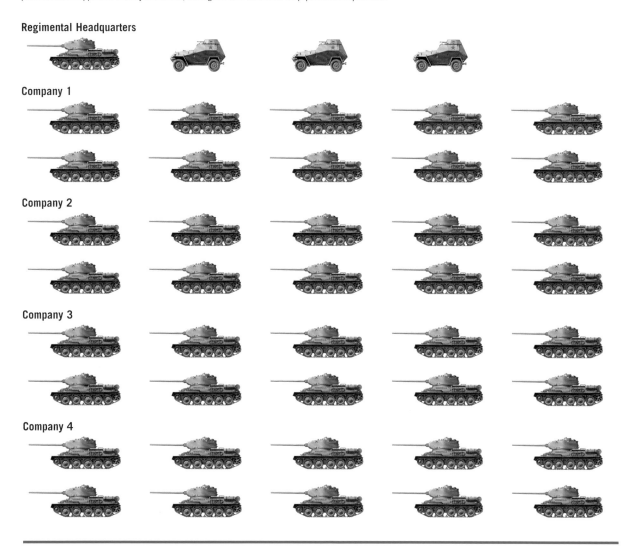

Regimental Headquarters

Company 1

Company 2

Company 3

Company 4

Operation *Jassy-Kishinev*
20–29 AUGUST 1944

By May 1944, German Army Group South Ukraine had been pushed back towards the Rumanian frontier along the River Dniester. The Red Army prepared for its next offensive.

THE RED ARMY HELD two bridgeheads across the river, and STAVKA now planned a double envelopment of the German and Rumanian armies by the 2nd and 3rd Ukrainian Fronts. The 2nd Ukrainian Front was to break through north of Jassy and then seize the crossings over the River Prut to cut

Specifications

Crew: 5	Speed: 48km/h (30mph)
Weight: 33.3 tonnes (32.77 tons)	Range: 161km (100miles)
Length: 7.6m (24ft 10in)	Radio: 9R (When fitted)
Width: 2.62m (8ft 7in)	Armament: 1 x 76mm (3in) M1A1 gun,
Height: 2.97m (9ft 9in)	1 x 12.7mm (0.5in) Browning HMG on turret
Engine: 279.4kW (375hp) General Motors	AA mount, 2 x 7.62mm (0.3in) Browning MGs,
12-cylinder in-line diesel	1 coaxial, 1 bow

▲ **M4A2 (76mm) Sherman medium tank**

2nd Ukrainian Front / Sixth Guards Tank Army / 5th Mechanized Corps.

By mid-1944, the M4A2 (76mm) formed the entire tank strength of V Mechanized Corps – several more mechanized and tank corps were entirely equipped with the type by the end of the war.

off the German Sixth Army. The Sixth Tank Army was to seize the bridges across the River Siret and the fortified Focsani Gap between the Siret and the Danube. The 3rd Ukrainian Front would break out from its bridgehead at Tiraspol, then head north to meet the 2nd Ukrainian Front and trap the German and Rumanian forces. After sealing the pocket, the Sixth Tank Army and IV Guards Mechanized Corps were to take Bucharest and the Ploesti oil fields.

Soviet forces were formidable – more than 1,340,000 men and at least 1800 AFVs to face about 500,000 Germans and 405,000 Rumanians supported by only 170 tanks and assault guns. The Red Army now had a huge qualitative superiority over the Rumanian forces, whose AFVs and AT weapons were unable to counter T-34/85s and JS-2s.

The attacks by the 2nd and 3rd Ukrainian Fronts were made on narrow frontages supported by the fire of almost 250 guns per kilometre. This superiority ensured rapid breakthroughs, leading to a double envelopment of the German Sixth Army and elements of the Eighth Army. By 22 August, the Axis front-line collapsed and VI Guards Mechanized Corps was inserted to exploit the breakthrough.

The next day, a *coup d'etat* led by King Michael of Rumania deposed the pro-German dictator, Marshal Antonescu, and the country changed sides. German forces guarding the Ploesti oilfields were attacked by Rumanian troops and withdrew into Hungary.

The equivalent of 18 German divisions had been destroyed and Germany's last major source of crude oil was lost. Fuel shortages caused by the Allied bombing campaign had already badly affected the *Luftwaffe's* operations and the loss of Rumanian oil would soon cripple the *Wehrmacht's* efforts to repulse future Soviet offensives.

▲ **Tank ferry**

Red Army engineers ferry a T-34/85 across the Donetz River as part of the massive Soviet summer offensive in 1944.

Specifications

Crew: 7	Engine: 95kW (128hp) White 160AX
Weight: 10.16 tonnes (10 tons)	6-cylinder petrol
Length: 6.14m (20ft 3in)	Speed: 64km/h (45mph)
Width: 2.49m (8ft 2in)	Range: 280km (200miles)
Height: 2.44m (8ft)	Armament: 1 x 37mm (1.46in) M1A2 gun, 2 x
	coaxial 12.7mm (0.5in) Browning HMGs

▲ **Combination Gun Motor Carriage M15A1**

3rd Ukrainian Front / Thirty-Seventh Army / AA Regiment

As late as 1944/45, the Luftwaffe's ground-attack units still posed a significant threat to Soviet armoured forces. (It has been estimated that air attacks were responsible for 6 per cent of the Red Army's tank losses, equating to 90 tanks a month during 1944.) Roughly 100 M15A1s were supplied under Lend-Lease and were enthusiastically received, as their armour protection and cross-country mobility allowed them to operate far more effectively with armoured and mechanized units than earlier truck-mounted AA guns.

▶ **GAZ-67 4X4 command car**

HQ 3rd Ukrainian Front

Intended as a Soviet equivalent of the Lend-Lease jeep, the GAZ-67 was never as popular, primarily due to its high fuel consumption and weak brakes.

Specifications

Crew: 1 driver	Engine: 37.25kW (50hp) 4-cylinder petrol
Weight: 1.32 tonnes (1.3 tons)	Speed: 90km/h (56mph)
Length: 3.35m (11ft)	Range: 450km (280miles)
Width: 1.685m (5ft 6in)	Radio: Name
Height: 1.7m (5ft 7in)	

To the Baltic
14 SEPTEMBER – 24 NOVEMBER 1944

In February 1944, the *Wehrmacht* was forced to retreat from the approaches of Leningrad to the Panther Line on the borders of Estonia. In June–August, Operation *Bagration* had decimated Army Group Centre and pushed it back into Poland.

THIS CREATED THE opportunity for a Red Army offensive (the Shyaulyay Offensive Operation) which reached the Baltic on 31 July, severing the land connection between the German Army Groups. Although Operation *Doppelkopf*, a German counter-offensive launched in August, temporarily reopened land links between the Army Groups, the 'corridor' was never more than 30km (18.6 miles) wide. It was always vulnerable and was quickly cut by a new Soviet offensive launched on 14 September by the

1st and 3rd Baltic Fronts. This made rapid progress towards Riga, despite counter-attacks by XXXIX Panzer Corps.

Memel offensive

On 5 October, the 1st Baltic Front launched the Memel Offensive Operation, which destroyed the Third Panzer Army and finally cut the land link between Army Groups North and Centre, isolating Schoerner's forces in Riga and Courland. Initially, it

seemed that Memel would soon fall, but the German XXVIII Corps was able to hold a perimeter around the port, supported by naval gunfire from heavy units of the *Kriegsmarine,* including the pocket battleship *Lützow* and the heavy cruiser *Prinz Eugen.*

Insignia of the 1219th Self-Propelled Artillery Regiment. Many Soviet armoured units adopted similar simple geometric symbols.

▲ **JSU-122 heavy self-propelled gun**

1st Baltic Front / Fifth Guards Tank Army / 1219th Self-Propelled Artillery Regiment

The JSU-122 was developed purely to take advantage of the ready availability of 122mm (4.7in) guns and was identical to the JSU-152 except for the main armament and ammunition stowage.

Specifications

Crew: 5	Speed: 37km/h (23mph)
Weight: 45.5 tonnes (44.78 tons)	Range: (Road) 220km (136.7miles), (Terrain)
Length: 9.85m (32ft 3in)	80km (49.7miles)
Width: 3.07m (10ft 1in)	Radio: 10RF (When fitted)
Height: 2.48m (8ft 1in)	Armament: 1 x 122mm (4.7in) A-19S gun,
Engine: 447kW (600hp) V-2 diesel	plus 1 x 12.7mm (0.5in) DShK HMG

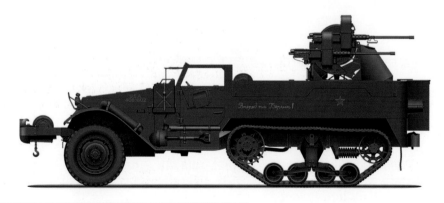

Specifications

Crew: 5	Engine: 106.54kW (143hp) International
Weight: 8.94 tonnes (8.8 tons)	Harvester RED-450-B; 6 cylinder, in-line petrol
Length: 6.49m (21ft 4in)	Speed: 68km/h (42mph)
Width: 2.17m (7ft 1in)	Range: 320km (200miles)
Height: 2.3m (7ft 6in)	Armament: 4 x 12.7mm (0.5in) Browning HMGs

▲ **M17 Multiple Motor Gun Carriage**

3rd Baltic Front / Sixty-First Army / AA Regiment / HQ

As many as 1000 M17s were issued to Soviet forces by 1945. The impressive firepower of the vehicle's four 12.7mm (0.5in) HMGs endeared it to the Red Army, which found it as useful for infantry support as in its AA role.

Hitler did not accept Schoerner's proposal to use forces freed by evacuating Riga in an attack towards Memel to attempt to re-establish the land connection, but his position was rapidly becoming untenable. Soviet forces were advancing and Riga was taken by the 3rd Baltic Front on 13 October, forcing Army Group North to retreat into the Courland Peninsula (where it held out until May 1945).

The success of these operations prompted *Stavka* to attempt a new offensive into East Prussia by Chernyakhovsky's 3rd Belorussian Front. The plan was for the Fifth and Eleventh Guards Armies to break through the German defences, after which II Guards Tank Corps and the Twenty-Eighth Army would advance on Königsberg, with the Thirty-First and Thirty-Ninth Armies providing flank protection. *Stavka* was becoming over-confident, however, and it failed to appreciate that the defenders had been

Specifications

Crew: 2, plus 11 passengers	Engine: 106.54kW (143hp) International
Weight: 9.3 tonnes (9.15 tons)	Harvester RED-450-B; 6-cylinder, in-line petrol
Length: 6.33m (20ft 9in)	Speed: 68km/h (42mph)
Width: 2.2m (7ft 2in)	Range: 320km (200miles)
Height: 2.74m (9ft)	Armament: 1 x 12.7mm (0.5in) Browning HMG

▲ **M5 halftrack**

2nd Baltic Front / Third Shock Army / HQ

In common with the other US armoured personnel carrier (APC) halftracks, the majority of the 342 M5s sent to Soviet forces were appropriated by formation HQs for use as command vehicles.

▲ **M2 halftrack**

3rd Baltic Front / Second Shock Army / HQ

With only a canvas tilt for protection against the elements, the open-topped US halftracks were not ideally suited to the extreme conditions of Russian winters.

Specifications

Crew: 2, plus 8 passengers	Engine: 109.5kW (147hp) White 160AX;
Weight: 8.89 tonnes (8.75 tons)	6 cylinder, in-line petrol
Length: 6.14m (20ft 2in)	Speed: 72km/h (45mph)
Width: 2.22m (7ft 3in)	Range: 320km (200miles)
Height: 2.7m (8ft 10in)	Armament: 1 x 12.7mm (0.5in) Browning HMG

heavily reinforced and would be aided by substantial fortifications.

On 16 October, the Fifth and Eleventh Guards Armies began their attacks, making an 11km (6.8-mile) penetration of the outer German defences and crossing the East Prussian border within the first 24 hours. However, it soon became clear that the German defences had been underestimated – it took four days to break through the first defensive line and the second was so strong that II Guards Tank Corps had to be committed.

The second line was finally broken at the cost of very heavy casualties, but it took the addition of the Front's reserve, the Twenty-Eighth Army, to push

back the defending units, which had been reinforced by the 18th Flak Division, whose guns inflicted heavy losses on the Soviet tanks. Gumbinnen was taken on 22 October, but was recaptured two days later.

There was equally fierce fighting around Goldap on the southern flank of the Soviet offensive. The town was retaken by the Germans on 25 October, successfully assaulted by the Soviet Thirty-First Army in a surprise attack on 28 October, and finally recaptured by the 5th Panzer Division on 3 November. The Soviet offensive had been a bloody failure, sustaining an estimated 79,500 casualties. The Red Army would not re-enter East Prussia in strength until January 1945.

▼ Heavy Assault Gun Regiment (1944)

The JSU-122 equipped regiments were formidable units, equally capable of acting as tank destroyers or in an infantry support role. Their high-velocity 122mm (4.8in) guns were capable of destroying even the heavily armoured Tiger IIs at normal combat ranges.

Regiment Headquarters

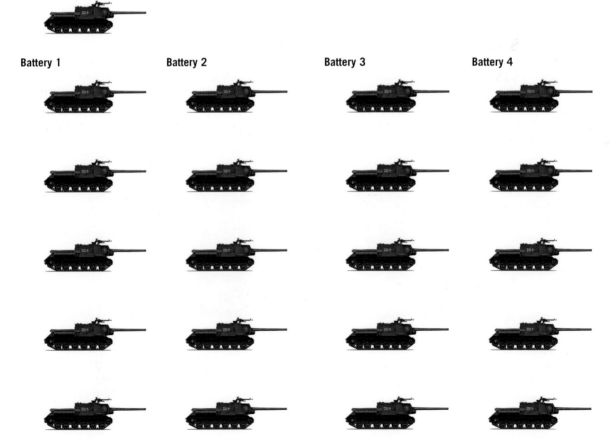

Battery 1 **Battery 2** **Battery 3** **Battery 4**

Specifications*

Crew: 1 driver

Weight: 3.1 tonnes (3.42 tons)

Length: 6.1m (20ft)

Width: 2.25m (7ft 4.5in)

Height: 2.16m (7ft 1in)

Engine: 54/57kW (73/76hp) ZiS-5M

Speed: 60km/h (37.3mph)

*Data for the basic ZiS-5 truck. Dimensions
and weight of the tanker version are likely
to be somewhat greater.

▲ **ZiS-5-BZ fuel tanker**

2nd Baltic Front / Supply Battalion

Even with the vast influx of Lend-Lease trucks, there were never enough supply
vehicles, and priority always had to be given to ammunition and fuel.

Into the Balkans

14 SEPTEMBER – 24 NOVEMBER 1944

**In September 1944, the two German Army Groups (E and F) in the Balkans were in danger of
being cut off by the rapid advance of the Red Army and the defection of former German satellite
forces. The Soviet victory at Jassy-Kishinev had forced Bulgaria and Romania to change sides,
adding them to Germany's list of enemies. *Stavka* now planned to carry the war into Yugoslavia
and take Belgrade.**

B Y THE END OF September 1944, the 3rd Ukrainian
Front (with the Second Bulgarian Army under
command) had moved up to the Bulgarian-Yugoslav
border in preparation for an advance on Belgrade.
In Rumania, elements of the 2nd Ukrainian Front
were assembling in readiness for an attack to cut
the rail link between Belgrade and Hungary. Tito's

Specifications

Crew: 2/3

Weight: 3.81 tonnes (3.75 tons)

Length: 3.65m (12ft)

Width: 1.92m (6ft 4in)

Height: 1.57m (5ft 2in)

Engine: 63.3kW (85hp) Ford V-8 petrol

Speed: 48km/h (30mph)

Range: 250km (150miles)

Armament: 1 x 12.7mm (0.5in) DShK HMG,
plus 1 x 7.7mm (0.303in) Bren Gun

▶ **Universal Carrier Mark II**

3rd Ukrainian Front / Fourth Guards Army / IV Guards Mechanized Corps /
14th Mechanized Brigade

Although the Red Army preferred US halftracks due to their far greater carrying
capacity, it employed 2500 Lend-Lease Universal Carriers in a variety of roles.
While retaining its Bren Gun, this example has been fitted with a 12.7mm (0.5in)
DShK HMG for the infantry fire support role.

▲ **Balkan victory**

A T-34/85 of the 3rd Ukrainian Front's IV Guards Mechanized Corps pauses for a halt in Belgrade, October 1944. The extra kit accumulated by tank crews on active service is much in evidence.

partisans now controlled large swathes of territory in Yugoslavia and Tito himself flew to Moscow for a meeting with Stalin to co-ordinate plans for the offensive.

Before the start of ground operations, the 3rd Ukrainian Front's Seventeenth Air Army carried out a week-long series of air attacks against German units withdrawing from Greece and southern Yugoslavia. The offensive began in late September – the 2nd Bulgarian Army's advance was contested by the 7th SS Mountain Division *Prinz Eugen*, which was overwhelmed and forced to withdraw. The Bulgarian forces then moved on Kosovo in an attempt to cut Army Group E's line of retreat from Greece. The Soviet Fifty-Seventh Army led the 3rd Ukrainian Front's attack towards Belgrade, with considerable support from Tito's partisans and the gunboats of the

Danube Military Flotilla. By 12 October, IV Guards Mechanized Corps was moved up from Bulgaria in preparation for a breakthrough to Belgrade.

Further north, the 2nd Ukrainian Front's Forty-Sixth Army advanced in an attempt to outflank the German Belgrade defensive position from the north, by cutting the river and rail supply lines running along the River Tisa. With close air support from the Fifth Air Army, its X Guards Rifle Corps made rapid progress to threaten the main rail routes from Belgrade.

On 14 October, IV Guards Mechanized Corps and the Yugoslav XII Corps broke through the German defences south of Belgrade. Although the assault on the city was delayed by the need to clear German forces holding out in the surrounding area, Belgrade was finally liberated on 20 October by combined Soviet and Yugoslav forces. At this time, the Bulgarian Second Army and Yugoslav XIII Corps were still advancing from the southeast. Their operations had forced Army Group E to retreat through Montenegro and Bosnia, preventing it from reinforcing German formations in Hungary. By late November, German forces had been cleared from virtually the whole of Yugoslavia and the Red Army was poised for its next offensives, riding high on a growing wave of victories. While its military successes had been spectacular, they were overshadowed by their political results – a new Soviet empire to rival that of the Tsars was rapidly being formed.

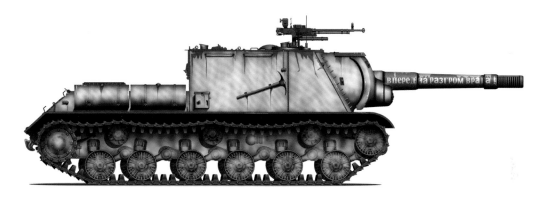

Specifications

Crew: 5

Weight: 46 tonnes (45.27 tons)

Length: 9.18m (30ft 1in)

Width: 3.07m (10ft 1in)

Height: 2.48m (8ft 1in)

Engine: 447kW (600hp) V-2 diesel

Speed: 37km/h (23mph)

Range: (Road) 220km (136.7 miles),

(Terrain) 80km (49.7 miles)

Radio: 10RF (When fitted)

Armament: 1 x 152mm (5.9in) ML-20S

howitzer, plus 1 x 12.7mm (0.5in) DShK HMG

on an AA mount

▲ JSU-152 heavy SP gun

2nd Ukrainian Front / Sixth Guards Tank Army / Independent Heavy Self-Propelled Artillery Regiment

Although officially designated as an artillery weapon, the JSU-152 was primarily used as a direct-fire assault gun, relying on its good armour protection to engage targets at close range.

Specifications

Crew: 4

Weight: 30.9 tonnes (30 tons)

Length: 5.92m (19ft 5in)

Width: 3.00m (9ft 8in)

Height: 2.44m (8ft)

Engine: 373kW (500hp) V-2-34 V-12 cylinder

diesel

Speed (road): 53km/h (33mph)

Range: 465km (290 miles)

Armament: 1 x 76mm (3in) L-40 gun; 2 x

7.62mm (0.3in) DT MGs (bow and coaxial)

▲ T-34 Model 1943

2nd Ukrainian Front / Sixth Tank Army

As the Red Army undertook increasingly large-scale offensives during 1944, ever-expanding numbers of its AFVs were fitted with 'drum type' long-range fuel tanks to extend their radius of action and ease demands on the supply columns.

Chapter 12

Victory
in Europe

By 1945, the Red Army was rapidly closing the
'technology gap' that had opened up in 1943 with the
Panzerwaffe's introduction of the Tiger and Panther.
The T-34/85 had entered service in 1944 and was steadily
replacing earlier T-34s, while the JSU-122 and JSU-152 had
proved to be exceptionally useful both as heavy assault guns
and as tank destroyers. The Germans attempted to maintain
their qualitative edge with improved versions of the Panther
and new types such as the Tiger II, Jagdpanzer IV and
Jagdpanther, but were unable to produce them in sufficient
numbers to make a significant impact. Ironically, in the last
months of the war one of the greatest threats to Soviet AFVs
would not be the impressive German Jagdpanzers, but the
simple, deadly *Panzerfausts* and *Panzerschrecks*.

◀ **Tank victory**
JS-2s roll through central Berlin, May 1945 – after the ceasefire, judging by the casual attitude of the tank
commanders.

Vistula–Oder Offensive
12 January – 2 February 1945

The Vistula–Oder operation was originally intended as a major element of a series of offensives to be launched in late January 1945, with the objective of ending the war in 45 days.

HOWEVER, IN RESPONSE to US and British requests for action to ease the pressure from the Ardennes offensive, Stalin ordered a less ambitious operation, which was launched on 12 January. The Soviet objective was now limited to securing the line of the River Vistula, which would bring them to within 60km (37 miles) of Berlin.

Zhukov's 1st Byelorussian Front and Konev's 1st Ukrainian Front fielded 163 divisions for the offensive, with a total of 2,203,000 troops, 4529 tanks, 2513 assault guns, 13,763 field artillery weapons (76mm/3in or more), 14,812 mortars, 4936 AT guns, 2198 'Katyusha' salvo rocket launchers and 5000 aircraft.

They were opposed by Army Group A, which could muster no more than 400,000 troops, 4100 guns and 1150 AFVs. (As usual, the Soviet numerical superiority was increased by massive

Tank Corps, Personnel (1945)	Strength
Corps Headquarters	32
Signal Battalion	253
Motorcycle Battalion	451
Tank Brigade x 3	1362
Motorized Rifle Brigade	3222
Heavy Assault Gun Regiment (SU-152)	374
Assault Gun Regiment (SU-85/100)	318
Light Assault Gun Regiment (SU-76)	225
Light Artillery Regiment	625
Rocket Launcher Battalion	203
Mortar Regiment	596
Anti-Aircraft Regiment	397
Pioneer Battalion	455
Trains Elements	298

▲ **JS-1 heavy tank**

2nd Ukrainian Front / Sixth Guards Tank Army

Only small numbers of the JS-1 were built. It was quickly replaced by the JS-2 after combat experience showed that a better gun was needed to deal with the heavy armour of the Tiger II and Jagdpanther.

Specifications

Crew: 4

Weight: 46 tonnes (45.3 tons)

Length: 8.32m (27ft 3in)

Width: 3.25m (10ft 8in)

Height: 2.9m (9ft 6in)

Engine: 38.8kW (510hp) V-2 12-cylinder diesel

Speed: 40km/h (24.9mph)

Range: 250km (155miles)

Radio: 10R

Armament: 1 x 85mm (3.35in) D-5T gun, plus

   2 x 7.62mm (0.3in) DT MGs, 1 coaxial,

   1 ball-mounted in turret rear

concentrations of troops and artillery at key sectors – Eighth Guards Army had 350 guns and mortars per kilometre, one gun every 3m (10ft).

The offensive was launched on 12 January 1945 by Konev's 1st Ukrainian Front from the Soviet bridgehead near Sandomierz. The assault quickly broke through the sketchy defences of the Fourth Panzer Army, which largely comprised isolated strongpoints since it lacked the infantry to hold a continuous front-line. Within 12 hours, Third Guards and Fourth Tank Armies with a combined strength of over 1700 tanks and SP guns were able to exploit the breakthrough and the Fourth Panzer Army had lost over 60 per cent of its artillery and 25 per cent of its troops.

Zhukov attacks

On 14 January, Zhukov's attack began with a 25-minute preliminary artillery barrage in which 315,000 rounds were fired (almost 5500 tonnes/ 5413 tons). Once again, the German defences virtually disintegrated: within a few hours, the First and Second Guards Tank Armies' 1635 tanks and SP guns were driving into the German rear areas, towards Lodz. Indeed, the speed of the Soviet advance was such that Panzer Corps *Grossdeutschland*, hastily transferred from East

▲ **Marshall Konev**

Konev (left) was an able and exceptionally ruthless commander. By 1944, his rivalry with Zhukov was exploited by Stalin to hasten the capture of key objectives.

▲ **T-34/85**

1st Ukrainian Front / Third Guards Tank Army / IX Mechanized Corps

By 1945, the T-34/85 was increasingly supplanting the earlier T-34s, especially in guards units, which tended to get priority for new equipment.

Specifications

Crew: 5	Speed (road): 55km/h (33mph)
Weight: 32 tonnes (31.5 tons)	Range: 360km (223 miles)
Length: 6m (19ft 7in)	Radio: 9R (When fitted)
Width: 3m (9ft 9in)	Armament: 1 x 85mm (3.4in) ZiS-S-53 cannon;
Height: 2.60m (8ft 6in)	2 x 7.62mm (0.3in) DT MGs (bow and coaxial)
Engine: 1 x V-2 V-12 cylinder 372 kW (493hp) diesel engine	

Prussia, was brushed aside before it could fully deploy and was forced to retreat.

Warsaw was taken on 17 January by the 1st Byelorussian Front's First Polish Army, whilst Konev's forces overran the industrial area of Upper Silesia by the end of the month. (Stalin had personally briefed Konev on the vital importance of capturing the region's factories and mines intact. All Soviet operations in the area carefully left escape routes open for retreating German forces to avoid destructive combat in key industrial centres.) While many towns and cities were captured quickly, some by-passed centres held out for prolonged periods, considerably complicating the work of the over-stretched Soviet supply units. Nonetheless, by 31 January the 1st

Byelorussian Front's I Mechanized Corps had secured bridgeheads over the frozen Oder, roughly 30km (18.6 miles) apart, one south of Frankfurt-an-der-Oder and the other north of Kustrin. They were only 60km (37 miles) from Berlin.

Although both Zhukov and Konev pressed for permission to go on to Berlin, *Stavka* closed down the offensive on 2 February. Both Fronts had advanced roughly 500km (311 miles) on a 500km (311-mile) frontage in little more than three weeks and their supply lines were stretched to breaking point. Furthermore, despite their weakened state, German forces in East Pomerania posed a real threat to the exhausted Soviet troops and would have to be dealt with – Berlin would have to wait.

 JSU-152 Heavy Self-Propelled Gun

1st Ukrainian Front / Third Guards Tank Army / IV Guards Tank Corps / 385th Guards Heavy Self-Propelled Artillery Regiment

This JSU-152 has unusually elaborate winter camouflage – roughly applied coats of whitewash were far more common.

Specifications

Crew: 5	Range: (Road) 220km (136.7miles),
Weight: 46 tonnes (45.27 tons)	(Terrain) 80km (49.7miles)
Length: 9.18m (30ft 1in)	Radio: 10RF (When fitted)
Width: 3.07m (10ft 1in)	Armament: 1 x 152mm (5.9in) ML-20S
Height: 2.48m (8ft 1in)	howitzxer, plus 1 x 12.7mm (0.5in) DShK HMG
Engine: 447kW (600hp) V-2 diesel	on an AA mount
Speed: 37km/h (23mph)	

▶ **Willys MB 4x4 ¼-ton Truck, Command Reconnaissance**

1st Ukrainian Front / Third Guards Tank Army / HQ

The extremes of the Russian climate led to many jeeps being fitted with 'hard tops' as a field modification.

Specifications

Crew: 1 driver	Engine: 44.7kW (60hp) 4-cylinder petrol
Weight: 1.04 tonnes (1.02 tons)	Speed: 88.5km/h (55mph)
Length: 3.33m (10ft 11in)	Range: n/k
Width: 1.58m (5ft 2in)	Radio: n/a
Height: 1.83m (6ft)	

▲ **The war's last winter**
Soviet troops ride on the warm rear deck of an JSU-152, Poland, January 1945.

▲ **Studebaker US6 BZ-35S 6x4 2½-ton fuel tanker**
1st Ukrainian Front / Third Guards Tank Army / Special Transport Regiment
A proportion of the thousands of Lend-Lease Studebakers received by the Red
Army were converted to fuel tankers under the designation BZ-35S. The advances
of 1945 stretched logistics to the limit, as each tank army required 600–750
tonnes (591–738 tons) of fuel per day – 270 to 300 tanker loads.

Specifications

Crew: 2	Engine: JXD 6 cylinder Hercules
Weight: 4.33 tons (9555lbs)	Speed: not known
Length: 6.55m (21ft 6in)	Range: not known
Width: 2.23m (7ft 4in)	Radio: none
Height: 2.76m (9ft 1in)	

HQ 1 x T-70 light tank   **5 Batteries each with 4 x SU-76 assault guns**

HQ 1 x T-70 light tank   **5 Batteries each with 4 x SU-76 assault guns**

HQ 1 x T-70 light tank   **5 Batteries each with 4 x SU-76 assault guns**

◀ Light Assault Gun Brigade

Although their thinly armoured, open-topped SU-76Ms were very vulnerable to air-burst artillery, light assault gun brigades were highly mobile formations with considerable firepower. (The low ground pressure of the SU-76M allowed it to cross swampy ground that was impassable to heavier AFVs.)

Specifications

Crew: 4	Engine: 2 x GAZ 6-cylinder petrol 52+52kW
Weight: 10.8 tonnes (11.9 tons)	(70+70hp)
Length: 4.88m (16ft)	Speed (road): 45km/h (28mph)
Width: 2.73m (8ft 11.5in)	Range: 450km (280miles)
Height: 2.17m (7ft 1.4in)	Armament: one 76mm (3in) gun and one
	7.62mm (0.3in) MG

▲ SU-76M

1st Ukrainian Front / Third Guards Tank Army / VII Guards Tank Corps

The open-topped SU-76M was a particularly uncomfortable vehicle in the depths of an Eastern Front winter.

▲ Forest cover

A JSU-122S moves up for the assault on Berlin, April 1945.

Austria and Hungary

FEBRUARY–APRIL 1945

By the summer of 1944, the Hungarian regime of Admiral Horthy was an increasingly reluctant German ally as the Red Army advanced towards the Carpathians. Hitler was determined to keep control of the oilfields around Lake Balaton, which were the Reich's last major source of oil.

GERMAN TROOPS HAD occupied key points throughout Hungary since March 1944, when Hitler had first learned of Admiral Horthy's initial 'peace feelers' to the Allies. On 16 October, renewed Hungarian attempts to negotiate with the Allies provoked Operation *Panzerfaust*, which deposed Admiral Horthy and set up a puppet fascist government led by Ferenc Szalasi.

Siege of Budapest

While the Germans had secured their rear areas, their defences in Hungary were rapidly crumbling as Malinovsky's 2nd Ukrainian Front advanced on Budapest. The first Red Army units penetrated the city's eastern suburbs on 7 November, but were halted by the German/Hungarian garrison that had

just received major reinforcements, including the 1st, 3rd, 6th and 8th Panzer Divisions.

During the next six weeks, the Soviet forces were joined by Tobulkhin's 3rd Ukrainian Front and on 18 December both Fronts launched a new offensive to encircle Budapest. Despite fierce counter-attacks by several Panzer divisions, 3rd Ukrainian Front's XVIII Tank Corps linked up with 2nd Ukrainian Front on 26 December to seal off the city. Although the garrison of 76,000 was heavily outnumbered by the opposing 300,000 strong Soviet Fronts, the cover provided by the urban terrain went a long way towards balancing the odds. (The city was divided by the Danube – Buda lay on the hills of the river's west bank and Pest covered the relatively flat ground to the east of the river.)

Specifications

Crew: 5	Range: (Road) 220km (136.7miles),
Weight: 45.5 tonnes (44.78 tons)	(Terrain) 80km (49.7miles)
Length: 9.85m (32ft 3in)	Radio: 10RF (When fitted)
Width: 3.07m (10ft 1in)	Armament: 1 x 122mm (4.8in) D-25 gun,
Height: 2.48m (8ft 1in)	plus 1 x 12.7mm (0.5in) DShK HMG on
Engine: 447kW (600hp) V-2 diesel	an AA mount
Speed: 37km/h (23mph)	

▲ **JSU-122S heavy SP gun**

3rd Ukrainian Front / Sixth Guards Tank Army / V Guards Tank Corps / Independent Heavy Assault Gun Regiment

The JSU-122S was an updated JSU-122 that began to enter service in 1945. The main improvements were the D-25 122mm (4.8in) gun, with a revised breech mechanism to increase the rate of fire and a muzzle brake that reduced recoil. The D-25 was mounted in a new ball mantlet that improved traverse arcs.

Hungary, January 1945	T-34	IS-2	SU-76	SU-85	SU-100	ISU-122	ISU-152	M4A2 Sherman
XVIII Tank Corps	120	19	–	11	–	–	–	–
I Gds Mechanized Corps	–	–	–	–	62	–	–	184
II Gds Mechanized Corps	35	8	–	11	–	–	–	–
VII Mechanized Corps	–	65	12	14	10	–	–	–
I Gds Fortified Region	7	–	4	–	–	–	–	–
V Gds Cavalry Corps	2	–	13	–	–	–	–	–
XXIII Tank Corps	–	174	–	–	–	–	19	–

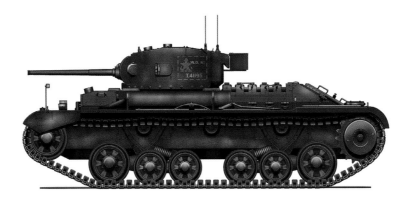

Specifications

Crew: 3

Weight: 17.27 tonnes (17 tons)

Length: 5.89m (19ft 4in)

Width: 2.64m (8ft 8in)

Height: 2.29m (7ft 6in)

Engine: 100kW (135hp) GMC 6004 diesel

Speed: 24km/h (14.9mph)

Range: 0km (0miles)

Radio: n/a

Armament: 1 x 2pdr (40mm), plus 1 x coaxial
7.92mm (0.31in) Besa MG

▲ Infantry Tank Mark III, Valentine Mark VII

2nd Ukrainian Front / 1st Guards Mechaniszd Cavalry Group

The Valentine was still in service with the Red Army in the final months of the war. As late as March 1945, a total of 41 Valentines were operational with the 1st Guards Mechanized Cavalry Group.

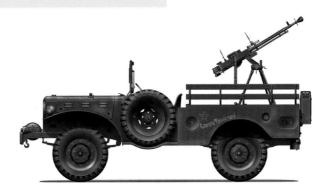

Specifications

Crew: 1 driver + 2/3 gun crew

Weight: 2.69 tonnes (5940lbs)

Length: 2.69m (14ft 8in)

Width: 2.10m (6ft 10in)

Height: 1.7m (5ft 7in)

Engine: 6 cylinder 68.6kW (92hp) petrol

Speed: not known

Range: not known

Armament: 1 x DShK 12.7mm (0.5in) HMG

▲ Dodge WC52 4x4 ¾-ton weapons carrier with DShK 12.7mm (0.5in) HMG

3rd Ukrainian Front / Sixth Guards Tank Army

From 1943 onwards, the Soviet Union received almost 25,000 of these vehicles, which were primarily used as gun tractors and troop carriers. However, a number were armed with the DShK 12.7mm (0.5in) HMG for use in the AA role and to protect AFVs against Panzerfaust ambushes.

The Soviet offensive began in the eastern suburbs, advancing into Pest itself along the broad main streets. The outnumbered German and Hungarian defenders fought delaying actions, slowly withdrawing to more defensible positions in the city centre. Soviet armoured units quickly discovered that *Panzerfausts* represented the greatest single threat to their tanks in street fighting. This was especially true when the defenders managed to pin down their accompanying infantry, before stalking the isolated tanks to make close range shots against their relatively thin side

◀ **Waiting to advance**

A column of IS-2 heavy tanks from the 1st Byelorussian Front sits outside a town on the Polish-Hungarian border, March 1945.

AFV Units (Operational Strength), Hungary, March 1945	T-34	IS-2	SU-76	SU-85	SU-100	ISU-122	ISU-152	M4A2 Sherman
XVIII Tank Corps	42	–	12	–	–	16	6	–
208th SPGBr	2	–	3	–	63	–	–	–
XXIII Tank Corps	20	1	–	–	–	–	–	–
207th SPGR	2	–	–	–	20	–	–	–
366th Gds SPGR	–	2	–	–	–	–	4	–
I Gds Mechanized Corps	–	–	–	–	17	–	–	47
V Gds Cavalry Corps	7	–	8	–	–	–	–	2
1891st SPGR	–	–	2	–	–	–	–	–
1513rd SPGR	–	–	24	–	–	–	–	–
1523rd SPGR	–	–	25	–	–	–	–	–
1524th SPGR	–	–	25	–	–	–	–	–
SSPGB (4th Gds Army)	–	–	2	–	–	–	–	–
432nd SSPGB	–	–	7	–	–	–	–	–
1202nd SPGR	–	–	14	–	–	–	–	–
1201st SPGR	1	–	–	12	–	–	–	–
72nd SSPGB	–	–	–	–	–	–	–	–
32nd Gds Mot Rifle Bde	19	–	–	–	–	–	–	–
249th Tank Reg	–	10	–	–	–	–	–	–
854th SPGR	1	–	21	–	–	–	–	–
1094th SPGR	–	–	–	–	20	–	–	–
1922nd SPGR	–	–	–	–	16	–	–	–
3rd Gds SSPGB	10	–	–	–	–	–	–	–
58th SSPGB	10	–	–	–				
SSPGB (27th Army)	–	–	22	—				
209th SPGBr	2	–	–	–				
XXII Tank Corps	6	–	–	2	–			

KEY
SPGBr   Self-Propelled Gun Brigade
SPGR   Self-Propelled Gun Regiment
SSPGB   Separate Self-Propelled Gun Battalion

and rear armour. Stalin was rapidly losing patience with the Red Army's slow progress and Malinovsky ordered the formation of a special combat group, including heavy weapons and assault engineers equipped with flamethrowers, to spearhead assaults. Rifle divisions were assigned attack sectors up to 700m (2297ft) wide, with regiments advancing fronts of no more than 300m (984ft). Large numbers of guns, including 122mm (4.8in), 152mm (5.9in), and 203mm (8in) howitzers, were brought up to support attacks with direct fire.

While Malinovsky was struggling to crush resistance in the city, three attempts by IV SS Panzer Corps to raise the siege (Operations *Konrad* I, II and III) came tantalizingly close to success before being blocked by hastily reinforced Soviet units. On 18 January, the corps launched a further attack after redeploying to the south, penetrating 32km (20 miles) in the first 24 hours, beating off a counterattack by VII Mechanized Corps.

The next day, further counterattacks by XVIII Tank Corps and CXXXIII Rifle Corps were broken up, largely due to the fire of the 3rd SS Panzer Division *Totenkopf*'s AT battalion, equipped with the new Jagdpanzer IV tank destroyers. Within three days, the leading German units had advanced 100km

▲ T-44 medium tank

Trials Unit

The T-44 entered production in 1945 as the replacement for the T34/85. Between 150 and 200 vehicles were produced by the end of the war, although it seems unlikely that any went into combat. (In 1947, the type was itself superseded by the T-54 which was armed with a 100mm gun.)

▼ M4A2 Sherman medium tank

3rd Ukrainian Front / I Guards Machanized Corps

By the end of the War, Shermans equipped three Guards mechanized corps and a Guards tank corps.

Specifications

Crew: 4

Weight: 31.9 tonnes (31.4 tons)

Length: 7.65m (25ft 1in)

Width: 3.15m (10ft 4in)

Height: 2.45m (8ft)

Engine: 372.5kW (500hp) V-44 12-cylinder

diesel

Speed: 51km/h (31.69mph)

Range: 300km (186.4 miles)

Armament: 1 x 85mm (3.35in) D-5T gun, plus

2 x 7.62mm (0.30in) DTM MGs, 1 coaxial and

1 fixed forward-firing

Specifications

Crew: 5

Weight: 32.28 tonnes (35.58 tons)

Length: 5.92m (19ft 5in)

Width: 2.62m (8ft 7in)

Height: 2.74m (9ft)

Engine: 280kW (375hp) General Motors 6046

12- cylinder diesel

Speed: 48km/h (30mph)

Range: 240km (150miles)

Armament: 1 x 75mm (2.9in) M3 L/40 gun;

1 x 12.7mm (0.5in) l Browning M2HB MG,

1 x turret mounted 12.7mm 0.50 cal MG

(62 miles) and had reached the Danube, cutting into the rear of the 3rd Ukrainian Front's Fifty-Seventh Army. By 24 January, the force had advanced to within 24km (15 miles) of Budapest and inflicted heavy losses on I Guards Mechanized Corps and V Guards Cavalry Corps. It was only with the arrival of the last Soviet reserve formation, XXIII Tank Corps, that the German advance was halted.

By 28 January, IV SS Panzer Corps was forced to withdraw, abandoning Budapest. Amazingly, some parts of the city held out until 13 February, largely due to air-dropped supplies, supplemented by larger shipments brought in at night by small river craft. Losses on both sides were heavy – an estimated 100,000 Soviet casualties to set against over 75,000 Germans and Hungarians killed or captured. Only 785 survivors managed to safely cross the 40km (25 miles) to reach the German lines.

The Lake Balaton offensive

Code-named Operation *Frühlingserwachen* ('Spring Awakening'), this was the last significant German offensive of the war. It was ordered by Hitler in a typically unrealistic attempt not only to secure the Hungarian oilfields, but to retake Budapest and destroy the 3rd Ukrainian Front.

Good operational security (and an understandable Soviet belief that the Germans were incapable of launching any major offensive) ensured that complete surprise was achieved. Spearheaded by Sepp Dietrich's Sixth Panzer Army, the attack went in on 6 March and made good progress.

An early thaw, however, had turned the entire region into a muddy morass and the appalling ground conditions posed as many problems for the Panzers as the Soviet forces. In some sectors, Tiger IIs sank up to their turrets in the thick mud and at least 15 had to be abandoned. Delays imposed by these conditions gave time for Tolbukhin to call in reinforcements from the Ninth Guards Army and launch a counterattack on 16 March, which pushed the German forces back to their start-lines within 24 hours.

By the end of the month, the remnants of the Sixth Panzer Army had retreated into Austria in an attempt to protect Vienna. (Sepp Dietrich remarked with only slight exaggeration and no doubt a great

▲ **SU-85 and T-34**
The SU-85 was a well-designed tank destroyer based on the T-34 hull and armed with an 85mm (3.3in) gun, which entered service in late 1943. In the summer of 1944, production switched to the SU-100 armed with a far more powerful 100mm (3.9in) gun.

deal of bitterness that 'Sixth Panzer Army is well named — we have just six tanks left!')

Vienna

The 3rd Ukrainian Front followed up Sixth Panzer Army's retreat and quickly assembled around Vienna, which was garrisoned mainly by II SS Panzer Corps. The Soviet assault began on 2 April with attacks by Fourth and Ninth Guards Armies, but made only limited progress until Sixth Guards Tank Army was committed on 8 April. The additional pressure forced German units westwards to avoid being trapped and

the city surrendered on 13 April. (As II SS Panzer Corps withdrew on 12 April, a single Panther commanded by *Leutnant* Arno Giesen knocked out 14 T-34s and JS-2s while holding one of the Danube bridges – a sharp reminder of German AT talents.)

This inscription 'Liberated Kirovgrad' is typical of many carried on Soviet AFVs. While some were undoubtedly designed and applied by the crews themselves, it seems likely that many of the more 'political' slogans were the work of the NKVD.

▲ **JSU-152 heavy SP gun**

2nd Byelorussian Front / HQ Fiftieth Army / Independent Heavy Assault Gun Regiment

The JSU-152 proved invaluable in the fierce street fighting prevalent at the end of the war, as its 40kg (88lb) HE shells were highly effective against even heavily fortified strrongpoints.

Specifications

Crew: 5	Speed: 37km/h (23mph)
Weight: 46 tonnes (45.27 tons)	Range: (Road) 220km (136.71miles),
Length: 9.18m (30ft 1in)	(Terrain) 80km (49.71 miles)
Width: 3.07m (10ft 1in)	Radio: 10RF (When fitted)
Height: 2.48m (8ft 1in)	Armament: 1 x 152mm (5.9in) ML-20S howitzer
Engine: 447kW (600hp) V-2 diesel	

▲ **SU-152 heavy SP gun**

1st Byelorussian Front / First Guards Tank Army / XI Guards Tank Corps / HQ 362nd Guards Assault Artillery Regiment

Although production of the SU-152 ended in late 1943, surviving vehicles remained in service until the end of the war.

Specifications

Crew: 5	Speed: 43km/h (26.72mph)
Weight: 45.5 tonnes (44.78 tons)	Range: (Road) 330km (205miles),
Length: 8.95m (29ft 4in)	(Terrain) 120km (74.57miles)
Width: 3.25m (10ft 8in)	Radio: 9R (When fitted)
Height: 2.45m (8ft 0in)	Armament: 1 x 152mm (5.9in) ML-20S howitzer
Engine: 447kW (600hp) V-2 diesel	

Seelow Heights and Berlin
APRIL–MAY 1945

During the second week of April 1945, a massive Soviet force was assembled in the small bridgehead on the west bank of the Oder near Kustrin. Zhukov's 1st Byelorussian Front was preparing to attack the Seelow Heights, the last natural defence line before Berlin.

THE 1ST BYELORUSSIAN Front had 908,000 men, 3155 AFVs and 16,934 guns and had stockpiled over 7,000,000 rounds of artillery ammunition. On its northern flank was Rokossovsky's 2nd Byelorussian

▲ **Into the suburbs**
JSU-122 heavy assault guns move into the suburbs of Berlin, April 1945.

Front. Zhukov's forces were opposed by General Gotthard Heinrici's Army Group Vistula – its Ninth Army, which would bear the brunt of the assault on the Seelow Heights, fielded 14 divisions, 512 AFVs, 344 guns and 300–400 AA guns. Further south the front was held by the Fourth Panzer Army, which faced Konev's 1st Ukrainian Front.

Although heavily outnumbered, Heinrici had done much to reduce the odds against him. Correctly anticipating that the main Soviet attacks would be made on the Seelow Heights along the line of the main east–west autobahn, he had thinned out other sectors of the front to reinforce the area. The Heights themselves were well fortified, forming part of three defence lines up to 25km (15.5 miles) deep. The Oder's flood plain, already saturated by the spring thaw, was turned into a swamp by water released

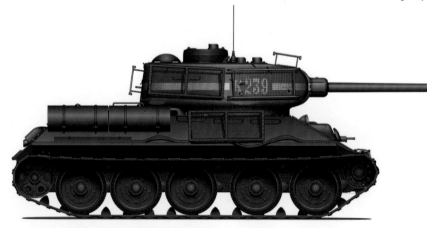

▲ **T-34/85**

1st Byelorussian Front / Second Guards Tank Army

This T-34/85 has been fitted with wooden-framed wire mesh panels as protection against German Panzerfausts and Panzerschrecks, which were responsible for almost 23 per cent of the T-34s lost during the battle of Berlin. It bears the white turret band adopted in April 1945 as a recognition marking to minimize the risk of friendly fire incidents between Western Allied tanks and Soviet AFVs.

Specifications

Crew: 5	Speed (road): 55km/h (33mph)
Weight: 32 tonnes (31.5 tons)	Range: 360km (223 miles)
Length: 6m (19ft 7in)	Radio: N/A
Width: 3m (9ft 9in)	Armament: 1 x 85mm (3.4in) ZiS-S-53 cannon;
Height: 2.60m (8ft 6in)	2 x 7.62mm (0.3in) DT MGs (bow and coaxial)
Engine: 1 x V-2 V-12 cylinder 372 kW (493hp)	
diesel engine	

from a reservoir upstream and minefields were laid in to protect key points.

At 0500 on 16 April, the offensive began with a massive bombardment by thousands of guns and 'Katyushas' of the 1st Byelorussian Front before the main assault went in. Almost immediately, things started to go wrong – the debris and smoke from the massive bombardment meant that the glare of the 140-plus searchlights intended to blind the Germans was reflected and blinded the attackers. (It also turned them into easy targets, silhouetted against the light.) Worse still, the bombardment had been largely

Specifications

Crew: 5

Weight: 42.5 tonnes (41.83 tons)

Length: 6.8m (22ft 4in)

Width: 3.25m (10ft 8in)

Height: 2.64m (8ft 8in)

Engine: 447kW (600hp) V-2 diesel

Speed: 45km/h (28mph)

Range: (Road):250km (155miles), (Terrain)

160km (99 miles)

Radio: 9R (When fitted)

▲ **KV1S Heavy Tank**

1st Byelorussian Front / First Guards Tank Army / XI Guards Tank Corps / HQ / 362nd Guards Assault Artillery Regiment

A few KV heavy tanks survived until the end of the war, usually as command vehicles in JSU-122 or JSU-152 units.

Mechanized Corps (May 1945)	Strength
Personnel	16,438
Armoured Vehicles:	
Light tanks	–
Medium tanks	183
Heavy tanks	–
Light assault guns	21
Medium assault guns	21
Heavy assault guns	21
Guns and Mortars:	
82mm (3.2in) mortars	100
120mm (4.7in) mortars	54
45mm (1.8in) AT guns	36
57mm (2.2in) AT guns	8
37mm (1.5in) AA guns	16
76mm (3in) guns	36
BM-13 rocket launchers	8

Tank Corps (May 1945)	Strength
Personnel	11,788
Armoured Vehicles:	
T-60 light tanks	–
T-70 light Tanks	–
T-34 medium Tanks	207
KV heavy tanks	–
SU-76	21
SU-85	21
SU-152/ISU-152	21
Guns and Mortars:	
82mm (3.2in) mortars	52
120mm (4.7in) mortars	42
45mm (1.8in) AT guns	12
57mm (2.2in) AT guns	16
37mm (1.5in) AA guns	16
76mm (3in) guns	36
M-13 rocket launchers	8

wasted on empty defences – a Soviet prisoner had revealed the timing of the attack and Heinrici had pulled his forces back to their second defensive line. Taking advantage of the slow and confused Soviet advance, the Germans reoccupied their forward defences and brought down a murderous fire on the attackers. By the next day, the 1st Byelorussian Front

had advanced no more than 8km (5 miles) and was still bogged down in the German defences.

An enraged Zhukov committed the 1337 AFVs of his two tank armies to the attack, but the huge number of vehicles deployed on a narrow front caused a massive traffic jam, providing more targets for the German artillery.

▲ JS-2 heavy tank

1st Ukrainian Front / Third Guards Tank Army / 57th Guards Heavy Tank Regiment

Even the heavily armoured JS-2 was vulnerable in the Berlin fighting, where hazards ranged from 128mm (5in) Flak guns to HEAT AT grenades lobbed from upper-floor windows.

Specifications

Crew: 4	Speed: 37km/h (23mph)
Weight: 46 tonnes (45.27tons)	Range: 240km (149 miles)
Length: 9.9m (32ft 6in)	Radio: 10R
Width: 3.09m (10ft 2in)	Armament: 1 x 122mm (4.8in) D-25T gun, plus
Height: 2.73m (8ft 11in)	3 x 7.62mm (0.3in) DT MGs (1 coaxial, 1 fixed
Engine: 382.8kW (513hp) V-2 12-cylinder diesel	in bow, 1 ball-mounted in turret rear)

Specifications

Crew: 4	Speed: 47km/h (29mph)
Weight: 29.2 tonnes (28.74 tons)	Range: (Road):400km (248.55 miles),
Length: 8.15m (26ft 9in)	(Terrain) 200km (124.27miles)
Width: 3m (9ft 10in)	Radio: 9R (When fitted)
Height: 2.45m (8ft)	Armament: 1 x 85mm (3.4in) D5-S gun
Engine: 372.5kW (500hp) V-2 diesel	

▲ SU-85 tank destroyer

3rd Ukrainian Front / VII Mechanised Corps

Most self-propelled guns developed for the Red Army during the war were intended to operate in both the anti-tank and close support roles. The SU-85 (and its successor, the SU-100) were exceptions to this rule, being deployed almost exclusively as tank destroyers.

Konev advances

In contrast to the bloody confusion at the Seelow Heights, Konev's attack, launched at almost the same time, made excellent progress – by 17 April, the 1st Ukrainian Front's forward units had broken through the main German defences and had crossed the River Spree. Konev seized the opportunity and obtained Stalin's permission to make straight for Berlin.

ORDER OF BATTLE: THE ASSAULT ON BERLIN (APRIL 1945)			
Front	Army	Corps	Brigade/Regiment
2nd Byelorussian	Fifth Guards Tank	XXIX Tank	1st Tank & 4th Mech Bdes
1st Byelorussian	First Polish		4th Polish Heavy Tank, 13th Polish SP Assault Artillery
	Forty-Seventh		70th Guards Independent Tank Rgt
		IX Tank	23rd Tank, 95th Tank, 108th Tank
	Fifth Shock		11th Tank, 67th Guards Tank, 220th Tank, 92nd Independent Tank Rgt
	Eighth Guards		7th Guards Tank, 84th Guards Tank, 65th Independent Tank, 259th Independent Tank Rgts
	Sixty-Ninth		68th Tank, 12th SP Assault Artillery
	Thirty-Third		257th Independent Tank Rgt, 360th SP Assault Artillery, 361st SP Assault Artillery
	First Guards Tank	VIII Guards Mech	19th, 20th & 21st Guards Mechanized, 1st Guards Tank Bde, 48th Guards Tank, 353rd & 400th Guards SP Assault Artillery Rgts
		XI Guards Tank	40th, 44th & 45th Guards Tank, 27th Guards Mechanized, 362nd, 399th Guards, 1454 SP Assault Artillery Rgts
		XI Tank	20th, 36th & 65th Tank, 12th Motorized Rifle, 50th Guards Tank Rgt, 1461st & 1493rd SP Assault Artillery Rgts, 64th Guards Tank, 19th SP Assault Artillery, 11th Guards Independent Tank Rgt
	Second Guards Tank	I Mechanized	19th, 35th & 37th Mechanized, 219th Tank, 347th Guards, 75th & 1822nd SP Assault Artillery Rgts
		IX Guards tank	47th, 50th & 65th Guards Tank, 33rd Guards Mechanized, 341st, 369th & 386th Guards SP Assault Artillery Rgts
		XII Guards Tank	48th, 49th & 66th Guards Tank, 34th Guards Mechanized, 79th Guards Tank Rgt, 387th & 393rd Guards SP Assault Artillery Rgt, 6th Guards Independent Tank Rgt
	Third	XXXV, XL & XLI Rifle	1812th, 1888th & 1901st SP Assault Artillery Rgts
		II, III & VII Guards Cavalry	
		III & VIII Guards Tank	244th Independent Tank Rgts, 31st, 39th, 51st & 55th Independent Armoured Train

With the Third Tank Army and Fourth Guards Tank Army in the lead, his forces charged along the autobahn towards the city.

On 19 April, Zhukov's forces finally broke through the last defences on the Seelow Heights and were also on their way to Berlin. The cost had been appalling – over 700 Soviet AFVs had been destroyed in the battle for the Heights and the Red Army had sustained at least 30,000 casualties (three times the German total).

Assault on Berlin

On 26 April, Soviet forces completed the encirclement of Berlin – the city had been under artillery bombardment since 20 April and attacks on the suburbs had begun on 24 April. (The initial attack was made by the First Guards Tank Army under cover of a barrage from 3000 guns and heavy mortars – 650 guns per kilometre of front) Stalin had finally decided that both Fronts should combine to assault the city, but that Zhukov would have the honour of taking the Reichstag, which Soviet propaganda portrayed as the symbol of Hitler's Reich.

The defenders of Berlin were a very 'mixed bag', ranging from hard-bitten veterans to hastily raised, virtually untrained *Volkssturm* militia, totalling possibly 60,000 men and 50–60 AFVs, supported by police and fanatical Hitler Youth units. The Soviet forces assembling for the attack on the city comprised five armies and four tank armies – 464,000 men, 12,700 guns and mortars, at least 2000 Katyushas and 1500 AFVs.

Between 24 April and 28 April, both Fronts slowly ground their way through the Berlin suburbs

ORDER OF BATTLE: THE ASSAULT ON BERLIN (APRIL 1945) – continued			
Front	Army	Corps	Brigade/Regiment
1st Ukrainian	Third Guards	XXV Tank	87th Guards Independent Tank Rgt, 938th SP Assault Artillery Rgt
	Thirteenth		88th Independent Tank Rgt, 327th, 372nd Guards, 768th & 1228th SP Assault Artillery Rgts
	Fifth Guards	IV Guards Tank	
	Second Polish	I Polish Tank	16th Polish Tank Bde, 5th Polish Independent Tank Rgt, 28th Polish SP Assault Artillery Rgt
	Fifty-Second	VII Guards Mechanized	8th SP Assault Artilleryt, 124th Independent Tank, 1198th SP Assault Artillery Rgt
	Third Guards Tank	VI Guards Tank	51st, 52nd & 53rd Guards Tank, 22nd Guards Motorized Rifle, 385th Guards, 1893rd & 1894th SP Assault Artillery Rgt
		VII Guards Tank	54th, 55th & 56th Guards Tank, 23rd Guards Motorized Rifle Bdes, 384th Guards, 702nd & 1977th SP Assault Artillery Rgts
		IX Mechanized	69th, 70th & 71st Mechanized, 91st Tank Bdes, 383rd Guards, 1507th & 1978th SP Assault Artillery Rgts, 16th SP Assault Artillery Bde, 57th Guards & 90th Independent Tank Rgts
	Fourth Guards Tank	V & VI Guards Mech	
		X Guards Tank	68th Guards Tank, 70th Guards SP Assault Artillery, 13th & 119th Guards Independent Tank Rgts
	Thirty-First		152nd Tank Bde, 98th Independent Tank, 368th Guards, 416th & 1976th SP Assault Artillery Rgts

against fierce resistance – the Third Shock Army took three days to advance 3km (1.8 miles). All Soviet units took heavy casualties, largely due to poor co-ordination between tanks, infantry and artillery. (General Chuikov's Eighth Guards Army initially sent unsupported columns of its tanks straight down main streets – *Panzerfausts* and AT guns trapped these columns by knocking out the lead and rear vehicles, before infantry AT teams moved in to destroy the remaining AFVs.)

As Chuikov ruefully remarked, 'A battle within a city is a battle of firepower.' Units quickly developed

▶ Street fighting

The mobility and power of the SU-76M light assault gun proved very useful in the infantry support role in the confined streets of Berlin.

▲ T-34/85 medium tank

1st Ukrainian Front / Third Guards Tank Army / IX Mechanized Corps

In addition to its improved armour-piercing performance compared to earlier 76.2mm weapons, the T-34/85's 85mm gun fired a far more effective 9.2kg (20.28lb) HE shell.

Specifications

Crew: 5	Speed (road): 55km/h (33mph)
Weight: 32 tonnes (31.5 tons)	Range: 360km (223 miles)
Length: 6m (19ft 7in)	Radio: 9R (When fitted)
Width: 3m (9ft 9in)	Armament: 1 x 85mm (3.4in) ZiS-S-53
Height: 2.60m (8ft 6in)	cannon; 2 x 7.62mm (0.3in) DT MGs (bow
Engine: 1 x V-2 V-12 cylinder 372 kW (493hp)	and coaxial)
diesel engine	

▶ GAZ-67 4x4 command car

1st Byelorussian Front / HQ

The GAZ-67 was the result of a programme to develop a Soviet equivalent of the jeep. However, the total produced from 1943 to 1945 was barely more than 5500, compared to over 50,000 Lend-Lease jeeps received by the end of the war.

Specifications

Crew: 1 driver	Engine: 37.25kW (50hp) 4-cylinder petrol
Weight: 1.32 tonnes (1.3 tons)	Speed: 90km/h (56mph)
Length: 3.35m (11ft)	Range: 450km (280miles)
Width: 1.685m (5ft 6in)	Radio: n/a
Height: 1.7m (5ft 7in)	

special assault teams comprising an infantry platoon or company, a tank platoon, a section of SP guns, a section of 'Katyushas' and a detachment of assault engineers.

The assault drills almost invariably involved artillery and 'Katyushas' smothering the objective with smoke and close-range direct fire before the infantry attacked. A Soviet war correspondent described how the gunners 'sometimes fired a thousand shells on to one small square, a group of houses, or even a tiny garden.' As the Red Army reached the city centre, the larger government buildings proved to have been turned into 'improvised fortresses', which were supported by fire from Berlin's three enormous flak towers. These were six storeys high, each with a thousand-strong garrison to man the tower's four twin 128mm (5in) and 12 quadruple 20mm (0.79in) guns. Dealing with

▼ 57th Guards Heavy Tank Regiment

The 21 JS-2s of a heavy tank regiment were a formidable striking force, but even these well-armoured vehicles proved to be vulnerable to well handled Panzerfausts and Panzershrecks. In response to this threat, many JS-2s were fitted with thin sheet metal panels as 'stand-off armour' similar to those fitted to contemporary Panzer IVs.

1 x T-34/85 command tank and 21 x IS-2s

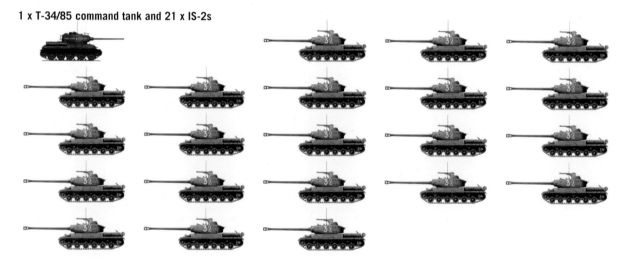

Third Guards Tank Army, AFVs	BM-13	T-34/76	T-34/85	IS-2	SU-57	SU-76	SU-85	ISU-122
VI Gds Tank Corps	8	–	207	–	–	21	21	21
VII Gds Tank Corps	8	–	207	–	–	21	21	21
IX Mechanized Corps	8	–	182	–	–	21	21	21
50th Motorcycle Rgt	–	–	10	–	–	–	–	–
1381st AA Rgt	–	–	–	–	–	–	–	–
1394th AA Rgt	–	–	–	–	–	–	–	–
91st Rocket Launcher Rgt	24	–	–	–	–	–	–	–
16th Assault Gun Bde	–	–	–	–	65	–	–	–
199th Light Artillery Bde	–	–	–	–	–	–	–	–
57th Guards Heavy Tank Rgt	–	–	1	21	–	–	–	–
90th Engineer Tank Rgt	–	18	4	–	–	–	–	–
19th Engineer Mine Bde	–	–	–	–	–	–	–	–
Army Troops	–	–	20	–	–	1	1	1

▶ **Streets of Berlin**
Accompanied by infantry, a T-34/85 advances down a leafy Berlin street, April 1945.

these demanded exceptional measures – at one stage, 500 Soviet guns were firing from a 1km (0.6-mile) section of the Unter den Linden.

Despite such massive firepower, Soviet losses continued to rise – at least 108 tanks were destroyed in the city centre by weapons ranging from 128mm (5in) AA guns to the ubiquitous *Panzerfaust*. As always, infantry casualties were the heaviest – between 19 and 30 April, one infantry company was reduced from 104 men to just 20 exhausted survivors after bitter street fighting.

Suicide and Surrender

By the time that the last German units surrendered on 2 May after Hitler's suicide and the capture of the battered shell of the Reichstag, the losses on both sides had been horrendous. Soviet casualties totalled over 352,000, including more than 78,000 dead – in addition, the First and Second Polish Armies lost almost 9000 men. The 'best estimate' of Soviet AFV losses is 2000 vehicles, while the two air armies supporting the offensive lost 527 aircraft – the majority to intensive AA fire.

The fall of Berlin effectively marked the end of the Red Army's war in Europe, but Stalin was already planning to unleash it against an old enemy half a world away – Japan.

Third Guards Tank Army, Personnel (1945)	Strength
VI Gds Tank Corps	12,010
VII Gds Tank Corps	12,010
IX Mechanized Corps	16,442
50th Motorcycle Rgt	–
1381st AA Rgt	396
1394th AA Rgt	396
91st Rocket Launcher Rgt	695
16th Assault Gun Bde	1112
199th Light Artillery Bde	–
57th Guards Heavy Tank Rgt	374
90th Engineer Tank Rgt	–
19th Engineer Mine Bde	–
Army Troops	–

▼ **British BSA M-20**

2nd Byelorussian Front / III Guards Tank Corps / HQ

Even by 1945, Soviet formations did not have the lavish scale of radio equipment of their Western counterparts, forcing them to rely more heavily on motorcycle dispatch riders than British or American forces.

Specifications

Crew: 1
Weight: 0.185 tonnes (0.182 tons)
Length: 2.18m (7ft 2in)
Width: 0.73m (2ft 5in)

Height: 0.99m (3ft 3in)
Engine: 8.94kW (12hp), BSA 1-cylinder petrol
Speed: 104.6km/h (65mph)
Range: 280km (175miles)

Chapter 13

Victory in the East

After prolonged negotiations, the Soviet-Japanese Neutrality Pact was signed in Moscow on 13 April 1941 to formalize the uneasy peace that had lasted since the battle of Khalkin Gol. Both sides recognized the existing frontiers between Manchukuo, Mongolia and Siberia. Equally importantly, they both agreed to remain neutral if either should go to war with any other powers. Japan seriously considered breaking the treaty to join Hitler's war on Soviet Russia during the German run of victories in 1941/42, but was too heavily committed to its own war in the Pacific and Southeast Asia. As the tide of war turned against Germany, Stalin began to plan an attack on Japan to extend the Soviet empire into the Far East.

◀ **Briefing**
The commander of a T-34/85 unit briefs his crews. Armoured units deployed to Manchuria included many veterans of the European campaign, whose combat skills far outclassed those of the many raw recruits in the Kwantung Army.

Operation *August Storm*
8 AUGUST – 1 SEPTEMBER 1945

Even in the darkest days of the war against Germany, the Soviet Union had retained substantial forces (averaging 40 divisions) to protect its borders with Manchuria, which had become the Japanese puppet state of Manchukuo, held by the 700,000-strong Kwantung Army.

THE NEUTRALITY PACT with Japan might theoretically guarantee Soviet security in the region, but after his experience with the Russo-German Non-Aggression Pact, Stalin was sceptical of the value of such treaties.

Stalin was determined to enter the war against Japan eventually to achieve long-standing strategic aims in the Far East. A key objective was to re-establish Russian dominance of Manchuria, which had been lost as a result of the humiliating defeat by Japan in 1905. Other aims included the consolidation of the Soviet hold on Mongolia and

the seizure of the entire Sakhalin peninsula and Kurile Islands from Japan. As the Pacific war dragged on, Britain and the United States were increasingly anxious for Soviet involvement in the war against Japan, especially as it seemed likely that it would take an invasion of the Japanese home islands to end the war, which could entail a horrifying 250,000 US casualties. (The actual American death toll for the entire war was 292,000.)

In April 1945, the Soviets abrogated the Neutrality Pact and began a massive redeployment effort that doubled the Soviet forces in the Far East to

▶ **T-26 Model 1935 light tank**

Trans-Baikal Front / Thirty-Sixth Army / 205th Tank Brigade

Although the T-26 was hopelessly outdated in terms of Western European armoured warfare by 1945, it was at least as good as the vast majority of Japanese AFVs.

Specifications

Crew: 3	Speed: 28km/h (17mph)
Weight: 10.4 tonnes (10.3 tons)	Range: 200km (124 miles)
Length: 4.8m (15ft 8in)	Armament: 1 x 45mm (1.77in) AT gun; 1
Width: 2.39m (7ft 10in)	x 7.62mm (0.3in) DT MG; 2 x additional
Height: 2.33m (7ft 8in)	7.62mm (0.3in) DT MG ball-mounted into
Engine: 68kW (91hp) GAZ T-26 8-cylinder petrol	turret rear and turret hatch

▶ **T-26 Model 1940 light tank**

2nd Far Eastern Front / Second Red Banner Army / 73rd Tank Brigade

Well over 1200 operational T-26s had been held by Soviet units in the Far East throughout the war. Supplemented by more modern AFVs shipped from the European theatre, they played a useful role in Manchuria.

Specifications

Crew: 3	Speed: 28km/h (17mph)
Weight: 10.4 tonnes (10.3 tons)	Range: 200km (124 miles)
Length: 4.8m (15ft 8in)	Radio: N/A
Width: 2.39m (7ft 10in)	Armament: 1 x 45mm (1.8in) AT gun;
Height: 2.33m (7ft 8in)	1 x 7.62mm (0.3in) DT MG
Engine: 68kW (91hp) GAZ T-26 8-cylinder petrol	

80 divisions. Between May and July 1945, at least 40 infantry, tank and mechanized divisions plus artillery and combat support units were transferred from Europe to the Far East. This massive undertaking stretched the capacity of the Trans-Siberian railway to the limit – 136,000 railway wagons were used for the transfer of men and equipment. As the movements peaked in June and July, 20–30 trains a day were despatched on the 9,000–12,000km (5500–7500-mile) journey to Mongolia.

Secret build-up

Surprise was an essential element of Red Army planning – after the abrogation of the Neutrality Pact, the Japanese were anticipating a Soviet attack, but Soviet security was so good that the offensive was expected either in the autumn, when the ground had dried out after the summer rains, or in the spring of 1946. The security measures themselves were simple but highly effective – whenever possible, units moved at night into assembly areas as far back from the frontier as possible, while senior officers travelled under assumed names, wearing the uniforms of junior officers. Some formations, such as the Sixth Guards Tank Army, left all their AFVs and heavy equipment behind in Europe and re-equipped with new tanks, assault guns and artillery straight off the production lines of the Urals armament factories.

A total of 11 combined-arms armies, one tank army and three air armies were assembled for the offensive, with a combined strength of some 1,577,725 men and 5556 AFVs, supported by

AFVS, FAR EAST, AUGUST 1945	Registered	Operable	Mid-life Repair	Thourough Repair	Discarded
BT-5	190	101	–	23	66
BT-7	1030	797	41	179	13
T-26	1461	1272	33	122	34
T-37	52	52	–	–	–
T-38	325	304	20	1	–
T-60/70	46	14	–	28	4
T-34	1899	1794	32	70	3
KV	77	47	5	23	2
IS	19	6	1	12	–
M4A2 Sherman	250	250	–	–	–
Mk III Valentine	81	78	3	–	–
M3 Stuart	1	–	1	–	–
M3 Lee	1	–	1	–	–
T-27	56	56	–	–	–
Tankettes	52	52	–	–	–
Other	5	5	–	–	–
Total Tanks	**5545**	**4828**	**137**	**458**	**122**
SU-76	952	944	9	–	–
SU-85	6	1	–	5	–
SU-100	262	261	1	–	–
SU-122	6	2	–	3	1
ISU-122	1	1	–	–	–
SU-152	11	–	–	11	–
ISU-152	197	188	1	8	–
Total SP Guns	**1435**	**1397**	**11**	**27**	**1**
Total	**6980**	**6225**	**148**	**485**	**123**

26,137 guns, mortars and rocket launchers. The air armies committed to the operation totalled 3800 aircraft while the Soviet Navy (the Pacific Fleet and Amur River Flotilla) had 600 warships and a further 1500 aircraft. Overall, the Soviet forces significantly outnumbered the Japanese – the ratios were a 2.2:1 advantage in men, 4.8:1 in artillery and tanks and a 2:1 advantage in aircraft.

Japanese weakness

Across the frontier in Manchukuo, the Kwantung Army was a shadow of its former self. In early 1941, it had numbered approximately 1,000,000 men and included some of the best units in the Imperial Japanese Army. In the opening stages of the Pacific War, it was regarded as a strategic reserve and kept up to strength to take advantage of any sudden Soviet collapse as a result of Operation *Barbarossa*. (It was considered equally important to maintain it as a strong garrison for the puppet state of Manchukuo, which had been built up as the primary industrial and agricultural centre of the Japanese Empire.)

However, as the Allies went over to the offensive in the Pacific war, Japanese Imperial General Headquarters began to withdraw elite divisions from the Kwantung Army to reinforce other theatres of war. By early 1943, Japanese strength in Manchukuo had been reduced to 600,000 men facing an estimated 750,000 Soviet troops deployed on its borders. Further units were withdrawn during 1944, and in March 1945 most of the remaining elite

formations, including the 1st Armoured Division, were transferred to the Japanese home islands.

The steady decline in the strength of the Kwangtung Army forced drastic changes in the contingency plans for the defence of Manchukuo. These had originally concentrated on the northern and eastern border areas, as it was believed that the western frontier was impassable for any major force due to the vast Mongolian desert and the natural barrier of the Grand Khingan mountains. In accordance with this assessment, the Japanese were busily constructing 17 fortified areas covering likely invasion routes along 1000km (621 miles) of the northern and eastern borders.

By May 1945, it was recognized that it was unrealistic to believe that a major Soviet offensive could be held at the frontier and a revised plan was adopted. This plan was based on fighting delaying actions on the borders before a phased retreat to a succession of defensive lines and finally to a fortified zone in south-eastern Manchuria approximately 650km (404 miles) from the northern and western borders. Despite the evidence of recent operations in Europe, Japanese planners believed that a combination of difficult terrain and the limitations of the Soviet transport system would force any major offensive to halt to resupply after 400km (249 miles) or so, giving defending forces the chance to regroup and counterattack. Based on these assumptions, only one-third of the Kwantung Army would remain in the border zones and the remainder would redeploy to man the

Specifications	
Crew: 3	Engine: 103kW (138bhp) GMC diesel
Weight: 17.69 tonnes (19.5 tons)	Speed (road): 24km/h (15mph)
Length: 5.41m (17ft 9in)	Range: 145km (90 miles)
Width: 2.63m (8ft 7.5in)	Armament: 1 x 40mm (1.57in) gun;
Height: 2.27m (7ft 5.5in)	1 x 7.92mm (0.31in) Besa MG

▲ **Infantry Tank Mark III Valentine Mk II**

2nd Far Eastern Front / Second Red Banner Army / 73rd Tank Brigade

The Manchurian campaign marked the swansong of the Valentine, which had seen action in almost all theatres of war, from the Western Desert to the Pacific.

defence lines in the interior. The unexpectedly early Soviet attack caught Japanese units in the midst of the redeployment programme and struck largely incomplete border fortifications.

To mask its fragility, the Kwangtung Army mobilized reservists and conscripts, forming new divisions and brigades to maintain the appearance of a capable fighting force. By early July 1945, it had expanded from 11 infantry divisions to over 24 divisions. However, a substantial proportion of

its entire combat force (eight out of 24 divisions and seven out of nine brigades) was mobilized only 10 days before the Soviet attack. One of its two weak tank brigades was not formed until July 1945, and both brigades were stationed in south-central Manchukuo far away from the areas targeted by the Soviet offensive. Of the 24 divisions in the Kwangtung Army, the Japanese themselves considered only seven or eight to be fully combat ready. The remaining formations were in terrible

▲ **BT-5 Model 1935 fast tank**

Trans-Baikal Front / Sixth Guards Tank Army / VII Guards Mechanized Corps

The 'BT contingent' of the Sixth Guards Tank Army was itself a strange variety of types, including BT-5s.

Specifications

Crew: 3	Speed: 86km/h (53mph)
Weight: 14 tonnes (13.2 tons)	Range: 250km (155 miles)
Length: 5.66m (18ft 6in)	Radio: N/A
Width: 2.29m (7ft 6in)	Armament: 1 x 45mm (1.8in) Model 1932 gun;
Height: 2.42m (7ft 10in)	1 x 7.62mm (0.3in) coaxial DT MG
Engine: 373kW (500hp) Model M-17T	

Specifications

Crew: 5	Speed (road): 55km/h (33mph)
Weight: 32 tonnes (31.5 tons)	Range: 360km (223 miles)
Length: 6m (19ft 7in)	Radio: N/A
Width: 3m (9ft 9in)	Armament: 1 x 85mm (3.4in) ZiS-S-53 cannon;
Height: 2.60m (8ft 6in)	2 x 7.62mm (0.3in) DT MGs (bow and coaxial)
Engine: 1 x V-2 V-12 cylinder 372 kW (493hp) diesel engine	

▲ **T34/85**

Trans-Baikal Front / Sixth Guards Tank Army / IX Guards Mechanised Corps

The T-34/85 was largely immune to Japanese tank and AT guns deployed in Manchuria, while its 85mm (3.3in) gun could easily destroy any of the Kwantung Army's AFVs.

condition – eight of the infantry divisions were assessed as being only 15 per cent combat effective while all nine independent mixed brigades were rated at 15 per cent combat effectiveness or less.

These alarming ratings were largely due to hopelessly inadequate levels of equipment – the newly formed 149th Infantry Division did not have a single piece of artillery at the time of the Soviet invasion. Equally serious was the obsolescence of much of the equipment that had been issued. Japanese war industries had lacked both the resources and the management skills to mass-produce modern weapons, and as a result the Kwantung Army of 1945 was seriously deficient in heavy artillery, tanks and AT weapons. (It was rumoured that some units even lacked sufficient rifles and were reduced to arming their men with bamboo spears.) By August 1945, the Japanese strength in Manchukuo stood at 1155 tanks, 5360 guns and 1800 aircraft, most of which were obsolete. Apart from Japanese garrisons in South Sakhalin, Korea and the Kuriles, Soviet forces faced an inexperienced army totalling little more than 710,000 men.

Poor intelligence

Despite excellent security, the Soviet build-up of forces was detected by the Japanese, but its scale and pace were grossly under-estimated. The Kwantung Army's intelligence reports failed to note any concentrations on the western border of Manchukuo (where more than 650,000 men were massing) and estimated that there were only eight infantry and two tank divisions with 1000 supporting aircraft on the eastern border (where the Red Army attacked with 31 infantry divisions and 12 tank brigades). Even after greatly increased Soviet activity in July 1945, the Imperial General HQ's last situation report on 31 July 1945 was inaccurate: 'Russian relations with Japan will reach a crisis in the early autumn. Recent Russian war preparations against Japan have made unexpected progress. The Soviet Union will be ready to launch hostile action by the end of August. Because of military considerations, it is highly probable that she will enter war against Japan in the early autumn.'

Soviet plan

The Soviet operation was well-planned. The experience gained from the war in Europe was applied to solve the problems of staging an offensive across terrain that included mountains, forests, marshland, steppe and deserts. Specialized tasks were assigned to formations that had relevant experience – the Fifth Army, which had assaulted the German fortifications at Königsberg, was to break through the Japanese fortified zone in eastern Manchukuo, while the Sixth Guards Tank Army was to make use of mountain warfare skills gained in the Carpathians

▲ **T-70 Light Tank**

Trans-Baikal Front / Thirty-Ninth Army / 735th Self-propelled Artillery Regiment

By 1945, surviving T-70s had mostly been assigned to SU-76M units as command vehicles.

Specifications

Crew: 2	Speed: 45km/h (28mph)
Weight: 5.8 tonnes (5.7 tons)	Range: 360km (224 miles)
Length: 4.29m (14ft 1in)	Radio: N/A
Width: 2.32m (7ft 7in)	Armament: 1 x 45mm (1.8in) Model 38 gun;
Height: 2.04m (6ft 7in)	1 x 7.62mm (0.3in) coaxial DT MG
Engine: 2 x GAZ-202 52+52kW (70+70hp)	

in crossing the Grand Khingan mountains. Even horsed cavalry had a role – 16,000 Mongolian cavalry formed part of Issa Pliev's Soviet-Mongolian KMG, which was to protect the right flank of the offensive by a massive raid, summarized in Pliev's briefing from Marshal Vasilevsky:

'You, Issa Aleksandrovich, will execute a raid in your favourite style across the Gobi Desert and the

Grand Khingan mountains. Your cavalry mechanized group will conduct a vigorous offensive on the axis Kalgan-Beijing, and will subsequently exploit success as far as the Gulf of Liadong. That is where our main forces will concentrate ... your mission – to secure the Front's forces against attack from the south.'

This was a strategic mission that would have been appreciated by Genghis Khan, using cavalry with

Specifications

Crew: 5
Weight: 32.28 tonnes (35.58 tons)
Length: 5.92m (19ft 5in)
Width: 2.62m (8ft 7in)
Height: 2.74m (9ft)
Engine: 280kW (375hp) General Motors 6046 12-cylinder diesel
Speed: 48km/h (30mph)
Range: 240km (150miles)
Armament: 1 x 75mm (2.9in) M3 L/40 gun; 1 x 12.7mm (0.5in)
l Browning M2HB MG, 1 x turret mounted 12.7mm 0.50 cal MG

▲ **M4A2 Sherman medium tank**

1st Far Eastern Front / Fifth Army / 72nd Tank Brigade

This Sherman carries a pair of logs to act as 'unditching beams' – if the tank bogged down in soft ground, these were pushed under the tracks to give it the necessary grip to haul itself out.

▲ **JS-3 Heavy Tank**

Sixth Guards Tank Army / III Guards Mechanized Corps / 35th Guards Tank Bde

The JS-3 was the last Soviet heavy tank to enter production before the end of the war. The 122mm (4.8in) main armament was mounted in new hemispherical turret and it had a pointed bow, which gave rise to the nickname 'Shchuka' (Pike). As many as 350 JS-3s may have been produced in the first half of 1945, but it seems unlikely that any saw action before VE-Day. However, a detachment may have undergone combat trials in the Manchurian campaign.

Specifications

Crew: 3
Weight: 45.77 tonnes (45.05 tons)
Length: 9.85m (32ft 4in)
Width: 3.09m (10ft 2in)
Height: 2.45m (8ft)
Engine: 447kW (600hp) V-2-JS V-12 diesel

Speed: 40km/h (25mph)
Range: 185km (115 miles)
Radio: 10R (when fitted)
Armament: 1 x 122mm (4.8in) D-25T gun,
plus 1 x coaxial 7.62mm (0.3in) DT MG and
1 x 12.7mm (0.5in) DShK HMG on AA mount

▲ SU-76M SP gun

Trans-Baikal Front / Thirty-Ninth Army / 735th Self-propelled Artillery Regiment

The lightweight SU-76M was well suited to operating on the poor roads and weak bridges encountered in Manchuria.

Specifications

Crew: 4	Engine: 2 x GAZ 6-cylinder petrol 52+52kW
Weight: 10.8 tonnes (11.9 tons)	(70+70hp)
Length: 4.88m (16ft)	Speed (road): 45km/h (28mph)
Width: 2.73m (8ft 11.5in)	Range: 450km (280miles)
Height: 2.17m (7ft 1.4in)	Armament: one 76mm (3in) gun and one
	7.62mm (0.3in) MG

▶ Harley-Davidson 42WLA, with M-72 sidecar and DP MG

Trans-Baikal Front / Sixth Guards Tank Army / 14th Guards Motorcycle Battalion

Motorcycle reconnaissance battalions covered vast distances during the brief Manchurian campaign.

Specifications

Crew: 2/3	Range: 201km (125 miles)
Engine: 17kW (23hp) V-2	Armament: 1 x 7.62mm (0.3in) DT MG
Speed: 105km/h (65.2mph)	

Specifications

Crew: 2	Engine: JXD 6 cylinder Hercules
Weight: 4.33 tons (9555lbs) (without fuel)	Speed: not known
Length: 6.55m (21ft 6in)	Range: not known
Width: 2.23m (7ft 4in)	Radio: none
Height: 2.76m (9ft 1in)	

▲ Studebaker US 6x6 U-5, 2½-ton fuel tanker

Trans-Baikal Front / Sixth Guards Tank Army / Supply Battalion

Formations tasked with seizing objectives deep inside Manchuria received the pick of logistical support, such as Studebaker 6x6 fuel tankers. Even so, the distances involved were such that air re-supply proved to be the only way to sustain the advance.

which he would have been familiar in conjunction with the latest tanks – the military technologies of the thirteenth and twentieth centuries working together.

The Last Battles

The Soviet plan was essentially simple – virtually all Manchukuo, a territory three times the size of France, would be seized in a gigantic pincer movement. The Trans-Baikal Front would attack eastwards across the Grand Khingan mountains and advance into central Manchukuo within 10–15 days.

The 1st Far Eastern Front was to form the second arm of the pincer movement, attacking westwards from the area north of Vladivostock to link up with Trans-Baikal Front. The third major Soviet force, the 2nd Far Eastern Front, was to pin Japanese troops in northern Manchukuo, preventing them withdrawing southwards to reinforce other units.

On 9 August, the Trans-Baikal Front's attacks were launched. More than 654,000 men, 2400 AFVs and 49,000 other vehicles moved forward on a front of 2300km (1429 miles). The Sixth Guards Tank Army spearheaded the advance against very light opposition, as the Japanese considered the region impassable by major armoured formations. The tank army's planned rate of advance was 70km (43 miles) per day for its armoured units, but it reached its objectives after covering more than 350km (217 miles) on 12 August – a full 24 hours ahead of schedule. By this time, its supply lines were stretched to breaking point; its leading units were over 700km (435 miles) from their supply dumps. The tanks were virtually 'running on empty' and the advance had to be halted for 48 hours until 400 transport aircraft could fly in sufficient fuel to allow the resumption of operations.

On the Front's left flank, the Japanese put up fierce resistance around Hailar. Although assessed as only 15 per cent combat effective, the 80th Independent Mixed Brigade withstood repeated attacks by two Soviet divisions with heavy artillery support for several days before the surviving 3287 defenders surrendered on 18 August.

The 1st Far Eastern Front faced stronger opposition since it had to penetrate major Japanese defences and extensive areas of marshy terrain before linking up with the Trans-Baikal Front. Despite these obstacles, it advanced 150km (93 miles) in five days, fixing Japanese forces in eastern Manchukuo. The fortresses of the so-called 'concrete belt' were largely by-passed and pounded into surrender by supporting Soviet forces.

Away to the north, the 2nd Far Eastern Front's offensive had to cross two rivers – the Amur and the Ussuri – and their broad marshlands. In recognition of the problems posed by the terrain, the Front was relatively lightly equipped with only 1280 AFVs and barely 6000 guns and mortars. In compensation, it had the support of the Amur Red Banner Flotilla, a force of 200 naval craft that provided invaluable fire support in both river crossings. The Front had to fight its way through determined resistance, which slowed an advance already hampered by appalling terrain. Nonetheless, it was completely successful in preventing any major Japanese forces withdrawing into the interior.

The opening of the Soviet offensive coincided with the second atomic bomb strike against Nagasaki and reports of the collapse of Manchukuo probably hastened the Japanese surrender. Although the Kwantung Army formally surrendered on 17 August, Stalin ordered the advance to continue, exploiting the confusion caused by the difficulties of communicating the news to isolated Japanese units. This ensured Soviet control of key strategic objectives – the whole of the former Manchukuo, now once again Manchuria, North Korea, the Kurile Islands and southern Sakhalin. A planned invasion of the northern Japanese home island of Hokkaido was cancelled at the last minute for fear of antagonizing the United States.

Postscript

The last battles of the war were a strange mixture of old and new – horsed cavalry fought alongside modern tanks and armoured trains went into action for almost the last time. In another, more sinister way they were the shape of things to come. By the end of the war, the largely ineffective Japanese tanks and AT guns had forced the adoption of drastic, but sometimes highly effective, AT measures. In accordance with the spirit of *bushido* ('way of the warrior'), *kamikaze* ('divine wind') attacks were adopted – suicidal attacks by infantry using demolition charges, AT grenades and lunge mines. Soviet accounts of these attacks in the Manchurian campaign provide a chilling foretaste of the suicide bombers of the twenty-first century.

'Katyusha' salvo rocket launchers
1941–45

In June 1938, the Red Army's Main Artillery Directorate (GAU) ordered the Soviet Jet Propulsion Research Institute (RNII) to develop a multiple rocket launcher for the new 82mm (3.2in) RS-82 and 132mm (5.2in) RS-132 air-launched rockets.

INITIAL EFFORTS WERE concentrated on the RS-132 (RS: *Reaktivnyy Snaryad*, 'rocket-powered shell'), which was fitted with a larger warhead and redesignated M-13. A total of 233 prototype rockets were test-fired in late 1938 from ZiS-5 trucks and it was found that a salvo could straddle an area target at a range of 5500m (18,044ft). These test-firings were made from 24-rail launchers firing over the sides of ZiS-5 trucks, but this configuration was unstable and the problem was solved only when longitudinally mounted launch rails were adopted. The modified vehicles were completed in August 1939 as the BM-13 (BM: *Boyevaya Mashina*, 'combat vehicle' for M-13 rockets). Further trials took place throughout 1940 and the BM-13-16 with launch rails for 16 rockets was ordered into production, but only 40 vehicles were completed by the time of the German invasion in 1941.

Rocket Artillery Regiment, personnel	Strength
Regiment HQ	58
Battalion x 3	250
AA Platoon x 2	–
Rocket Battery x 2	–

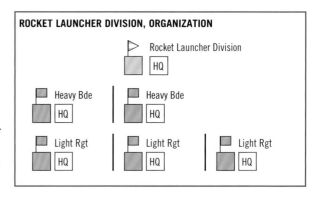

ROCKET LAUNCHER DIVISION, ORGANIZATION

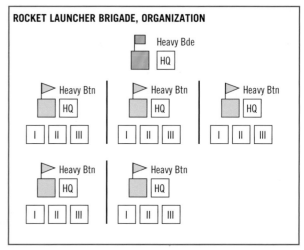

ROCKET LAUNCHER BRIGADE, ORGANIZATION

▶ **Willys MB Jeep with BM-8-8 82mm (3.2in) 'Katyusha' salvo rocket launcher**

3rd Ukrainian Front / IV Guards Mechanized Corps / 15th Guards Mech Bde

As the Soviet offensives approached the Carpathians, it became clear that the existing 'Katyusha' vehicles could not cope with such mountainous terrain. So the jeep was adapted to mount a light eight-rail launcher for 82mm (3.2in) rockets.

Specifications*

Crew: 1 driver

Weight: 1.04 tonnes (1.02 tons)

Length: 3.33m (10ft 11in)

Width: 1.58m (5ft 2in)

Height: 1.83m (6ft)

Engine: 44.7kW (70hp) 4-cylinder petrol

Speed: 88.5km/h (55mph)

Range: n/k

Armament: 8 x 82mm (3.2in) M8 rockets

(* For standard jeep)

The system consisted of an elevating frame that carried a bank of eight parallel rails on which the rockets were mounted (eight on top of the rails and a further eight hung beneath them). The 132mm (5.2in) diameter M-13 rocket of the BM-13 system had an overall length of 180cm (70in) and weighed 42kg (92lb). It was stabilized by pressed-steel cruciform fins and powered by a solid nitrocellulose-based propellant, venting through a single central nozzle at the base. Maximum range was just under 8500m (27,887ft), but the M-13-DD rocket, introduced in 1944, used two standard motors that

Specifications

Crew: 1 driver	Engine: 6 cylinder 75.3kW (101hp) engine
Weight: 3.9 tons (8700lb) (vehicle only)	Speed: not known
Length: 8m (26ft 3in)	Range: not known
Width: 2.21m (7ft 3in)	Armament: 16 x 132mm (5.2in) M13 rockets
Height: 2.4m (7ft 10in)	

▲ **International K7 ('Inter'), 2½-ton, 4x2 with BM-13-16 'Katyusha' salvo rocket launcher**

3rd Ukrainian Front / Fifth Shock Army

Although there is very little hard evidence, it seems highly likely that limited Lend-Lease deliveries of this vehicle were made and that some examples were adapted to carry the BM-13-16.

Specifications

Crew: 1 driver	Engine: 6 cylinder 82.77kW (111hp) engine
Weight: 5.1 tons (11,250lbs) (vehicle only)	Speed: not known
Length: 6.8m (22ft 6in)	Range: not known
Width: 2.22m (7ft 4in)	Armament: 16 x 132mm (5.2in) M13 rockets
Height: 2.33m (7ft 8in)	

▲ **International M-5-6-318 ('Inter'), 2½-ton, 6x6, with BM-13-16 'Katyusha' salvo rocket launcher**

1st Ukrainian Front / Fourth Tank Army

A total of 500 of these trucks were produced by International Harvester on a Quartermaster Corps foreign aid order from 1941, with most being sent to the Soviet Union. A number were fitted with the BM-13-16.

gave a maximum range of 11,800m (38,73ft). Most warheads were simple 22kg (48.4lb) impact-fused high-explosive (HE) fragmentation types, although there is a possibility that high-explosive anti-tank (HEAT) warheads may have been developed for use against tank concentrations. (Some reports indicate that illuminating and incendiary warheads were also used in small numbers.)

While the weapon was slow to reload and was less accurate than conventional artillery, it had immense firepower. In 7–10 seconds, a battery of four BM-13 launchers could fire a salvo delivering 4.4 tonnes (4.35 tons) of HE over a 4-hectare (10-acre) impact zone. Well-trained crews could then redeploy within minutes to avoid counter-battery fire.

The multiple rocket launchers were top secret at the beginning of the war and were operated under close NKVD supervision. They were assigned various code names such as 'Kostikov Guns', before being officially designated Guards Mortars. However, to

the troops they were 'Katyushas', the name coming from a popular song of the time and this was the title by which they would become world-famous.

On 7 July 1941, an experimental battery of seven launchers was first used in combat at Orsha

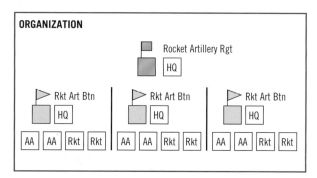

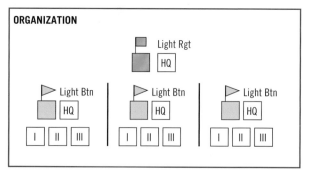

Mobile Rocket Launcher Production	1941	1942	1943	1944	1945
BM-8	400	900	400	500	200
BM-13	600	2400	2900	900	–
BM-31-12	–	–	–	1200	600

▲ **Fordson WOT8 30-cwt 4x4 with BM-13-16 'Katyusha' salvo rocket launcher**

South-Western Front / Sixth Army / 5th Guards Mortar Breakthrough Regiment

The WOT8, developed from the 3-ton WOT6, was the only British 30-cwt 4x4 wartime truck. Small numbers were included in the early deliveries to Russia in 1942, some of which were converted to carry the BM-13-16.

Specifications

Crew: 1 driver

Weight: 3.048 tons (3 tons) (vehicle only)

Length: 5.09m (16ft 8in)

Width: 2.28m (7ft 6in)

Height: 2.8m (9ft 2)

Engine: V8 cylinder 63.38kW (85hp) petrol

Speed: not known

Range: not known

Armament: 16 x 132mm (5.2in) M13 rockets

– the bombardment was spectacular, destroying the important railway junction together with German troop and supply trains. Following this success, the Red Army began priority production of the system and developed additional types of 'Katyusha'. In August 1941, the 82mm (3.2in) M-8 rocket entered service. Much smaller and lighter than the M-13, it could be fired from vehicles as small as a jeep, which could carry eight M-8s. Medium trucks mounted a bank of rails for no less than 48 rockets. The M-8's overall length was 66cm (26in), weight 8kg (17.6lb) (including a 5.4kg/11.8lb HE-fragmentation

Specifications

Crew: 1 driver	Engine: 8 cylinder 70.84kW (95hp) petrol
Weight: not known	Speed: not known
Wheelbase: 3.4m (11ft 2in)	Range: not known
Width: 2.13m (7ft)	Armament: 16 x 132mm (5.2in) M13 rockets
Height: 2.54m (8ft 4in)	

▲ **Ford/Marmon-Herrington ('Ford-Marmon') HH6-COE4 4x4 1½-ton with BM-13-16 'Katyusha' Salvo Rocket Launcher**

1st Ukrainian Front / Third Guards Tank Army / 115th Guards Mortar Breakthrough Regiment

Some of the 500 Ford/Marmon-Herrington 4x4 cab-over-engine (COE) conversions, delivered to Soviet Russia under Lend-Lease from late 1941 to 1942 were used to carry BM-13-16 rocket launchers, possibly the first foreign chassis used in this role.

▲ **Chevrolet G-7117 4x4 1½-ton with BM-13-16 'Katyusha' salvo rocket launcher**

1st Belorussian Front / Forty-Seventh Army

Approximately 60,000 Chevrolet '1½-tonners' were supplied under Lend-Lease. While most were used as troop transporters and artillery prime movers, a number were converted to mount the BM-8-48 and BM-13-16.

Specifications

Crew: 1 driver	Engine: 6 cylinder 63.38kW (85hp) 4F1R petrol
Weight: not known	Speed: not known
Length: 5.69m (18ft 7in)	Range: not known
Width: 2.18m (7ft 2in)	Armament: 16 x 132mm (5.2in) M13 rockets
Height: 2m (6ft 6in)	

▲ Studebaker US6 U3 2½-ton 6x6 with BM-8-48 'Katyusha' salvo rocket launcher

4th Ukrainian Front / Second Guards Army / 133rd Guards Mortar Breakthrough Regiment

In mid-1943, the Red Army adopted the Studebaker 6x6 as the standard vehicle to mount the BM-8 and BM-13 salvo rocket launchers. With almost 105,000 such vehicles delivered to the Soviet Union by 1945, the Studebaker was available in quantity and gave the 'Katyusha' a high degree of cross-country mobility.

Specifications

Crew: 1 driver	Engine: 6 cylinder 64.8kW (87hp) petrol
Weight: 4.53 tonnes (10,000lbs) (vehicle only)	Speed: not known
Length: 6.19m (20ft 4in)	Range: not known
Width: 2.23m (7ft 4in)	Armament: 48 x 82mm (3.2in) M8 rockets
Height: 2.79m (9ft 2in)	

Specifications

Crew: 1 driver	Engine: 6 cylinder 64.8kW (87hp) petrol
Weight: 4.53 tonnes (10,000lbs) (vehicle only)	Speed: not known
Length: 6.19m (20ft 4in)	Range: not known
Width: 2.23m (7ft 4in)	Armament: 12 x 300mm (11.81in) M-31
Height: 2.79m (9ft 2in)	rockets

▲ Studebaker US 6x6 U3 2½-ton 6x6 with BM-31-12 'Katyusha' salvo rocket launcher

1st Belorussian Front / Third Shock Army / IV Breakthrough Artillery Corps / 12th Breakthrough Artillery Division

The M-31 was a longer-ranged derivative of the M-30 heavy rocket. Initially both types were fired from static launchers, but in March 1944 a mobile version of the BM-31 entered service mounted on the Studebaker US6 chassis. The M-31's 28.9kg (63.5lb) warhead proved to be highly effective during the fierce street fighting in Budapest and Berlin.

warhead) and its maximum range was just over 5000m (1640ft). In 1944, an improved version of the rocket came into service with a maximum range of 5500m (18,044ft).

These light and medium rockets were highly effective, but there was a need for a heavier version, which was initially met by the M-30. This used a modified version of the M-13's rocket motor, which was fitted with a bulbous 300mm (11.8in) HE warhead containing 28.9kg (63.5lb) of explosive. Maximum range was only 2800m (9186ft), but this was considered acceptable in view of the warhead's devastating blast effect. The M-30 was fired directly from its packing case, four of which could be mounted on a firing frame, referred to as a 'Rama'. In late 1942, the improved M-31 was adopted. This was very similar to its predecessor, but a new rocket motor gave it a maximum range of 4300m (14,107ft). (The later M-13-UK was modified to give a degree of spin-stabilization, which greatly improved

▲ **Waiting to move out**

A brief rest halt for a BM-13-16 'Katyusha' battery. The rocket launchers are mounted on US Studebaker truck chassis.

▲ **Load**

Loading the 42kg (92lb) M-13 rockets was a lengthy task, not to be undertaken while under counter-battery fire.

▲ **Aim**

The launcher has been aligned on the target area and the crew take cover away from the vehicle prior to firing.

accuracy.) Initially the firing method was the same as that of the M-30, but in March 1944 a mobile version entered service consisting of launchers for 12 M-31s on a ZiS-6 6x6 truck.

Later production batches were mounted on Lend-Lease Studebaker US-6 6x6 trucks. These had such a good cross-country performance that in 1943 they were adopted as the standard mount for the BM-13 under the designation BM-13N (*Normalizovanniy*, 'standardize'), and more than 1800 of this type were produced by the end of the war.

Cheap, effective manufacture

All 'Katyushas' were simple, cheap weapons and could be manufactured in workshops and small factories that lacked the specialist machinery for producing conventional artillery or ammunition. This simplicity allowed fast construction – more than 3000 launchers of all types were produced during 1942. By the end of the year, 57 regiments

were operational – together with the independent battalions, they equated to 216 batteries: 21 per cent BM-8 light launchers, 56 per cent BM-13, and 23 per cent M-30 heavy launchers. While the majority of Katyushas were truck-mounted, a bewildering variety of other vehicles were also used in small numbers, including STZ-5 artillery tractors, plus the hulls of T-60 and KV-1 tanks. A few launchers were even fitted to armoured trains and river gunboats.

The Red Army's initial enthusiasm for the new weapon led to the creation of a large number of small units. The very first batteries had seven launchers each, but this was soon reduced at four per battery. On 8 August 1941, *Stavka* ordered the formation of eight rocket regiments, each of three battalions, with three four-vehicle batteries per battalion. (A total of 36 launchers per regiment.)

By the end of 1941, a total of 554 launchers were operational, equipping eight regiments, 35 independent battalions and two independent batteries. The increasing numbers of BM-13s allowed a battalion of eight launchers to be added to each tank corps from July 1942.

In June 1942, 20 independent battalions were formed to operate the new M-30 rockets, with each having 96 launchers in three batteries. These units were gradually concentrated into larger formations, finally leading to the establishment of seven full divisions in 1943, each of which had 864 launchers firing a total of 3456 rockets. (By 1944, these divisions

▲ **Fire**

Fire! A four-vehicle BM-13 battery unleashes its 64 rockets, carrying a total of over 300kg (660lb) of HE to a maximum range of 8500m (27,887ft).

were supplemented by motorized heavy battalions, each of which were equipped with 48 BM-31 launchers.)

Close combat role

While 'Katyushas' were assembled *en masse* for carefully orchestrated preparatory bombardments for 'set-piece' battles, they were increasingly used in smaller numbers in the bitter street fighting of the last months of the war. Their employment in this role developed as the Red Army began to appreciate the problems posed by the heavily defended cities of central Europe.

Specifications

Crew: 1 driver	Engine: 6 cylinder 64.8kW (87hp) petrol
Weight: 4.53 tonnes (10,000lbs) (vehicle only)	Speed: not known
Length: 6.19m (20ft 4in)	Range: not known
Width: 2.23m (7ft 4in)	Armament: 16 x 132mm (5.2in) M13 rockets
Height: 2.79m (9ft 2in)	

▲ **Studebaker US 6x6 U3 2½-ton with BM-13-16 'Katyusha' salvo rocket launcher**

1st Ukrainian Front / Third Guards Tank Army / 91st Guards Mortar Breakthrough Regiment

By 1945, 'Katyushas' were an essential part of the fire plan for every major Soviet artillery bombardment.

Specifications

Crew: 1 driver	Engine: 6 cylinder 77.55kW (104hp) petrol
Weight: 4.76 tonnes (10,500lbs) (vehicle only)	Speed: not known
Length: 5.86m (19ft 3in)	Range: not known
Width: 2.23m (7ft 4in)	Armament: 16 x 132mm (5.2in) M13 rockets
Height: 2.76m (9ft)	

▲ **GMC CCKW-352M-13 6x6 2½-ton with BM-13-16 'Katyusha' salvo rocket launcher**

2nd Belorussian Front / Forty-Eighth Army

Roughly 6700 Lend-Lease GMC trucks were shipped to the Red Army, a proportion of which were fitted with the BM-13-16.

Lend-Lease support vehicles

Lend-Lease came into existence on 11 March 1941 with the passage of the Lend-Lease Act, which permitted the President of the United States to 'sell, transfer title to, exchange, lease, lend, or otherwise dispose of, to any such government (whose defense the President deems vital to the defense of the United States) any defense article'.

ORIGINALLY DEVISED TO ALLOW the transfer of essential war supplies to Britain, it was extended to cover the Soviet Union in November 1941. It was a highly controversial plan that had been 'sold' to the American public by Franklin D Roosevelt's well-publicized explanation that his plan was comparable to one neighbour lending another a garden hose to put out a fire in his home.

'What do I do in such a crisis?' the president asked at a press conference. 'I don't say... "Neighbor, my garden hose cost me $15; you have to pay me $15 for it." ...I don't want $15 – I want my garden hose back after the fire is over.' By the end of June 1941, Stalin was bombarding Britain and the United States with increasingly urgent requests for war matériel – a typical early request listed 3000 fighters, 3000 bombers, 20,000 light AA guns, 3,000,000 pairs of boots and vast quantities of raw material. Although expressed as requests, there was always the implied threat that the Soviet Union could not continue the war if the supplies were not delivered. Gradually, the early extreme requests were moderated in recognition of what was actually available and, equally importantly, of what could be shipped to Russia.

British aid

Initially, Britain provided most of the matériel as

US Vehicles	Lend-Lease exports	Total exports	Arrived	Lost en route	Diverted	En route Sept 1945
Trucks:						
¾-ton	25,240	25,240	24,564	78	598	–
1½-ton	153,415	159,494	148,664	6660	1826	2344
2½-ton	190,952	193,603	182,938	4300	1130	5235
2½-ton amphibious	589	589	586	3	–	–
5-ton and over	852	858	814	–	–	44
Special purpose	2792	2792	2784	8	–	–
Truck tractors w/o trailer	1941	1960	1938	6	–	16
Truck Subtotal	**375,781**	**384,536**	**362,288**	**11,055**	**3554**	**7639**
Jeeps:						
¼-ton 4x4	47,993	48,993	43,728	3657	1378	230
Amphibious	3510	3510	3510	–	–	–
Trucks & Jeeps Subtotal	**427,284**	**437,039**	**409,526**	**14,712**	**4932**	**230**
Ordnance Service Vehicles:						
Field repair trucks	1543	1543	1534	9	–	–
Tank recovery units	130	130	130	–	–	–
Tank transporters	655	655	629	26	–	–
Motor Vehicle Total	**429,612**	**439,367**	**411,819**	**14,747**	**4932**	**7869**
Motorcycles	35,170	35,170	32,200	1870	11	–
Track-laying tractors	8071	8074	7570	253	11	–

the United States had only just begun the process of converting to a war economy and was straining to equip its own rapidly expanding forces. (A further factor was that until the Soviet Union was included in the coverage of the Lend-Lease Act in November 1941, all US-supplied items had to be paid for in gold.) The problems of actually

'delivering the goods' were, however, daunting. At first, the 'Arctic convoys' were the only practical way and the first of these docked at Archangel in August 1941. At much the same time, British and Soviet forces jointly occupied Iran, opening up a land route to southern Russia from the Persian Gulf. A further option was to ship in supplies

Specifications

Crew: 1	Engine: 53.7kW (72hp) Bedford 6-cylinder
Weight: 7 tonnes (6.89 tons)	petrol
Length: 5.99m (19ft 8in)	Speed: 61km/h (38mph)
Width: 2.26m (7ft 5in)	Range: 370 km (230 miles)
Height: 3m (9ft 10in)	

▲ Bedford QLD 4x4 3-ton general service

2nd Baltic Front / Twenty-Second Army / Supply Battalion

A total of 1100 Bedford trucks were delivered to Soviet Russia in 1942, including some batches of QLD General Service vehicles.

▲ Chevrolet C60L CMP 4x4 3-ton general service

1st Ukrainian Front / HQ Sixtieth Army / Supply Battalion

The Chevrolet C60L, built by General Motors Products of Canada from 1942 onwards, was a 'Canadian Military Pattern' (CMP) vehicle, a purpose-built military design. Although the total production ran to 209,000 vehicles, only a small number were taken into service with Soviet forces.

Specifications

Crew: 1 driver	Engine: 6 cylinder kW (85hp) petrol
Weight: not known	Speed: not known
Wheelbase: 4m (13ft 2in)	Range: not known
Width: 2.23m (7ft 4in)	Radio: none
Height: 3.04m (10ft)	

British and Canadian Vehicles	Shipped	Lost at Sea	Arrived
Lorries:			
Albion 3-ton	35	–	35
Austin 30-cwt	147	–	147
Austin 3-ton	333	–	333
Bedford 30-cwt	110	–	110
Bedford 3-ton	1662	275	1387
Dodge 30-cwt	157	–	157
Ford 30-cwt	868	137	731
Ford 3-ton	582	–	582
GMC	106	–	106
Total	**4000**	**412**	**3588**
Ambulances:			
Austin K-2	12	–	12
Motorcycles:			
BSA	685	–	685
Matchless	255	–	255
Norton	1	–	1
Velocette	225	–	225
Make unspecified	45	–	45
Total	**1223**	**–**	**1223**

(continued)	Shipped	Lost at Sea	Arrived
Machine Lorries:			
Albion 3-ton 4-wheel	42	5	37
Albion 3-ton, Ford 4-wheel	11	2	9
Other 3-ton	17	1	16
Leyland 3-ton 4-wheel	19	2	17
Albion 3-ton, Ford 4-wheel	11	–	11
Albion 3-ton 4-wheel	6	–	6
Albion 3-ton 4-wheel	1	–	1
Canadian 3-ton, Ford 4-whl	16	–	16
Ford 3-ton 4-wheel	3	–	3
Leyland 3-ton 6-wheel	2	–	2
Ford 3-ton 4-wheel	20	–	20
Ford 15-cwt 4-wheel	15	–	15
3-ton	2	–	2
Ford 3-ton 4-wheel	44	4	40
Albion 3-ton 4-wheel	5	–	5
Leyland 3-ton 6-wheel	7	–	7
Leyland 3-ton 4-wheel	9	–	9
Bedford 15-cwt Ford 4-whl	31	5	26
Ford 3-ton 4-wheel	2	–	–
Total	**263**	**19**	**242**

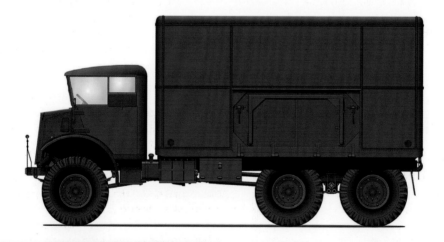

Specifications

Crew: 1

Weight: 8.7 tonnes (8.56 tons)

Length: 6.44m (21ft 1in)

Width: 2.28m (7ft 5in)

Height: 3.25m (10ft 8in)

Engine: 77.48kW (104hp) GMC 6-cylinder
petrol

Speed: 80.46km/h (50mph) (estimated)

▲ **General Motors C60X 6x6 3-ton mobile workshop**

HQ 2nd Ukrainian Front / Maintenance Battalion

The GM C60X, produced by General Motors Products of Canada from 1942 to 1944, was basically a lengthened version of the Chevrolet C60L. It was designed to carry various special body types, including the mobile workshop shown here. The Soviet Union received almost 1500 of the 2710 built from 1943 onwards, mainly through the Pacific route and the Persian Corridor.

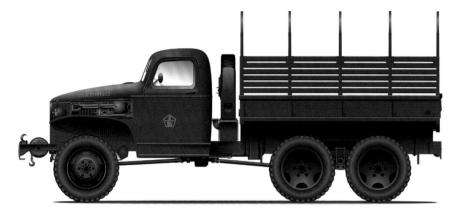

▲ GMC CCKW-352 6x6 2½-ton steel cargo body

1st Byelorussian Front / HQ Sixty-Fifth Army / Supply Battalion

The GMC CCKW-352 and 353 were the standard medium trucks of the US Army throughout the war. More than half a million were produced from 1941 as the short 3.68m (145in) wheelbase (illustrated) and the long 4.2m (164in) wheelbase of the CCKW-353. The Red Army received only 6700 as Lend-Lease vehicles, almost all being the CCKW-352 type.

Specifications	
Crew: 1 driver	Engine: 6 cylinder 77.55kW (104hp) petrol
Weight: 4.76 tonnes (10,500lbs) (vehicle only)	Speed: not known
Length: 5.86m (19ft 3in)	Range: not known
Width: 2.23m (7ft 4in)	Radio: none
Height: 2.76m (9ft)	

through Vladivostock for distribution via the Trans-Siberian railway, but Japan's entry into the war made this impractical until late 1942. (When it did come into operation, it became the route for roughly 50 per cent of all US Lend-Lease.) A final route for warplanes, transport aircraft, small high-value items and VIPs was the Alaska–Siberia Air Route, known as Alsib, which was used from October 1942.

Although initial Soviet requests were primarily for aircraft, tanks, AA and AT guns, the emphasis switched as Soviet war production revived in 1942. By this time, the factories evacuated to the Urals to escape the German invasion were supplying rapidly increasing numbers of tanks, artillery and aircraft. Resources were concentrated on the production of these top-priority weapons at the expense of support vehicles, which were in critically short supply following the massive losses sustained in the first year or so of the war. While the British vehicles supplied in 1941/42 were not well-suited to Russian conditions, they provided the Red Army with a critical degree of mobility that it would otherwise have lacked.

As US deliveries increased, the Soviets rapidly came to appreciate the sheer quality of the vehicles supplied. The vast majority of their own trucks were licence-built copies of antiquated US civilian

designs of the late 1920s. These were of extremely rugged construction and were well-suited to coping with the appalling Russian roads.

Their engines were also designed to run efficiently in the depths of Russian winters and to tolerate very low octane fuel, which was all that was available for most road vehicles. These qualities could not disguise the fact that such vehicles were at best obsolescent compared to the US-supplied vehicles, which were modern military designs.

A further bonus was that many of these American trucks had all-wheel drive, which gave a useful degree of cross-country mobility. These advantages were partially off-set by a number of drawbacks. Vehicles such as the Studebaker demanded more careful servicing and better fuel than their Soviet counterparts, and performance was often reduced due to constant overloading, insufficient maintenance and the use of low octane fuels.

By 1944–45, nearly two-thirds of the truck strength of the Red Army was US-built. Without these vehicles, the great offensives of the period, such as the advance from the Vistula to the Oder would have been impossible. During this offensive, four tank armies were routinely operating up to 90km (56 miles) ahead of the remaining Soviet forces – each army used 600–750 tonnes (591–738 tons) of fuel per day, which required 270–300 trucks to carry it.

Despite the huge numbers of trucks supplied, there were never enough – only three of the four tank armies could be assigned special motor transport units, each with almost 600 trucks.

Amphibious units

Whilst the 586 DUKWs supplied represented only a small percentage of the total Lend-Lease shipments, they were highly valued. All were concentrated in nine 'independent special-purpose motorized battalions' (see organizational table, right), which were part of the Red Army's armour branch. Each battalion had approximately 60 DUKWs and these units were extensively used in the many river crossings undertaken during 1944/45, notably by the 2nd Byelorussian Front in its assault crossing of the Oder. (One battalion was assigned to the 2nd Far Eastern Front for the Manchurian

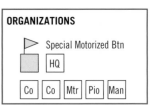

ORGANIZATIONS

Special Motorized Btn

HQ

Co | Co | Mtr | Pio | Man

Specifications

Crew: 1	Height: 1.75m (5ft 9in)
Weight: 1.63 tonnes (1.6 tons)	Engine: 44.7kW (60hp) 4-cylinder petrol
Length: 4.62m (15ft 2in)	Speed: 104.6km/h (65mph)
Width: 1.63m (5ft 4in)	

▲ **Ford GPA 4x4 ¼-ton amphibian**

3rd Ukrainian Front / Thirty-Seventh Army / LCVI Rifle Corps / Reconnaissance Company

3500 of the 12,000 GPAs produced between 1942 and 1943 were sent to the USSR under Lend-Lease. The Red Army found them so useful that a close copy of the design was manufactured in Soviet Russia in the immediate post-war period.

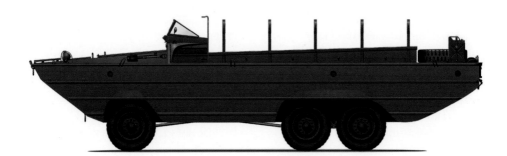

▲ **GMC DUKW-353 6x6 2½-ton amphibious truck**

3rd Ukrainian Front / HQ Fifth Shock Army / Supply Battalion

A total of 586 Lend-Lease DUKWs were supplied to the Red Army in 1943/45 and a copy of the design was put into production in the Soviet Union after the war.

Specifications

Crew: 1	Height: 2.69m (8ft 10in)
Weight: 6.75 tonnes (6.64 tons)	Engine: 62.8kW (91.5hp) GMC Model 270
Length: 9.75m (32ft)	Speed: 80km/h (50mph)
Width: 2.51m (8ft 3in)	

Campaign, taking part in the crossings of the Amur and Ussuri rivers.) The Ford GPA 'amphibious jeep' was supplied in larger numbers (roughly 3500 vehicles) and was primarily used by reconnaissance units, although some may well have equipped the independent special-purpose motorized battalions.

US Lend-Lease support vehicles had considerable influence on post-war Soviet designs and were supplied in such vast numbers that they became a common sight throughout Soviet Russia and eastern Europe. (In Russia, the popular belief grew up that the stencilled 'USA' prefixed serial numbers which were left on most vehicles stood for 'Ubiyat

Sukinsyna Adolfa' – Kill that Son-of-a-Bitch Adolf.) Lend-Lease supplies to the Soviet Union continued to be sent until 12 May 1945, but, under the 'Milepost' agreement, deliveries continued for the duration of the war with Japan. (The scheme formally terminated on 20 September, but it is probable that the last shipments were made at the end of the month.) Total Lend-Lease aid exceeded $50 billion, of which the USSR received over $11 billion.

The scale of the Lease-Lend programme is vividly illustrated by the lists of war matériel shipped to the Soviet Union between November 1941 and 30 September 1945.

▲ **Austin K2/Y 4x2 2-ton ambulance**

Voronezh Front / Fortieth Army / Medical Battalion

It is likely that a small number of these ambulances were included in British deliveries to Russia in 1941/42.

Specifications

Crew 2	Height: 2.79m (9ft 2in)
Weight: not known	Engine: 44.7kW (60hp) Austin 6-cylinder petrol
Length: 5.49m (18ft)	Speed: 80km/h (50mph)
Width: 2.21m (7ft 3in)	

▶ **Dodge WC51 4x4 weapons carrier**

2nd Byelorussian Front / HQ Seventieth Army / Supply Battalion

Almost 25,000 WC series vehicles were supplied to the Red Army between 1943 and 1945.

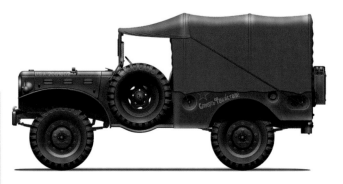

Specifications

Crew: 1	Engine: 68.54kW (92hp) Dodge T214 6-
Weight: 3.3 tonnes (3.25 tons)	cylinder petrol
Length: 4.47m (14ft 8in)	Speed: not known
Width: 2.1m (6ft 11in)	Range: 384km (240 miles)
Height: 2.15m (7ft 1in)	

Lend-Lease production figures

The total of Lend-Lease AFVs supplied to the Red Army equalled approximately 16 per cent of Soviet wartime tank production and 12 per cent of SP gun production.

THE FIRST SOVIET UNITS equipped with Valentines and Matilda went into action in December 1941. By 1943, units solely equipped with Lend-Lease vehicles accounted for as much as 17 per cent of the total Red Army tank force. Large-scale deliveries of the M4A2 Sherman in 1944/45 led to entire tank and mechanized corps being equipped with the type, including I Guards Mechanized Corps.

Official Soviet sources heavily criticized the quality of Lend-Lease tanks, often comparing them unfavourably to the T-34 and KV-1. While this was undoubtedly true of many types such as the Valentine and Matilda, they were all that British factories could supply at the time and were far superior to the T-60 and T-70 that were in volume production at the time.

PORT OF DELIVERY, %

Year	1941	1942	1943	1944	1945	Total
Northern	0.4	17.0	8.3	33.6	12.8	72.1
Iran	0	10.1	58.9	92.6	19.4	181.0
Far East	0	5.4	27.9	13.4	12.8	59.5
Total	0.4	32.5	95.1	139.6	45.0	312.6

BRITISH & CANADIAN AFVS, LEND-LEASE (1941–45)	Sent	Lost	Arrived
Brit Inf Tk Mk II Matilda	1184	–	–
Matilda Mk III	113	–	113
Matilda Mk IV	915	221	694
Matilda Mk IV CS	156	31	126
Brit Inf Tk Mk III Valentine	2394	–	–
Valentine Mk II	161	25	136
Valentine Mk III	346	–	346
Valentine Mk IV	520	71	559
Valentine Mk V	340	113	227
Valentine Mk IX	836	18	818
Valentine Mk X	74	8	66
Valentine Bridgelayer	25	–	25
Brit Inf Tk Mk IV Churchill	301	–	–
Churchill Mk II	45	19	26
Churchill Mk III	151	24	127
Churchill Mk IV	105	–	105
Cromwell	6	–	6
Tetrarch	20	–	20
Universal Carriers	1212	–	–
Canadian Valentine Mk VII	1388	180	1208
Canadian Universal Carriers	1348	–	–
Total Valentine	**3782**	**320**	**3462**
Total Universal Carrier	**2560**	**224**	**2336**

AMERICAN AFVS, LEND-LEASE (1942–45)	Sent	Lost	Arrived
M3/M3A1 Stuart	1676	–	–
M5 Stuart	5	–	–
M24 Chaffee	2	–	–
Total Light Tanks	**1682**	**443**	**1239**
M3 Lee medium tank	1386	–	–
M4A2 Sherman (75mm/2.9in)	2007	–	–
M4A2 Sherman (76mm/3in)	2095	–	–
Total Medium Tanks	**5374**	**417**	**4957**
M26	1	–	–
M31B2 ARV	115	–	–
M15A1 MGMC SP AA	100	–	–
M17 MGMC SPG AA	1000	–	–
T48 SPG (SU-57)	650	–	–
M18 tank destroyer	5	–	–
M10 3in GMC TD	52	–	–
M2 halftrack	342	–	–
M3 halftrack	2	–	–
M5 halftrack	421	–	–
M9 halftrack	413	–	–
Total Halftracks	**1158**	**54**	**1104**
Universal Carrier T16	96	–	–

SOFT VEHICLES, LEND-LEASE	1941	1942	1943	1944	1945	Total
Towing Vehicles						
Studebaker	–	3800	34,800	56,400	19,200	114,200
GM	–	1400	4900	400	–	6700
International	–	900	1800	100	300	3100
Chevrolet	–	2700	13,100	25,100	6800	47,700
Ford	–	400	500	–	100	1000
Dodge 3/4	–	–	4300	10,700	4600	19,600
Trucks						
Ford-6	–	7600	18,600	29,000	5800	61,000
Dodge 1 1/2 ton	–	8000	1500	100	–	9600
Dodge 3 ton	–	–	1400	300	–	1700
Bedford	–	1100	–	–	–	1100
Ford Marmon	200	300	–	–	–	500
Austin	200	300	–	–	–	500
Light Vehicles						
Willys	–	5400	13,900	14,300	6200	39,800
Bantam	–	500	100	–	–	600
Chevrolet	–	–	–	–	200	200
Special Auto						
Dodge Staff Car	–	–	–	100	100	200
Ford Amphibian	–	–	–	1900	300	2200
GM Amphibian	–	–	–	–	300	300
Trailer	–	–	–	600	200	800
Mack Diesel	–	–	–	–	900	900
Other	–	–	200	300	–	500
Total	400	32,400	95,100	139,300	45,000	312,200

▶ **Studebaker 'Katyushas'**
With their launch rails protected by canvas covers, US-supplied Studebaker 2.5-ton trucks of the 4th Ukrainian Front carry their M13 salvo rocket launchers through a town in Czech Moravia, March 1945.

Tractors and towing vehicles

While not as 'glamorous' as the tank arm, the Red Army's tractors and artillery played a vital role in supporting armoured operations throughout the war.

T HE MOTLEY COLLECTION of home-produced and Lend-Lease tractors gave mobility to increasingly powerful artillery formations, whose firepower paved the way for the tank armies to spearhead the spectacular advances of 1944/45.

As the twentieth century began, the problems of moving increasingly heavy artillery were becoming acute. Horse teams could not draw guns weighing much in excess of 4.5 tonnes (4.4 tons), while traction engines and early trucks lacked cross-country mobility. The most promising solution, a prototype tracked artillery tractor, was produced by Hornsby, an engineering firm based in Grantham, UK. It was first tested by the British Army as early as 1909, but required further development. The disillusioned developers sold the patent for

▶ **Industrial might**

The principal Soviet tank factories, mostly built under the two Five Year Plans that laid the foundations of Soviet war industry. The Kharkov and Izhorskiy complexes were lost in 1941, and the sieges of Leningrad and Stalingrad severely disrupted production in these cities.

their caterpillar tracks to a US company, Holt Tractors (which later became the Caterpillar Tractor Company).

Agricultural use

Holt developed the tracks for a series of agricultural tractors, some of which were bought by the British Army in 1915 as artillery tractors. By 1918, some 2100 Holts were in British service and others had been sold to the Soviet Union.

▶ **T-26T**

First Army Group / VI Tank Brigade, Khalkin-Gol, 1939

The T-26T was a fully armoured variant of the T-26T2, which was issued to a handful of artillery units in 1933. Small numbers of both types remained in service until 1945, with a few even participating in the Manchurian Campaign.

Specifications

Crew: 2	Height: 1.83m (6ft) (Estimated)
Weight: 8.5 tonnes (8.36 tons) (Estimated)	Engine: 66.2kW (90hp) 4-cylinder petrol
Length: 4.8m (15ft 9in)	Speed: 30km/h (18.6mph)
Width: 3.41m (11ft 2in)	Range: 175km (108.75 miles)

▶ **Heavy Tractor *Stalinez* – ChTZ S-60**

Bryansk Front / Fiftieth Army / 151st Corps Artillery Regiment

The *Stalinez* S-60 was a close copy of the US Caterpillar 60, designed for industrial and agricultural use. It was issued to Red Army artillery units during the mid 1930s as a prime mover for medium and heavy artillery.

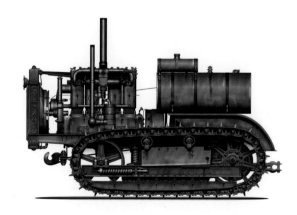

Specifications

Crew: 1	Height: not known
Weight: 9.5 tonnes (9.35 tons)	Engine: 44.7kW (60hp) 4-cylinder petrol
Length: not known	Speed: 7km/h (4.35mph)
Width: not known	Range: 80km (49.71 miles)

SOVIET VEHICLE FACTORIES

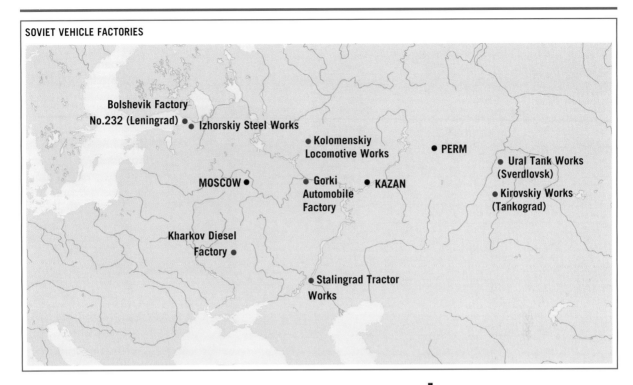

Bolshevik Factory
No.232 (Leningrad) ●
● Izhorskiy Steel Works
● Kolomenskiy
Locomotive Works
● PERM
● Ural Tank Works
(Sverdlovsk)
MOSCOW ●
● Gorki
Automobile
Factory
● KAZAN
● Kirovskiy Works
(Tankograd)
Kharkov Diesel
Factory ●
● Stalingrad Tractor
Works

▶ **Heavy Tractor** *Stalinez* – **ChTZ S-65**
Western Front / Nineteenth Army / 596th Corps Artillery Regiment
The S-65 was another derivative of the Caterpillar 60 design. Although initially intended as a civilian vehicle, many of the 37,626 S-65s built from 1937 to 1941 were brought into service as artillery tractors.

Specifications

Crew: 1	Height: 2.151m (7ft 1in)
Weight: 11.2 tonnes (11.02 tons)	Engine: 55.87kW (75hp) diesel
Length: 4.086m (13ft 5in)	Speed 7km/h (4.35mph)
Width: 2.416m (7ft 11in)	Range: 90km (55.82 miles)

▶ **Heavy Tractor** *Stalinez* – **ChTZ S-65 with cab**
Western Front / Twenty-Second Army / 56th Corps Artillery Regiment
A high proportion of S-65 artillery tractors were fitted with a variety of cabs to allow them to operate efficiently in the extremes of the Russian climate.

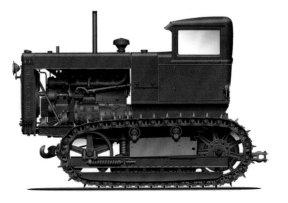

Specifications

Crew: 1	Height: not known
Weight: 11.2 tonnes (11.02 tons)	Engine: 55.87kW (75hp) diesel
Length: 4.086m (13ft 5in)	Speed: 7km/h (4.35mph)
Width: 2.416m (7ft 11in)	Range: 90km (55.82 miles)

Track-laying Tractors, Lend-Lease program	Strength
Heavy, M1, Prime Mover, Class 2:	
Allis-Chalmers HD10W	413
Caterpillar D7	243
International TD18	494
Others	1082
Subtotal	2232
Medium Heavy, Prime Mover, Class 3:	
Allis-Chalmers HD7W	2106
Caterpillar D6	296
International TD14	246
Others	2393
Subtotal	5041
Others:	
Tractor, Crawler type, Class 2	836
Tractor, Crawler type, Class 3	10
Tractor, Crawler type, Class 4	157
Tractor, Elec. Light Duty, 2000 & 2500lbs	115
Subtotal	1118
Cranes and Shovels:	
Crawler type, Class I	17
Crawler type, Class II	27
Crawler type, Class III	405
Crawler type, Class IV	62
Crawler type, Class V	43
Crawler type, Class VI	6
Subtotal	560
Total	8951

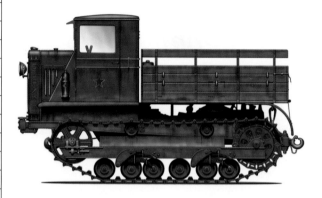

▲ **High-Speed Tractor** *Stalinez* – **S-2** *skorostnoy*
Southern Front / Eighteenth Army / LV Rifle Corps / 437th Corps
Artillery Regiment
A total of 1263 S-2s were produced between 1939 and 1942. Unlike most earlier types, the S-2 was a purpose-built artillery tractor, although its 'S' (skorostnoy – fast) designation was something of a misnomer since its maximum towing speed was no more than 16km/h (10mph) on roads.

Specifications

Crew: 1	Engine: not known
Weight: 11.7 tonnes (11.51 tons)	Speed: 24km/h (14.91mph)
Length: not known	Range: 180km (111.85 miles)
Width: not known	

▶ **Medium Tractor M1 – Allis-Chalmers HD-7W**
1st Byelorussian Front / First Polish Army / 5th Heavy Artillery Brigade
A total of 2100 HD-7W Lend-Lease artillery tractors were supplied to the Red Army and the Polish formations on the Eastern Front, where they were extensively used as tractors for the 152mm (5.9in) ML-20 howitzer.

Specifications

Crew: 1	Engine: 33.6kW (45hp) General Motors
Weight: 6.35 tonnes (6.25 tons)	3-cylinder diesel
Length: 3.25m (10ft 8in)	Speed: not known
Width: 2.05m (6ft 8in)	Range: not known
Height: 1.75m (5ft 9in)	

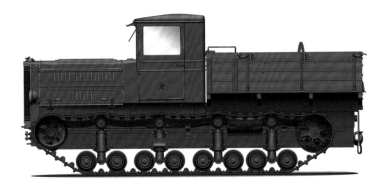

Specifications

Crew: 1

Weight: 10.5 tonnes (10.33 tons)

Length: 5.767m (18ft 11in)

Width: 2.21m (7ft 3in)

Height: 2.54m (8ft 4in)

Engine: 96.85kW (130hp) 4-cylinder diesel

Speed: 30km/h (18.64mph)

Range: 170km (105.6 miles)

▲ Heavy Tractor *Komintern*

Southern Front / Twelfth Army / XIII Rifle Corps / 468th Heavy Howitzer Regiment

The Komintern used the suspension of the T-24 medium tank and it proved capable of towing even the 18.3-tonne (18-ton) B-4 203mm (8in) howitzer. Roughly 2000 vehicles were produced between 1935 and 1941.

Specifications

Crew: 1

Weight: 15.5 tonnes (15.25 tons)

Length: 6.22m (20ft 5in)

Width: 2.35m (7ft 8in)

Height: 2.74m (9ft)

Engine: 260.75kW (350hp) diesel

Speed: 36km/h (22.37mph)

Range: 270km (167.77 miles)

▲ Heavy Tractor *Voroshilovyets*

Kalinin Front / Third Shock Army / 429th Howitzer Regiment

The Voroshilovyets was intended to supersede the Komintern artillery tractor. As many as 450 may have been produced between 1939 and 1942.

▶ Heavy Tractor M1 – Allis-Chalmers HD-10W

3rd Ukrainian Front / Fourth Guards Army / 41st Guards Rifle Division

Over 400 HD-10W tractors were issued to Red Army heavy artillery units.

Specifications

Crew: 1

Weight: 9.731 tonnes (9.58 tons)

Length: 3.81m (12ft 6in)

Width: 2.38m (7ft 9in)

Height: 1.98m (6ft 6in)

Engine: 48.5kW (65hp) General Motors 4-cylinder diesel

Speed: not known

Range: not known

Specifications

Crew: 1

Weight: 6.55 tonnes (6.45 tons)

Length: not known

Width: not known

Height: not known

Engine: GM 4-71 diesel

Speed: 38km/h (23.61mph)

Range: 290km (180 miles)

▲ High-Speed Artillery Tractor Ya-12

1st Ukrainian Front / Third Guards Tank Army / 199th Light Artillery Brigade

The YA-12 was the first of a new generation of artillery tractors, combining the suspension of the T-60 light tank and the Lend-Lease GM4-71 diesel engine. A total of over 1600 vehicles were completed between 1943 and 1945.

▶ Heavy Tractor M1 – International TD-18

4th Ukrainian Front / Second Guards Army / LV Rifle Corps / 2nd Guards Breakthrough Artillery Division.

Almost 500 Lend-Lease TD-18s were shipped to the Soviet Union, primarily for use as heavy artillery prime movers.

Specifications

Crew: 1

Weight: 9.75 tonnes (9.6 tons)

Length: 4.21m (13ft 10in)

Width: 2.41m (7ft 11in)

Height: 2.69m (8ft 10in)

Engine: 78.97kW (106hp) International Harvester 6-cylinder diesel

Speed: not known

Range: not known

▶ Heavy Tractor M1 – Caterpillar D-7

4th Ukrainian Front / Fifty-First Army / 26th Artillery Division

The 7500 Lend-Lease tractors supplied to the Red Army by 1945 included roughly 240 D-7s.

Specifications

Crew: 1

Weight: 14.34 tonnes (14.11 tons)

Length: 4.1m (13ft 5in)

Width: 2.5m (8ft 2in)

Height: 2.44m (8ft)

Engine: 68.54kW (92hp) Caterpillar 4-cylinder diesel

Speed: not known

Range: not known

In 1918, 2000 Bolshevik tractors were ordered for the Red Army. These were copies of the World War I vintage Holts supplied to the Tsar's army. The chaos of the Russian Civil War meant that only eight had been produced by 1922, when production switched to an improved type, the Nr. 75, which was also based on a Holt design. This type remained in production throughout the 1920s and was primarily used by AA units.

Between 1922 and 1930, roughly 3500 tracked artillery tractors based on the German Hanomag WD-50 were produced as the *Kommunar* series. The rapid expansion of Soviet industry and the obsession with production targets led to an ill-trained workforce turning out appallingly bad vehicles – an American engineer who visited the factory in the late 1920s commented, 'If they run at all, their life is limited to a few hours.'

Licensed production

In 1932, the ChTZ factory began licence production of the US Caterpillar 60 design as the S-60, completing almost 69,000 in five years. Production was then switched to a diesel-powered derivative, the S-65, over 37,000 of which were completed before the German invasion. From 1937, these were supplemented by the first Soviet-designed tractor, the STZ-3, which like the earlier types was essentially a slow agricultural vehicle with

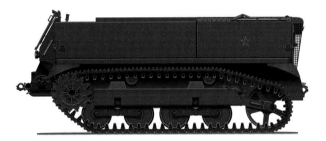

▲ **High-Speed Tractor M5**

1st Ukrainian Front / Thirteenth Army / 17th Artillery Division

The M5 was a purpose-built artillery tractor, capable of road speeds of up to 56km/h (35mph) while towing medium artillery. Almost 200 Lend-Lease vehicles were sent to the Soviet Union in 1944.

Specifications

Crew: 1	Engine: 154kW (207hp) Continental R6572
Weight: 13.8 tonnes (13.58 tons)	6-cylinder petrol
Length: 5.03m (16ft 6in)	Speed: 48km/h (30 mph)
Width: 2.54m (8ft 4in)	Range: 290km (180 miles)
Height: 2.69m (8ft 10in)	

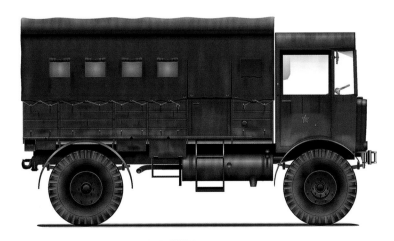

Specifications

Crew: 1	Height: 3.1m (10ft 2in)
Weight: 7.189 tonnes (7.07 tons)	Engine: 70.8kW (95hp) AEC 6-cylinder diesel
Length: 6.32m (20ft 9in)	Speed: 58km/h (36mph)
Width: 2.4m (7ft 10.5in)	Range: 579km (360 miles)

▲ **AEC Matador 0853 4x4 medium artillery tractor**

1st Byelorussian Front / 4th Artillery Corps

Small numbers of Matadors were included in the early consignments of British vehicles sent to Russia on the Arctic convoys.

a maximum speed of 6–7km/h (3.7–4.3mph). Despite the obvious drawbacks of such low speeds, all these models were issued to the Red Army as well as civilian industries and state farms.

The STZ-3 was considered to be a marked improvement on earlier tractors – 4000 were issued for military use by 1941 and a militarized version was produced as the STZ-5. This had the cab repositioned at the front of tractor to create space for a rear-mounted cargo compartment and was a far more effective artillery tractor than the earlier types, especially as it had a top speed of 20km/h (12.4mph). However, production fell well short of the Red Army's needs and it received only 7000 vehicles before the German invasion.

Military tractors

As early as 1930, it had been recognized that civilian-based tractor designs were far from ideal for army use and the first exclusively military type, the *Komintern*, went into production shortly thereafter, based on the suspension of the T-12 medium tank. Only 50 or so vehicles were completed before production switched to an improved version using T-24 suspension in 1935. Approximately 2000 were issued to the Red Army, primarily to medium artillery regiments. By the late 1930s, it was becoming apparent that a more modern design of heavy artillery tractor was needed and the *Voroshilovyets* was developed with an improved suspension and a 261kW (350hp) diesel engine that gave it a road speed of 36km/h (22.4mph). In service, it met all expectations, proving to be a capable towing vehicle for the massive 203mm (8in) B-4 howitzer.

In the era of military modernization and experimentation between 1931 and 1937, considerable efforts were made to produce a family of fully tracked and at least partially armoured support vehicles, many based on the hull of the T-26. Prototypes of APCs, ammunition transporters and command vehicles were all tested, but the only versions to enter limited production were the fully armoured T-26T artillery tractor and the very similar, but only partially armoured, T-26T2. Only very small numbers of both types were built, in contrast to the final pre-war artillery tractor, the *Komsomolyets*. This was primarily intended as a towing vehicle for 45mm (1.8in) AT guns and had a fully enclosed two-man armoured cab with a hull-mounted MG, plus six open seats for the gun crew. Over 4400 were built between 1937 and 1941.

Huge numbers of all these pre-war tractors were lost in the opening stages of Operation *Barbarossa* and many civilian vehicles had to be hastily impressed for use by artillery units, tank

▲ Scammell Pioneer SV2S 6x4 heavy breakdown tractor
Voronezh Front / HQ Sixtieth Army / Maintenance Battalion
The Scammell Pioneer was another British vehicle supplied to the Red Army in small quantities early in the war. With its relatively powerful diesel engine and the ability to convert it to halftrack configuration by fitting tracks over the rear wheels, it was well suited to Russian conditions.

Specifications

Crew: 3

Weight: 9.74 tonnes (9.58 tons)

Length: 6.17m (20ft 3in)

Width: 2.64m (8ft 8in)

Height: 2.87m (9ft 5in)

Engine: 80kW (102hp) Gardner diesel

Speed: not known

Range: 690km (430 miles)

recovery teams and a wide range of other military duties. The supply of a wide variety of (mainly) US Lend-Lease tractors from late 1941 eased the situation, but there were never enough to go round until 1943–44.

By that time, the pressure on Soviet war industries had eased to the extent that resources were available to start work on a new artillery tractor design, which went into production as the Ya-12 in late 1943. This used the suspension of the now obsolete T-60 light tank and the Lend-Lease GM 4-71 diesel engine, and over 1600 were completed by the end of the war in May 1945.

While many of the older vehicles were scrapped or turned over to civilian use following the war, production of the newer models (notably re-engined variants of the YA-12) continued until at least the late 1940s.

▲ **Reo 28XS 6x4 truck tractor**

1st Ukrainian Front / Third Guards Tank Army / Maintenance Battalion

The Red Army's need for tank transporters was partially met by 190 Reo 28XS vehicles during 1943–44. However, the type's usefulness was limited by its 18-tonne (20-US ton) semi-trailer, which restricted it to carrying lighter AFVs.

Specifications

Crew: 1 driver	Engine: Hercules HXD 6 cylinder 134.2kW
Weight: 8.6 tons (18,960lbs) (without load)	(180hp)
Length: 7.18m (23ft 7in)	Speed: not known
Width: 2.43m (8ft)	Range: not known
Height: 2.64m (8ft 7in)	Radio: none

Specifications

Crew: 1	Engine: 149.75kW (201hp) Hercules
Weight: 20.4 tonnes (20.07 tons)	DFXE diesel
Length: 7.1m (23ft 3in)	Speed: not known
Width: 2.6m (8ft 6in)	Range: 250km (156 miles)
Height: 2.97m (9ft 9in)	

▲ **Diamond T-980 6x4 truck tractor**

1st Ukrainian Front / Third Guards Tank Army / 6th Guards Tank Corps

After the limitations of the Reo became apparent, 295 Diamond Ts and 40.8-tonne (45-US ton) M9 trailers were supplied to the Red Army to transport the heavier AFVs coming into service in the last year of the war.

Tank divisions, 1941

In June 1941, the vast majority of the Red Army's armoured divisions were well below strength. Many of their tanks were unserviceable or poorly maintained, largely due to abysmal levels of crew training. Unsurprisingly, these formations were massacred by the veteran panzer divisions in the summer of 1941. The reconstruction of Soviet armoured forces was going to be a long, hard struggle.

SOVIET TANK DIVISIONS (JUNE 1941)					
Division	Commander	Tank Regiment	Assigned	Destruction	Site
1 TD	Maj-Gen V.I. Baranov	1, 2	Independent	24 April 42	–
2 TD	Maj-Gen E.N. Solyankin	3, 4	III Mech Corps	12 July 41	Minsk
3 TD	Col K.Yu. Andreev	5, 6	I Mech Corps	7 Dec 41	–
4 TD	Maj-Gen A.G. Potaturchev	7, 8	VI Mech Corps	4 July 41	Bialystok
5 TD	Col F.F. Fedorov	9, 10	III Mech Corps	27 June 41	Olita
6 TD	Col V.M. Alekseev	11, 12	XXVIII Mech Corps	24 July 41	–
7 TD	Maj-Gen S.V. Borzilov	13, 14	VI Mech Corps	17 July 41	Disna
8 TD	Col P.S. Fotchenkov	15, 16	IV Mech Corps	24 Sept 41	–
9 TD	Col V.G. Burkov	17, 18	XXVII Mech Corps	–	–
10 TD	Maj-Gen S.Ya. Ogurtsov	19, 20	XV Mech Corps	23 Sept 41	–
11 TD	Col G.I. Kuzmin	21, 22	II Mech Corps	8 Sept 41	South Russia
12 TD	Maj-Gen T.A. Mishanin	23, 24	VIII Mech Corps	13 Sept 41	Dneipropyetrovsk
13 TD	Col F.U. Grachev	25, 26	V Mech Corps	4 Aug 41	Smolensk
14 TD	Col I.D. Vasil'ev	27, 28	VII Mech Corps	5 Oct 41	–
15 TD	Col V.I. Polozkov	29, 30	XVI Mech Corps	8 Aug 41	Uman
16 TD	Col M.I. Mindro	31, 149	II Mech Corps	8 Aug 41	Uman
17 TD	Col I.P. Korchagin	33, 34	V Mech Corps	4 Aug 41	Smolensk
18 TD	Maj-Gen F.T. Remizov	35, 36	VII Mech Corps	20 Oct 41	Viazma
19 TD	Maj-Gen K.A. Semenchenko	37, 38	XXII Mech Corps	24 Sept 41	Kiev
20 TD	Col M.E. Katukov	39, 40	IX Mech Corps	29 Sept 41	Kiev
21 TD	Col L.V. Bunin	41, 42	X Mech Corps	4 April 42	–
22 TD	Maj-Gen V.P. Puganov	43, 44	XIV Mech Corps	5 July 41	Slutsk
23 TD	Col T.S. Orlenko	45, 144	XII Mech Corps	28 Sept 41	–
24 TD	Col M.I. Chesnokov	48, 49	X Mech Corps	9 Sept 41	Luga
25 TD	Col N.M. Nikiforov	50, 113	XIII Mech Corps	28 June 41	Bialystok
26 TD	Maj-Gen V.T. Obukhov	51, 52	XX Mech Corps	14 July 41	–
27 TD	Col A.O. Akhmanov	54, 140	XVII Mech Corps	–	–
28 TD	Col I.D. Chernyakhovskiy	55, 56	XII Mech Corps	3 Jan 42	–
29 TD	Col N.P. Studnev	57, 59	XI Mech Corps	6 July 41	Minsk
30 TD	Col S.I. Bogdanov	60, 61	XIV Mech Corps	3 July 41	–
31 TD	Col S.A. Kalikhovich	46, 148	XIII Mech Corps	5 July 41	Bialystok
32 TD	Col E.G. Pushkin	63, 64	IV Mech Corps	17 July 41	Volodorka

SOVIET TANK DIVISIONS (JUNE 1941)

Division	Commander	Tank Regiment	Assigned	Destruction	Site
33 TD	Col M.F. Panov	65, 66	XI Mech Corps	–	–
34 TD	Col I.V. Vasil'ev	67, 68	VIII Mech Corps	30 June 41	Dubno
35 TD	Maj-Gen N.A. Novikov	69, 70	IX Mech Corps	24 Sept 41	Kiev
36 TD	Col S.Z. Miroshnikov	71, 72	XVII Mech Corps	–	–
37 TD	Col F.G. Anikushkin	73, 74	XV Mech Corps	17 July 41	–
38 TD	Col S.I. Kapustin	75, 76	XX Mech Corps	15 July 41	–
39 TD	Col N.V. Starkov	77, 78	XVI Mech Corps	6 Aug 41	–
40 TD	Col M.V. Shirobokov	79, 80	XIX Mech Corps	29 Sept 41	Kiev
41 TD	Col P.P. Pavlov	82, 81	XXII Mech Corps	24 Sept 41	Kiev
42 TD	Col N.I. Voeikov	83, 84	XXI Mech Corps	18 Aug 41	–
43 TD	Col I.G. Tsibin	85, 86	XIX Mech Corps	29 Sept 41	Kiev
44 TD	Col V.P. Krimov	87, 88	XVIII Mech Corps	–	–
45 TD	Col M.D. Solomatin	89, 90	XXIV Mech Corps	8 Aug 41	Uman
46 TD	Col V.A. Koptsov	91, 92	XXI Mech Corps	2 Aug 41	Chola
47 TD	Col G.S. Rodin	93, 94	XVIII Mech Corps	24 Sept 41	Kiev
48 TD	Col D.Ya. Yakovlev	95, 96	XXIII Mech Corps	26 Aug 41	Velikiye Luki
49 TD	Col K.F. Shvetsov	97, 98	XXIV Mech Corps	8 Aug 41	Uman
50 TD	Col B.S. Bakhorov	99, 100	XXV Mech Corps	7 Sept 41	–
51 TD	Col P.G. Chernov	101, 102	XXIII Mech Corps	13 Aug 41	–
52 TD	Col G.M. Mikhailov	104, 105	XXVI Mech Corps	–	–
53 TD	Col A.S. Beloglazov	106, 107	XXVII Mech Corps	–	–
54 TD	Col M.D. Sinenko	108, 109	XXVIII Mech Corps	–	–
55 TD	Col V.M. Badanov	110, 111	XXV Mech Corps	29 July 41	–
56 TD	Col I.D. Illarionov	112, 113	XXVI Mech Corps	–	–
57 TD	Col V.A. Mishulin	114, 115	Independent	4 Aug 41	–
58 TD	Maj-Gen(?) A.A. Kotlyarov	116, 117	XXX Mech Corps	2 Dec 41	–
59 TD	Col S.P. Chernoba	118, 119	Independent	–	–
60 TD	Maj-Gen(?) A.F. Popov	120, 121	XXX Mech Corps	10 Feb 42	–
61 TD	Col B.M. Skvortsov	141, 142	Independent	1946	disbanded, Far East
69 TD	–	–	–	20 Oct 41	Viazma
101 TD	–	202	–	20 Oct 41	Viazma
102 TD	–	204	–	20 Oct 41	Viazma
104 TD	–	208, 209	–	16 Aug 41	disbanded
105 TD	–	210, 211	–	4 Sept 41	disbanded
107 TD	–	–	–	20 Oct 41	Viazma
108 TD	–	216, 217	–	29 Nov 41	disbanded
109 TD	–	218, 219	–	1 Sept 41	disbanded
110 TD	–	220, 221	–	12 Sept 41	North Russia
111 TD	–	–	–	1946	disbanded, Far East
112 TD	–	–	–	6 Nov 42	–

Soviet tank strengths

Stavka analysts frequently 'fine-tuned' the official organization of armoured units, but the reality was often very different from the neat tables prepared by staff officers. Mechanical breakdowns and combat losses could quickly reduce a unit to a fraction of its authorized strength.

IN 1941–42, many formations had a bizarre appearance, as they were equipped with a strange collection of whatever tanks were available. As an example, in October 1941, the 24th Tank Brigade's strength stood at:

- 4 x KV-1
- 22 x T-34
- 1 x BT
- 9 x T-26
- 22 x T-40

Captured vehicles were also used in some numbers, notably StuG III assault guns and Panther tanks, which were available in sufficient quantities to equip whole units by the final year of the war.

▲ **Fighting the propaganda war**
A column of KV-1 heavy tanks from the 6th Soviet Tank Regiment pose for a propoganda photograph.

Causes of T-34 Tank Losses (as percentage)

T-34 Tank Losses	20mm (0.78in)	37mm (1.5in)	short 50mm (2in)	long 50mm (2in)	75mm (2.9in)	88mm (3.5in)	105mm (4.1in)	128mm (5in)	AT rocket	Unknown
Up to September 42	4.7	10.0	7.5	54.3	10.1	3.4	2.9	–	–	7.1
Stalingrad operation	–	–	25.6	26.5	12.1	7.8	–	–	–	28.0
Central Front, Operation 1943	–	–	10.5	23.0	40.5	26.0	–	–	–	–
1st Byelorussian Front Jun–Sep 44	–	–	–	–	39.0	38.0	–	–	9.0	14.0
1st Byelorussian Front Jan–Mar 45	–	–	–	–	29.0	64.0	–	1.0	5.5	0.5
1st Ukrainian Front Jan–Mar 45	–	–	–	0.5	19.0	71.0	0.6	–	8.9	–
4th Ukrainian Front Jan–Mar 45	–	–	–	–	25.3	51.5	0.9	–	9.0	13.5
1st Byelorussian Front Oder–Berlin 1945	–	–	–	1.4	69.2	16.7	–	–	10.5	2.2
2nd Guards Tank Army, Berlin 1945	–	5.4	–	–	36.0	29.0	6.6	–	22.8	–

Soviet and German AFV Strength on the Eastern Front

AFVs: Eastern Front	Jun 41	Mar 42	May 42	Nov 42	Mar 43	Aug 43	Jun 44	Sep 44	Oct 44	Nov 44	Dec 44	Jan 45
Soviet	28,800	4690	6190	4940	7200	6200	11,600	11,200	11,900	14,000	15,000	14,200
German	3671	1503	3981	3133	2374	2555	4470	4186	4917	5202	4785	4881

These figures include tanks and all kinds of SP guns, but the number of serviceable vehicles on both sides was less than the figures shown. The Soviet figures do not include the permanent armoured force held on the Manchurian Front.

Eastern Front: Tank Balance	1941	1942	1943	1944	1945	Total
Soviet tank production	6274	24,639	19,959	16,975	4384	72,231
German tank production	3256	4278	5966	9161	1098	23,759
Production ratio (German:Soviet)	1:2	1:5.6	1:3.3	1:1.85	1:4	1:3
Soviet tank losses	20,500	15,000	22,400	16,900	8700	83,500
German tank losses	2758	2648	6362	6434	7382	25,584
Tank exchange ratio* (German:Soviet)	1:7	1:6	1:4	1:4	1:1.2	1:4.4

* German tank losses here include all fronts; the tank exchange ratio shown is an estimate of the Soviet-German loss ratio.

Soviet and German AFV Strength at the Beginning of Seleted Major Offensives

AFVs: Major Offensives	Date	Formation		Strength	
Sector		German	Soviet	German	Soviet
Leningrad	14 Jan 44	18 Army	Leningrad Fr; Volkov Fr	200	1200
Krivoi Rog/Nikopol	30 Jan 44	6 Army	3 Ukrainian Fr; 4 Ukrainian Fr	250	1400
R. Pripet/Nikolaev	4 Mar 44	1 Pz Army; 4 Pz Army; 6 Army; 8 Army	1 Ukrainian Fr; 2 Ukrainian Fr; 3 Ukrainian Fr	1300	6400
Uman/Kirovrad	5 Mar 44	8 Army	2 Ukrainian Fr	310	2400
Crimea	8 Apr 44	17 Army	4 Ukrainian Fr; Ind Cst Army	70	900
Vitebsk/R. Pripet	22 Jun 44	Army Group Centre	1 Baltic Fr; 1 Byelo Fr; 2 Byelo Fr; 3 Byelo Fr	800	4100
Kovel/Tamopol	12 Jul 44	A Group N Ukraine	1 Ukrainian Fr	700	2040
Chelm/Rava Russkaya	18 Jul 44	4 Pz Army	3 Gds Army; 13 Army; 1 Gds Tk Army	174	550
Mariampol/Daugavpils	19 Jul 44	3 Pz Army	1 Baltic Fr; 3 Byelo Fr (parts)	95	1100
Bendory/Chemovitsy	20 Aug 44	A Group S Ukraine	2 Ukrainian Fr; 3 Ukrainian Fr	400	1880
Narva	14 Sep 44	Army Group North	Leningrad Fr;1 Baltc Fr; 2 Baltic Fr; 3 Baltic Fr	400	3000
Warsaw/Tarnow	12 Jan 45	Army Group A	1 Byelo Fr; 1 Ukrainian Fr	770	6460
E. Prussia	13 Jan 45	Army Group Centre	2 Byelo Fr; 3 Byelo Fr	750	3300
Pomerania	1 Mar 45	3 Pz Army	1 Byelo Fr (parts)	70	1600
Oder/Neisse confluence to Stettin	16 Apr 45	A Group Vistula	1 Byelo Fr; 2 Byelo Fr	750	4100
R. Neisse	16 Apr 45	4 Pz Army	1 Ukrainian Fr	200	2150

Soviet tank production

Improved Soviet war production was achieved at the expense of civilian living standards – the most thorough application of the principle of total war – and with the help of Lend-Lease supplies. Germany's advantages in good-quality engineering and skilled labour were offset by greater Soviet efficiency in using their often limited resources. Soviet factories were ordered to concentrate on the production of low-cost, low-maintenance AFVs in contrast to German attempts to gain decisive qualitative superiority by producing sophisticated, costly designs such as the Panther. All major Soviet types were incrementally upgraded while simplified and refined manufacturing processes increased production.

TANK PRODUCTION BY TYPE AND YEAR	1941	1942	1943	1944	1945	Total
Light Tanks						
T-40	41	181	–	–	–	222
T-50	48	15	–	–	–	63
T-60	1818	4474	–	–	–	6292
T-70	–	4883	3343	–	–	8226
T-80	–	–	120	–	–	120
Sub-total	**1907**	**9553**	**3463**	**–**	**–**	**14,923**
Medium Tanks						
T-34	3014	12,553	15,529	2995	–	34,091
T-34/85	–	–	283	11,778	7230	19,291
T-44	–	–	–	–	200	200
Sub-total	**3014**	**12,553**	**15,812**	**14,773**	**7430**	**53,582**
Heavy Tanks						
KV-1	1121	1,753	–	–	–	2874
KV-2	232	–	–	–	–	232
KV-1S	–	780	452	–	–	1232
KV-85	–	–	130	–	–	130
IS-2	–	–	102	2252	1500	3854
Sub-total	**1353**	**2533**	**684**	**2252**	**1500**	**8322**
Total Tanks	**6274**	**24,639**	**19,959**	**17,025**	**8930**	**76,827**
Assault Guns						
SU-76	–	26	1928	7155	3562	12,671
SU-122	–	25	630	493	–	1148
SU-85	–	–	750	1300	–	2050
SU-100	–	–	–	500	1175	1675
SU-152	–	–	704	–	–	704
ISU-122/ISU-152	–	–	35	2510	1530	4075
Sub-total	**–**	**51**	**4047**	**11,958**	**6267**	**22,323**
Total AFVs	**6274**	**24,690**	**24,006**	**28,983**	**15,197**	**99,150**

Soviet AFV production history – all theatres

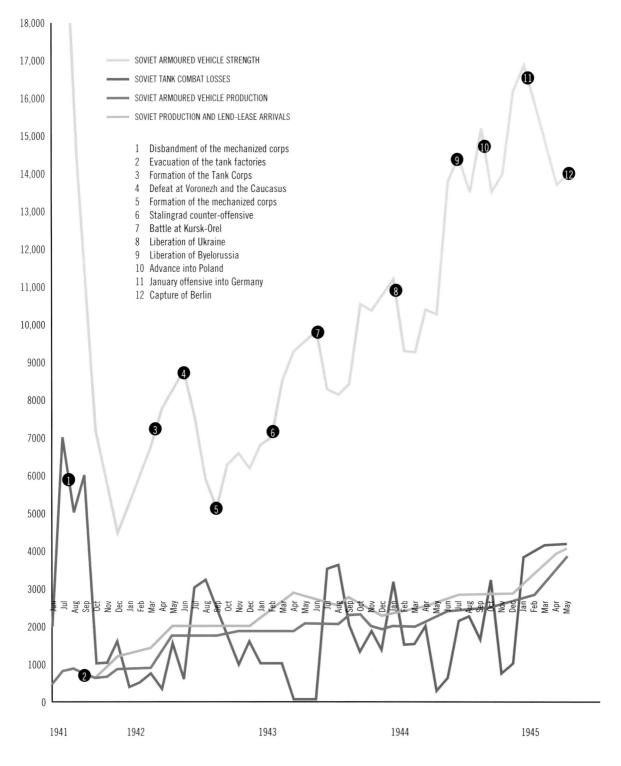

- SOVIET ARMOURED VEHICLE STRENGTH
- SOVIET TANK COMBAT LOSSES
- SOVIET ARMOURED VEHICLE PRODUCTION
- SOVIET PRODUCTION AND LEND-LEASE ARRIVALS

1 Disbandment of the mechanized corps
2 Evacuation of the tank factories
3 Formation of the Tank Corps
4 Defeat at Voronezh and the Caucasus
5 Formation of the mechanized corps
6 Stalingrad counter-offensive
7 Battle at Kursk-Orel
8 Liberation of Ukraine
9 Liberation of Byelorussia
10 Advance into Poland
11 January offensive into Germany
12 Capture of Berlin

Glossary

Ammunition A complete unit of fire, consisting of primer, case, propellant and projectile.

AP Armour Piercing. Ammunition designed to penetrate and destroy armoured targets. Term usually reserved for solid shot fired at high velocity.

APC Armoured Personnel Carrier. APCs, usually armed with machine guns, generally transport infantry to the battle before the troops dismount to fight on their own.

Armour (1) Generic term for all armoured vehicles.

Armour (2) Protection. Armour was originally one material throughout, usually specially hardened steel. Modern armour is a laminated series of layers, which can include metals and related composites (e.g. titanium diboride), ceramics and related composites (e.g. crystal whiskers in a bonded matrix), organic fibres and composites (e.g. arrays of woven cloth), and layered and honeycombed combinations of these.

Armoured Car Wheeled vehicle protected by armour.

AT Anti-Tank. Applied to weapons and weapon systems whose primary function is to destroy heavy armour.

AVRE Armoured Vehicle Royal Engineers. British term for combat engineer vehicle.

Ballistics The science of studying projectiles and their paths. Ballistics can be 'interior' (inside the gun), 'exterior' (in-flight), or 'terminal' (at the point of impact).

Barbette Open gun mounting – normally with front and side protection.

Blindé French term meaning 'Armoured'

Bore The interior of the barrel of any firearm, forward of the chamber.

Bullet Projectile fired by small arms and machine guns. Can be anti-personnel or anti-armour. usually solid, but can also be filled – tracer, incendiary, or a combination of both.

Cal Calibre (caliber in USA)

Calibre (1) Internal diameter of gun or bullet or shell expressed in inches (e.g. a .30-calibre machine gun fires bullets 0.3in in diameter), centimetres or millimetres.

Calibre (2) Length of a tank or artillery gun barrel expressed as a multiple of the internal calibre of the weapon.

Carrier Wheeled or tracked armoured vehicle used to transport supplies and ammunition to the front line.

CGMC Combination Gun Motor Carriage.

Char French expression for 'tank'. Literally 'Chariot'.

Chassis Lower part of a tank's hull, containing the engine, transmission and suspension and on to which the tracks are attached.

Christie suspension Designed by J. Walter Christie in the 1920s. Independently sprung road wheels on tall vertical helical springs.

Coaxial Two guns mounted in the same turret or mantlet, rotating together and firing along the same axis.

Cruiser Tanks Prewar and WWII British medium tanks for rapid advance and exploitation after a breakthrough. Fast, lightly armed and armoured, and used by cavalry.

Depression Angle by which a tank's gun can point below the horizontal. Limited by length of gun inside turret, where the gun is mounted in the turret, and the height of the inside of the turret.

Direct fire Line-of-sight fire directly towards a target, as opposed to indirect fire. Most tanks use direct fire exclusively in battle.

Ditched A tank is ditched when the trench it is being driven across is too wide or the ground beneath is too soft or waterlogged to allow the tracks to grip.

DP Dual-purpose. When a weapon is intended for more than one job, or a round of ammunition has more than one effect, it is said to be dual-purpose.

Elevation Angle by which a tank's gun can point above the horizontal – the greater the angle the greater the range.

GMC Gun Motor Carriage. WWII US army name for self-propelled gun, mounted on wheeled, half-tracked or tracked platforms. Also applied to tank destroyers, which were lightly armoured tank hunters armed with powerful guns in open-topped turrets.

GP General-Purpose

GPMG General-Purpose Machine Gun. MG used as both infantry LMG and for sustained fire. Variants adapted as coaxial guns for tanks and as anti-aircraft guns on many different kinds of armoured vehicle.

HE High Explosive

Howitzer Artillery piece with short barrel capable of high angle fire. Originally a low-velocity short-range weapon, though modern self-propelled howitzers have a long range. Howitzers are usually used for indirect fire.

Hull Main part of armoured vehicle, comprising chassis and superstructure, onto which tracks/wheels and turret are mounted.

Infantry As applied to tanks, denoting vehicles used for infantry support and assault. Often applied to slow, heavily armoured vehicles before World War II.

Light tanks One of the original classes of tanks. Thinly armoured fast tanks designed primarily for reconnaissance.

LMG Light Machine Gun. Squad support weapon which can often be fired from the gun ports of infantry fighting vehicles.

Low profile The bigger a tank, the bigger a target it makes. Tank designers strive to give their designs a low profile to make them less easy to identify on the battlefield.

LVT Landing Vehicle, Tracked. The original amphibious assault vehicles used by the Allies in Europe and the Pacific during World War II.

Machine Guns Rifle-calibre small arms capable of automatic fire, used as primary or secondary armament of armoured vehicles.

Mk. Mark. used to denote major variants of any military design.

Muzzle velocity Speed of projectile as it leaves the muzzle. Air friction means velocity drops rapidly once in flight.

Obstacle Given in specification of a vehicle's performance, indicating maximum height of obstacle that it can negotiate without assistance.

Ordnance Military equipment, specifically tube artillery.

Panzerwagen 'Armoured vehicle' (German)

Periscope Optical device which enables viewer to see over obstacles. Enables tank crew to look out while remaining protected.

QF or **Quick Firing** Fixed ammunition – cartridge case and projectile joined.

Rate of fire Number of rounds which can be fired in a period of time, usually expressed in rounds per minute.

Running gear The transmission, suspension, wheels and tracks of a tank.

Sabot French word for 'wooden shoe', describing the cladding around an APDS round.

Semi-automatic Firearm which fires, extracts, ejects and reloads only once for each pull and release of the trigger.

Shell Hollow projectile normally fired from a rifled gun. Shell can have a number of fillings, including HE, submunitions, chemical and smoke.

Shot Solid projectile, usually armour-piercing.

Sloped Armour Angled armour – projectiles will either ricochet or be forced to penetrate diagonally.

SMG Sub machine-gun. Small fully automatic weapon often carried as personal arm by armoured crewmen.

Smoothbore Cannon without rifling, designed to fire unrotated fin-stabilized projectiles.

Snorkel Breather pipe delivering air to the engines of armoured vehicles; allows vehicle to run submerged.

SP Self-Propelled

SPG Self-Propelled Gun

Sponson Gun mounting that projects from the side of the hull. Traverse is limited

Spring Part of suspension which absorbs vertical movement when on rough ground. It also enables the driven parts of the suspension to remain in contact with the ground.

Tank Heavily armed and armoured full-tracked fighting vehicle. Originally called tank as a disguise during early development.

Tank Destroyer US army WWII lightly armoured tracked vehicle armed with a powerful gun. Designed to ambush enemy armour.

Track Endless belt circling the sprocket, idler, roadwheels and return rollers of a tracked suspension and providing the surface for the wheels to run on.

Trajectory The curved path of a projectile through the air.

Transmission Means by which the power of the engine is converted to rotary movement of wheels or tracks. Transmission can be hydraulic mechanical or electrical.

Traverse The ability of a gun or turret to swing away from the centreline of a vehicle. A fully rotating turret has a traverse of 360 degrees.

Tread Distance between the centrelines of a vehicle's tracks or wheels.

Turret Revolving armoured box mounting a gun. Usually accommodates commander and other crew.

Velocity The speed of a projectile at any point along its trajectory, usually measured in feet per second or metres per second.

Bibliography

Forty, George. *US Army Handbook, 1939–1945.* Stroud, UK: Sutton Publishing, 2003.

Macksey, Kenneth. *Tank versus Tank.* London: Grub Street, 1999.

Man, John. *The Penguin Atlas of D-Day and the Normandy Campaign.* London: Viking, 1994

Perret, Bryan. *Iron Fist, Classic Armoured Warfare Case Studies.* Brockhampton Press, 1999.

Porter, David 'Armour in Battle' articles in *Miniature Wargames* Magazine. Issues (February 2000) 176, 177, 178 (January-March 1998) 186 (November 1998) and 201), 187, 188 (December 1998 – January 1999) and 200 (January 2000)..

Zaloga, Steven J. & Grandsen, James. *Soviet Tanks and Combat Vehicles of World War Two.* Arms and Armour Press, 1984.

Zaloga, Steven J. & Grandsen, James. *The Eastern Front, Armour, Camouflage and Markings, 1941 to 1945.* Arms and Armour Press, 1989.

Zaloga, Steven J. & Ness, Leland S. *Red Army Handbook 1939–1945.* Sutton Publishing Ltd, 1998.

Websites

http://www.o5m6.de/ – Oliver Missing's excellent website 'Engines of the Red Army in WW2', which contains superb illustrations of an ever-increasing range of Soviet and Lend-Lease AFVs. (Our thanks to Oliver for providing so many of the colour profiles for this book.)

http://rkkaww2.armchairgeneral.com/index.htm – 'RKKA in World War II'. Another extremely useful website covering the equipment and operations of the Red Army during World War II.

http://www.winterwar.com/mainpage.htm – 'The Battles of the Winter War'. This website provides fascinating details of all aspects of Finland's 'Winter War' against the Red Army.

http://derela.republika.pl/armcarpl.htm
An excellent English language website covering Polish AFVs (and armoured trains) from 1918 to 1939.

http://france1940.free.fr/en_index.html#AdA
A treasure house of technical information on French AFVs of 1939/40.

http://www.wwiivehicles.com/default.asp
A very useful website for illustrations and technical data on a wide range of AFVs of all nationalities.

http://www.btinternet.com/~ian.a.paterson/main.htm
A highly detailed account of 7th Armoured Division from its formation in 1940 to the end of the war in Europe.

http://www.royaltankregiment.com/9th_RTR/TT/CONTENTS.HTM
This covers the war service of 9 RTR from its formation in 1940 to VE Day. Extracts from the unit's war diary and veterans' accounts are combined to give a remarkable account of life in a wartime tank regiment.

http://www.royaltankregiment.com/9th_RTR/tech/reichswald/Reichswald%20Report.htm
A report by 34 Armoured Brigade on operations in the Reichswald, February 1945. This provides an invaluable insight into some of the problems facing Allied armoured operations in the winter of 1944–45.

http://afvdb.50megs.com/
A highly detailed collection of technical data on almost all US AFVs.

Index

Page numbers in *italics* refer to illustrations, photographs and tables.